Postsecondary Transition for College- or
Career-Bound Autistic Students

Kathleen D. Viezel
Susan M. Wilczynski • Andrew S. Davis
Editors

Postsecondary Transition for College- or Career-Bound Autistic Students

Editors
Kathleen D. Viezel
School of Psychology and Counseling
Fairleigh Dickinson University
Teaneck, NJ, USA

Susan M. Wilczynski
Department of Special Education
Ball State University
Muncie, IN, USA

Andrew S. Davis
Department of Educational Psychology
Ball State University
Muncie, IN, USA

ISBN 978-3-030-93949-6   ISBN 978-3-030-93947-2   (eBook)
https://doi.org/10.1007/978-3-030-93947-2

© Springer Nature Switzerland AG 2022
This work is subject to copyright. All rights are reserved by the Publisher, whether the whole or part of the material is concerned, specifically the rights of translation, reprinting, reuse of illustrations, recitation, broadcasting, reproduction on microfilms or in any other physical way, and transmission or information storage and retrieval, electronic adaptation, computer software, or by similar or dissimilar methodology now known or hereafter developed.

The use of general descriptive names, registered names, trademarks, service marks, etc. in this publication does not imply, even in the absence of a specific statement, that such names are exempt from the relevant protective laws and regulations and therefore free for general use.

The publisher, the authors and the editors are safe to assume that the advice and information in this book are believed to be true and accurate at the date of publication. Neither the publisher nor the authors or the editors give a warranty, expressed or implied, with respect to the material contained herein or for any errors or omissions that may have been made. The publisher remains neutral with regard to jurisdictional claims in published maps and institutional affiliations.

This Springer imprint is published by the registered company Springer Nature Switzerland AG
The registered company address is: Gewerbestrasse 11, 6330 Cham, Switzerland

Acknowledgments

This project would not have been possible without the Autistic individuals who have educated us during our professional careers. Special thanks are due to past and current Autistic people with whom we have worked as well as scholars and practitioners who are dedicated to ensuring Autistics experience meaningful, self-determined outcomes as well as a high quality of life. We are sincerely grateful to all of the authors who contributed chapters to this volume, all of whom worked on their contribution during the COVID-19 pandemic. We appreciate the dedication you displayed to this project as we all re-learned the meaning of "multitasking." Thank you to the publishing team at Springer for your assistance in bringing this book to light.

Author Note

We have no conflicts of interest to disclose

Correspondence concerning this manuscript should be directed to Kathleen D. Viezel. Email: viezel@fdu.edu

Contents

College- or Career-Bound Autistic Adolescents: An Introduction   1
Kathleen D. Viezel, Susan M. Wilczynski, and Andrew S. Davis

Barriers to Successful Transition 13
Darlene D. Unger, Frank J. Sansosti, and Allison M. Novotny

Neuropsychological Considerations of Adolescents and Young Adults with High-Functioning Autism Spectrum Disorder for School Psychologists 39
Andrew S. Davis, D. J. Bernat, and Michele D. Shetter

Core Academic Skills Considerations, Evaluation Methods, and Intervention Approaches for Autistic Adolescents 63
Maria E. Hernández Finch, Aimee Wildrick, and Jenna M. Pittenger

Social Emotional and Behavioral Assessment and School-Based Intervention for Adolescents with High Functioning ASD 89
Brittany A. Dale, Maria B. Sciuchetti, and David E. McIntosh

Self-Management for Transition-Aged College-Bound Autistic Students 111
Susan M. Wilczynski, Robin A. Snyder, Amanda J. Kazee,
Shawnna Sundberg, Cori A. Conner, Brandon N. Miller,
and Sam Johnson

Understanding Autistic College Students 137
Kathleen D. Viezel and Elizabeth Froner

Considering College Alternatives 159
Beth A. Trammell, Amanda Kazee, Susan M. Wilczynski,
Evette Simmons-Reed, Anita Kraft, and Shawnna Sundberg

Addressing Transition Preparation in Middle and High Schools 179
Erik W. Carter and Michele A. Schutz

Obtaining Appropriate Services in College 201
Elizabeth Williams

Preparation for Successful Employment 217
Jennifer M. Cullen

**Considerations for School Psychology University Faculty: Developing
and Implementing Services for Students with ASD**.................. 243
Jennifer Cleveland and Elizabeth Williams

**The Need for Relationship and Sexuality Education
for Transition-Aged Autistic Youth** 259
Susan Wilczynski, Shawnna Sundberg, Brandon Miller,
and Sam Johnson

Index... 283

College- or Career-Bound Autistic Adolescents: An Introduction

Kathleen D. Viezel, Susan M. Wilczynski, and Andrew S. Davis

Abstract School psychologists and those in related professions need to provide a variety of services to Autistic students as they prepare for postsecondary life, including assessment, intervention, and consultation. Similarly, school psychology professionals in postsecondary settings ought to be prepared to meet the needs of Autistic college students. Many Autistic high-schoolers have the abilities to enter college or competitive employment and often have the same goals as their neurotypical peers; however, individual and systemic barriers may impede their success. This introductory chapter reviews foundational concepts relevant to the context of this text, including diagnostic considerations, use of appropriate terminology, and the role school psychologists have in supporting college- or career-bound Autistic students. Finally, summaries of the chapters included in this book are provided.

Keywords Autism · Transition planning · Postsecondary

Increasing prevalence rates of autism spectrum disorder (ASD) suggest those working in high schools can expect to see more Autistic students in their classrooms and on their caseloads. The dual demand on schools to meet the current needs of students (e.g., academic, social, and behavioral skills) and to prepare these students for their postsecondary futures means school psychologists need to be prepared to provide expansive direct and consultative services that support the self-determined goals of transition-aged Autistic students. Given 38% of high school students take advanced placement courses (College Board, 2021), school psychologists will need

K. D. Viezel (✉)
School of Psychology and Counseling, Fairleigh Dickinson University, Teaneck, NJ, USA
e-mail: viezel@fdu.edu

S. M. Wilczynski
Department of Special Education, Ball State University, Muncie, IN, USA
e-mail: smwilczynski@bsu.edu

A. S. Davis
Department of Educational Psychology, Ball State University, Muncie, IN, USA
e-mail: davis@bsu.edu

© Springer Nature Switzerland AG 2022
K. D. Viezel et al. (eds.), *Postsecondary Transition for College- or Career-Bound Autistic Students*, https://doi.org/10.1007/978-3-030-93947-2_1

to support college-bound Autistic students while they are in high school as well as prepare them for postsecondary life. Autistic high school students often have the cognitive ability, academic potential, and most importantly the desire to follow similar postsecondary trajectories as their non-Autistic peers. Despite these protective factors, it is often difficult for neurodivergent adolescents to navigate systems which are not optimally designed for them. Autistic students without comorbid intellectual disability (ID) who desire to live and work independently (often historically referred to in the literature as having "high-functioning" autism spectrum disorder, or HFASD) would therefore benefit from the assistance of experts in the educational system, such as school psychologists. Practitioners, however, may not feel adequately prepared to help these students meet their postsecondary goals. Similarly, practitioners serving postsecondary students should be prepared to meet the needs of Autistic college students and professors must adequately train graduate students to work with transition-age Autistic students. It is also often necessary for vocational supervisors and/or college administrators and faculty to be provided with psychoeducation about how best to help Autistic workers and students. Our aim in producing this book was to help school psychologists, and those in related professions, support Autistic students and their families so they can effectively prepare and execute meaningful and appropriate postsecondary transition plans and interventions. Information in this book will also be useful for families and Autistic self-advocates as they navigate the transition to college or a career.

Autism Spectrum Disorder

The Diagnostic and Statistical Manual of Mental Disorders (DSM) has always been written using the medical model, in which clusters of deficits or excesses are applied to human beings, as opposed to the mismatch between individuals and the environments in which they live (American Psychiatric Association, 2013). We believe the deficit model of ASD in which psychologists are often trained fails to adequately account for the strengths associated with ASD and to reflect that many of the challenges Autistics experience result from a poor match between the environment and their unique needs, rather than constitutional deficits associated with ASD. However, given the central role that the DSM has played across disciplines, we would be remiss in eliminating the diagnostic criteria consistently being applied by health and school professionals. The fifth and most recent edition of the Diagnostic and Statistical Manual of Mental Disorders (DSM-5; American Psychiatric Association, 2013) contains two major categories of diagnostic criteria for autism spectrum disorder. The first is deficits in social communication/ interaction; the individual must have (or previously had) difficulty with reciprocity, nonverbal communication, and with social relationships. The second criterion focuses on restricted or repetitive behavior or interests, such as stereotyped movements, resistance to change in routine, restricted/fixated interests, and/or being either over- or under-reactive to sensory input. These deficits must have occurred during the individual's early development, cause significant impairment, occur across settings, and are not better accounted for by another developmental disability (although they can co-occur; APA, 2013). The reader is directed to the DSM-V for full diagnostic criteria.

Of note, many practitioners may be familiar with other autism spectrum disorders, such as Asperger's disorder, or pervasive developmental disorder not otherwise specified (PDD-NOS). The current DSM does not differentiate between these disorders and autism (called "Autistic disorder" in the previous edition of the DSM); instead, the text notes that individuals who previously met criteria for these disorders should now be considered to warrant a diagnosis of ASD. Thus, the contents of this book do not differentiate between people diagnosed with "autism" or "Asperger's." However, Autistic individuals may still identify as having Asperger's (the label "Aspie" is sometimes used by people who self-identify as such), although the elimination of the PDD-NOS category seems to be well-received within the autism community (Linton et al., 2014).

Perhaps in an effort to recognize the "spectrum" nature of ASD without the existence of heterogeneous categories, the DSM includes specifiers for severity level for both social communication and restricted/repetitive behaviors. These levels range from 3 ("requiring very substantial support") to 1 ("requiring support"). The population of interest in this book will mostly be individuals without co-occurring ID, and likely fall within levels 1–2. However, it should be noted these distinctions are somewhat subjective and may not sufficiently describe differences across environments that often result from poorly structured supports in some environments. For example, 51% of college-bound Autistic high school students reported being recently bullied. In addition, college-bound Autistic high school students whose parents reported they experienced bullying had much higher rates of social anxiety (van Schalkwyk et al., 2017). The same student may have been described as not requiring supports prior to bullying but requiring more substantial supports in school once the bullying and resulting anxiety increase. Thus, school psychologists should withhold judgment about the identified level of support required for new students on their caseload until they understand the environmental conditions that may be attenuating independence. Further discussion on the use of terminology to describe the level of functioning is provided below. Readers of this volume may also be familiar with the educational classification of autism. Different states may define this category differently, and it should be noted that a DSM-V diagnosis of ASD is not required for special education services.

A Discussion of Terminology

There is some debate in the field about how to describe Autistic individuals and, in particular, how to distinguish groups with different needs. One issue arises with person-first (e.g., "person with autism") versus identity-first (e.g., "Autistic person") language. Most psychologists and school psychologists were, at one point, trained to exclusively use person-first language when discussing individuals with any diagnosis, including autism or a learning disability (e.g., "person with a learning disability," not learning-disabled person). However, a number of self-advocates have objected to person-first language (Botha, Hanlon, & Williams, 2020), and it appears the much of the autism community has made the shift to self-identify as "Autistic." Therefore, the editors of this book have decided to use identify-first language in this chapter. However, we do not speak for Autistics as a whole, and other researchers, practitioners, and self-advocates may still view person-first language as more respectful. Therefore, some chapter authors have mindfully chosen to use person-first language. Inconsistencies in this book are not due to carelessness but illustrate the current lack of consensus in the field and the struggle many scholars and practitioners experience as they seek to better understand how to effectively support Autistic people. By modeling the disparity in opinions in this book, we hope it will support readers as they make decisions about ableism and person-first language.

The terms "high-functioning" (including HFASD) and "low-functioning" have long been used to describe Autistic individuals without and with significant cognitive and adaptive impairment. However, recent research such as that conducted by Alvares et al. (2020) suggests these terms do not provide a useful characterization and should no longer be part of our lexicon. Perhaps more important, many Autistics are now coming forward with concerns that these terms may be pejorative and limiting. For example, the same person may demonstrate many characteristics of ASD under one condition and very few under different conditions. In addition, we would not use the term "high functioning" to describe a neurotypical group of people who were identified based on race or religion and many in the Autistic community ask that we reduce the ableism (i.e., discrimination based on the biased assumption that people without disabilities are superior) they face by basing our decisions on whether we would apply the same standard to neurotypical people. The recommendation is to describe a person's strengths and areas of need. When we first set out to write this book, we also used the term "high-functioning" to discuss the population of interest; however, we have shifted away from this terminology as we learn more about ableism and the role practitioners have in mitigating or perpetuating discrimination disabled people may face. We do acknowledge that the term "high-functioning" is common in the literature when discussing Autistic individuals without ID who have the potential to live independently with minimal or no assistance, and it has become an easily identifiable shorthand for researchers and professionals. Because Autistics are a diverse group of individuals, some may also still self-identify as "high-functioning." Therefore, like person-first language, some chapters in this volume may still use terms such as "high-functioning" or HFASD.

The Role of the School Psychologist

School psychologists work in many sectors, including pre-K-12 public schools, private schools, residential settings, hospitals, private practices, and colleges/universities. We include trainers of school psychologists (e.g., faculty) in this group. Although the topics presented in this book are most relevant to those working with Autistic students who are either planning their postsecondary transition (e.g., middle and high school settings) or those working in colleges, much of the information would be useful to anyone in other disciplines that support Autistic individuals who seek to enter fields dominated by neurotypical individuals, such as traditional colleges or careers. For example, the information in this text would likely be useful for professionals working in the field of vocational rehabilitation.

The Individuals with Disabilities Education Act (IDEA) mandates postsecondary transition planning (IDEA, 2004). Specifically, Part B specifies individualized education programs (IEPs) must include postsecondary goals by the time the student is 16 years old. These goals must be measurable, and related to several adult outcomes, including education and employment. Further, services need to be put into place to help the student achieve these goals (IDEA, 2004). Additionally, the National Association of School Psychologists (NASP) calls on school psychologists to use evidenced-based techniques to help students with postsecondary transition (NASP, 2020). This can be a difficult task when Autistic students are aiming for traditional college or careers because empirical research describing effective interventions for Autistic college students is still relatively scant (Anderson et al., 2019) and the vast majority of the literature on ASD and the workplace involves participants with intellectual disabilities (Baldwin et al., 2014).

The goal of entering traditional colleges or high paying positions in the workforce may be appropriate for a large percentage of Autistic students, as approximately 44% of children with ASD have average or above average intelligence (Christensen et al., 2016). Intelligence alone does not predict success in college or the workplace, however. Sufficient academic, social, self-regulation, and self-sufficiency skills must be developed for Autistic adolescents and young adults with ASD to be successful in either of these endeavors (Hendricks & Wehman, 2009). Additionally, the degree of success may, in part, also depend on the willingness of supervisors and professors to enact appropriate accommodations. Although this literature base is limited, high-quality evidence regarding related populations, settings, or skills should be used to guide both transition plans and service delivery. Unfortunately, extrapolating from other literature bases is a time-consuming process that is not feasible for the average school psychologist. It is our hope that the chapters in this volume can help school psychologists, and those in related fields, efficiently understand and learn about the characteristics and needs of Autistic college- and career-bound people.

Chapter Overviews

We selected several topics we felt would be most relevant and helpful to professionals, families, and self-advocates.

Prior to attempting to implement solutions, stakeholders must understand the problems Autistic adolescents face as they begin to navigate their postsecondary options. In *Barriers to Successful Transition*, Unger et al. explain difficulties these students may face as they prepare for increased independence from family and K-12 educational supports. They explain academic difficulties, with a focus on executive functioning skills that required across environments, specific social and emotional concerns, and behavioral barriers such as rigidity and skills associated with autonomy. It may be helpful to the reader to conceptualize behavioral skill deficits as opportunities for learning and growth, rather than problems to be solved for the benefit of others. Unger et al. also discuss how these barriers could translate into difficulties in vocational and postsecondary educational settings. Importantly, the authors point out that deficits are often found in the environment, and not in the Autistic individual, illustrating the need for professionals to address larger systemic issues in addition to individualized transition plans, interventions, and accommodations. This chapter also addresses the often-overlooked issue of the possibility of Autistic students' involvement in the criminal justice system and associated roles of, and preventative opportunities for, school-based professionals. Overall, this chapter goes beyond the DSM-V to help readers understand the contextual challenges many college- or career-bound Autistic students face.

School psychologists are experts in neurocognitive assessment and should be able to conduct high-quality psychoeducational evaluations of Autistic students. Even when the assessment is completed by another professional, school psychologists need to competently interpret the findings and apply them to effective interventions and postsecondary transition plans. In *Neuropsychological Considerations of Adolescents and Young Adults with High-Functioning Autism Spectrum Disorder for School Psychologists*, Davis et al. address topics related to the neurodevelopment and neuropsychological assessment of Autistic adolescents who aim to attend college or enter the competitive workforce. The authors explain how thorough assessments can be used to benefit the trajectories of these individuals, the potential-associated difficulties that ought to be considered (i.e., comorbid psychiatric and medical conditions), and the domains that should be addressed in the evaluation. School psychologists and other assessment professionals can use the information in this chapter to ensure their evaluations are comprehensive and contain information and recommendations useful to all stakeholders.

Hernández Finch et al. address educational considerations in *Core Academic Skills Considerations, Evaluation Methods, and Intervention Approaches for Autistic Adolescents*. Academic success is critical to the successful transition of many Autistic students, but particularly for those intended to attend universities. This chapter will be useful to those looking for specific details of well-designed transition plans. Many Autistic students will transition to postsecondary settings where they will be held to the same standards as their peers (i.e., traditional colleges), yet they often have unique needs. Hernández Finch and colleagues review common academic needs of Autistic people, including potential causes of these difficulties. Simultaneously, they address strengths many Autistic students may have while acknowledging that this population has diverse need. This chapter also includes detailed information on appropriate academic assessment, including potential test batteries, and associated interventions for the primary academic domains of reading, math, and writing. Information in this chapter is specific to the Autistic population, and includes a discussion of how one might need to modify standard approaches to educational assessment.

The mismatch between the school expectations for age-appropriate social and behavior skills and those demonstrated by many Autistic students reflects one of the primary challenges faced by Autistic students and their educators alike. School psychologists need to be aware of how these challenges may interfere with successful postsecondary transition, and how to help Autistic students increase social, coping, and behavioral skills. In *Social Emotional and Behavioral Assessment and School-Based Intervention for Adolescents with High Functioning ASD*, Dale et al. detail assessment and school-based intervention strategies. This chapter includes the discussion of both assessment tools used to diagnose the characteristics of ASD as well as associated comorbid and related domains, such as adaptive behavior, social skills, and internalizing concerns. As the authors note, assessment and intervention should be linked, and this chapter will also be a valuable resource for school professionals looking for evidence-based interventions for Autistic students. Because Autistic individuals have diverse needs, a variety of strategies and curriculums are described so professionals can best match the intervention to the needs of their population.

Transitioning to college requires all students to increase their level of independent goal-directed behavior. Autistic college students may experience some challenges with new expectations for self-sufficiency and self-advocacy. Wilczynski et al. address self-management through a lens of self-determination in *Self-Management for Transition-Aged College-Bound Autistic Students*. Readers will find specific steps with examples they can follow to help Autistic students with self-management, allowing the student to set their own goals and drive their own intervention techniques. Specific applications to college settings, such as working with campus offices, registering for classes, behaviors required for academic success, self-care, mental health, and college-specific social situations are highlighted. Those working with Autistic students in K-12 settings can also use these flexible strategies with students in their caseload as they help them build self-management skills over time.

The rise in the prevalence of ASD diagnoses has led to a corresponding increase in research and professional interest in working with Autistic children. Less research, however, has been conducted with young Autistic adults. In *Understanding Autistic College Students*, Viezel and Froner comprehensively describe the state of research and the need for practitioners to apply their professional judgment when serving this population by assembling essential information about Autistic adolescents and adults who plan to, or are attending, college. As discussed throughout this text, Autistic college students sometimes have a different pathway to academic success compared to their peers. Although the field of psychology tends to use a deficit model, Viezel and Froner recognize it is equally important to examine the strengths Autistic college students have and the social barriers that sometimes are the source of challenges these students face. Viezel and Froner review these abilities to help practitioners understand how to use a strengths-based approach to support concurrent with accommodations for the challenges that are unique to this group of college students. Areas of cognitive, social-emotional, behavioral, and self-care needs are reviewed with a focus on practitioners' applying this knowledge. A summary of current research and recommendations for academic areas (e.g., reading, writing, and mathematics) is offered. An important consideration for those working with Autistic students currently attending, or preparing for college, is the discussion of the college community. This section highlights the importance of understanding that while it is important to work directly with the Autistic college student, it is also critical to work with individuals and systems with which the student will interact. This includes peers, instructors, and other college staff.

Even when students have the cognitive and academic abilities to succeed in traditional, four-year college, it is not always the best path towards their ultimate career goals. In *Considering College Alternatives*, Trammell et al. describe different options available to Autistic students within the context of effective transition planning. The authors detail specific steps in developing appropriate career goals, how to address barriers to these goals, and options for supported employment, all of which may help prevent unemployment, underemployment, or malemployment. For anyone looking to enter the career force, getting a job is only the first step; Trammell et al. describe how school psychologists can support Autistic students in maintaining employment. The specificity of their recommendations will be appealing to a variety of helping professionals. Also included in this chapter are recommendations regarding when and how to consider and plan for entering community college, trade/vocational school, or technical college. These alternative postsecondary educational settings are often excellent choices for some Autistic students and require unique considerations of benefits and drawbacks, including potential career outcomes, accommodations offered, and opportunities beyond course content, such as socialization and development of independent living skills.

School psychologists are ideal candidates to affect systems-level change. Carter and Shulz focus on comprehensive, high-quality, and team-based transition services at the middle- and high-school levels. Throughout *Addressing Transition Preparation in Middle and High Schools*, the authors highlight aspects of transition planning required by both law and best practice. Carter and Shulz build on the information about evaluation of cognitive and social/emotional domains offered in previous chapters by detailing transition-specific assessment practices. Specific recommendations are also provided for academic strategies with a focus on inclusive education supportive of postsecondary goals. Early (i.e., before leaving high school) career planning could help Autistic students actualize the goals in their transition plans. Carter and Shulz describe how schools can be supportive of increased skill-building and actual employment experience. Strategies are also offered for achieving goals around independent living and social skills and relationships. Interdisciplinary practice is essential for effective educational programs. A section of *Addressing Transition Preparation in Middle and High Schools* is devoted to outlining the roles and responsibilities of school personnel, including school psychologists, special and general educators, guidance counselors, transition specialists, and more. Readers will also find information to help strengthen community connections, including with family and adult/postsecondary programs.

If college is the goal for an Autistic student, knowledge of the typical accommodations and services offered by colleges is essential for successful transition planning. Yet, school psychologists and other educators are likely under-informed about how to help Autistic students and their families select an appropriate college. Some postsecondary schools may have specialty support programs with their own application requirements. Regardless of whether the student is interested in an ASD-specific support program, there are factors to consider when selecting a college and requesting appropriate accommodations. In *Obtaining Appropriate Services in College*, Williams describes considerations related to college selection, including both desirability (e.g., majors offered and social activities) and logistics (e.g., cost and location). Although these factors are important to anyone, there are sometimes unique considerations for Autistic students, particularly those receiving special education services. Relatedly, Williams details how school professionals can be better prepared to help students transition from accommodations offered in high school to those offered in college settings. Finally, information on specialty programs is presented, including common interventions and how to access these services.

If further education is not aligned with a student's goals, then transition planning should focus on meaningful employment. Appropriately supporting students during their final years in high school can mitigate some of the barriers to entering the workforce. Additionally, those working with Autistic college students should include post-college planning as part of their supports. In *Preparation for Successful Employment*, Cullen describes individual, family, and systemic factors that may be associated with employment, thereby helping determine domains to consider in transition planning. Like other chapters in this volume, Cullen provides specific recommendations for identifying appropriate goals for the student, as well as how to meet those goals. Career preparation goes beyond specific skills related to job searches and interviewing. Readers of this chapter will find information on a variety of domains, including course planning, social skills, independent living skills, self-determination, and building work experience. School psychologists are experts on consultation and collaboration, and Cullen describes how to bridge these skills to working with employment-based community stakeholders from a person-centered planning framework. Another important consideration for Autistic adolescents looking to enter the workforce is whether and how to access workplace-based supports, which, as noted by Cullen, actually begin with the hiring process. Employers should be aware of inclusive hiring practices, as neurodiverse individuals bring many benefits to the workforce. Support professionals are well-positioned to provide consultation and training about nondiscriminatory interviewing and hiring. Once hired, some employees may need workplace accommodations, to varied degrees. Cullen provides a description of some of these options, with a focus on self-advocacy.

School psychologists working at colleges or universities in service delivery and/or faculty roles are ideal candidates to help new Autistic undergraduate students successfully transition to college, as well as train future school psychologists on a variety of topics detailed in this volume. Although the previous chapters will also be beneficial for these professionals, *Considerations for School Psychology University Faculty: Developing and Implementing Services for Students with ASD* specifically focuses on information for school psychologists in postsecondary institutions. Cleveland and Williams detail factors relevant to those interested in starting (or adjusting) an ASD-specific support program, as well as how to support a college culture which is accepting of neurodiversity. Even, or perhaps especially, in postsecondary settings without an ASD support program, supporting faculty, staff, and peer self-efficacy in inclusive practice is essential. Effective consultation practices relevant to Autistic college students are especially highlighted by the authors.

High-quality and accurate sex education is important for health, safety, relationship building, and general quality of life. This is as true for Autistic students as it is for their neurotypical peers (and, due to their elevated risk of victimization and involvement in the justice system, perhaps even more so); however, their sex and relationship education is often impoverished. In *The Need for Relationship and Sexuality Education for Transition Aged Autistic Youth,* Wilczynski et al. address these issues within the context of school-based services. Because some professionals and families may be hesitant to discuss sensitive topics with students, the chapter opens with a frank discussion of why sex education is imperative for Autistics. A focus of the chapter is inclusivity and intersectionality, recognizing that Autistics are more likely to identify on the LGBTQIA+ spectrum. Even if they recognize the importance of comprehensive sex and relationship education, stakeholders cannot assume that curricula designed for neurotypical students will match the needs of Autistic students. Wilczynski et al. review the literature on available sexuality education programs, highlighting the potential benefits and limitations of each choice. Individualized programming and intervention may be the optimal solution for many students, and this chapter also includes important topics that should be covered, with specialized consideration for Autistics.

References

Alvares, G. A., et al. (2020). The misnomer of 'high functioning autism': Intelligence is an imprecise predictor of functional abilities. *Autism, 24,* 221–232.

American Psychiatric Association. (2013). *Diagnostic and statistical manual of mental disorders* (5th ed.). https://doi.org/10.1176/appi.books.9780890425596

Anderson, A. H., Stephenson, J., Carter, M., & Carlon, S. (2019). A systematic literature review of empirical research on postsecondary students with autism spectrum disorder. *Journal of Autism and Developmental Disorders, 49,* 1531–1558. https://doi.org/10.1007/s10803-018-3840-2

College- or Career-Bound Autistic Adolescents: An Introduction 11

Baldwin, S., Costley, D., & Warren, A. (2014). Employment activities and experiences of adults with high-functioning autism and Asperger's disorder. *Journal of Autism and Developmental Disorders, 44*(10), 2440–2449.

Botha, M., Dibb, B., & Frost, D. M. (2020). "Autism is me": An investigation of how Autistic individuals make sense of autism and stigma. *Disability & Society, 1–27.* https://doi.org/10.108 0/09687599.2020.1822782

Christensen, D. L., Baio, J., Braun, K. V., Bilder, D., Charles, J., Constantino, J. N., & Zahorodny, W. (2016). Prevalence and characteristics of autism spectrum disorder among children aged 8 years — Autism and developmental disabilities monitoring network, 11 sites, United States, 2012. *MMWR Surveillance Summaries, 65*(SS-3), 1–23.

College Board. (2021, February 25). *AP program results: Class of 2020.* https://reports.colleg-eboard.org/ap-program-results

Hendricks, D. R., & Wehman, P. (2009). Transition from school to adulthood for youth with autism spectrum disorders. *Focus on Autism and Other Developmental Disabilities, 24*(2), 77–88.

Individuals with Disabilities Education Act, 20 U.S.C. § 1400 (2004).

Linton, K. F., Krcek, T. E., Sensui, L. M., & Spillers, J. L. H. (2014). Opinions of people who self-identify with autism and Asperger's on DSM-5 criteria. *Research on Social Work Practice, 24*(1), 67–77. https://doi.org/10.1177/1049731513495457

National Association of School Psychologists. (2020). *The professional standards of the National Association of School Psychologists.* https://www.nasponline.org/standards-and-certification/nasp-practice-model

van Schalkwyk, G. V., Smith, I. C., Silverman, W. & Volkmar, F. (2017). Brief report: Bullying and anxiety in highfunctioning adolescents with ASD. *Journal of Autism and Developmental Disorders, 48, 1819–1824.* https://doi.org/10.1007/s10803-017-3378-8

Barriers to Successful Transition

Darlene D. Unger ⓘ**, Frank J. Sansosti** ⓘ**, and Allison M. Novotny**

Abstract Adolescents experience a variety of emotions as they transition from high school to postsecondary experiences across educational, employment, and community settings. For many individuals, these feelings may range from optimism and enthusiasm to uncertainty and apprehension, or anxiety as they interact with new acquaintances and new environments. Even with appropriate planning and individualized supports, these transitions can be intimidating and overwhelming for Autistic adolescents. The purpose of this chapter is to provide an overview of internal and external factors that may influence or hinder the Autistic individual's experiences in pursuing college and career goals. Challenges experienced by Autistic individuals related to academics, social, mental health, self-management, and interaction with law enforcement officials are documented. The chapter communicates these topics as potential barriers to favorable transition to increase awareness of potential challenges so professionals and those supporting Autistic youth can proactively plan and help prepare individuals for success as they exit secondary education.

Keywords Transition barriers · Self-sufficiency

Introduction

Many youth struggle during the transition to adulthood; this period of development appears particularly difficult for Autistic individuals (Shattuck et al., 2012) because this transition represents a fundamental shift in expectations for accessing supports from having professionals and caregivers direct the process to that of being a self-advocate. During this time, Autistic young adults lose access to federally mandated educational services, thereby cutting access to many formal supports available to them while in school. These young adults now are expected to make decisions about their lives when they may not understand their own idiosyncrasies or how to advocate for services to meet their unique needs. In addition, Autistic young adults may

---

D. D. Unger (✉) · F. J. Sansosti · A. M. Novotny
School of Lifespan Development and Educational Sciences, College of Education, Health, and Human Services, Kent State University, Kent, OH, USA
e-mail: dunger1@kent.edu; fsansot@kent.edu; anovotn4@kent.edu

© Springer Nature Switzerland AG 2022
K. D. Viezel et al. (eds.), *Postsecondary Transition for College- or Career-Bound Autistic Students*, https://doi.org/10.1007/978-3-030-93947-2_2

feel socially alienated (Eussen et al., 2013) while struggling with a host of cognitive, emotional, and behavioral difficulties that lead to further withdrawal from various situations (e.g., Bellini, 2006). As a result, many Autistic adults remain dependent on their families and may be unable to assume independent adult roles (Howlin et al., 2004; Wehman et al., 2009), increasing the likelihood of disengagement from postsecondary education or paid employment opportunities completely (Alverson et al., 2019; Ohl et al., 2017; Shattuck et al., 2012).

The purpose of this chapter is to provide an overview of variables that may interfere with the successful transition of Autistic adolescents to postsecondary education or the workplace. Topics explored include both internal and external challenges that affect the successful transition opportunities for this population. Specifically, we begin with an examination of the noteworthy academic, social, mental health, behavioral, and self-management characteristics of Autistic adolescents. Then, we provide an analysis of how these characteristics, combined with limited access to post-school services and supports, may interact with future employment and educational environments.

Academic Skills

Although Autistic adolescents and young adults typically do not display significant delays in cognitive development, they still may require significant academic supports (Sansosti et al., 2010). It may initially appear to educators that Autistic students know and/or understand more than they actually do because of their relatively fluent communication and advanced vocabulary, masking more advanced academic difficulty. Academic difficulties become increasingly apparent when instruction and instructional materials become more abstract, requiring higher-order thinking such as skills to interpret, integrate, and generalize information (Goldstein et al., 2008; Whitby & Mancil, 2009). Moreover, preoccupation with restricted interests, attention problems, limited problem-solving skills, and organizational challenges often make it difficult for Autistic individuals to benefit from advanced education without appropriate supports and/or accommodations.

Attention

Autistic adolescents and young adults frequently appear to be inattentive and easily distracted both during structured and unstructured academic activities. These students may appear to be daydreaming (i.e., staring into space) and unaware of their immediate environment. Attention is likely to be fleeting when they do attend to tasks (Hoffmann et al., 2016). For instance, an Autistic young adult may start to follow directions for a task but quickly lose focus. As a result, the student likely is perceived as purposefully inattentive and requiring frequent redirection (e.g., restating directions). High levels of inattention may be due to distractions in the environment, such as noises (e.g., chairs screeching across the floor, intercom announcements), objects (e.g., bulletin boards, highly decorated classrooms), and/or overstimulation of the senses (e.g., flickering of fluorescent lights, school bells). Autistic students tend to be easily distracted as they often view their environment as overstimulating and stressful due to aforementioned sensory reasons, as well as the social expectations of the classroom (Humphrey & Lewis, 2008).

Perhaps the most fundamental characteristic of inattention in Autistic adolescents and young adults is their difficulty in shifting attention, or the ability to move the focus of attention from one stimulus (i.e., cat) to another (i.e., dog). Attention shifting is one of several cognitive components that fall within the realm of executive functioning that enable individuals to achieve goals efficiently (Boucher, 2017; Ozonoff et al., 2010; Pennington & Ozonoff, 1996); and subsequent primacy theories consider attention and arousal to be central to many of the social and cognitive differences in Autistic individuals (e.g., Courchesne et al., 2011; Dawson & Faja, 2008). For many Autistic students, switching attention from one stimulus to another or from one sensory modality to another is a relatively slow process that results in a pause or delay of reaction.

Educators may observe an Autistic student struggling to follow along and communicate their lines in a timely manner during an oral reading or role-play activity. In this frequently occurring activity in a high school English literature class, students are assigned characters in a novel and must follow written text and then verbally communicate the lines attributed to their character. This task can be especially daunting to an Autistic individual who may sense they cannot keep up but lack instructional supports or self-management strategies to facilitate favorable participation. The lack of compensatory strategies to address insufficient attention shifting also contributes to challenges with problem-solving, organization, and planning, as well as with other skills related to executive functioning.

Problem-Solving

Autistic adolescents and young adults often exhibit problem-solving skills that are insufficient and inflexible. That is, they demonstrate difficulty in generalizing and applying knowledge and skills across multiple environments and situations. Instead, these students use the same rigid problem-solving method for all academic tasks even when this strategy has proven to be ineffective for them in the past. For example, a student who has learned the spelling rule of "I before E except after C" may adhere to this strategy rigidly, incorrectly spelling words such as *freight* and *weigh*. Poor problem-solving also may occur in reading tasks, exhibited by deficits in differentiating fact from fiction, extracting meaning from text, and discriminating relevant from irrelevant information (Loukusa & Moilanen, 2009). Consequently, these deficits lead to slower, or poor, comprehension of text. In fact, Nation et al. (2006) found that nearly 75% of their sample of Autistic students demonstrated below average comprehension skills. One possible explanation for limited problem-solving skills is that Autistic individuals may have difficulty applying contextual information into higher order cognitive representations, as well as integrating prior background knowledge into the construction of complex operations (Bogte et al., 2009; Sansosti et al., 2013).

Organization and Planning

Autistic adolescents and young adults may demonstrate difficulties with organizing, planning, and prioritizing, a critical executive functioning skill needed to persist in postsecondary education and employment. For example, they tend to misplace academic supplies (e.g., writing instruments, notebooks), fail to plan ahead regarding what materials are necessary in order to complete assignments, and incorrectly allocate time and energy to their work (e.g., Martin et al., 2010). Likewise, they may have messy desks, workstations, backpacks, or lockers so finding anything in these areas becomes a daunting and challenging task. As a result, these students often have difficulty completing academic assignments on time or fail to turn them in at all (Sansosti et al., 2010).

Poor organization often goes beyond the placement of academic materials and supplies. Many Autistic individuals also demonstrate poor organization of thoughts, as well as actions. For example, a high school student, Matt, often (almost daily) forgot the combination of his locker. When teachers provided Matt with a card with his locker combination on it, he often forgot the card at home. When they wrote the combination of the locker on his backpack, Matt frequently forgot that it was there. When Matt was able to get into his locker, he often forgot what he needed. Subsequently, these behaviors often led Matt to be late for class and not to have the correct materials. Although this example may seem overstated, this pattern of forgetfulness and lack of planning is somewhat common and presents challenges to favorable experiences in postsecondary education (Getzel & Thoma, 2008; White et al., 2016) and employment for Autistic young adults (Baldwin & Costley, 2016; Lee & Carter, 2012).

Despite what often appears as a general display of average to above-average cognitive abilities, and at times, superior intellectual skills of Autistic adolescents, many obstacles may hinder their academic success, making the prospect of postsecondary transition tenuous. The heightened level of abstraction may increase the frequency and intensity of successive behavioral reactions. Academically, problem-solving becomes more difficult in middle and high school contexts because more abstract concepts are involved (e.g., word problems, advanced comprehension, geometry). Abstraction often requires increased focus and additional problem-solving strategies that Autistic students may not understand or even know exist. As a consequence, academic subjects requiring flexibility in reasoning (e.g., English language arts, philosophy, social studies) may cause significant confusion for the student (Sansosti et al., 2010), limiting their potential for grasping "real-world" content necessary for postsecondary success. Thus, many Autistic adolescents underachieve academically (Estes et al., 2010) and are at high risk for dropping out of college or avoiding postsecondary education completely (Alverson et al., 2019; Shattuck et al., 2012). In some instances, Autistic students may even be dissuaded from pursuing postsecondary education (Zimmerman, 2017). Similarly, job attainment remains significantly lower for Autistic young adults than those with other disabilities (Chen et al., 2015), which may be due to gaps in earlier teaching.

Social, Emotional, and Behavioral Issues

Social Relationships and Independence

Deficits in social communication and social interactions are the defining characteristic of Autistic individuals (American Psychological Association [APA], 2013; Volkmar et al., 2014). Autistic adolescents and young adults tend to have few friends, and they prefer to be on the periphery of social networks within school and community settings (Locke et al., 2010). In comparison to neurotypical peers (Stanish et al., 2017) and peers with other disabilities (Orsmond et al., 2013), Autistic adolescents report a higher level of social isolation and are less likely to participate in social or recreational activities such as making phone calls, having friends over, or attending activities/clubs. Perhaps the most critical challenge to social relationships lies in the basics of social understanding and problem-solving. In general, Autistic young adults exhibit difficulties in understanding nonverbal cues such as facial expressions, gestures, and tone of voice (Kuzmanovic et al., 2011; Uljarevic & Hamilton, 2013), making it difficult for them to decipher thoughts, feelings, intentions, and perspectives of others.

Difficulty understanding nonverbal cues means increased challenges when attempting to interpret when another is upset, happy, or uninterested. It is unlikely that an Autistic individual will engage in all expected nonverbal behaviors when communicating. For example, they may demonstrate poor eye contact (or have a stiff, staring gaze), display awkward or clumsy body posture and limited or inappropriate facial expressions, and/or fail to use gestures while interacting and communicating with others. As a result of limited social understanding, Autistic young adults frequently appear unaware of how to physically engage and respond in social interactions (Volkmar et al., 2014). They may violate social conventions and engage in a large amount of socially inappropriate behavior(s). For example, an Autistic individual may infringe upon another's personal space (e.g., touching a shirt that has a picture the individual likes), ask extremely personal questions (e.g., "Why are your parents divorced?"), or share thoughts and/or opinions that are better left unsaid (e.g., blurting out "you have really ugly shoes"). A lack of understanding of the social world, combined with socially inappropriate behavior(s), often results in numerous social errors.

Friendship is often described in terms of common interests and may wane when the focus of activities deviates from the shared interest. For example, an Autistic individual may continue to talk about the latest Spiderman movie while seemingly ignoring the listener's signs of boredom (e.g., looking away, or attempting to leave). This failure may appear as disregard for others' feelings and may come across as insensitive, despite this not being the individual's intention. Instead, Autistic young adults experience difficulties recognizing, relating to, and understanding the feelings of others, making it challenging for them to understand why others do not share their same level of passion (APA, 2013; Webb et al., 2017).

Challenges in understanding the social world combined with a tendency to make social errors are likely to impact the development of social independence. Adolescence can be challenging for all youth as they navigate physical, emotional, and social changes but even more so for Autistic young adults due to difficulties engaging socially with peers. The demands of social situations combined with social anxiety will likely impact the progression toward social independence. In fact, Autistic adults often achieve lower levels of socially independent functioning than would be expected from their cognitive and language skills (Howlin & Moss, 2012). This translates to developing romantic relationships. Some Autistic individuals may have limited social knowledge and independence to pursue and engage in romantic relationships appropriately (Dewinter et al., 2015). They may initiate behaviors viewed or received by others as inappropriate or intrusive given the situation and context (e.g., touching without consent, making sexual comments) when engaging with potential romantic partners (Strunz et al., 2017). See the Wilczynski et al. (chapter "The Need for Relationship and Sexuality Education for Transition Aged Autistic Youth") chapter on relationship and sexuality education in this book.

Anxiety, Depression, and Suicidal Ideation

Recent research and clinical information suggests that Autistic individuals may be more susceptible to anxiety and other affective mood problems. In fact, Autistic young adults demonstrate higher levels of anxiety and depression than neurotypical peers. Prevalence rates for comorbid anxiety range between 11% and 85% (White et al., 2009) and 1.4% and 38% for depression (Magnuson & Constantino, 2011). The higher risk of these psychiatric disorders increases throughout adolescence for Autistic individuals who are older, possess higher IQ (>85), and self-report more Autistic traits (Merikangas et al., 2010; van Steensel & Heeman, 2017).

One hypothesis for increased rates of affective disorders is that Autistic individuals may be more socially aware, but also experience increased anxiety as their deficits become more apparent and they experience more social failures (Bellini, 2006; Kerns & Kendall, 2013). Alternatively, as Autistic adolescents become more socially aware, they may increasingly recognize incidents of bullying, mistreatment, and disrespect from peers and other people. Autistic adolescents experience the highest rate of bullying in comparison to peers with intellectual disabilities and neurotypical peers (Tipton-Fisler et al., 2018). Although they may minimize the severity of bullying incidents, they also withdraw socially from peer relationships, contributing further to social isolation and other internalizing symptoms such as anxiety, depression, and suicidality (Fisher & Taylor, 2016). Findings also demonstrate the relationship between being bullied and suicidality for neurotypical adolescents as well as Autistic adolescents (Holden et al., 2020).

Initial anxiety may emerge at early ages for Autistic individuals due to: (1) preoccupation with possible violations of routines and rituals, (2) being placed in situations without clear schedules or expectations, or (3) anticipation of failed social encounters. These anxieties may evolve into more depressive symptoms during adolescence and early adulthood (Eussen et al., 2013). This typically occurs when an Autistic individual begins to develop a greater insight into their differences from others and experience a growing desire for friendships (Eussen et al., 2013). Many Autistic adolescents desire and frequently seek friendships; however, they may lack the skills to acquire and maintain such relationships. Continued rejections and/or history of negative social interactions may cause Autistic young adults to remove themselves from social opportunities. In turn, this may cause them to downwardly spiral, whereby they rarely encounter opportunities to learn how to interact appropriately with others, and, subsequently, fail to develop meaningful friendships (White et al., 2011). As a result, poor social competence may increase or exacerbate mental health problems as the individual ages (White et al., 2011).

It is likely that chronic frustration from repeated failure to engage others socially contributes to the development of deepening depression, especially during adolescence and young adulthood (Hedley et al., 2017). That is, as Autistic children enter adolescence, they become more ostracized from their peer group and experience greater isolation from society, and, consequently, depressive symptoms become pronounced (Hedley et al., 2017). Characteristics of depression may include worsening in behavior, inattention, social withdrawal, overreliance on obsessions and compulsions, hyperactivity, aggressive or oppositional behavior, agitation, and/or changes in eating and sleeping (Eussen et al., 2013). Once caught in this downward spiral, it is likely that depressive symptomatology will worsen, resulting in significant risks if left untreated by interventions targeting resiliency (Mackay et al., 2017).

Consistent with higher rates of anxiety and depression, rates of suicidal ideation in Autistic adults appear significantly higher than the general population. Cassidy et al. (2014) found the rate of suicidal ideation in adults with recent diagnoses of ASD was 9.6 times higher than the general population; and that 35% of their sample had planned or attempted suicide, especially in those who self-reported higher autism traits. Similarly, Hirvikoski et al. (2016) reported that suicide was the leading cause of premature death in Autistic individuals and this group was 9.4 times at greater risk of suicide compared to the general population. More recently, talk of death or suicide (as indicated via parent report) was reported to be common in 22% of Autistic young adults during inpatient psychiatric admission (Horowitz et al., 2017). Such data highlight the relationship between affective mood problems and autism symptomatology; and, consequently, it is equally important to understand why Autistic individuals with high self-perceptions of autism traits may be at an increased risk of suicide. For example, Pelton and Cassidy (2017) revealed that individuals most at-risk for suicide included those with high levels of autism traits who also experienced significant depression with *thwarted belonging* (i.e., feelings of loneliness, difficulties establishing reciprocal relationships) and *perceived burdensomeness* (i.e., poor self-esteem, agitation, unemployment).

Behavioral Rigidity

Autistic young adults often display an inflexible adherence to routines or rituals, desiring sameness, and requiring environmental predictability (APA, 2013). Change, surprise, chaos, and uncertainty are not easily tolerated or adapted to by many on the spectrum, and the lack of predictability or sameness can cause feelings of stress and/or anxiety (Gotham et al., 2013). Like most people, Autistic individuals prefer predictability in their environment; however, the extent to which a lack of predictability or sameness negatively influences Autistic people is likely much greater than the majority of the population (Goris et al., 2020). Although the specific cause of these behaviors are unclear, they are generally attributed to some type of neurological impairment and interpreted as attempts to cope with sensory factors, and others may relate to cognitive difficulties secondary to those neurological factors (Leekam et al., 2011).

Perhaps the most interesting feature of rigid behavior displayed by Autistic individuals is their obsessive and, at times, all absorbing interests (Harrop et al., 2019). These individuals may collect volumes of detailed, factual information and trivia related to a relatively narrow topic (e.g., Harry Potter, NASCAR racing). Regardless of the topic or the frequency with which it may change, Autistic individuals tend to focus most of their social advances and conversations on their specific topic of interest and talk about it to the point at which others become uninterested and disengaged.

Self-Sufficiency

As students advance through schooling, the characteristics of school programming and environments become more dynamic as expectations and demands around independent or autonomous behavior continually increase. The nature and context of middle and secondary schools require students to adapt and self-direct their behavior across increasingly less structured and more unpredictable interactions and educational experiences. One of the developmental achievements often associated with adolescence is an individual's ability to function independently across complex situations and dynamic environments, without supervision or monitoring (Hume et al., 2014; Sessa & Steinberg, 1991).

The dynamic nature of high schools with varying curricula choices, multiple classes, and teachers, as well as the independent nature of navigating the formal and informal structure and culture of schools, can be challenging for all students but even more so for Autistic students. Deficits associated with the core areas of autism (e.g., social/communication; restrictive, repetitive behavior, and/or stereotypical behavior) can impact progress toward independent functioning and self-sufficiency. The freedom and autonomy students experience in changing classes, managing multiple assignments, and increased social and behavioral expectations may contribute to increased anxiety and other challenges as Autistic students struggle with skills related to social cognition (e.g., perspective taking) and executive functioning (e.g., organization, time management, and flexibility).

Across their k-12 educational experiences and given appropriate instruction and supports, Autistic individuals continue to develop skills related to independent functioning and autonomous behavior. Yet, findings indicate this progress tends to slow during the late adolescent, young adult, and postsecondary transition years (Taylor & Seltzer, 2010). This occurs during a time when Autistic individuals are leaving federally mandated special education services and transitioning to eligibility-driven adult services, postsecondary education, and employment settings. Across these environments, Autistic individuals must demonstrate self-awareness and self-advocacy skills in an effort to receive accommodations, accentuating the need for independent functioning.

During a potentially stressful and uncertain time of life, it is probable that Autistic young adults will encounter difficulties maintaining supports and strategies they have relied on to compensate for challenges associated with social cognition and executive functioning (Smith et al., 2012). Students, caregivers, and other individualized education program (IEP) team members should monitor the extent to which instructional or behavioral supports and accommodations advance or impede the student's progress toward independent functioning and autonomous behavior (Hume et al., 2014).

Decisions made surrounding supports and accommodations should consider the feasibility of the support across multiple environments and contexts in addition to considering the student's personal functional and behavioral goals. For instance, when an educator, human service professional, or caregiver is needed to provide a cue, instruction, or support to the Autistic individual for them to use or implement the support, then an important consideration is whether the support is helping to move the individual toward independence. Beginning early in the Autistic individual's life and continuing throughout the lifespan decisions about the nature and intensity of supports should be informed by individual characteristics, preferences, and performance data well concurrently choosing those supports which are non-stigmatizing and increase one's self-sufficiency. Instructing children to use cues and supports available in their environment that are non-intrusive or stigmatizing should begin early to promote independence.

Given the variety of environmental, social, psychological, and physiological changes that occur during adolescence through early adulthood, self-sufficiency can be challenging or elusive for many young adults but even more so for Autistic individuals. Evaluating typical markers associated with self-sufficiency, such as obtaining a driver's license, employment, educational attainment, and residential status reveals disparate outcomes for Autistic young adults in comparison to peers. Autistic individuals also report higher rates of disengagement in postsecondary education and employment (Shattuck et al., 2012), and are less likely to reside outside of their childhood residence (Anderson et al., 2014) compared to peers with other disabilities (e.g., learning disabilities, intellectual disability, and emotional disturbance). Yet parents and Autistic young adults recognize living away from home as a step toward independence and a desirable transition outcome for Autistic individuals (Sosnowy et al., 2018).

Obtaining a driver's license is often viewed as a passport for increased freedom and independence for many teenagers. Autistic young adults are less likely to secure a driver's license, self-report lower ratings regarding their ability to drive, and experience a greater number of traffic accidents and citations relative to non-ASD drivers (Daly et al., 2014). Autistic individuals who have limited mobility depend on others or must find alternative means for getting around the community and accessing educational, employment, or social and recreational opportunities as well as needed medical or wellness services. For transition-age youth with disabilities, getting to and from work is frequently cited as a continued barrier to employment and remains through one's adult years (Lubin & Feeley, 2016; Rosenbloom, 2007).

The learning, social, emotional, and behavioral difficulties experienced by transition-age adolescents do not disappear as students leave federally funded special education services. Without effective strategies and supports, the challenges students encounter during secondary school will present in postsecondary education, employment, and community settings. Strategies and supports that move the student toward functional independence and autonomous behavior should be a critical component of educational programming.

Mismatch Between Goals and Supports in the Environment

Autistic individuals have much to contribute to the workforce and their communities. However, Autistic individuals are underrepresented in the competitive labor force. Reported rates of employment for Autistic individuals are low across studies, with 25–50% of Autistic adults participating in any type of paid employment (Hendricks, 2010). Yet, there is an evolving knowledge base that highlights workplace contributions of Autistic employees. The limited research conducted with employers suggests favorable experiences with hiring Autistic individuals (Hagner & Cooney, 2005; Scott et al., 2017). Autistic employees performed the same or better than neurotypical coworkers when rated on attention to detail, work ethic, and quality of work but were rated as less flexible or likely to follow instructions compared to coworkers (Scott et al., 2017). Several of the characteristics associated with the autism that can be viewed as challenges in an educational environment (e.g., rigidity of thought, insistence on consistency) may translate into desirable traits (e.g., attention to detail, insistence on consistency, strong adherence to procedures in repetitive process) for certain occupations. Through participation in early career and work experiences, Autistic adolescents have an opportunity to gain valuable employment-related social and industry-specific skills that should inform education and career decisions in addition to exposing them to a variety of workplace environments and demands.

Unfortunately, Autistic individuals tend to struggle in employment, postsecondary education, and engagement in community activities. They often underperform in relation to their perceived abilities. Deficits in social and communication skills as well as with areas of executive functioning (e.g., impulse control, emotional control, flexibility, planning, organization, goal setting, etc.) may become evident during workplace interactions; despite an individual meeting the requirements for the position, they may struggle with social-communicative engagement. Postsecondary goals related to employment or education may be developed based on limited exposure to performance expectations as well as limited knowledge of the daily routines and processes that occur in work settings or across college and university campuses (Szidon et al., 2015; Wehman et al., 2009). The limited self-awareness often associated with Autistic adolescents and young adults contributes to the selection of post-school goals that may be inconsistent with the strengths, preferences, interests, and needs of the individual (Alverson et al., 2019; Nuske et al., 2019).

Autistic secondary students may spend the majority of their school day in general education classes focused on the core curriculum, with limited opportunities for explicit instruction on building skills reflecting their unique social/communication and behavioral needs. Instruction related to adaptive behaviors such as social skills, problem solving, and self-regulation can occur in general education settings and be embedded within content-area classes. However, the practice is not widespread or individualized to address a student's unique cognitive and behavioral challenges associated with an activity and environment (Thomeer et al., 2019). Additionally, the teaching and learning strategies may not be consistent with the behavioral-based strategies documented to be effective for Autistic students.

Given the positive relationship between participation in paid employment while in high school and post-school employment, it is important for Autistic students to participate in work-based learning experiences or paid employment (Test et al., 2009). See the Lee and Carter (2012) chapter regarding employment for more details. School personnel may encounter scheduling or staffing difficulties in facilitating these opportunities for Autistic students, especially when students spend the majority of their day in general education classes. Caregivers may worry their son or daughter will miss time during the school day to participate in vocational experiences or they may believe part-time employment limits participation in other activities or needed services.

The benefits of vocational and work experiences for students with disabilities are well documented (Mazzotti et al., 2016). These activities allow students to participate in community businesses and facilitate an opportunity to assess environmental factors that may support or impede a student's future employment success. They also allow the individual to build important work-related and independence skills while also establishing a work history. Without participation in employment environments prior to establishing career or postsecondary goals, students experience difficulties making informed decisions about their future (Lee et al., 2019).

Authentic workplace experiences and interactions inform Autistic students and education professionals about how one's specific strengths and challenges interact with physical and social environments of workplaces and specific job duties and provide an opportunity to develop potential strategies and supports or to explore alternative career options more closely aligned with a student's skills and preferences. For instance, individuals may receive information related to career or soft skills needed in the workplace through texts, videos, or classroom-based instruction. Although these experiences are beneficial, they are likely guided by a person the student knows and occur in a contrived setting familiar to the student. As a result, these experiences do not provide for an authentic experience reflective of a dynamic workplace nor do they facilitate the gathering of data to inform the environmental characteristics of a workplace that might be supportive or conducive to the needs and interest of the Autistic adolescent. Thus, Autistic students and their IEP teams make decisions about postsecondary goals based on an incomplete understanding of the student based on a simulated work environment as opposed to data-based decisions gleaned from authentic experiences in post-school environments.

Analyzing or assessing prospective employment opportunities and postsecondary environments in relation to one's unique needs and interests can be challenging without guidance and support regarding performance expectations and the availability of potential supports in these environments. There is evidence some Autistic youth do not learn about their differences or unique needs during their k-12 experiences, such as reasons for receiving special education services and how these may advance or hinder progress toward individual goals (Camarena & Sarigiani, 2009). It is common for youth to struggle with self-acceptance and finding their strengths and challenges. The process of assessing future opportunities in college and workplaces is much more complex for Autistic individuals, even for Autistic students who may demonstrate an increased level of self-awareness and acceptance of their neurodiversity.

Autistic adolescents and young adults must consider the issue of disability disclosure, an often-overlooked and unaddressed area of secondary curricula but closely aligned to discussions around functional independence and autonomous behavior. To secure accommodations in the workplace or postsecondary education environments, individuals must disclose one's disability. There are benefits and challenges with disability disclosure for individuals with disabilities (von Schrader et al., 2014). Autistic individuals who disclosed their disability were more likely to be employed compared to individuals who did not disclose their disability (Ohl et al., 2017). From our experiences in coordinating a university program for Autistic students, Autistic individuals transitioning to postsecondary education may often initially choose not to disclose their disability but after a semester or year of courses decide to disclose in an effort to access supports and services beyond those available to all students. Findings from studies of Autistic students enrolled in postsecondary education (Marshak et al., 2010) and Autistic job seekers and employees (Johnson & Josie, 2014) also support the limited understanding and complexity around disability disclosure for Autistic individuals. This issue is also counterintuitive to a capacity-building approach to services and empowerment of Autistics embracing their neurodivergence.

The difficulties Autistic adolescents and young adults experience related to social cognition, such as understanding and appraising social and personal relations in educational and employment environments, compounds decisions around disability disclosure. Providing opportunities for Autistic adolescents and young adults to become more aware of their strengths, preferences, interests, and needs as well as experience potential postsecondary environments might improve consideration of their strengths, challenges, and support needs when making educational and occupational decisions. Instruction and experiences to improve self-awareness and the practice of disability disclosure in postsecondary education and employment settings are also needed (Bublitz et al., 2017; Munandar et al., 2020).

Readying or preparing the environment to support Autistic individuals is notably absent from many transition-focused planning discussions or explicitly identified as a barrier to postsecondary employment and education. For instance, adolescents and their caregivers reported existing support services available at college and universities are ill-equipped to meet the needs of Autistic college students (Camarena & Sarigiani, 2009; White et al., 2016). Autistic college students reported needs reflective of self-determination skills (e.g., self-advocacy, self-awareness, problem-solving) as well as strategies for effectively communicating with peers and instructors (White et al., 2016). There are also concerns about whether individuals working at colleges or universities, such as student service personnel and course instructors, understand the characteristics and needs of Autistic individuals. These perspectives speak to the increasing need for Autistic individuals to be well versed in self-advocacy and to understand the legally mandated supports and services versus those provided as student enticements or at additional costs. There are several resources available to school psychologists related to self-advocacy and disability disclosure to help them support Autistic young adults in making informed choices around disability disclosure. These resources are available from autism Speaks® (2018), the Job Accommodation Network (n.d.), the National Collaborative on Workforce Development for Youth (2005), and the US Department of Labor's Office of Disability and Employment Policy (n.d.).

Parents and Autistic young adults also believe employers underestimate the abilities of Autistic individuals and underutilize the skills they bring to the workplace (Barnhill, 2007; Hillier & Galizzi, 2014). Autistic employees may encounter multiple supervisors with different leadership styles and perceptions of expected workplace behaviors. The lack of consistency in processes or unanticipated changes can be a source of anxiety for Autistic employees as they try to adapt to different and sometimes evolving expectations. Multitasking, working in teams, or changing job tasks can also make it difficult for an Autistic individual to adapt or regulate their workplace behavior.

The federal/state vocational rehabilitation program is the primary agency that supports individuals with disabilities in finding employment. They also network and provide information to employers on strategies for hiring and supporting individuals with disabilities in the workplace. Over the past decade, some colleges and universities have expanded support services and/or developed programs that specialize in working with Autistic students (Lindstrom et al., 2009; Viezel et al., 2020). Representatives from these programs often interface with instructors and student affairs personnel. The focus of service through higher education or the federal/state vocational rehabilitation program is the student or the individual with a disability. In some situations, such as customized employment, services may be directed at the employer to address specific needs of an individual with a disability (Wehman et al., 2017).

Clearly, an argument can be made as to the need for greater awareness about the characteristics and needs of Autistic young adults across the general population of employers and postsecondary educational settings. However, no federal policy exists that necessitates employers or postsecondary institutions must educate their workforce about supporting Autistic individuals or preparing their environment for Autistic people at this time. Federal and state laws exist to address discriminatory behavior or the lack of accessibility but making a business or university disability or autism-friendly is not mandated. Although many businesses, educational environments, and community organizations are engaging in these efforts, the responsibility rests with the job seeker or Autistic student to advocate on their behalf. This can be a daunting task for any individual seeking their first job, but it speaks to the critical need to provide Autistic students with explicit instruction related to self-determination skills (e.g., self-awareness, self-advocacy, and self-management.) across their k-12 educational experience.

Correctional Systems

Several core characteristics of autism increase the possibility Autistic young adults may become both victims and offenders of criminal behavior. Social naivete, inability to understand and follow social rules, inappropriate touching of objects or people, challenges with environmental stimuli such as noise and lights, and several language and communication difficulties (e.g., information processing delays and perspective taking) may contribute to challenging interactions or situations with community members and representatives of the criminal justice system (e.g., law enforcement, attorneys, judges, and correction officials). Findings related to the experiences and outcomes of Autistic individuals and the criminal justice system in the United States are lacking. The limited research is plagued with methodological shortcomings and inconsistent findings making it difficult to draw conclusions about the prevalence, characteristics or symptomology, and offending behavior of Autistic individuals in the adult or juvenile justice system (Cheely et al., 2012; Helverschou et al., 2018; Vermeiren et al., 2006).

Autistic individuals are up to seven times more likely to intersect with the criminal justice system than people without ASD even though Autistic individuals are no more likely than the general population to commit criminal acts (Ghaziuddin et al.,

1991; Mouridsen et al., 2008). Autistic individuals can also be victims of crimes (see Wilczynski et al., chapter "The Need for Relationship and Sexuality Education for Transition Aged Autistic Youth" regarding sexuality education in this book), but the purpose of this section is to reflect the knowledge base concerning the risks of perpetration and the far-reaching consequences for those on the spectrum. Thus, much of the following information describes the experiences of Autistic individuals charged with illegal acts as well as concerns associated with the core deficits of autism and unlawful behavior.

Regarding the incidence and type of offending behavior, it is not surprising more crimes involved behaviors against people in comparison to property given the social and communication difficulties and poor problem-solving skills characteristic of the population. Findings from national data of youth served in juvenile residential facilities indicated the majority of crimes committed by youth, including youth with disabilities, involved crimes against persons (37.7%) as opposed to property crimes (21.7%; Hockenberry, 2018). Unlawful behavior against people included such acts as: robbery; aggravated, simple, or sexual assault; criminal homicide. Whereas unlawful behavior involving property included such acts as theft, vandalism, trespassing, arson, fraud, and illegal drug trade. Longitudinal data regarding the types of offending behaviors of Autistic youth (i.e., 12–18 years of age) from state-level data reflected similar results. Cheely et al. (2012) reported lower rates of overall charges for Autistic youth in comparison to the general youth population but significantly higher rates of person offenses and lower rates of property offenses than the general youth population in a state's criminal justice system over the 6 years reflected in the report.

Given these findings and in light of the core indications of autism, including communication and psychosocial challenges, this speaks to potential supports or strategies Autistic individuals may need across situations, contexts, and lifespan. It also suggests the need for early awareness and identification of behaviors that likely increase vulnerability to offending or engaging in unlawful acts and developing appropriate training and intervention plans across areas of immediate need and long-term support. It is probable that individuals on the spectrum are under-identified or inaccurately labeled within the criminal and juvenile justice system as well as during encounters with law enforcement officials.

Although findings in this area are limited, we know through anecdotal information and clinical experience, contributing factors include the underdeveloped self-awareness and self-advocacy skills, and communication challenges of Autistic individuals interacting with others under potentially provocative and tense circumstances. In some instances, adolescents on the spectrum may not identify as an Autistic individual so behavior or interactions may be interpreted without critical information that might be helpful to law enforcement professionals. It is also likely Autistic young adults may present or react differently in one environment or context than they might in another such as communicating with a police officer one-on-one or in front of a courtroom with a judge and several people. Given the difficulties Autistic individuals experience with social functioning, communication, restrictive behavior, and emotional regulation, these findings are disconcerting and raise important questions about the capacity to discriminate between potentially illegal acts and the ability to self-advocate.

Identifying areas of concerns related to potentially unlawful behavior by Autistic adolescents is helpful in planning proactive strategies to reduce the occurrences of such incidents. Several factors related to the core characteristics of autism and the high rates of psychiatric comorbidity (e.g., anxiety, depression; Mattila et al., 2011) warrant a discussion on potential contributors to offending behavior for Autistic adolescents and young adults that may ultimately interrupt or derail transition to prosocial postschool environments and activities.

Behaviors associated with the core characteristics of autism place Autistic adolescents at risk of being both victims and offenders of crime. Social skills and theory of the mind deficits (e.g., lacking understanding that others have independent thoughts and feelings), mood disturbances and poor emotional coping skills, impairments in moral reasoning, sensory processing challenges, and rigidity of thought or behavior may contribute to situations in which an individual's actions, or inactions, led to offending or criminal behavior (Browning & Caulfield, 2011; Newman & Ghaziuddin, 2008). For example, Chen et al. (2003) described an Autistic adolescent whose fixation and challenges with cognitive inhibition resulted in illegal behavior. The young man repeatedly stole items such as papers, boxes, and plastic bags from peers, resulting in expulsion from high school and dropping out of college. While living with his parents, the young adult also stole letters from neighbors' mailboxes (Chen et al., 2003).

Obsessions and preoccupations can lead Autistic individuals to not realize, or disregard, the social consequences of their behavior (Haskins & Silva, 2006). In instances when an Autistic individual may misinterpret the verbal or non-verbal behavior of others, such as from a member of the opposite sex or an online stranger, challenging or compromising situations may follow (e.g., sexual advances toward a minor). See Wilczynski et al. (chapter "The Need for Relationship and Sexuality Education for Transition Aged Autistic Youth") in this book for additional examples of why Autistic individuals may be at higher risk of sex-related crimes. Sensory processing challenges can produce strong responses that are unusual or atypical for the environment (Lane et al., 2010; Fernandez-Prieto et al., 2021) and this can produce potentially dangerous misinterpretations by community or members of law enforcement. For instance, when an Autistic individual who is sensitive to environmental stimuli reacts strongly to loud noises, his behavior is misinterpreted as threatening, aggressive, or attributed to use of alcohol or drugs.

Given that Autistic individuals may have challenges with communication, aggressive or externalizing behavior, combined with increased expectations for communication and self-direction associated with adult roles, potential challenges arise. The documented decline in adaptive behavior skills for adolescents on the spectrum, especially those students with no co-occurring intellectual disability, is well documented (Picci & Scherf, 2015; Pugliese et al., 2015). Adolescence is a period marked by increased risk-taking behavior and teenagers, including those on the spectrum and neurotypical peers challenge boundaries set by family members and other authority figures. These situations present unique challenges for Autistic teenagers and are especially acute when individuals encounter situations requiring perspective taking, in addition to situations outside of routine daily occurrences. For example, Autistic individuals with sensory sensitivity may provide an unusual response to yelling or physical reaction to questions raised, noises and lights from police or emergency vehicles, or a physical pat-down conducted by a security checkpoint worker at an event entrance potentially leading to a confrontational situation. Similarly, a police officer perceives an Autistic young male as not taking the officer's questions seriously or being noncompliant or stubborn as the individual fails to make eye contact and provides unrelated answers or engages in repetitive behavior (e.g., body rocking).

Challenges interpreting and processing information can contribute to fear and misunderstanding when questioned or arrested by police or other professionals involved in law enforcement or criminal justice professions (Freckelton & List, 2009). Similarly, individuals on the spectrum are likely guided and benefit from rule-governed behavior, so when instructions or advice from law enforcement officials or attorneys contradicts how an individual perceives the information, communication breakdowns may result and trigger strong flight/fight, or emotional responses. For example, during a semi-structured interview, a police officer reported an incident where an Autistic adolescent male acted aggressively when the police officer attempted to communicate with him (Railey et al., 2020).

For school psychologists supporting youth on the spectrum during their transition years, advocating for the inclusion of an array of strategies to increase areas of adaptive functioning during the transition years is critically important. Given these skills may not be explicitly taught in general education classes, exploring opportunities through peer groups that help role-play social-communication scenarios and strategies about potential complex community interactions and environments are needed. However, role-playing with Autistic secondary students about potential community situations, especially scenarios involving law enforcement, may be controversial with educators and parents. Resources used in secondary schools include an immersive virtual reality experience that provides students with an augmented experience in communicating with law enforcement (see, e.g., *Floreo*; McCleery et al., 2020) and social scripts.

In addition to the heightened risk for committing crimes, school psychologists should realize Autistic individuals are more likely to be victims of crimes than they are to commit them (Weiss & Fardella, 2018). Social emotional challenges can make interactions with peers difficult for Autistic students. Peers may view a student's rigid behavior or strong adherence to rule and school processes unfavorably. One study found prevalence estimates regarding bullying among Autistic adolescents to be 46.3% for victimization, 14.8% for perpetration, and 8.9% for behavior that combines victimization and perpetration (Sterzing et al., 2012). This compares to the CDC's overall prevalence of bullying on school property for students in grades 9–12 of 20.2% (Gladden et al., 2014). In certain cases (i.e., involving physical assault, death threats, or threats to do harm), bullying is categorized as criminal behavior resulting in involvement of law enforcement.

Information related to unlawful acts by Autistic individuals combined with knowledge about the characteristics and potential idiosyncratic behaviors exhibited by individuals on the spectrum may alert school psychologists, other professionals, and caregivers to behaviors or situations that place an individual at an increased risk of engaging in behavior that may rise to the level of a criminal act. The information speaks to the importance of early intervening and proactive strategies to address the behavior and prepare individuals for potentially vulnerable or compromising situations. For example, in the area of sexual expression and determining another individual's interest in sexual acts an Autistic individual's lack of early and proactive training on appropriate sexual expression and consent could potentially lead to problematic situations (Ballan & Freyer, 2017). Similar to Social Stories™, the use of social behavior mapping where students are required to identify appropriate and inappropriate behaviors but also discuss what the behaviors might look like or feel like to another individual such as would they be expected or unexpected and how each scenario might play out (Winner, 2007).

Conclusion

The transition from secondary schools to education, employment, or community settings is both a challenging and exciting time for adolescents and their families. Accurately representing potential challenges with the transition to adult life is particularly daunting because Autistic individuals vary significantly in the environments in which they live and learn as well as symptom presentation and severity. The information in the chapter provides an analysis of several internal and external variables that can potentially impede post-school opportunities. Findings regarding the transition outcomes of Autistic adolescents and young adults have been discouraging. Acknowledging potential barriers to favorable postsecondary outcomes should inform the planning and delivery of student-centered services and supports aimed at promoting independence and self-sufficiency. The chapters that follow extend the discussion and offer school psychologists and other professionals working with Autistic individuals strategies and resources to improve the preparation of Autistic individuals for post-school opportunities.

References

Alverson, C. Y., Lindstrom, L. E., & Hirano, K. A. (2019). High school to college: Transition experiences of young adults with autism. *Focus on Autism and Other Developmental Disabilities, 34*(1), 52–64. https://doi.org/10.1177/1088357615611880

American Psychiatric Association. (2013). *Diagnostic and statistical manual of mental disorders* (5th ed.). https://doi.org/10.1176/appi.books.9780890425596

Anderson, K. A., Shattuck, P. T., Cooper, B. P., Roux, A. M., & Wagner, M. (2014). Prevalence and correlates of postsecondary residential status among young adults with an autism spectrum disorder. *Autism: The International Journal of Research and Practice, 18*(5), 562–570. https://doi.org/10.1177/1362361313481860

Autism Speaks. (2018, August 27). *To disclose or not disclose: Employment toolkit.* https://www.autismspeaks.org/tool-kit-excerpt/disclose-or-not-disclose

Baldwin, S., & Costley, D. (2016). The experiences and needs of female adults with high-functioning autism spectrum disorder. *Autism: The International Journal of Research and Practice, 20*(4), 483–495. https://doi.org/10.1177/1362361315590805

Ballan, M. S., & Freyer, M. B. (2017). Autism spectrum disorder, adolescence, and sexuality education: Suggested interventions for mental health professionals. *Sexuality and Disability, 35*(2), 261–273. https://doi.org/10.1007/S11195-017-9477-9

Barnhill, G. P. (2007). Outcomes in adults with Asperger syndrome. *Focus on Autism and Other Developmental Disabilities, 22*(2), 116–126. https://doi.org/10.1177/10883576070220020301

Bellini, S. (2006). The development of social anxiety in high functioning adolescents with autism spectrum disorders. *Focus on Autism and Other Developmental Disabilities, 21*, 138–145.

Bogte, H., Flamma, B., Van der Meere, J., & Engeland, V. (2009). Divided attention capacity in adults with autism spectrum disorders with and without intellectual disability. *Autism, 13*, 229–243. https://doi.org/10.1177/1362361309103793

Boucher, J. (2017). *The autistic spectrum: Characteristics, causes and practical issues* (2nd ed.). Sage.

Browning, A., & Caulfield, L. (2011). The prevalence and treatment of people with Asperger's syndrome in the criminal justice system. *Criminology and Criminal Justice, 11*(2), 165–180. https://doi.org/10.1177/1748895811398455

Bublitz, D. J., Fitzgerald, K., Alarcon, M., D'Onofrio, J., & Gillespie-Lynch, K. (2017). Verbal behaviors during employment interviews of college students with and without ASD. *Journal of Vocational Rehabilitation, 47*(1), 79–92. https://doi.org/10.3233/JVR-170884

Camarena, P. M., & Sarigiani, P. A. (2009). Postsecondary educational aspirations of high-functioning adolescents with autism spectrum disorders and their parents. *Focus on Autism and Other Developmental Disabilities, 24*(2), 115–128. https://doi.org/10.1177/1088357609332675

Cassidy, S., Bradley, P., Robinson, J., Allison, C., McHugh, M., & Baron-Cohen, S. (2014). Suicidal ideation and suicide plans or attempts in adults with Asperger's syndrome attending specialist diagnostic clinic: A clinical cohort study. *Lancet Psychiatry, 1*, 142–147.

Cheely, C. A., Carpenter, L. A., Letourneau, E. J., Nicholas, J. S., Charles, J., & King, L. B. (2012). The prevalence of youth with autism spectrum disorders in the criminal justice system. *Journal of Autism and Developmental Disorders, 42*(9), 1856–1862. https://doi.org/10.1007/s10803-011-1427-2

Chen, J. L., Leader, G., Sung, C., & Leahy, M. (2015). Trends in employment for individuals with autism spectrum disorder: A review of the research literature. *Review Journal of Autism and Developmental Disorders, 2*, 115–127. https://doi.org/10.1007/s40489-014-0041-6

Chen, P. S., Chen, S. J., Yang, Y. K., Yeh, T. L., Chen, C. C., & Lo, H. Y. (2003). Asperger's disorder: A case report of repeated stealing and the collecting behaviours of an adolescent patient. *Acta Psychiatrica Scandinavica, 107*, 73–76. https://doi.org/10.1034/j.1600-0447.2003.01354.x

Courchesne, E., Campbell, K., & Solso, S. (2011). Brain growth across the life span in autism: Age-specific changes in anatomical pathology. *Brain Research, 1380*, 138–145. https://doi.org/10.1016/j.brainres.2010.09.101

Daly, B. P., Nicholls, E. G., Partick, K. E., Brinckman, D. D., & Schultheis, M. T. (2014). Driving behaviors in adults with autism spectrum disorders. *Autism and Developmental Disorders, 44*, 3119–3128. https://doi.org/10.1007/s10803-014-2166-y

Dawson, G., & Faja, S. (2008). Autism spectrum disorders: A developmental perspective. In T. P. Beauchaine & S. P. Hinshaw (Eds.), *Child and adolescent psychopathology*. Wiley.

Dewinter, J., Vermeiren, R., Vanwesenbeeck, I., Lobbestael, J., & Van Nieuwenhuizen, C. (2015). Sexuality in adolescent boys with autism spectrum disorder: Self-reported behaviours and attitudes. *Journal of Autism and Developmental Disorders, 45*, 731–741. https://doi.org/10.1007/s10803-014-2226-3

Estes, A., Rivera, V., Bryan, M., Cali, P., & Dawson, G. (2010). Discrepancies between academic achievement and intellectual ability in higher-functioning school-aged children with autism spectrum disorder. *Journal of Autism and Developmental Disorders, 41*, 1044–1058. https://doi.org/10.1007/s10803-010-1127-3

Eussen, M. L., Van Gool, A. R., De Verheij, F., Nijs, P. F. A., Verhulst, F. C., & Greaves-Lord, K. (2013). The association of quality social relations, symptom severity and intelligence with anxiety in children with autism spectrum disorders. *Autism, 17*, 723–735. https://doi.org/10.1177/1362361312453882

Fernandez-Prieto, M., Moreira, C., Cruz, S., Campos, V., Martinez-Regueiro, R., Taboada, M., Carracedo, A., & Sampaio, A. (2021). Executive functioning: A mediator between sensory processing and behaviour in autism spectrum disorder. *Journal of Autism and Developmental Disorders, 51*, 2091–2103. https://doi.org/10.1007/s10803-020-04648-4

Fisher, M. H., & Taylor, J. L. (2016). Let's talk about it: Peer victimization experiences as reported by adolescents with autism spectrum disorder. *Autism, 20*(4), 402–411. https://doi.org/10.1177/1362361315585948

Freckelton SC, I. & List, D. (2009). Asperger's Disorder, criminal responsibility and criminal culpability. *Psychiatry, Psychology and Law, 16*(1), 16–40. https://doi.org/10.1080/13218710902887483

Getzel, E. E., & Thoma, C. A. (2008). Experiences of college students with disabilities and the importance of self-determination in higher education settings. *Career Development for Exceptional Individuals, 31*(2), 77–84. https://doi.org/10.1177/0885728808317658

Ghaziuddin, M., Tsai, L., & Ghaziuddin, N. (1991). Brief report: Violence in Asperger syndrome, a critique. *Journal of Autism and Developmental Disorders, 21*, 349–354. https://doi.org/10.1007/BF02207331

Gladden, R. M., Vivolo-Kantor, A. M., Hamburger, M. E., & Lumpkin, C. D. (2014). *Bullying surveillance among youths: Uniform definitions for public health and recommended data elements, version 1.0*. National Center for Injury Prevention and Control, Centers for Disease Control and Prevention and U.S. Department of Education.

Goldstein, G., Allen, D. N., Minshew, N. J., Williams, D. L., Volkmar, D. L., & Klin, A. (2008). The structure of intelligence in children and adults with high functioning autism. *Neuropsychology, 22*, 301–312. https://doi.org/10.1037/0894-4105.22.3.301

Goris, J., Brass, M., Cambier, C., Delplanque, J., Wiersema, J. R., & Braem, S. (2020). The relation between preference for predictability and autistic traits. *Autism Research: Official Journal of the International Society for Autism Research, 13*(7), 1144–1154. https://doi.org/10.1002/aur.2244

Gotham, K., Bishop, S. L., Hus, V., Huerta, M., Lund, S., Buja, A., Krieger, A., & Lord, C. (2013). Exploring the relationship between anxiety and insistence on sameness in autism spectrum disorders. *Autism Research: Official Journal of the International Society for Autism Research, 6*(1), 33–41. https://doi.org/10.1002/aur.1263

Hagner, D., & Cooney, B. F. (2005). "I do that for everybody": Supervising employees with autism. *Focus on Autism and Other Developmental Disabilities, 20*(2), 91–97.

Harrop, C., Amsbary, J., Towner-Wright, S., Reichow, B., & Boyd, B. A. (2019). That's what I like: The use of circumscribed interests within interventions for individuals with autism spectrum disorder. A systematic review. *Research in Autism Spectrum Disorders, 57*, 63–86. https://doi.org/10.1016/J.RASD.2018.09.008

Haskins, B. G., & Silva, J. A. (2006). Asperger's disorder and criminal behavior: Forensic-psychiatric considerations. *Journal of the American Academy of Psychiatry and the Law Online, 34*(3), 374–384.

Hedley, D., Uljarević, M., Wilmot, M., Richdale, A., & Dissanayake, C. (2017). Brief report: Social support, depression and suicidal ideation in adults with autism spectrum disorder. *Journal of Autism and Developmental Disorders, 47*, 3669–3677. https://doi.org/10.1007/s10803-017-3274-2

Helverschou, S. B., Steindal, K., Nøttestad, J. A., & Howlin, P. (2018). Personal experiences of the criminal justice system by individuals with autism spectrum disorders. *Autism, 22*(4), 460–468. https://doi.org/10.1177/1362361316685554

Hendricks, D. (2010). Employment and adults with autism spectrum disorders: Challenges and strategies for success. *Journal of Vocational Rehabilitation, 32*(2), 125–134.

Hillier, A., & Galizzi, M. (2014). Employment outcomes for young adults with autism spectrum disorders. *Review of Disability Studies, 10*(1 & 2), 69–81.

Hirvikoski, T., Mittendorfer-Rutz, E., Boman, M., Larsson, H., Lichtenstein, P., & Bölte, S. (2016). Premature mortality in autism spectrum disorder. *The British Journal of Psychiatry, 208*, 232–238.

Hockenberry, S. (2018). *Juveniles in residential placement, 2015. Juvenile justice statistics, national report series bulletin.* U.S. Department of Justice, Office of Justice Programs, Office of Juvenile Justice and Delinquency Prevention.

Hoffmann, W., Weber, L., König, U., Becker, K., & Kamp-Becker, I. (2016). The role of the CBCL in the assessment of autism spectrum disorders: An evaluation of symptom profiles and screening characteristics. *Research in Autism Spectrum Disorders, 27*, 44–53. https://doi.org/10.1016/j.rasd.2016.04.002

Holden, R., Mueller, J., McGowan, J., Sanyal, J., Kikoler, M., Simonoff, E., Velupillai, S., & Downs, J. (2020). Investigating bullying as a predictor of suicidality in a clinical sample of adolescents with autism spectrum disorder. *Autism Research, 13*(6), 988–997. https://doi.org/10.1002/aur.2292

Horowitz, L. M., Thurm, A., Farmer, C., Mazefsky, C., Lanzillo, E., Bridge, J., Greenbaum, R., Pao, M., & Siegel, M. (2017). Talking about death or suicide: Prevalence and clinical correlates in youth with autism spectrum disorder in the psychiatric inpatient setting. *Journal of Autism and Developmental Disorders, 48*(11), 3702–3710. https://doi.org/10.1007/s10803-017-3180-7

Howlin, P., Goode, S., Hutton, J., & Rutter, M. (2004). Adult outcome for children with autism. *Journal of Psychology and Psychiatry, 45*(2), 212–249. https://doi.org/10.1111/j.1469-7610.2004.00215.x

Howlin, P., & Moss, P. (2012). Adults with autism spectrum disorders. *The Canadian Journal of Psychiatry, 57*(5), 275–283. https://doi.org/10.1177/070674371205700502

Hume, K., Boyd, B. A., Hamm, J. V., & Kucharczyk, S. (2014). Supporting Independence in adolescents on the autism spectrum. *Remedial and Special Education, 35*(2), 102–113. https://doi.org/10.1177/0741932513514617

Humphrey, N., & Lewis, S. (2008). Make me normal: The views and experiences of pupils on the autistic spectrum in mainstream secondary schools. *Autism, 12*, 1362–3613.

Job Accommodation Network. (n.d.). *Disability disclosure. Job accommodation network.* https://askjan.org/topics/Disability-Disclosure.cfm

Johnson, T. D., & Josie, A. (2014). Disclosure on the spectrum: Understanding disclosure among employees on the autism spectrum. *Industrial and Organizational Psychology, 7*(2), 278–281. https://doi.org/10.1111/iops.12149

Kerns, C. M., & Kendall, P. C. (2013). The presentation and classification of anxiety in autism spectrum disorder. *Clinical Psychology, 19*, 323–347.

Kuzmanovic, B., Schilbach, L., Lehnhardt, F. G., Bente, G., & Vogeley, K. (2011). A matter of words: Impact of verbal and nonverbal information on impression formation in high-functioning autism. *Research in Autism Spectrum Disorders, 5*, 604–613. https://doi.org/10.1016/j.rasd.2010.07.005

Lane, A. E., Young, R. L., Baker, A. E., & Angley, M. T. (2010). Sensory processing subtypes in autism: Association with adaptive behavior. *Journal of Autism and Developmental Disorders, 40*(1), 112–122. https://doi.org/10.1007/s10803-009-0840-2

Lee, E. A. L., Black, M. H., Tan, T., Falkmer, T., & Girdler, S. (2019). "I'm destined to ace this": Work experience placement during high school for individuals with autism spectrum disorder. *Journal of Autism and Developmental Disorders, 49*, 3089–3101. https://doi.org/10.1007/s10803-019-04024-x

Lee, G., & Carter, E. (2012). Preparing transition-age students with high-functioning autism spectrum disorders for meaningful work. *Psychology in the Schools, 49*(10), 988–1000. https://doi.org/10.1002/pits.21651

Leekam, S. R., Prior, M. R., & Uljarevic, M. (2011). Restricted and repetitive behaviors in autism spectrum disorders: A review of research in the last decade. *Psychological Bulletin, 137*(4), 562–593. https://doi.org/10.1037/a0023341

Lindstrom, L. E., Flannery, K. B., Benz, M. R., Olszewski, B., & Slovic, R. (2009). Building employment training partnerships between vocational rehabilitation and community colleges. *Rehabilitation Counseling Bulletin, 52*(3), 189–201. https://doi.org/10.1177/0034355208323946

Locke, J., Ishijima, E. H., Kasari, C., & London, N. (2010). Loneliness, friendship quality and the social networks of adolescents with high functioning autism in an inclusive school setting. *Journal of Research in Special Education Needs, 10*, 74–81.

Loukusa, S., & Moilanen, I. (2009). Pragmatic inference abilities in individuals with Asperger syndrome or high-functioning autism: A review. *Research in Autism Spectrum Disorders, 3*, 890–904.

Lubin, A., & Feeley, C. (2016). Transportation issues of adults on the autism spectrum: Findings from focus group discussions. *Transportation Research Record, 2542*(1), 1–8. https://doi.org/10.3141/2542-01

Mackay, B., Shochet, I. M., & Orr, J. A. (2017). A pilot randomized controlled trial of a school-based resilience intervention to prevent depressive symptoms for young adolescents with autism spectrum disorder: A mixed methods analysis. *Journal of Autism and Developmental Disorders, 47*, 3458–3478. https://doi.org/10.1007/s10803-017-3263-5

Magnuson, K. M., & Constantino, J. N. (2011). Characterization of depression in children with autism spectrum disorders. *Journal of Developmental and Behavioral Pediatrics, 32*(4), 332–340.

Marshak, L., Van Wieren, T., Ferrell, D. R., Swiss, L., & Dugan, C. (2010). Exploring barriers to college student use of disability services and accommodations. *Journal of Postsecondary Education and Disability, 22*(3), 151–165.

Martin, J. S., Poirier, M., & Bowler, D. M. (2010). Brief report: Impaired temporal reproduction performance in adults with autism spectrum disorder. *Journal of Autism and Developmental Disorders, 40*, 640–646.

Mattila, M. L., Kielinen, M., Linna, S. L., Jussila, K., Ebeling, H., Bloigu, R., Joseph, R. M., & Moilanen, I. (2011). Autism spectrum disorders according to DSM-IV-TR and comparison with DSM-5 draft criteria: An epidemiological study. *Journal of the American Academy of Child and Adolescent Psychiatry, 50*(6), 583–592.e11. https://doi.org/10.1016/j.jaac.2011.04.001

Mazzotti, V. L., Rowe, D. A., Sinclair, J., Poppen, M., Woods, W. E., & Shearer, M. L. (2016). Predictors of post-school success: A systematic review of NLTS2 secondary analyses. *Career Development and Transition for Exceptional Individuals, 39*(4), 196–215. https://doi.org/10.1177/2165143415588047

McCleery, J. P., Zitter, A., Solórzano, R., Turnacioglu, S., Miller, J. S., Ravindran, V., & Parish-Morris, J. (2020). Safety and feasibility of an immersive virtual reality intervention program for teaching police interaction skills to adolescents and adults with autism. *Autism Research, 13*, 1418–1424. https://doi.org/10.1002/aur.2352

Merikangas, K. R., He, J., Burstein, M., Swanson, S. A., Avenevoli, S., Cui, L., et al. (2010). Lifetime prevalence of mental disorders in US adolescents: Results from the national comorbidity survey replication-adolescent supplement (NCS-A). *Journal of the American Academy of Child and Adolescent Psychiatry, 49*, 980–989.

Mouridsen, S. E., Rich, B., Isager, T., & Nedergaard, N. J. (2008). Pervasive developmental disorders and criminal behaviour: A case control study. *International Journal of Offender Therapy and Comparative Criminology, 52*(2), 196–205.

Munandar, V. D., Morningstar, M. E., & Carlson, S. R. (2020). A systematic literature review of video-based interventions to improve integrated competitive employment skills among youth and adults with autism spectrum disorder. *Journal of Vocational Rehab, 53*, 29–41. https://doi.org/10.3233/JVR-201083

Nation, K., Clarke, P., Wright, B., & Williams, C. (2006). Patterns of reading ability in children with autism spectrum disorder. *Journal of Autism and Developmental Disorders, 36*, 911–919.

National Collaborative on Workforce Development for Youth. (2005, October 20). *The 411 on disability disclosure: A workbook for youth with disabilities.* http://www.ncwd-youth.info/publications/the-411-on-disability-disclosure-a-workbook-for-youth-with-disabilities/

Newman, S. S., & Ghaziuddin, M. (2008). Violent crime in Asperger syndrome: The role of psychiatric co-morbidity. *Journal of Autism and Developmental Disorders, 38*(10), 1848–1852.

Nuske, A., Rillotta, F., Bellon, M., & Richdale, A. (2019). Transition to higher education for students with autism: A systematic literature review. *Journal of Diversity in Higher Education, 12*(3), 280–295.

Ohl, A., Sheff, M. G., Small, S., Nguyen, J., Paskor, K., & Zanjirian, A. (2017). Predictors of employment status among adults with autism spectrum disorders. *Work, 56*, 345–355. https://doi.org/10.3233/WOR-172492

Orsmond, G. I., Shattuck, P. T., Cooper, B. P., Sterzing, P. R., & Anderson, K. A. (2013). Social participation among young adults with an autism spectrum disorder. *Journal of Autism and Developmental Disorders, 43*(11), 2710–2719. https://doi.org/10.1007/s10803-013-1833-8

Ozonoff, S., Iosif, A. M., Baguio, F., Cook, I. C., Hill, M. M., Hutman, T., Rogers, S. J., Rozga, A., Sangha, S., Sigman, M., Steinfeld, M. B., & Young, G. S. (2010). A prospective study of the emergence of early behavioral signs of autism. *Journal of the American Academy of Child and Adolescent Psychiatry, 49*(3), 256–66.e662.

Pelton, M. K., & Cassidy, S. A. (2017). Are autistic traits associated with suicidality? A test of interpersonal-psychological theory of suicide in a non-clinical young adult sample. *Autism Research, 10*, 1891–1904.

Pennington, B. F., & Ozonoff, S. (1996). Executive functions and developmental psychopathologies. *Journal of Child Psychology & Psychiatry, 37*, 51–87.

Picci, G., & Scherf, K. S. (2015). A two-hit model of autism: Adolescence as the second hit. *Clinical Psychological Science: A Journal of the Association for Psychological Science, 3*(3), 349–371. https://doi.org/10.1177/2167702614540646

Pugliese, C. E., Anthony, A., Strang, J. F., Dudely, K., Wallace, G. L., & Kenworthy, L. (2015). Increasing adaptive behavior skill deficits from childhood to adolescence in autism spectrum disorder: Role of executive function. *Journal of Autism and Developmental Disorders, 45*(6), 1579–1587. https://doi.org/10.1007/s10803-014-2309-1

Railey, K. S., Bowers-Campbell, J., Love, A., & Campbell, J. M. (2020). An exploration of law enforcement officers' training needs and interactions with individuals with autism spectrum disorder. *Journal of Autism and Developmental Disorders, 50*(1), 101–117. https://doi.org/10.1007/s10803-019-04227-2

Rosenbloom, S. (2007). Transportation patterns and problems of people with disabilities. In M. J. Field & A. M. Jette (Eds.), *The future of disability in America.* Institute of Medicine (US) Committee on Disability in America. National Academies Press (US); Available from: https://www.ncbi.nlm.nih.gov/books/NBK11420/

Sansosti, F. J., Powell-Smith, K. A., & Cowan, R. J. (2010). *High functioning autism/Asperger syndrome in schools: Assessment and intervention.* Guilford Press.

Sansosti, F. J., Was, C., Rawson, K. A., & Remaklus, B. L. (2013). Eye movements during processing of text requiring bridging inferences in adolescents with higher functioning autism spectrum disorders: A preliminary investigation. *Research in Autism Spectrum Disorders, 7*, 1535–1542. https://doi.org/10.1016/j.rasd.2013.09.001

Scott, M., Jacob, A., Hendrie, D., Parsons, R., Girdler, S., Falkmer, T., et al. (2017). Employers' perception of the costs and the benefits of hiring individuals with autism spectrum disorder in open employment in Australia. *PLoS One, 12*(5), e0177607. https://doi.org/10.1371/journal.pone.0177607

Sessa, F. M., & Steinberg, L. (1991). Family structure and the development of autonomy during adolescence. *Journal of Early Adolescence, 11*, 38–55. https://doi.org/10.1177/0272431691111003

Shattuck, P., Narendorf, S., Cooper, B., Sterzing, M., Wagner, M., & Taylor, J. (2012). Postsecondary education and employment among youth with an autism spectrum disorder. *Pediatrics, 129*, 1042–1049. https://doi.org/10.1542/peds.2011-2864

Smith, L. E., Maenner, M. J., & Seltzer, M. M. (2012). Developmental trajectories in adolescents and adults with autism: The case of daily living skills. *Journal of the American Academy of Child and Adolescent Psychiatry, 51*, 622–631. https://doi.org/10.1016/j.jaac.2012.03.001

Sosnowy, C., Silverman, C., & Shattuck, P. (2018). Parents' and young adults' perspectives on transition outcomes for young adults with autism. *Autism, 22*(1), 29–39. https://doi.org/10.1177/1362361317699585

Sterzing, P. R., Shattuck, P. T., Narendorf, S. C., Wagner, M., & Cooper, B. P. (2012). Bullying involvement and autism spectrum disorders: Prevalence and correlates of bullying involvement among adolescents with an autism spectrum disorder. *Archives of Pediatrics and Adolescent Medicine, 166*(11), 1058–1064. https://doi.org/10.1001/archpediatrics.2012.790

Strunz, S., Schermuck, C., Ballerstein, S., Ahlers, C. J., Dziobek, I., & Roepke, S. (2017). Romantic relationships and relationship satisfaction among adults with Asperger syndrome and high-functioning autism. *Journal of Clinical Psychology, 73*(1), 113–125. https://doi.org/10.1002/jclp.22319

Stanish, H. I., Curtin, C., Must, A., Phillips, S., Maslin, M., & Bandini, L. G. (2017). Physical Activity Levels, Frequency, and Type Among Adolescents with and Without Autism Spectrum Disorder. Journal of autism and developmental disorders, 47(3), 785–794. https://doi.org/10.1007/s10803-016-3001-4

Szidon, K., Ruppar, A., & Smith, L. (2015). Five steps for developing effective transition plans for high school students with autism spectrum disorder. *Teaching Exceptional Children, 47*(3), 147–152. https://doi.org/10.1177/0040059914559780

Taylor, J. L., & Seltzer, M. M. (2010). Change in the autism phenotype during the transition to adulthood. *Journal of Autism and Developmental Disorders, 40*, 1431–1446. https://doi.org/10.1007/s10803-010-1005-z

Test, D. W., Mazzotti, V. L., Mustian, A. L., Fowler, C. H., Kortering, L., & Kohler, P. (2009). Evidence-based secondary transition predictors for improving postschool outcomes for students with disabilities. *Career Development for Exceptional Individuals, 32*(3), 160–181. https://doi.org/10.1177/0885728809346960

Thomeer, M. L., McDonald, C. A., Rodgers, J. D., & Lopata, C. (2019). High-functioning autism spectrum disorder: A framework for evidence-based practice. *School Mental Health, 11*, 29–39. https://doi.org/10.1007/s12310-017-9236-1

Tipton-Fisler, L. A., Rodriguez, G., Zeedyk, S. M., & Blacher, J. (2018). Stability of bullying and internalizing problems among adolescents with ASD, ID, or typical development. *Research in Developmental Disabilities, 80*, 131–141. https://doi.org/10.1016/j.ridd.2018.06.004

Uljarevic, M., & Hamilton, A. (2013). Recognition of emotions in autism: A formal meta-analysis. *Journal of Autism and Developmental Disorders, 43*, 1517–1526. https://doi.org/10.1007/s10803-012-1695-5

US Department of Labor's Office of Disability and Employment Policy. (n.d.). *Youth, disclosure, and the workplace why, when, what, and how*. https://www.dol.gov/agencies/odep/publications/fact-sheets/youth-disclosure-and-the-workplace-why-when-what-and-how

van Steensel, F. J. A., & Heeman, E. J. (2017). Anxiety levels in children with autism spectrum disorder: A meta-analysis. *Journal of Child and Family Studies, 26*, 1753–1767. https://doi.org/10.1007/s10826-017-0687-z

Vermeiren, R., Jespers, I., & Moffit, T. (2006). Mental health problems in juvenile justice populations. *Child and Adolescent Psychiatry Clinics of North America, 15*, 333–351.

Viezel, K. D., Williams, E., & Dotson, W. H. (2020). College-based support programs for students with autism. *Focus on Autism and Other Developmental Disabilities, 35*(4), 234–245. https://doi.org/10.1177/1088357620954369

Volkmar, F. R., Reichow, B., Westphal, A., & Mandell, D. S. (2014). Autism and the autism spectrum: Diagnostic concepts. In F. R. Volkmar, R. Paul, S. J. Rogers, & K. A. Pelphrey (Eds.), *Handbook of autism and pervasive developmental disorders (volume 1): Diagnosis, development, and brain mechanisms*. Wiley.

von Schrader, S., Malzer, V., & Bruyère, S. (2014). Perspectives on disability disclosure: The importance of employer practices and workplace climate. *Employee Responsibility and Rights Journal, 26*, 237–255. https://doi.org/10.1007/s10672-013-9227-9

Webb, S. J., Neuhaus, E., & Faja, S. (2017). Face perception and learning in autism spectrum disorders. *Quarterly Journal of Experimental Psychology, 70*(5), 970–986. https://doi.org/10.108 0/17470218.2016.1151059

Wehman, P., Schall, C. M., McDonough, J., Graham, C., Brooke, V., Riehle, J. E., Brooke, A., Ham, W., Lau, S., Allen, J., & Avellone, L. (2017). Effects of an employer-based intervention on employment outcomes for youth with significant support needs due to autism. *Autism, 21*(3), 276–290. https://doi.org/10.1177/1362361316635826

Wehman, P., Smith, M. D., & Schall, C. M. (2009). *Autism and the transition to adulthood: Success beyond the classroom*. Paul Brookes.

Weiss, J. A., & Fardella, M. A. (2018). Victimization and perpetration experiences of adults with autism. *Frontiers in Psychiatry, 9*, 203. https://doi.org/10.3389/fpsyt.2018.00203

Whitby, P. J. S., & Mancil, G. R. (2009). Academic achievement profiles of children with high functioning autism and Asperger syndrome: A review of the literature. *Educational and Training in Developmental Disabilities, 44*, 551–560.

White, S. W., Elias, R., Salinas, C. E., Capriola, N., Conner, M., Asselin, S. B., & Getzel, E. E. (2016). Students with autism spectrum disorder in college: Results from a preliminary mixed methods needs analysis. *Research in Developmental Disabilities, 56*, 29–40. https://doi. org/10.1016/j.ridd.2016.05.010

White, S. W., Ollendick, T. H., & Bray, B. C. (2011). College students on the autism spectrum: Prevalence and associated problems. *Autism, 15*(6), 683–701. https://doi. org/10.1177/1362361310393363

White, S. W., Oswald, D., Ollendick, T., & Scahill, L. (2009). Anxiety in children and adolescents with autism spectrum disorders. *Clinical Psychology Review, 29*(3), 216–229. https://doi. org/10.1016/j.cpr.2009.01.003

Winner, M. G. (Ed.). (2007). *Social behavior mapping: Connecting behavior, emotions and consequences across the day*. Think Social.

Zimmerman, J. (2017, 5 May). *Student voice: They told me I'd never go to college but I just finished my freshman year—What about all the other students with autism?* Hechinger Report. https://hechingerreport.org/student-voice-told-id-never-go-college-just-finished-freshman-year-students-autism/

Neuropsychological Considerations of Adolescents and Young Adults with High-Functioning Autism Spectrum Disorder for School Psychologists

Andrew S. Davis, D. J. Bernat, and Michele D. Shetter

Abstract Neuropsychological assessment is a comprehensive evaluation of multiple domains of an individual's life including medical history, educational and vocational history, psychosocial and psychiatric history, sensory-motor abilities, and neurocognitive functioning. Although neuropsychological evaluations are often conducted to facilitate differential diagnosis, they can also be used for the determination of capacity in a number of different areas. This includes academic and vocational functioning and potential and ability to execute activities of daily living. This chapter explains how school psychologists can use neuropsychological assessment for the purpose of helping determine the capacity of older adolescents and young adults with high functioning autism spectrum disorder (ASD) to attend and succeed in college and vocational settings. This includes incorporating information about comorbid medical problems and information about neuropsychological domains into an evaluation. The chapter concludes with a discussion of future directions, including evolving technologies.

Keywords Autism spectrum disorders · Neuropsychological assessment · Transition planning

Recent years have seen a substantial rise in awareness of autism spectrum disorder (ASD) and a corresponding increase in the prevalence of the condition. As more children have been diagnosed with ASD over the past several years, there is an increased need for literature related to working with these individuals when they transition from high school. School psychologists are closely involved in this transition process and therefore should be aware of the options the adolescent has when

---

A. S. Davis (✉) · M. D. Shetter
Department of Educational Psychology, Ball State University, Muncie, IN, USA
e-mail: davis@bsu.edu

D. J. Bernat
Department of Pediatric Psychology and Neuropsychology, Nationwide Children's Hospital, Columbus, OH, USA

Department of Pediatrics, The Ohio State University, Columbus, OH, USA

© Springer Nature Switzerland AG 2022
K. D. Viezel et al. (eds.), *Postsecondary Transition for College- or Career-Bound Autistic Students*, https://doi.org/10.1007/978-3-030-93947-2_3

they leave high school based upon their strengths and weaknesses. After high school, residential options could include continuing to live with their caregivers, moving to a group home, or living independently. Vocational and volunteer options will also vary depending upon their level of independent functioning. Individuals with high functioning ASD (HFASD)[1] may attend college or enter the workforce after high school, which is the group discussed in this text. In these situations, many individuals are likely to benefit from at least minimal supports and accommodations to help cope with the novel social and neurocognitive demands of these settings. Concurrently, decisions regarding the degree to which the individual with ASD can independently manage their finances, operate a motor vehicle, and safely and effectively manage their home, and consent to medical treatment may need to be made.

Similar to children with other neurodevelopmental disorders, individuals with ASD can present with a heterogeneous trajectory as they age. This can range from needing 24-hour supervision throughout the lifespan to being desired for employment at a technology firm due to their "desirable qualities employers look for, such as careful attention to detail, commitment to high quality and accuracy, out of the box thinking, conscientiousness and diligence, and ability to work independently" (p. 3123, Knight et al., 2019). Indeed, the continuum of severity, neuropathology, comorbidity, and symptomology is extremely diverse in individuals identified with ASD and likely more so now that the myriad of pervasive developmental disorder conditions from *Diagnostic and Statistical Manual of Mental Disorders – Fourth Edition* (DSM-IV-TR American Psychiatric Association, 2000) have been collapsed into a single dimensional diagnosis with the publication of the *Diagnostic and Statistical Manual of Mental Disorders – Fifth Edition* (DSM-5; American Psychiatric Association, 2013). Given the varying prognoses of children with ASD as they enter adulthood, psychologists are often called upon to complete comprehensive evaluations with these adolescents. The role of the neuropsychologist in this process is to address these questions from a neurocognitive, academic, adaptive, psychiatric, psychosocial, sensory, and motor perspective. This typically consists of a comprehensive neuropsychological assessment involving a review of medical and educational records, diagnostic interview with the patient (and/or caregivers), a battery of tests, and consultation with other professionals working with the patient. The entire process of neuropsychological assessment is beyond the scope of this chapter and readers interested in this topic are directed to resources such as Davis (2011),

---

[1] At the time of the writing of this chapter, there was emerging discussion about terminology for individuals with ASD. There is a convincing case to be made for using the term "autistic individual" vs. "individual with ASD." There has also been discussion about the use of the term "High Functioning" with some preferring to not delineate a specific group based on inconsistent terminology. These issues are discussed elsewhere in this text as well. Given the literature review in this chapter was based primarily on sources using the person first language and referring more to individuals who attend college and engage in more independent vocational tasks, that is the language that was used in this chapter. We, however, acknowledge that moving forward there may be increased consensus for different language. Regardless, our recommendation in any clinical, social, or school-based interaction is to ask the individual for their preference and defer to their judgment in conversation and any written document.

Lezak et al. (2012); Yeates et al. (2009). Much has also been written about the diagnosis of children and adults with ASD, and readers interested in diagnostic evaluations should consider resources such as Matson, 2016; Saulnier & Ventola, 2012; Wolff et al., 2018. Instead of focusing on diagnostic assessment, this chapter will review neurodevelopmental concerns and the concept of neuropsychological evaluations for high school students with HFASD who are considering entering the workforce or attending college, with a focus on how school psychologists should consider this information.

The somewhat recent changes to the DSM-5 have resulted in modifications to the procedures of how neuropsychologists approach the assessment and diagnosis of individuals with ASD. Neuropsychologists were previously confronted with what was largely a two-step process of diagnosis in which they first had to decide if the patient's symptomology was consistent with the category of behavior labeled as a pervasive developmental disorder. If so, the second step was to provide a differential diagnosis among those conditions. Although there were some obvious differences between these disorders, there were enough patients, particularly those who were considered high-functioning, who did not cleanly meet one set of criteria. This led to the frequent use of the "Pervasive Developmental Disorder, Not Otherwise Specified" (PDD-NOS) for those individuals. The change to consolidate several of the PDD-NOS disorders from the DSM-IV-TR conditions into the umbrella category of ASD has somewhat negated the second step of the two-step process described above. As such, it is now easier to determine, from a description and/or observation of the patient's behavior, whether or not they meet the diagnostic criteria for ASD without the need to differentiate between Asperger's disorder, Autistic disorder, and PDD-NOS. This change in the DSM-V, while helpful in determining which neurodevelopmental condition is present, did not obviate the need for a comprehensive assessment of neurodevelopmental status. Indeed, the inclusion of ASD in a category of conditions deemed to fall under the umbrella of neurodevelopmental disorders suggests the involvement of central nervous system (CNS) dysfunction, and a neuropsychological evaluation is ideally suited to determine how the patient's organic concerns are contributing to or interfering with their functioning.

Neuropsychological assessments can be used to answer a number of questions (Lezak et al., 2012). In one case, the neuropsychologist collects a variety of data and uses the assessment findings to determine a diagnosis based upon the neuropsychological profile. Another question neuropsychologists address refers to the capability of the individual. For example, the referral question may be if the patient can live independently, drive a car, manage their finances, be successful vocationally or academically, or consent (or refuse) medical treatment. When working with children with congenital neurodevelopmental disorders, pediatric neuropsychologists often tend to focus more on addressing capacity issues as opposed to addressing diagnostic questions. This is because, increasingly, genetic markers are being identified for neurodevelopmental conditions (e.g., Fragile X Syndrome, Rett's Disorder), which means clinicians do not need to rely upon a caregiver's description of the child's behavior and their own observations to make a primary diagnosis. Of course, neuropsychologists and school psychologists may still be the first to recognize the signs of these neurodevelopmental genetic disorders and refer the child for genetic testing. Neuropsychological assessment can facilitate differential diagnosis in these children when an additional condition is suspected to be present which may have overlapping symptoms with the primary neurodevelopmental genetic disorder. For example, it is typical for children with Fragile X Syndrome to present with inattention and executive dysfunction (Kogan et al., 2009) to such an extent that an additional diagnosis of attention-deficit hyperactivity disorder (ADHD) may be warranted.

As of now, there are a multitude of neurodevelopmental conditions, including ASD, which still require a description and/or observation of the patient's behavior for diagnosis. As such, while it is easier to determine if a patient has ASD (as opposed to *which* PDD condition is present), neuropsychological assessment for both differential diagnosis and determination of functional abilities is still warranted in many cases. Individuals with higher-functioning ASD, however, may be more likely to be diagnosed later in life as they may not exhibit the type of severe behavior symptomology that places them in conflict with societal conventions that may necessitate an earlier referral to a specialist. For individuals with HFASD, determining what cognitive capabilities and/or limitations are present can help the individual, their family, health care providers, and school psychologists and other educators to ensure that they are making safe choices as well as guide decision making.

Prevalence and Presentation

Determining the incidence and prevalence of ASD, particularly HFASD, is complicated by several factors although there appears to be little doubt that the last several years have seen an increase in the number of children diagnosed with ASD. According to the Centers for Disease Control and Prevention website on autism spectrum disorder (https://www.cdc.gov/ncbddd/autism/data.html), prevalence rates for ASD in the United States went from 1 in 150 in 2000 to 1 in 54 in 2016 (Maeneer et al., 2020). The increase in awareness and knowledge of ASD is likely driving the increase in new diagnoses as opposed to an increase in the number of people born each year with this neurodevelopmental disorder. Another consideration is that the DSM-5 does not specify a diagnostic classification for HFASD; and thus different health care professionals, researchers, individuals with ASD, and their families may have different criteria for what constitutes "high functioning." For example, the term may be used with individuals with ASD who have at least average intelligence (e.g., Giambattista, 2018) while others refer to an overall IQ score above 70 (e.g., Bennett et al., 2008). For the purpose of this chapter, HFASD will refer individuals with at least the intellectual functioning to attend college or enter the workforce with some degree of independence, albeit with accommodations.

Readers are directed to the DSM-5 for a complete list of diagnostic criteria for ASD. The severity and extent of symptomology of ASD can vary across a number of factors, including intellectual functioning (Rommelse, 2015). Although individuals with HFASD may present with higher intellectual functioning than others with ASD, they are still likely to present with difficulties in social interactions (i.e., a key component of ASD) that probably will need accommodations in the workplace and college. The challenges with social interactions can result in distress, creating academic and vocational difficulties for adolescents and young adults with HFASD. These concerns can render many typical college and vocational interactions challenging such as participating in group discussions, appropriately approaching the professor with questions, understanding the hierarchical relationships present in college and the workplace, and picking up on nonverbal cues that are often important in understanding task directions.

Medical Problems to Be Considered During Neuropsychological Assessment

In any neuropsychological assessment, a key consideration is determining how a patient's health affects their functioning, including any contributions, sometimes reciprocal, of the effect medical conditions have on the individual's central nervous system. This is the case for individuals with neurodevelopmental disorders, such as ASD, as adolescents and young adults with ASD are at a significantly increased risk of other medical problems. This includes that individuals with ASD often exhibit intellectual deficits which place them at an increased risk of accidents (Lee et al., 2008), as well as a reduced ability to independently execute activities of daily living. For young adults who are newly independent, limitations in cognitive functioning and social reciprocity could also render them vulnerable to the risk of sexual, financial, and other exploitation.

Comorbid psychiatric disorders and psychiatric symptomology are frequently seen in individuals with ASD, including intellectual disability disorder (American Psychiatric Association, 2013; Matson & Shoemaker, 2009). Additionally, ADHD symptomology frequently is present in individuals with ASD (Brentani, 2013; Llanes et al. 2020; Leitner, 2014) which is not surprising given less interest or inappropriate levels of focus on external stimuli could alter attention. Neuropsychological assessment should carefully consider the wide range of ADHD symptomology potentially displayed in these adolescents and young adults, particularly as there is a wealth of intervention literature for these concerns (e.g., Dawson & Guare, 2009; DuPaul & Kern, 2011; Sibley, 2016). Other psychiatric concerns for which individuals with ASD may be at risk include depression, anxiety, developmental coordination disorder, learning disorder, and anxiety (APA, 2013; Mayes et al., 2010). Having HFASD, compared to lower functioning ASD, does not appear to be a protective factor for depression and concerns are present that it may be more common in individuals with HFASD than lower functioning ASD, though similar levels of anxiety have been found between the two groups (Mayes et al., 2010). Alexithymia also appears to play a role in the severity of depression and anxiety in individuals with ASD (Morie et al., 2019). These types of concerns, along with difficulties in social communication, place adolescents and young adults with HFASD at an increased risk of failure in college and vocational settings, particularly when the often-high level of support that was provided in special education in high school is removed.

In addition to comorbid psychiatric concerns, other medical conditions are common in individuals with ASD at an increased rate when compared to their peers. These comorbid medical conditions have the potential to interrupt neurodevelopment and can synergistically interact with the already present risk factors of ASD symptomology to exacerbate neurocognitive, social, academic, emotional, and behavioral concerns in college and the workplace. One of the reasons understanding the impact of these comorbid conditions is so important for adolescents and young adults with HFASD is that they may be tasked with increased responsibility as they gain independence. In many instances, it may have been their caregivers who ensured the adolescent with HFASD attended regular medical appointments, took prescribed medication, attended treatment sessions, and followed up with specialist appointments. Once the adolescent gains independence, they may not see as clearly the reason for attending these appointments; this could be exacerbated for those individuals with ASD who have significant reluctance to engage in novel non-comfortable acts given their adherence to routine. For those in college, this may be the case as a college health center can be a different experience compared to their primary medical provider's office and individuals with HFASD may need extra help and support to both schedule and attend these appointments. This scenario provides a good illustration of the rationale for school psychologists obtaining this information and integrating it with neuropsychological assessment results to design and monitor interventions.

Common medical problems associated with ASD that have the potential to further interfere with neurodevelopment are gastrointestinal (GI) disorders (Lefter et al., 2020; McElhanon et al., 2014), seizure disorders (Canitano, 2007), sleep dysfunction (Richdale & Schreck, 2009), sensory processing problems (Behrmann & Minshew, 2015), and pica (Goldschmidt, 2018). Sleep problems have been shown to result in significant impairments in a number of domains, including executive functions, attention, memory, and academic performance (Astill et al., 2012; Blunden et al., 2005; Dewald et al., 2010). In adolescents, lower levels of sleep have been associated with higher levels of risky behaviors such as drinking and driving, texting while driving, as well as motor vehicle and vocational accidents (Wheaton et al., 2016). On average, individuals with ASD appear to demonstrate abnormal sleep architecture (Limoges et al., 2005) and sleep problems seem to exacerbate social and emotional concerns in individuals with ASD (Goldman et al., 2011). School psychologists and other professionals working with children and adolescents with ASD may benefit from the use of sleep measures such as the *Sleep Disorders Inventory for Students* (SDIS; Luginbuehl, 2004).

Seizure disorders are associated with a wide array of neurocognitive difficulties including problems with attention, executive functioning, processing speed, memory, and intellectual difficulties (Hermann et al., 2007; Parisi et al., 2010); some have argued that these problems may cause social difficulties (e.g., Steiger & Jokeit, 2017), an area where individuals with ASD often struggle. Seizure disorders are typically reflective of an underlying neurological concern and thus it is not surprising that approximately 20–25% of individuals with ASD will also have seizures (Brentani, 2013) and the level of developmental functioning has been associated with the presence of seizures (Burns & Matson, 2018). The concerns about GI disorders is noteworthy as individuals with ASD, even those with developed verbal skills, may have difficulty adequately explaining their symptoms to health care providers and other caregivers (Buie et al., 2010). This is a good example of the role school psychologists can play in consulting with college health care centers to help providers understand how best to communicate with an unfamiliar adolescent and young adult with HFASD. An instrument that measures adaptive functioning via a performance approach such as the *Independent Living Scales* (ILS; Loeb, 1996) could be considered as examinees must solve practical problems including those that measure the ability to make health and safety decisions, manage finances, and manage the home.

The Neuropsychological Evaluation for Adolescents and Young Adults with HFASD

A comprehensive neuropsychological evaluation typically proceeds in the following fashion after a referral question: review of records, diagnostic interview with the patient and/or caregiver, administration, scoring and interpreting of tests, consultation with other professionals when warranted, writing a report, meeting with the patient and/or caregiver to provide results (feedback), and possibly consultation with the referral source. Neuropsychologists may conduct serial or longitudinal assessments, when the situation warrants it, repeating the process every year or so. Below we review domains that practitioners conducting assessments of adolescents and young adults with HFASD should consider.

Social and Behavioral Functioning.

Some of the barriers adolescents and young adults with HFASD face arise as a result of challenges with social communication and interaction, adherence to nonfunctional routines, a restricted range of interests, and flexibility of thinking. These skills are essential for interacting and problem-solving with others, particularly with authority figures and when in novel situations. Interacting with professors and supervisors requires a significantly different set of skills as compared to interacting with caregivers and high school teachers, all of whom likely have gotten to know the individual well. Limitations in executive functions could result in increased disinhibition and problems with cognitive set-shifting which contribute to difficulty with problem solving, particularly under pressure. When combined with the less structural support found in most college and vocational settings compared to high school, this can result in awkward, disruptive, inefficient, or maladaptive relationships. The social exclusion of individuals with ASD, including HFASD, may persist in college (Chown & Beavan, 2012) and early adulthood (Sasson et al., 2017). School psychologists are encouraged to look for the type of programs discussed elsewhere in this book to provide guidance to caregivers and adolescents with HFASD considering college.

Individuals with ASD typically do better in social situations that are calm, consistent, and follow a typical routine which may be present in some college and vocational situations; school psychologists should foster this environment when possible for adolescents and young adults with HFASD. However, unstructured situations may be present in dorm rooms, workplace break rooms, and other vocational and academic circumstances. In these instances, there could be an increase in distress and associated social and behavioral problems. The importance of this is magnified by the finding that a majority of high school teachers agreed to the importance of their students with ASD having peer relationships to foster a sense of well-being; however, many of their students were not engaging in these relationships (Danker et al., 2019). As such, an integral component of the neuropsychological evaluation for adolescents and young adults with HFASD is the determination of social and behavioral barriers that could interfere with functioning. Clinicians could consider measures such as the *Behavioral Assessment Scales for Children – Third Edition* (BASC-3; Reynolds & Kamphaus, 2015), which yields valuable information about the social and behavioral functioning of young adults up to the age of 21:11. For individuals with adequate reading levels, the *Minnesota Multiphasic Personality Inventory Adolescent* (MMPI-A; Butcher et al., 1992) or *Minnesota Multiphasic Personality Inventory-3* (MMPI-3; Ben-Porath & Tellegen, 2020) could be considered for measures of personality and psychopathology.

Academic Abilities

Academic assessment is a key component of the neuropsychological assessment when working with adolescents and young adults with HFASD. A multitude of research has demonstrated that children with ASD present with difficulty with reading, writing, and math relative to their same aged peers (e.g., Wei et al., 2015; Mayes & Calhoun, 2008). This is not surprising given the array of cognitive and sensory-motor deficits with which this population can present. In addition to the obvious concerns in college that can present when academic difficulties are present, many vocations also require adequate or better reading, writing, and math skills. School psychologists should ensure there are up-to-date standardized measurements of these abilities, such as the *Kaufman Tests of Educational Achievement – Third* Edition (KTEA-3; Kaufman & Kaufman, 2014), *Wechsler Individual Achievement Test – Fourth Edition* (WIAT-4 Wechsler, 2020), or *Wide Range Achievement Test – Fifth Edition* (WRAT-5; Wilkinson & Robertson, 2017). Relying upon grades may not be as effective as recent scores from standardized measures given grades may be reflecting accommodations that may not be present in college or the workplace.

Intelligence

At the core of many neuropsychological and psychoeducational assessment batteries is a test of intelligence, and school psychologists often consider a measure of general intellectual functioning as part of a psychoeducational assessment battery. Neuropsychological evaluations, however, typically go far beyond this type of interpretation as the clinician may be just, if not more, interested in performance on other indexes and subtests as well as intraindividual comparisons. Measures of general intellectual functioning may be reflective of impairment, but it does not inform the neuropsychologist as to the localization of the neurological impairment or even if it is an organic etiology given the sensitivity of the FSIQ to culture, SES, and other demographic factors (e.g., Davis et al., 2018). Thus, it is common for neuropsychologists to consider scores on tests that go beyond a measure of g and where research has elucidated their relationship to neurofunctional difficulty. For a review of various intelligence tests from a neuropsychological perspective see Davis (2011) as well as Lezak et al. (2012). In essence, the measurement of intelligence for adolescents and young adults with HFASD is an important component of a neuropsychological battery given the ability to measure a broad array of functions that are necessary for vocational and academic success.

While it has been argued that no exact neuroanatomical correlates for general intelligence exist (e.g. Sattler, 2008), there are some known associations between intelligence and brain structure. Regardless of the exact model applied, the general consensus appears to be that intellectual functioning is governed by multiple brain regions working in concert. As such, it is not surprising that patients with neurodevelopmental conditions, such as ASD, as well as with acquired brain lesions consistently have been found to present with intellectual compromise. Two long-standing associations between intelligence and neuroanatomy are overall brain size and cortical thickness. Cortical thickness has been shown to be associated with g in a number of studies, including those in neurotypical children and adolescents (Karama et al., 2011). These studies are also of interest for children with ASD as they appear to show abnormal patterns of cortical thickness, with increases in some areas (e.g., left precuneus) and decreases in others (e.g., left medial orbitofrontal gyrus; Jiao et al., 2010). Zielinski et al. (2014) found that "abnormal cortical development in autism spectrum disorders undergoes three distinct phases: accelerated expansion in early childhood, accelerated thinning in later childhood and adolescence, and decelerated thinning in early adulthood." (p. 1799). These types of finding within this population are important as they emphasize the biological and longitudinal nature of the condition.

There is a wealth of literature describing intellectual findings for individuals with pervasive developmental disorders such as Autistic disorder and Asperger's disorder as defined by the DSM-IV. Now that these types of conditions are encapsulated in an umbrella term of ASD, there is quite likely a bit of variability of IQ to be found in these individuals given the history of differences. For example, Bennett et al. (2008) found children with Asperger's disorder scored nearly a standard deviation higher than children with high functioning autism (defined as an ASD diagnosis with a full-scale score higher than 70 on an intelligence on a standardized nonverbal intelligence test). Charman et al. (2011) found that 28% of children aged 10–14 with ASD had average intelligence and about 3% were above average; in other words, about one-third of children can be considered "high-functioning" based on a definition of average range or higher intelligence as measured by a standardized cognitive assessment. In sum, particularly now that a broad range of presentations are under a single diagnosis, individuals with ASD are unlikely to present with a unitary profile of IQ scores and comprehensive assessment also likely is necessary for adolescents and young adults with HFASD to elicit a pattern of strengths and weaknesses.

Although the measurement of intelligence has obvious advantages, it does not appear to solely capture the neurocognitive variability exhibited by individuals with HFASD. This is consistent with long-standing findings regarding other cognitive measures exhibiting unique variance when compared with measures of intelligence (i.e. D'Amato et al., 1988; Davis et al., 2011). A study by Kenworthy et al. (2010) found individuals with HFASD showed greater impairment in social skills as measured by the *Adaptative Behavior Assessment System – Second Edition* (ABAS-II; Harrison & Oakland, 2006) compared to a group of typically developing peers with comparable performance on standardized intelligence measures such as the *Wechsler Intelligence Scales for Children – Fourth Edition* (WISC-IV; Wechsler, 2003). This shows that when individuals with ASD have similar intellectual levels, they may still exhibit adaptive functioning differences. Black et al. (2009) found that a significant split between performance on verbal and nonverbal measures, where NVIQ was 11 or more standard score points higher, was associated with social symptoms of autism in an HFASD sample. Performance on VIQ also showed statistically significant correlations with social and communication symptoms of autism. Given these findings, while measures of IQ are certainly likely to be important in determining the current level of functioning, simply relying on an overall measure of IQ is unlikely to capture an individual with HFASD's full range of neurocognitive abilities. As such, examining the underlying factors that help determine IQ scores should be useful for this population which likely becomes less homogenous as the level of functioning increases. Oliveras-Rentas et al. (2012) found individuals with HFASD (those with an FSIQ >70) showed pronounced deficits in processing speed and on the Comprehension subtest as measured by the WISC-IV. The authors also found processing speed performance accounted for communication impairment and that processing speed was positively associated with social communication skills as measured by the *Autism Diagnostic Observation Schedule* (ADOS; Lord et al., 2000). Another notable finding comes from a study of 127 pre-school-aged children with ASD, which found that, using scores obtained from the *Wechsler Preschool and Primary Scale of Intelligence – Fourth Edition* (WPPSI-IV; Wechsler, 2012), a higher PIQ was associated with better fine motor skills, while a higher VIQ was associated with fine motor impairment (Yu et al., 2018). This is particularly useful information for early intervention, particularly given the potential for motor difficulties to interfere with children's ability to interact with their environment.

Memory

Two neurological regions most frequently associated with memory, and particularly emotional aspects of memory, are the amygdala and hippocampus and surrounding areas (e.g., "parahippocampal"; McDonald & Mott, 2017). These areas are particularly of interest to this chapter given neuroimaging findings showing limbic system anomalies in individuals with ASD when compared to typically developing peers (e.g., Ameis et al., 2013; Pugliese et al., 2009). A meta-analysis of nearly 100 studies involving children and adolescents with HFASD found consistent evidence for moderate impairment of verbal and spatial working memory (Lai et al., 2017). Kercood et al. (2014) reached a similar conclusion, writing "results suggest that persons with autism score lower on measures of working memory than do typical controls. They make more errors, use fewer strategies, and demonstrate lower performances on tasks that require cognitive flexibility, planning, greater working memory load, and spatial working memory, especially with increasing task complexity and in dual task conditions. They also score lower on the WM [Working Memory]-Math component of IQ tests, such as digit symbol" (p. 326). Snow et al. (2011) conducted research of eye movements in neurotypical children and children with HFASD and found significant differences in the HFASD group's ability to remember faces, but not inanimate, non-social objects. The authors noted that the HFASD group tended to focus on the eyes, nose, and mouth but allotted less attention to other facial features. These types of memory concerns are likely to require intervention when present in both college and workplace settings. Another consideration for school psychologists is that instructions and lectures to individuals in their late teens/early 20s are typically multi-step in nature and presume adequate working memory abilities as previous sentences are typically assumed by the speaker to have been integrated into current statements. Clearly, memory and working memory should be thoroughly assessed in this population.

Language

Deficits in social communication are a key aspect of ASD, and thus adolescents and young adults with HFASD may present with some degree of language impairment. Given the importance of both receptive and expressive language in college settings and many vocational settings, any deficits in language functions are likely to need substantial accommodations. Indeed, the primary modality of college instruction in the classroom may be language-based, and even for jobs which don't require extensive public interactions, instructions on how to complete tasks may be either language-based or workers may be required to ask questions. The area of the brain most frequently associated with language is the Perisylvian area in the dominant (usually left) hemisphere, named for its close proximity to the Sylvian fissure. The Perisylvian area includes key areas of the posterior frontal and temporal lobes, perhaps most notably Broca's area in the frontal lobe, Wernicke's area in the temporal lobe, and the subcortical structure known as the arcuate fasciculus, which connects these two regions. Damage to one or more of these areas is often indicated in the various forms of aphasia, and consistent with the behavioral presentation, research has suggested that atypical structure and function of the arcuate fasciculus plays a role in language impairment in ASD (Fletcher et al., 2010). A thorough meta-analysis conducted by Kwok et al. (2015) challenged the traditional belief that individuals with ASD show a pronounced pattern of expressive language abilities exceeding receptive language abilities. The authors did not find evidence for this argument; indeed, on average individuals with ASD showed a pattern of both expressive and receptive language skills which fell about 1.5 standard deviations below the performance of neurotypical peers.

Gold and Faust (2010) found evidence implicating the right hemisphere in poor metaphor comprehension in individuals with Asperger's disorder. Given the contributions of both dominant and non-dominant hemisphere performance to communication, school psychologists should widely explore language with measures such as the *Clinical Evaluation of Language Fundamentals – Fourth Edition* (CELF-4; Semel et al., 2003), as well as measures such as the Seashore Rhythm test from the *Halstead Reitan Neuropsychological Battery* (Reitan and Wolfson, 1993), the latter of which can be useful in assessing non-dominant hemisphere functioning. Indeed, given the role pragmatics (i.e., social aspects of language) play in successful social interactions, school psychologists are encouraged to consider careful assessment of the non-dominant hemisphere for those individuals who will independently interact with peers in workplace and college settings where metaphor and sarcasm are likely to be commonplace. Gold & Faust (2010) found that individuals with Asperger's disorder showed marked impairment in understanding metaphors, while Whyte et al. (2014) found that individuals with ASD performed worse on idiom comprehension than a sample of age and non-verbal IQ-matched typically developing peers.

Attention

As with other constructs such as memory, attention is understood to be an umbrella term which includes numerous subtypes such as sustained attention, divided attention, selective attention, and vigilance as well as domain-specific forms of attention such as auditory and visual attention. With that said, many have argued that evidence supports a hierarchical attention network (Lezak et al., 2012). This network appears to encapsulate a number of cortical and subcortical areas, primarily those in the frontal and parietal lobes. Adolescents with ASD appear to show impairments in sustained attention that are correlated with reduced activity in regions of the striatum, thalamus, left dorsolateral prefrontal cortex (DLPFC), and superior parietal cortex as well as greater activation in the precuneus and cerebellum compared to controls (Christakou et al., 2013). Other areas indicated in sustained attention include the subcortical white matter of the right parietal cortex and superior longitudinal fasciculus (SLF), and successful communication between the right frontal and parietal cortices appears particularly important to sustained attention (Klarborg et al., 2013; Sarter et al., 2001) as well as redirection of attention (Monge et al., 2016). Freeth et al. (2010) found significant differences in how children with high-functioning ASD directed their attention to the faces of human figures compared to neurotypical peers, including less overall time used observing the individual's face. A meta-analysis by Chita-Tegmark (2016) found individuals with ASD spend less time attending to social stimuli than neurotypical peers, yielding a mean effect size of 0.55; the effect was most salient when observing stimuli with multiple human figures. Another area where individuals with ASD seem to struggle is in engaging in joint attention with adults (Mundy et al., 2016). An area of assessment which may yield useful information for clinical decisions is tests of inhibitory control; studies suggest that children with ASD tend to show less impairment in this area than children with ADHD (Bühler et al., 2011; Sinzig et al., 2008).

School psychologists should attempt to use instruments which make minimal use of stimuli that use human-like stimuli when attempting to measure attention, as they may artificially inflate attention issues. One such test is the *Conners Continuous Performance Test – Third Edition* (CPT-3; Conners, 2013). Additionally, should rating scales be used, the role of social deficits should be factored into interpretations; for example, disinterest in conversation with same age peers or other individuals could be inadvertently viewed as inattention by some raters, and this should be taken into account. Indeed, this seeming disinterest is likely to broadly affect social interactions in both vocational and academic settings.

Executive Functioning

Executive functioning is an umbrella term which encapsulates a broad variety of cognitive abilities including, but not limited to, cognitive set-shifting, verbal fluency, planning, judgment, reasoning, organization, and inhibition. An agreed-upon definition of executive functions remains elusive (Cirino & Willcutt, 2017; Otero & Barker, 2014), but after reviewing more than two dozen existing definitions, Goldstein et al. (2014) identified several common characteristics. For example, the authors argued there appears to be consensus that executive functioning involves the application of knowledge but is separate from knowledge itself and that executive functioning involves completion of goal-oriented tasks. The frontal lobes, and particularly prefrontal cortex, (PFC) have consistently been identified as the primary neuroanatomical area associated with executive functions (e.g. Goldstein et al., 2014; McCloskey

& Perkins, 2012), and abnormalities in the structure and function of the PFC have been consistently found in individuals with ASD (Geurts et al., 2014). More specific executive functions have also been associated with particular brain areas. For example, verbal fluency is largely correlated with the left inferior frontal gyrus (Costafreda et al., 2006). In a review of the extant literature, Geurts et al. (2014) found that inhibition, cognitive flexibility, and planning are common EF deficits in individuals with ASD, though they also cautioned that many individuals with ASD do not experience these deficits.

Some have argued that difficulties with executive functioning may be the root of difficulties with flexibility and non-literal thinking that are some of the hallmark symptoms of ASD (Pellicano, 2012). A study by Sinzig et al. (2008) found adolescents with ASD tended to show impairment in planning and flexibility, while youth with ADHD showed greater impairment in working memory and inhibition. Begeer et al. (2014) found that while their strategies varied from neurotypical peers, children and adolescents with ASD performed similarly (e.g., total number of words) on a verbal fluency task. Demetriou et al. (2018) found that individuals with ASD tended to show significant EF impairment, though no clear pattern of impairment emerged, a finding that has been supported by past research and conceptualizations of ASD (Geurts et al., 2014). Of note for ASD in particular, there appears to be a relationship between EF and theory of mind, or the ability to infer what another individual is thinking and/or how they may react in a given social situation. McAlister & Peterson (2013) found that improvements in EF appeared to benefit theory of mind and vice versa. Another notable finding of this study is that the presence of neurotypical siblings appeared to aid in the development of both skills, suggesting that interaction with neurotypical peers is an easily accessible form of intervention. It should be noted, however, that Hughes and Ensor (2007) found this relationship was not equal bidirectionally. Namely, increases in EF led to greater increases of theory of mind compared to the ability of ToM to increase performance on EF measures. While these studies focused primarily on younger children, Lagattuta et al. (2015) argued that the relationship between ToM and EF is likely to persist well into adolescence and perhaps beyond, and Stichter et al. (2010) found that a targeted social intervention for children aged 11–14 was able to improve ToM and EF performance.

Future Directions and Conclusions

Evolving technology is likely to change the way clinicians approach neuropsychological assessment in the future. For example, a number of computer-aided diagnosis systems (CADS) have been developed with the aim of improving the accuracy and speed with which ASD can be diagnosed. These methods include multiple forms of artificial intelligence (AI) including deep learning (DL; Khodatars et al., 2020). A detailed explanation of deep learning methodology is beyond the scope of this writing, but the method has proven successful in completing a number of complex medical tasks (Chartrand et al., 2017). The goal of decreasing the amount of clinical time needed to diagnose ASD is admirable given extensive wait times sometimes required to receive a formal autism evaluation (Kanne & Bishop, 2021) as well as concerns about the age of onset than the age of recognition. Even in major metropolitan areas where multiple options are available, it is not uncommon for ASD clinics to have waitlists of several months or even 1–2 years (Bernat, personal communication). Indeed, the wait list problem is so pronounced there is at least one study analyzing the benefits of providing a support group for parents during this stressful and uncertain period (Connolly & Gersch, 2013). Another, related tool for using data to aid in classification is functional connectomics, or the study of whole brain synchronization maps, including how these mappings vary across different neurodevelopmental and related conditions (Schirmer et al., 2021).

Niu et al. (2020) developed a multichannel deep attention neural network (DANN), which they used to analyze a large dataset collected as part of the Autism Brain Imaging Data Exchange (ABIDE). The authors found that their DANN was able to achieve an accuracy rate of 0.732 for ASD classification. Of note, data in this model outside of resting state fMRI (rs-fMRI) included personal characteristics of participants including scores on cognitive measures and the Social Responsiveness Scale (SRS; Constantino & Gruber, 2012). The authors noted the decision to include performance on cognitive measures including Full Scale IQ, Performance IQ, and Verbal IQ was based on existing literature which suggests that a split between PIQ and VIQ can be a useful diagnostic tool, particularly for individuals with ASD (see Ankenman et al., 2014; Black et al., 2009 for further reading). The DANN model which made use of PC data including neuropsychological measures achieved the highest degree of accuracy of all models evaluated, suggesting that even if clinicians begin to move towards the use of tools such as CADS to aid with clinical decision making, psychological and neuropsychological measures are likely to remain an important tool which can provide additional discriminative validity above and beyond neuroimaging data alone (Khodatars et al., 2020). Neuropsychological test data such as FSIQ is also recognized as a possible confound (or in the language of machine learning "unseen data") and is often used when trying to control for group differences in developing such models and is recognized as a valuable research tool for this reason (Schirmer et al., 2021). This is consistent with recommendations from a review article by Song et al. (2020) which suggested that deep learning techniques be viewed as a potential way to strengthen and augment diagnostic decision making as part of an evaluation (as opposed to a substitute for a traditional diagnostic evaluation). Despite the significant potential of such models, there are notable limitations of this approach to diagnosis at this time and "significant improvements are necessary in order to translate functional connectivity into clinical practice" (Schirmer et al., 2021, p. 22). The high rate of comorbidities and other confounding factors seen in individuals with neurodevelopmental disabilities such as ASD is a complication that also contributes to the challenges of development and limited generalizability of such models (Schirmer et al., 2021).

Neuroimaging data suggests that differences in the default mode network (DMN) can be found when comparing individuals with ASD to healthy controls. For example, Chen et al. (2020) found that individuals with ASD demonstrated areas of both significantly increased and decreased areas of functional connectivity within the DMN. This included significantly decreased nodal centralities in the bilateral anterior medial prefrontal cortex and increased nodal centralities in the right lateral temporal cortex and the right retro splenial cortex. Foss-Feig et al. (2016) completed a study aimed at elucidating the neurological bases of restricted interests and expertise seen in ASD which found that children and adolescents with ASD showed higher levels of recruitment of the fusiform face area (FFA) when compared to controls. This was a novel study which used peers with similar levels of restricted interest and/or expertise but did not otherwise display symptoms consistent with ASD as assessed by the *Social Communication Questionnaire* (SCQ; Rutter et al., 2003). Controls also had no first-degree relatives with ASD. Members of the same lab previously reported evidence for enhanced insula and anterior cingulate response to individuals' own specialized/restricted interests in individuals with ASD compared to typically developing (TD) peers (Cascio et al., 2014). Kilroy et al. (2021) found that individuals with ASD show a unique pattern of hypoactivity in the inferior frontal gyrus and pars opercularis when observing motor movements compared to both TD peers and individuals with developmental coordination disorder (DCD). Both the ASD and DCD groups showed reduced activity in the same areas when imitating motor actions. Bilateral activation of the inferior frontal gyrus and pars opercularis was also found to positively correlate with performance of motor tasks as measured by the total score on the *Movement Assessment Battery for Children – Second Edition* (MABC-2; Henderson et al., 2007).

Adolescents with HFASD who leave high school and enter the workforce and college are likely to need accommodations in some or many areas to be successful given that even individuals with ASD with strong intellectual functioning are still likely to demonstrate deficits in social communication (APA, 2013). Additionally, concerns are present that adults with HFASD struggle with occupational or vocational outcomes (Taylor et al., 2015). As such, school psychologists who are working in schools assisting these individuals with transition, as well as psychologists working with them in college and in the workforce, need to conduct a careful and thorough neuropsychological evaluation. The purpose of this evaluation may be for diagnosis of ASD or other comorbid conditions but also to determine the patient's capacity to attend college or enter the workforce and determine what interventions and accommodations are likely to be useful. School psychologists should also consider research (e.g., Lee et al., 2019) that looks at factors in vocational success. Evaluations should include components consistent with a typical neuropsychological evaluation, including measures of symptom validity testing (particularly when academic and/or testing accommodations are being sought) and assessing the wide array of domains detailed in this chapter.

References

Ameis, S. H., Fan, J., Rockel, C., Soorya, L., Wang, A. T., & Anagnostou, E. (2013). Altered cingulum bundle microstructure in autism spectrum disorder. *Acta neuropsychiatrica, 25*(5), 275–282.

American Psychiatric Association. (2000). *Diagnostic and statistical manual of mental disorders: DSM-IV-TR*. Author.

American Psychiatric Association. (2013). *Diagnostic and statistical manual of mental disorders (DSM-5)*. Author.

Ankenman, K., Elgin, J., Sullivan, K., Vincent, L., & Bernier, R. (2014). Nonverbal and verbal cognitive discrepancy profiles in autism spectrum disorders: Influence of age and gender. *American Journal on Intellectual and Developmental Disabilities, 119*(1), 84–99.

Astill, R. G., Van der Heijden, K. B., Van Ijzendoorn, M. H., & Van Someren, E. J. (2012). Sleep, cognition, and behavioral problems in school-age children: A century of research meta-analyzed. *Psychological Bulletin, 138*(6), 1109.

Begeer, S., Wierda, M., Scheeren, A. M., Teunisse, J. P., Koot, H. M., & Geurts, H. M. (2014). Verbal fluency in children with autism spectrum disorders: Clustering and switching strategies. *Autism, 18*(8), 1014–1018.

Behrmann, M., & Minshew, N. J. (2015). Sensory processing in autism. *Autism Spectrum Disorders, 180*, 54–67.

Bennett, T., Szatmari, P., Bryson, S., Volden, J., Zwaigenbaum, L., Vaccarella, L., … Boyle, M. (2008). Differentiating autism and Asperger syndrome on the basis of language delay or impairment. *Journal of Autism and Developmental Disorders, 38*(4), 616–625.

Ben-Porath, Y., & Tellegen, A. (2020). *Minnesota multiphasic personality Inventory-3*. Pearson.

Black, D. O., Wallace, G. L., Sokoloff, J. L., & Kenworthy, L. (2009). Brief report: IQ split predicts social symptoms and communication abilities in high-functioning children with autism spectrum disorders. *Journal of Autism and Developmental Disorders, 39*(11), 1613–1619.

Blunden, S., Lushington, K., Lorenzen, B., Martin, J., & Kennedy, D. (2005). Neuropsychological and psychosocial function in children with a history of snoring or behavioral sleep problems. *The Journal of Pediatrics, 146*(6), 780–786.

Brentani, H. S. (2013). Autism spectrum disorders: An overview on diagnosis and treatment. *Revista Brasileira de Psiquiatria*, S62–S72.

Bühler, E., Bachmann, C., Goyert, H., Heinzel-Gutenbrunner, M., & Kamp-Becker, I. (2011). Differential diagnosis of autism spectrum disorder and attention deficit hyperactivity disorder by means of inhibitory control and 'theory of mind'. *Journal of Autism and Developmental Disorders, 41*(12), 1718–1726.

Buie, T., Campbell, D. B., Fuchs, G. J., Furuta, G. T., Levy, J., Van De Water, J., … Winter, H. (2010). Evaluation, diagnosis, and treatment of gastrointestinal disorders in individuals with ASDs: A consensus report. *Pediatrics, 125*, 1–18.

Burns, C. O., & Matson, J. L. (2018). An investigation of the association between seizures, autism symptomology, and developmental functioning in young children. *Developmental Neurorehabilitation, 21*, 188–196.

Butcher, J. N., Williams, C. L., Graham, J. R., Archer, R. P., Tellegen, A., … Kaemmer, B. (1992). *Minnesota multiphasic personality inventory – Adolescent*. University of Minnesota Press.

Canitano, R. (2007). Epilepsy in autism spectrum disorders. *European Child & Adolescent Psychiatry, 16*(1), 61–66.

Cascio, C. J., Foss-Feig, J. H., Heacock, J., Schauder, K. B., Loring, W. A., Rogers, B. P., … Bolton, S. (2014). Affective neural response to restricted interests in autism spectrum disorders. *Journal of Child Psychology and Psychiatry, 55*(2), 162–171.

Centers for Disease Control. Data & statistics on Autism Spectrum Disorder | CDC. (n.d.). Retrieved March 25, 2019, from https://www.cdc.gov/ncbddd/autism/data.html

Charman, T., Pickles, A., Simonoff, E., Chandler, S., Loucas, T., & Baird, G. (2011). IQ in children with autism spectrum disorders: Data from the special needs and autism project (SNAP). *Psychological Medicine, 41*(3), 619–627.

Chartrand, G., Cheng, P. M., Vorontsov, E., Drozdzal, M., Turcotte, S., Pal, C. J., … Tang, A. (2017). Deep learning: A primer for radiologists. *Radiographics, 37*(7), 2113–2131.

Chen, L., Chen, Y., Zheng, H., Zhang, B., Wang, F., Fang, J., … Zhang, S. (2020). Changes in the topological organization of the default mode network in autism spectrum disorder. *Brain Imaging and Behavior*, 1–10.

Chita-Tegmark, M. (2016). Social attention in ASD: A review and meta-analysis of eye-tracking studies. *Research in Developmental Disabilities, 48*, 79–93.

Chown, N., & Beavan, N. (2012). Intellectually capable but socially excluded? A review of the literature and research on students with autism in further education. *Journal of Further and Higher Education, 36*(4), 477–493.

Christakou, A., Murphy, C. M., Chantiluke, K., Cubillo, A. I., Smith, A. B., Giampietro, V., … Rubia, K. (2013). Disorder-specific functional abnormalities during sustained attention in youth with attention deficit hyperactivity disorder (ADHD) and with autism. *Molecular Psychiatry, 18*(2), 236.

Cirino, P. T., & Willcutt, E. G. (2017). An introduction to the special issue: Contributions of executive function to academic skills. *Journal of Learning Disabilities, 50*(4), 355–358.

Conners, C. K. (2013). *Conners' CPT 3: Conners' continuous performance test* (3rd edn.) [computer software]. Multi Health Systems.

Connolly, M., & Gersch, I. (2013). A support group for parents of children on a waiting list for an assessment for autism spectrum disorder. *Educational Psychology in Practice, 29*(3), 293–308.

Constantino, J. N., & Gruber, C. P. (2012). *Social responsiveness scale: SRS-2*. Western Psychological Services.

Costafreda, S. G., Fu, C. H., Lee, L., Everitt, B., Brammer, M. J., & David, A. S. (2006). A systematic review and quantitative appraisal of fMRI studies of verbal fluency: Role of the left inferior frontal gyrus. *Human Brain Mapping, 27*(10), 799–810.

D'Amato, R. C., Gray, J. W., & Dean, R. S. (1988). A comparison between intelligence and neuropsychological functioning. *Journal of School Psychology, 26*(3), 283–292.

Danker, J., Strnadova, I., & Cumming, T. M. (2019). "They don't have a good life if we keep thinking that they're doing it on purpose!": Teachers' perspectives on the well-being of students with autism. *Journal of Autism and Developmental Disorders, 49*, 2923–2934.

Davis, A. S. (Ed.). (2011). *Handbook of pediatric neuropsychology*. Springer.

Davis, A. S., Pierson, E. E., & Finch, W. H. (2011). A canonical correlation analysis of intelligence and executive functioning. *Applied Neuropsychology, 18*(1), 61–68.

Davis, A. S., Bernat, D. J., & Reynolds, C. R. (2018). Estimation of premorbid functioning in pediatric neuropsychology: Review and recommendations. *Journal of Pediatric Neuropsychology*, 1–14.

Dawson, P., & Guare, R. (2009). *Smart but scattered: The revolutionary "executive skills" approach to helping kids reach their potential*. Guilford Press.

Demetriou, E. A., Lampit, A., Quintana, D. S., Naismith, S. L., Song, Y. J. C., Pye, J. E., … Guastella, A. J. (2018). Autism spectrum disorders: A meta-analysis of executive function. *Molecular Psychiatry, 23*(5), 1198.

Dewald, J. F., Meijer, A. M., Oort, F. J., Kerkhof, G. A., & Bögels, S. M. (2010). The influence of sleep quality, sleep duration and sleepiness on school performance in children and adolescents: A meta-analytic review. *Sleep Medicine Reviews, 14*(3), 179–189.

DuPaul, G. J., & Kern, L. (2011). *Young children with ADHD: Early identification and intervention*. American Psychological Association.

Fletcher, P. T., Whitaker, R. T., Tao, R., DuBray, M. B., Froehlich, A., Ravichandran, C., ... Lainhart, J. E. (2010). Microstructural connectivity of the arcuate fasciculus in adolescents with high-functioning autism. *NeuroImage, 51*(3), 1117–1125.

Foss-Feig, J. H., McGugin, R. W., Gauthier, I., Mash, L. E., Ventola, P., & Cascio, C. J. (2016). A functional neuroimaging study of fusiform response to restricted interests in children and adolescents with autism spectrum disorder. *Journal of Neurodevelopmental Disorders, 8*(1), 15.

Freeth, M., Chapman, P., Ropar, D., & Mitchell, P. (2010). Do gaze cues in complex scenes capture and direct the attention of high functioning adolescents with ASD? Evidence from eye-tracking. *Journal of Autism and Developmental Disorders, 40*(5), 534–547.

Geurts, H. M., de Vries, M., & van den Bergh, S. F. (2014). Executive functioning theory and autism. In S. Goldstein & J. A. Naglieri (Eds.), *Handbook of executive functioning* (pp. 121–141). Springer.

Giambattista, C. V. (2018). Subtyping the autism spectrum disorder: Comparison of children with high functioning autism and asperger syndrome. *Journal of Autism and Developmental Disorders, 49*, 138–150.

Gold, R., & Faust, M. (2010). Right hemisphere dysfunction and metaphor comprehension in young adults with Asperger syndrome. *Journal of Autism and Developmental Disorders, 40*(7), 800–811.

Goldman, S. E., McGrew, S., Johnson, K. P., Richdale, A. L., Clemons, T., & Malow, B. A. (2011). Sleep is associated with problem behaviors in children and adolescents with autism spectrum disorders. *Research in Autism Spectrum Disorders, 5*(3), 1223–1229.

Goldschmidt, J. (2018). A broad view: Disordered eating on the autism spectrum. *Eating Disorders Review, 29*(3).

Goldstein, S., Naglieri, J. A., Princiotta, D., & Otero, T. M. (2014). Introduction: A history of executive functioning as a theoretical and clinical construct. In S. Goldstein & J. A. Naglieri (Eds.), *Handbook of executive functioning* (pp. 3–12). Springer.

Harrison, P., & Oakland, R. (2006). Adaptive behavior assessment system-(ABAS-II.). : Harcourt Assessment, Inc.

Henderson, S. E., Sugden, D. A., & Barnett, A. L. (2007). *Movement assessment battery for children–second edition*. Harcourt Assessment.

Hermann, B., Jones, J., Dabbs, K., Allen, C. A., Sheth, R., Fine, J., ... Seidenberg, M. (2007). The frequency, complications and aetiology of ADHD in new onset paediatric epilepsy. *Brain, 130*(12), 3135–3148.

Hughes, C., & Ensor, R. (2007). Executive function and theory of mind: Predictive relations from ages 2 to 4. *Developmental Psychology, 43*(6), 1447.

Jiao, Y., Chen, R., Ke, X., Chu, K., Lu, Z., & Herskovits, E. (2010). Predictive models of autism spectrum disorder based on brain regional cortical thickness. *NeuroImage, 50*, 589–599.

Kanne, S. M., & Bishop, S. L. (2021). Editorial perspective: The autism waitlist crisis and remembering what families need. *Journal of Child Psychology and Psychiatry, 62*(2), 140–142.

Karama, S., Colom, R., Johnson, W., Deary, I. J., Haier, R., Waber, D. P., Lepage, C., Ganjavi, H., Jung, R., & Evans, A. C. (2011). Cortical thickness correlates of specific cognitive performance accounted for by the general factor of intelligence in healthy children aged 6 to 18. *NeuroImage, 55*, 1443–1453.

Kaufman, A. S., & Kaufman, N. L. (2014). *KTEA-3: Kaufman test of educational achievement*. Pearson.

Kenworthy, L., Case, L., Harms, M. B., Martin, A., & Wallace, G. L. (2010). Adaptive behavior ratings correlate with symptomatology and IQ among individuals with high-functioning autism spectrum disorders. *Journal of Autism and Developmental Disorders, 40*(4), 416–423.

Kercood, S., Grskovic, J. A., Banda, D., & Begeske, J. (2014). Working memory and autism: A review of literature. *Research in Autism Spectrum Disorders, 8*(10), 1316–1332.

Khodatars, M., Shoeibi, A., Ghassemi, N., Jafari, M., Khadem, A., Sadeghi, D., ... & Khosravi, A. (2020). Deep learning for neuroimaging-based diagnosis and rehabilitation of autism spectrum disorder: A review. *arXiv preprint* arXiv:2007.01285.

Kilroy, E., Harrison, L., Butera, C., Jayashankar, A., Cermak, S., Kaplan, J., ... Aziz-Zadeh, L. (2021). Unique deficit in embodied simulation in autism: An fMRI study comparing autism and developmental coordination disorder. *Human Brain Mapping, 42*(5), 1532–1546.

Klarborg, B., Skak Madsen, K., Vestergaard, M., Skimminge, A., Jernigan, T. L., & Baaré, W. F. (2013). Sustained attention is associated with right superior longitudinal fasciculus and superior parietal white matter microstructure in children. *Human Brain Mapping, 34*(12), 3216–3232.

Knight, V. F., Wright, J., Wilson, K., & Hooper, A. (2019). Teaching digital, block-based coding of robots to high school students with autism spectrum disorder and challenging behaviors. *Journal of Autism and Developmental Disorders, 49*, 3113–3126.

Kogan, C. S., Boutet, I., Cornish, K., Graham, G. E., Berry-Kravis, E., Drouin, A., & Milgram, N. W. (2009). A comparative neuropsychological test battery differentiates cognitive signatures of Fragile X and Down syndrome. *Journal of Intellectual Disability Research, 53*(2), 125–142.

Kwok, E. Y., Brown, H. M., Smyth, R. E., & Cardy, J. O. (2015). Meta-analysis of receptive and expressive language skills in autism spectrum disorder. *Research in Autism Spectrum Disorders, 9*, 202–222.

Lagattuta, K. H., Kramer, H. J., Kennedy, K., Hjortsvang, K., Goldfarb, D., & Tashjian, S. (2015). Beyond Sally's missing marble: Further development in children's understanding of mind and emotion in middle childhood. In *Advances in child development and behavior* (Vol. 48, pp. 185–217). JAI.

Lai, C. L. E., Lau, Z., Lui, S. S., Lok, E., Tam, V., Chan, Q., ... Cheung, E. F. (2017). Meta-analysis of neuropsychological measures of executive functioning in children and adolescents with high-functioning autism spectrum disorder. *Autism Research, 10*(5), 911–939.

Lee, L. C., Harrington, R. A., Chang, J. J., & Connors, S. L. (2008). Increased risk of injury in children with developmental disabilities. *Research in Developmental Disabilities, 29*(3), 247–255.

Lee, E. A. I., Black, M. H., Tan, T., Falkmer, T., & Girdler, S. (2019). "I'm Destined to Ace This": Work experience placement during High School for individuals with autism spectrum disorder. *Journal of Autism and Developmental Disorders, 49*, 3089–3101.

Lefter, R., Ciobica, A., Timofte, D., Stanciu, C., & Trifan, A. (2020). A descriptive review on the preveleance of gastrointestinal disturbances and their multiple associations in autism spectrum disorder. *Medicina, 56.* https://doi.org/10.3390/medicina56010011

Leitner, Y. (2014). The co-occurrence of autism and attention deficit hyperactivity disorder in children-what do we know. *Frontiers in Human Neuroscience, 8*, 1–8.

Lezak, M. D., Howieson, D. B., Bigler, E. D., & Tranel, D. (2012). *Neuropsychological assessment* (5th ed.). Oxford University Press.

Limoges, E., Mottron, L., Bolduc, C., Berthiaume, C., & Godbout, R. (2005). Atypical sleep architecture and the autism phenotype. *Brain, 128*(5), 1049–1061.

Llanes, E., Blacher, J., Stavropoulos, K., & Eisenhower, A. (2020). Parent and teacher reports of comorbid anxiety and ADHD symptoms in children with ASD. *Journal of Autism and Developmental Disorders, 50*, 1520–1531.

Loeb, P. A. (1996). *Independent living scales manual.* Pearson.

Lord, C., Risi, S., Lambrecht, L., Cook, E. H., Leventhal, B. L., DiLavore, P. C., et al. (2000). The autism diagnostic observation schedule-generic: A standard measure of social and communication deficits associated with the spectrum of autism. *Journal of Autism and Developmental Disorders, 30*, 205–223.

Luginbuehl, M. (2004). *Sleep disorders inventory for students.* Pearson.

Maeneer, M. J., Shaw, K. A., Baio, J. et al. (2020). Prevalence of autism spectrum disorder among children aged 8 years-autism and developmental disabilities monitoring network, 11 sites, United States. *MMWR Surveill Summ 2020, 69*(No ss-4), 1–12.

Matson, J. L. (Ed.). (2016). *Handbook of assessment and diagnosis of autism spectrum disorder.* Springer.

Matson, J. L., & Shoemaker, M. (2009). Intellectual disability and its relationship to autism spectrum disorders. *Research in Developmental Disabilities, 30*(6), 1107–1114.

Mayes, S. D., & Calhoun, S. L. (2008). WISC-IV and WIAT-II profiles in children with high- functioning autism. *Journal of Autism and Developmental Disorders, 38*(3), 428–439.

Mayes, S. D., Calhoun, S. L., Murray, M. J., Ahuja, M., & Smith, L. A. (2010). Anxiety, depression, and irritability in children with autism relative to other neuropsychiatric disorders and typical development. *Research in Autism Spectrum Disorders, 5*, 474–485. https://doi.org/10.1016/j.rasd.2010.06.012

McAlister, A. R., & Peterson, C. C. (2013). Siblings, theory of mind, and executive functioning in children aged 3–6 years: New longitudinal evidence. *Child Development, 84*(4), 1442–1458.

McCloskey, G., & Perkins, L. A. (2012). *Essentials of executive functions assessment.* Wiley.

McDonald, A. J., & Mott, D. D. (2017). Functional neuroanatomy of amygdalohippocampal interconnections and their role in learning and memory. *Journal of Neuroscience Research, 95*(3), 797–820.

McElhanon, B. O., McCracken, C., Karpen, S., & Sharp, W. G. (2014). Gastrointestinal symptoms in autism spectrum disorder: A meta-analysis. *Pediatrics, 133*(5), 872–883.

Monge, Z. A., Greenwood, P. M., Parasuraman, R., & Strenziok, M. (2016). Individual differences in reasoning and visuospatial attention are associated with prefrontal and parietal white matter tracts in healthy older adults. *Neuropsychology, 30*(5), 558.

Morie, K. P., Jackson, S., Zhai, Z. W., Potenza, M. N., & Dritschel, B. (2019). Mood disorders in high functioning autism: The importance of alexithymia and emotional regulation. *Journal of Autism and Developmental Disorders, 49*, 2935–2945.

Mundy, P., Kim, K., McIntyre, N., Lerro, L., & Jarrold, W. (2016). Brief report: Joint attention and information processing in children with higher functioning autism spectrum disorders. *Journal of Autism and Developmental Disorders, 46*(7), 2555–2560.

Niu, K., Guo, J., Pan, Y., Gao, X., Peng, X., Li, N., & Li, H. (2020). Multichannel deep attention neural networks for the classification of autism spectrum disorder using neuroimaging and personal characteristic data. *Complexity, 2020.*

Oliveras-Rentas, R. E., Kenworthy, L., Roberson, R. B., Martin, A., & Wallace, G. L. (2012). WISC-IV profile in high-functioning autism spectrum disorders: Impaired processing speed is associated with increased autism communication symptoms and decreased adaptive communication abilities. *Journal of Autism and Developmental Disorders, 42*(5), 655–664.

Otero, T. M., & Barker, L. A. (2014). The frontal lobes and executive functioning. In *Handbook of executive functioning* (pp. 29–44). Springer.

Parisi, P., Moavero, R., Verrotti, A., & Curatolo, P. (2010). Attention deficit hyperactivity disorder in children with epilepsy. *Brain and Development, 32*(1), 10–16.

Pellicano, E. (2012). The development of executive function in autism. *Autism Research and Treatment, 2012.*

Pugliese, L., Catani, M., Ameis, S., Dell'Acqua, F., de Schotten, M. T., Murphy, C., … Murphy, D. G. (2009). The anatomy of extended limbic pathways in Asperger syndrome: A preliminary diffusion tensor imaging tractography study. *NeuroImage, 47*(2), 427–434.

Reitan, R. M., & Wolfson, D. (1993). *The Halstead-Reitan neuropsychological test battery: Theory and clinical interpretation* (2nd ed.). Neuropsychology Press.

Reynolds, C. R., & Kamphaus, R. W. (2015). *Behavior assessment system for children* (3rd edn.) (BASC-3). Pearson.

Richdale, A. L., & Schreck, K. A. (2009). Sleep problems in autism spectrum disorders: Prevalence, nature, & possible biopsychosocial aetiologies. *Sleep Medicine Reviews, 13*(6), 403–411.

Rommelse, N. L. (2015). Intelligence may moderate the cognitive profile of patients with ASD. *Cognitive Deficits in Autism Spectrum Disorder as a Function of IQ, 1*–17.

Rutter, M., Bailey, A., & Lord, C. (2003). *The social communication questionnaire*. Western Psychological Services.

Sarter, M., Givens, B., & Bruno, J. P. (2001). The cognitive neuroscience of sustained attention: Where top-down meets bottom-up. *Brain Research Reviews, 35*(2), 146–160.

Sasson, N. J., Faso, D. J., Nugent, J., Lovell, S., Kennedy, D. P., & Grossman, R. B. (2017). Neurotypical peers are less willing to interact with those with autism based on thin slice judgments. *Scientific Reports, 7,* 40700.

Sattler, J. (2008). *Assessment of children: Cognitive foundations* (5th ed.). JM Sattler.

Saulnier, C. A., & Ventola, P. E. (2012). *Essentials of autism spectrum disorders evaluation and assessment*. Wiley.

Schirmer, M. D., Venkataraman, A., Rekik, I., Kim, M., Mostofsky, S. H., Nebel, M. B., ... Chung, A. W. (2021). Neuropsychiatric disease classification using functional connectomics-results of the connectomics in neuroimaging transfer learning challenge. *Medical Image Analysis, 70,* 101972.

Semel, E., Wiig, E. H., & Secord, W. A. (2003). *Clinical evaluation of language fundamentals (CELF-4)*. The Psychological Corporation.

Sibley, M. H. (2016). *Parent-teen therapy for executive function deficits and ADHD: Building skills and motivation*. Guilford Publications.

Sinzig, J., Morsch, D., Bruning, N., Schmidt, M. H., & Lehmkuhl, G. (2008). Inhibition, flexibility, working memory and planning in autism spectrum disorders with and without comorbid ADHD-symptoms. *Child and Adolescent Psychiatry and Mental Health, 2*(1), 4.

Snow, J., Ingeholm, J. E., Levy, I. F., Caravella, R. A., Case, L. K., Wallace, G. L., & Martin, A. (2011). Impaired visual scanning and memory for faces in high-functioning autism spectrum disorders: it's not just the eyes. *Journal of the International Neuropsychological Society, 17*(6), 1021–1029.

Song, J. W., Yoon, N. R., Jang, S. M., Lee, G. Y., & Kim, B. N. (2020). Neuroimaging-based deep learning in autism Spectrum disorder and attention-deficit/hyperactivity disorder. *Journal of the Korean Academy of Child and Adolescent Psychiatry, 31*(3), 97.

Steiger, B. K., & Jokeit, H. (2017). Why epilepsy challenges social life. *Seizure, 44,* 194–198.

Stichter, J. P., Herzog, M. J., Visovsky, K., Schmidt, C., Randolph, J., Schultz, T., & Gage, N. (2010). Social competence intervention for youth with Asperger syndrome and high- functioning autism: An initial investigation. *Journal of Autism and Developmental Disorders, 40*(9), 1067–1079.

Taylor, J. L., Henninger, N. A., & Mailick, M. R. (2015). Longitudinal patterns of employment and postsecondary education for adults with autism and average-range IQ. *Autism, 19,* 785–793. https://doi.org/10.1177/1362361315585643

Wechsler, D. (2003). *Wechsler intelligence scale for children*(4th edn.) (WISC-IV). The Psychological Corporation.

Wechsler, D. (2012). *Wechsler preschool and primary scale of intelligence* (4th ed.). The Psychological Corporation.

Wechsler, D. (2020). *Wechsler individual achievement test* (4th ed.). NCS Pearson.

Wei, X., Christiano, E. R., Yu, J. W., Wagner, M., & Spiker, D. (2015). Reading and math achievement profiles and longitudinal growth trajectories of children with an autism spectrum disorder. *Autism, 19*(2), 200–210.

Wheaton, A. G., Olsen, E. O., Miller, G. F., & Croft, G. B. (2016). *Sleep duration and injury-related risk behaviors among high school students—United States, 2007–2013* (p. 65). MMWR.

Whyte, E. M., Nelson, K. E., & Scherf, K. S. (2014). Idiom, syntax, and advanced theory of mind abilities in children with autism spectrum disorders. *Journal of Speech, Language, and Hearing Research, 57*(1), 120–130.

Wilkinson, G. S., & Robertson, G. J. (2017). *Wide range achievement test* (5th ed.). Pearson.

Wolff, M., Bridges, B., & Denczek, T. (Eds.). (2018). *The complexity of autism Spectrum disorders*. Routledge.

Yeates, K. O., Ris, M. D., Taylor, H. G., & Pennington, B. F. (Eds.). (2009). *Pediatric neuropsychology: Research, theory, and practice*. Guilford Press.

Yu, T. Y., Chou, W., Chow, J. C., Lin, C. H., Tung, L. C., & Chen, K. L. (2018). IQ discrepancy differentiates levels of fine motor skills and their relationship in children with autism spectrum disorders. *Neuropsychiatric Disease and Treatment, 14*, 597–605.

Zielinski, B. A., Prigge, M. B., Nielsen, J. A., Froehlich, A. L., Abildskov, T. J., Anderson, J. S., ... Alexander, A. L. (2014). Longitudinal changes in cortical thickness in autism and typical development. *Brain, 137*(6), 1799–1812.

Core Academic Skills Considerations, Evaluation Methods, and Intervention Approaches for Autistic Adolescents

Maria E. Hernández Finch, Aimee Wildrick, and Jenna M. Pittenger

Abstract This chapter discusses the importance of assessment and intervention of academic skills for Autistic individuals. Using the available literature and a developmental approach, the chapter highlights the academic needs of Autistic adolescents who are planning to enter college or a vocation and reviews present day outcomes. Key constructs such as executive function, theory of mind, and others are related to achievement. Numerous useful assessment tools and formal standardized measures in reading, math, and written expression are reviewed within the context of evaluations to assist Autistic individuals to have more positive outcomes and transitions. Interventions keyed to Autistic students in the areas of reading, math, and written expression are discussed in-depth. Finally, co-occurring learning disabilities are examined. Throughout this chapter, we use identity-first language in solidarity with the preference of the neurominoritized Autistic community.

Keywords Autism achievement assessment · Autism transitions · Autism academic skills · Work readiness autism

Autism spectrum disorder (ASD) is characterized by difficulties in social interaction, repetitive and inflexible behaviors, and an onset early in development (American Psychiatric Association, 2013). According to a recently available Centers for Disease Control and Prevention survey, an estimated 1 in 59 8-year-old children in 2014 had ASD (Baio et al., 2018). Autistic people make up a significant and growing portion of the population. Unfortunately, members of this portion of the population commonly face underemployment and low wages during their lifetimes when compared to other adults with disabilities (Roux et al., 2015; Burgess & Cimera, 2014). In fact, Autistic adults in their 20s have lower rates of employment than any other disability category (Roux et al. 2015). These outcomes may be, in part, due to low levels of higher education attainment. Around 43% of Autistic individuals attend postsecondary education, and completion rates are 38.8% (Newman et al.,

---

We have no known conflict of interest to disclose.

M. E. Hernández Finch (✉) · A. Wildrick · J. M. Pittenger
Department of Educational Psychology, Ball State University, Muncie, IN, USA
e-mail: mefinch@bsu.edu; awildrick@bsu.edu; jmpittenger@bsu.edu

© Springer Nature Switzerland AG 2022
K. D. Viezel et al. (eds.), *Postsecondary Transition for College- or Career-Bound Autistic Students*, https://doi.org/10.1007/978-3-030-93947-2_4

2011). In terms of employment outcomes, only around one-third of Autistic adults receiving services through vocational rehabilitation were employed in the United States from 2004 to 2014, and those who were employed generally earned wages below the poverty line (Burgess & Cimera, 2014). Academic success is a significant predictor of lifetime success for Autistic people (Nasamran et al., 2017). Because of this, after considering the importance of appropriate educational transitioning to adult life more generally, this chapter will consider the academic profiles of this population, along with interventions that may improve academic achievement and life outcomes.

Transition Planning

Academic achievement currently plays a central role in transition planning for Autistic adolescents. Though some families of Autistic students have mentioned an overemphasis on academic performance in transition planning (Anderson & Butt, 2017), the importance of functional reading, mathematics, and writing skills for employment and postsecondary education cannot be overstated (Benz et al., 2000). Basic employability skills include the ability to read and interpret text, express thoughts through writing, and solve problems mathematically (Hunter et al., 2019). Furthermore, to successfully function in society, being able to read to learn and to write to communicate are necessary (Alfassi, 2006). This application piece of academic skills is where Autistic individuals tend to struggle.

The interplay of executive dysfunction and difficulty with specific academic concepts and skills may lead to low achievement in higher education and contribute to high levels of college non-completion within this population. Autistic college students may have difficulty with written expression, abstract academic concepts, time management, and organization of class assignments (Anderson et al., 2017). Academic supports to address these deficits have been ranked by Autistic college students as being among the most helpful supports for them to receive (Anderson et al., 2018). Building academic competencies in primary school may support the skills needed for future academic endeavors and successful functioning in day-to-day life.

While school individualized education plans (IEPs) for special education students must formally begin addressing transition by the youth's fourteenth birthday, academic preparation for transitions will vary depending on the career path and should be centered on individualized guidance for Autistic adolescents. For optimal outcomes, transition planning should begin early. When transition services begin prior to age 14, preliminary research suggests that the likelihood of employment increases and wages increase (Cimera et al., 2013). This may be because early preparation provides the time needed to explore career paths, identify necessary competencies, and build relevant skills. Any postsecondary path chosen will involve increased independence for Autistic adolescents, who should be prepared with the skills needed to function independently. Explicit instruction may be needed on how to self-monitor and plan for large assignments or tasks, how to self-advocate for accommodations, and how to seek out additional support when needed.

For Autistic students mainstreamed or included in the general education classroom, academic planning tends to be generalized, rather than personalized based on situations they are likely to encounter in their careers or postsecondary education. It may behoove stakeholders in the transition process to advocate for incorporating real-world experiences into the school day during secondary school. For students planning on enrolling in college, taking a college class while in high school may help in acclimating to the environment and academic demands (VanBergeijk et al., 2008; Lee et al., 2014).

Oftentimes there is a disconnect between practical skills needed for postsecondary functioning and skills taught in secondary school. For example, the ability to use a computer is a basic skill, needed for higher education, employment, and day-to-day life. But Newman (2007) found that approximately 45% of Autistic students in primary school "rarely" or "never" use computers in the classroom to access the internet or use word processing. In a recent large study, Hedges et al. (2018) found that of the 472 Autistic adolescents surveyed, fully one-third indicated that they did not know how to use technology to learn, 30% did not have an educator helping them use technology, and 44% indicated that they were not allowed to use it in their classes. Furthermore, 58% indicated that technology could be distracting at school. This is problematic considering computer-aided instruction has been identified as more efficacious for this population (Abidoğlu et al., 2017) and Autistic students will need to learn to navigate websites that are not designed in a way that is sensitive toward their unique sensory needs (Pavlov, 2014).

Compared to Autistic adults with an intellectual disability, one study found that Autistic adults without an intellectual disability are three times more likely to have no activities during the daytime (Taylor & Seltzer, 2010). Thus, current transitional services do not appear to be fully meeting the needs of this population. Dismal employment and educational attainment outcomes are a multifaceted problem. Unmet needs may involve social difficulty, inadequate planning for transitions, adaptive functioning deficits, insufficient self-advocacy skills, and academic skill deficits (Matthews et al., 2015; Anderson & Butt, 2017; Lee et al., 2014). A multi-measure, multi-informant approach to assess abilities in these areas will help to facilitate the development of individualized planning and transition supports.

Academic Strengths and Weaknesses

Learning core academic concepts often initially requires concrete thinking about what can be directly seen followed by the application of those concepts to solve problems, which requires abstract thought and inference generation. A literature review of the academic profiles of Autistic children and adolescents finds that the ability of this population to complete rote learning tasks, where information and steps to complete a task can be memorized, is intact (Schaefer Whitby & Richmond

Mancil, 2009). Rote learning may include basic reading, math, and spelling tasks with concrete steps that can be committed to memory. Difficulties are more apparent when the complexity of tasks increases, and abstract thinking is required. Autistic students may be able to decode words while reading, though they may struggle when asked to make inferences or identify the focus of the passage. Likewise, Autistic students may be able to complete computational math problems with step-by-step instructions, though they may be unable to apply this skillset to a real-world scenario. Difficulty with complexity and abstraction contributes to an academic achievement gap between Autistic individuals and neurotypical individuals and tends to widen in adolescence (Goldstein et al., 1994). As tasks begin to require in-depth and abstract thought, Autistic students often fall behind their peers academically.

Though there are commonalities in academic abilities, it is important to note there is significant heterogeneity in academic ability among Autistic individuals. There are inter-individual differences in cognitive profiles and intra-individual differences across academic domains in this population. Academic performance incommensurate with what would be expected based on general intelligence is commonly found among Autistic youth (Estes et al., 2011; Jones et al., 2009; Wei et al., 2014). Estes et al. (2011) assessed the academic and cognitive ability of 30 nine-year-old Autistic children using the core subtests of the Differential Ability Scales (DAS), which reflects reasoning and conceptual abilities, and three subtests of the DAS Achievement Tests (basic number skills, spelling, and word reading). In 90% of the participants assessed, there was at least one significant discrepancy between their cognitive and academic scores. These results suggest that their scores for over-all reasoning ability were not aligned with performance in specific academic facets. Similarly, Jones et al. (2009) assessed the reading and math abilities of 100 four-teen- to sixteen-year-old Autistic adolescents using the Wechsler Objective Reading Dimensions (WORD), Test of Word Reading Efficiency (TOWRE), and Wechsler Objective Numerical Dimensions (WOND). These scores were compared to participants' cognitive ability, as measured by the Wechsler Abbreviated Scale of Intelligence (WASI). These authors found that 73% of participants had reading or math scores that were significantly different than expected, based on their Full-Scale Intelligence Quotient, a measure of global cognitive ability. The most common discrepancy found was in reading comprehension scores that were below the predicted values. In childhood and adolescence, Autistic youth have been found to attain discrepant scores on academic assessments compared to expectations based on their cognitive abilities.

Executive dysfunction theory (see Dementriou et al., 2018) may provide a framework to understand strengths and weaknesses in academic ability. Executive function, which refers to cognitive abilities including attention, working memory, planning, inhibitory control, and cognitive flexibility, is predictive of academic achievement (Samuels et al., 2016). Executive function deficits manifest as trouble executing many of the tasks necessary for academic success. Difficulty with cognitive flexibility may result in trouble with task switching and perseveration on the current task (Pellicano, 2012; Rosenthal et al., 2013). Working memory deficits restrict the amount of information some Autistic students are able to process at once, leading to difficulty with actively holding all information necessary for problem-solving, reasoning, and comprehending. Trouble paying attention may result in Autistic individuals not learning during classroom instruction and difficulty with completing academic tasks. The high degree to which Autistic students display deficits in executive function and that these difficulties may increase in real-world secondary education settings (Rosenthal et al., 2013) could in part account for low academic performance among these individuals.

Reading

To discuss reading profiles of Autistic individuals, it is important to acknowledge the different skills and abilities that make up reading. Reading involves a large set of skills, any of which may contribute to comprehension deficits. Important skillsets include word decoding, language comprehension, phonological knowledge, semantic understanding, mentalization, and background knowledge (Gunning, 2020). Comprehension involves an understanding of the language used and ability to visualize what is happening.

As noted in the simple view of reading theory, oral language ability and word recognition are considered to be foundational skills in reading comprehension (Gough & Tunmer, 1986). The simple view of reading has been substantiated as an explanation for comprehension difficulty among Autistic individuals (Norbury & Nation, 2011; Jones et al., 2009; Ricketts et al., 2013). However, Ricketts et al. (2013) note that social behavior and mental state understanding may need to be added to this theory in order to account for their association with reading comprehension in this population. To understand what we read, we first need to recognize the words used and understand the meaning of the language. Beyond foundational skills, higher-order abilities may determine the extent to which we comprehend what we are reading. Deficits in higher-order language skills, such as integrating background knowledge during reading, generating inferences, verbal reasoning, and focusing on the main ideas of the text are found to explain many of the difficulties in reading for this population (McIntyre et al., 2017a).

Autistic students are perhaps best characterized by heterogeneity of reading ability. In a meta-analysis of 36 studies examining the reading profiles of 1487 Autistic individuals, Brown et al. (2012) found high variability in reading comprehension, beyond what would be expected by error within studies. Over half of this variability was independently explained by participants' decoding skills and semantic knowledge. This heterogeneity may be conceptualized as several distinct reading profiles within this population. Research on reading profiles for school-aged Autistic individuals using a comprehensive evaluation of cognitive abilities, phonological processing, rapid automatized naming, word recognition, linguistic comprehension, and reading comprehension has found relatively consistent reading profiles (Solari et al., 2019; McIntyre et al., 2017b). Reading profiles included average scores across all reading, cognitive, and language measures; comprehension disturbance with other reading abilities intact; global disturbance with below average scores on all measures; and either below average with intact receptive vocabulary or severe global disturbance (Solari et al., 2019; McIntyre et al., 2017b). autism symptom severity, as measured by the ADOS-2, was related to profile membership (Solari et al., 2019; McIntyre et al., 2017b).

Comprehension difficulty among children with ASD is the most well-validated reading deficit within this population (Estes et al., 2011; Jones et al., 2009; Jacobs & Richdale, 2013; Norbury & Nation, 2011). However, comprehension difficulties are not necessarily stable across time. Solari et al. (2019) found that reading comprehension disturbance as measured by the Gray Oral Reading Test, Fifth Edition was the least stable reading profile across a 30-month period for school-aged Autistic children and adolescents. Of the 68.8% of participants in their sample with comprehension disturbance at time point one, only 57% still demonstrated comprehension disturbance at time point two.

In addition to the differences in skill development between Autistic individuals and their neurotypical peers, differences in brain activation patterns may help explain the comprehension disturbance profile within this population. The brain activation patterns of this population while reading were found to differ from neurotypical peers (Just et al., 2004). Among Autistic participants, Wernicke's area, important for language comprehension, had increased activation and Broca's area, important for language production, had decreased activation when compared to neurotypical controls. Just et al. (2004) suggest this pattern of activation could be indicative of extensive processing of the meaning of individual words and a lowered integration of the combined meaning of the words. These findings may be understood through the weak central coherence theory (Frith, 1989). This theory suggests that Autistic people have a bias to process at the local level, rather than integrating parts of concepts and perceiving them as a whole (Happé & Frith, 2006). The weak central coherence theory combined with brain activation pattern findings in the Just et al. study suggests that while reading, Autistic individuals may focus their attention on the individual, rather than combined, meaning of words.

Nuske and Bavin (2010) explored narrative comprehension and weak central coherence in an early elementary sample. Verbal comprehension of typically developing and Autistic children was assessed using the understanding spoken paragraphs test from the Clinical Evaluation of Language Fundamentals-3. Prior to this task, children were primed with the name of the story. Inferential processing was assessed using a paradigm developed based on previous research where children were read short stories and asked to answer factual, script, and propositional questions. On the verbal comprehension task, there were no differences between groups on responses to main idea questions. However, local processing biases were observed in the children's responses to globally based passage comprehension questions, with an inclination to list details and difficulty in expressing overarching concepts. While generating inferences, Autistic children did not automatically connect parts of the story.

Similar results were found among Autistic adults on bridging inferences and sentence interpretation tasks where participants were asked to select the most logical inference for a scenario and the meaning of an ambiguous sentence using context (Jolliffe & Baron-Cohen, 1999). In both tasks, participants had significant impairments in comparison to control participants matched on age and cognitive functioning. According to Jolliffe and Baron-Cohen (1999), results indicate that Autistic individuals do not comprehend globally without explicit instruction or deliberate effort to do so. Therefore, without training, Autistic children and adults may not spontaneously combine sentences to consider the global meaning of a text.

When considering where strengths and weaknesses lie in reading comprehension of Autistic people, the social aspects of the story present an important variable. The number of social aspects can affect an individual's comprehension in ways that are not present in neurotypical individuals. For example, Autistic children and adults have demonstrated comparable comprehension ability to peers when reading texts that require limited social understanding (Brown et al., 2012). This difficulty with understanding the stories with social content may be understood in part through differences in theory of mind.

Theory of mind (ToM) refers to the ability to attribute mental states to the self and others to understand and predict behavior (Premack & Woodruff, 1978). This is usually present in typically developing children by age 3 or 4 and follows a protracted period of development among Autistic children (Kimhi, 2014). Autistic children in elementary school consistently show deficits in explicit ToM tests (Kimhi, 2014; Pellicano, 2007; Kimhi et al., 2014). By adolescence, Autistic participants with average verbal and cognitive abilities have scored the same as neurotypical peers on explicit ToM tasks (Kimhi, 2014; Livingston et al., 2018; Happé et al., 2017). When more advanced naturalistic ToM paradigms are used, findings are inconsistent. ToM abilities range from no deficits to significant impairments (Roeyers & Demurie, 2010; Spek et al., 2009; Scheeren et al., 2013). Among Autistic adults who pass ToM measures, their ability to infer mental states does not necessarily transfer to real-world interactions. Autistic individuals reportedly fail to infer mental states spontaneously during conversations, even when able to do so during ToM measures (Kimhi, 2014; Peterson et al., 2008).

While reading, ToM deficits may manifest in difficulty with understanding the behaviors and intentions of story characters and subsequent development of inaccurate conclusions. Moreover, Autistic individuals may struggle to shift from the perspective of one character to another when characters interact in stories (Kimhi, 2014). White et al. (2009) investigated reading comprehension across different types of stories among Autistic children aged 7 to 12. Participants were split into the following groups: good ToM, poor ToM, and control (neurotypical individuals). The good and poor theory of mind groups were decided based on whether they performed above or below the 1.65 standard deviation (fifth percentile) on a ToM task. For Autistic children in the poor theory of mind group, deficits were seen across all story types. Importantly, both groups of Autistic children showed substantially stronger ability to answer questions in stories with little to no social aspects and need for mentalization than in stories with these elements. Among Autistic children who had good ToM, the ability to answer questions about stories that did not require social understanding was the same as in neurotypical individuals. Notability of reading comprehension deficits among Autistic people may depend on the story content and the individual's theory of mind ability. Without the additional demand of using social knowledge for information processing, Autistic individuals may improve their ability to understand stories.

In general, among Autistic individuals, word decoding tends to be intact while the meaning of words and story comprehension are challenging. Several interconnected factors contribute to this difficulty. Limited language proficiency and vocabulary knowledge may contribute to limited understanding of individual words. A lack of global processing and difficulty understanding the thoughts of characters may result in weaknesses in story comprehension. Depending on theory of mind ability, reading deficits may only be seen when stories require social understanding.

Reading Assessment

In addition to the three global achievement tests discussed in the *General Achievement Assessment* section, this section highlights measures focused specifically on reading. The Test of Word Reading Efficiency – Second Edition (TOWRE-2) and The Woodcock Reading Mastery Tests – Third Edition (WRMT-III) included individuals with disabilities in their normative samples matched with US census data (McCauley, 2017; Brunsman, 2014). The TOWRE-2 assesses basic word reading skill, fluency, and word recognition for ages 6:0 through 24:11 (Torgesen et al., 2012). This assessment may be used to identify reading disabilities and determine the need for early intervention services. The TOWRE-2 is based on the simple view of reading, which emphasizes the ability to identify words and comprehend their meaning (McCauley, 2017). The WRMT-III assesses reading comprehension, fluency, phonics, and vocabulary for ages 4:6 to 79:11 and may be used to assess deficits in reading ability and guide intervention plans (Woodcock, 2011). Similar to the TOWRE-2, the WRMT-III is "designed to measure the building blocks of reading" (Brunsman, 2014, para. 9).

Reading Intervention

The effectiveness of reading comprehension interventions is inconclusive and thus caution should be given to putting too much emphasis on any single intervention strategy (El Zein et al., 2014; McClain et al., 2021). Nonetheless, research on reading intervention strategies do provide insight into what strategies may work to enhance reading skills among Autistic individuals. To date, the strongest evidence to support Autistic students in primary school exists for student grouping strategies, graphic organizers, and explicit instruction (El Zein et al., 2014).

Interventions that pair peers may help in addressing deficits in oral language ability and social skills that underlie difficulty in reading comprehension among Autistic individuals. In examining three studies that used cooperative learning, where eight Autistic students aged 8 to 13 were assessed in total, effects were generally moderately effective, though ranged from no improvement to significant improvement in reading comprehension (El Zein et al., 2014). The strategies used in these studies included a combination of peer tutoring with one-on-one academic tutoring and free playtime, class wide peer tutoring, and cooperative learning groups. Mixed results may be the result of low sample sizes and heterogeneity in ASD.

Graphic organizer interventions may help Autistic students to understand the connections between topics discussed in the text (Finnegan & Mazin, 2016). Finnegan and Mazin (2016) synthesized the results from five studies that assessed graphic organizer interventions. These studies assessed a total of 32 eight- to twelve-year-old Autistic students. Graphic organizer interventions included instruction on how to use a graphic organizer, thinking maps, character maps, or Venn diagrams. Effectiveness was measured using the percentage of non-overlapping data points, and scores of 90% or higher were considered highly effective whereas 70–90% was considered moderately effective. Graphic organizers had moderate-to-strong effects on improving the accuracy of comprehension question responses. Improvements were seen in answering literal questions, inferential questions, and "wh" questions. In all studies assessing graphic organizers, the skills gained from the intervention were maintained and able to be generalized to other stories.

The use of explicit instruction, where reading comprehension is directly taught, may reduce cognitive load while reading as it guides Autistic individuals toward effective strategies. The combination of explicit instruction with visual representations has yielded a large effect size, with three studies, assessing a total of 28 Autistic students aged 6 to 14 in the intervention condition. Improvements were found in the ability to make inferences, comprehending analogies, and making deductions while reading (Accardo, 2015). Randi et al. (2010) noted that Autistic individuals are often placed in general education classrooms where questions assessing reading comprehension are common, though direct instruction on how to read for meaning is limited. Reading comprehension deficits may be, in part, due to a lack of understanding of the steps involved in reading for meaning. Direct instruction clarifies the thought processes that underlie reading comprehension.

In an intervention combining peer interaction, direct instruction, and use of graphic organizers, two out of the three Autistic high school students aged 15 to 17 demonstrated increased confidence, improvements in reading comprehension, increased interaction, and decreased negative behaviors (Reutebuch et al., 2015). For these two students, mean scores on reading comprehension question accuracy increased from a range of 50–100% to a range of 75–100%. This intervention utilizes the collaborative strategic reading strategy, which combines cognitive psychology with sociocultural theory to teach students cognitive strategies to improve reading. Tasks during the peer-instruction sessions involved clarifying story meaning, answering questions, generating and responding to questions, and using a graphic organizer. When considering intervention strategies, it may behoove practitioners to consider the effectiveness of combining interventions.

Math

In conducting a literature review of the math abilities of Autistic individuals, Chiang and Lin (2007) found that average math ability was the most common math profile, weak mathematical abilities were less common, and math giftedness was the least prevalent profile among a total of 837 individuals aged 3 to 51. One study of 27 Autistic adolescents aged 12 to 17 found an estimated 4% had a gifted math ability whereas an estimated 22% had a math-related learning disability (Oswald et al., 2016).

The computational ability of Autistic individuals depends on the complexity of the problems. The performance of Autistic individuals tends to decline as computational problems become more complex and involve multiple steps (Peklari, 2019). On single-digit arithmetic and simple addition and subtraction problems, Autistic children have performed significantly better than typically developing individuals (Iuculano et al., 2014; Titeca et al., 2014). For procedural calculation where number splitting and regrouping during addition and subtraction, Autistic first-grade children have performed significantly below average and second through fourth graders have performed average when compared to neurotypical peers (Titeca et al., 2015). Because these calculations involved regrouping, and not simply rote memorization, lowered scores may be the result of an increase in complexity.

For Autistic adolescents, performance on numerical operations, which included arithmetic, multiplication, division, and algebra, has been found to significantly exceed mathematical reasoning ability as measured by the Wechsler Objective Numerical Dimensions (Jones et al., 2019; WOND[UK]: Rust, 1996). Autistic youth are more likely to make errors in math reasoning while completing word problems that include day-to-day scenarios and irrelevant information (Jones et al., 2019; Bae et al., 2015). In contrast, word problems presented in short, clear sentences, have resulted in performance beyond that of neurotypical peers among Autistic elementary-aged children (Titeca, et al., 2014, 2015). Autistic individuals thus may have the mathematical knowledge to complete a problem, but pictures or extraneous scenario information may act as confounding elements that impede them from applying that knowledge. Moreover, word-problem solving among Autistic children has a strong association with math vocabulary, everyday knowledge, and sentence comprehension (Bae et al., 2015). Because of restricted interests and limited experiences, Autistic children often have not participated in activities represented in word problems that would be considered common among neurotypical children. Autistic children have limited involvement in leisure activities, including "social, physical, and informal activities" and most often engage in activities alone at home (Hochhauser & Engel-Yeger, 2010, p. 746). Limited exposure may explain an increase in errors when solving math problems that relate to money, paying restaurant tips, and sports (Bae et al., 2015). Solving a word problem involves first understanding the content of the problem and what is being asked, then accurately applying the correct math procedure. Without the background knowledge of the situation being described, it may be difficult to conceptualize what is being asked.

The nature of mathematical language and steps to solving problems may also be difficult to comprehend. As described by Yakubova et al. (2015), the understanding of math vocabulary requires that an individual understand how context can change the meaning of the word. A number of math words have different meanings outside of a math context. For example, the word "odd" can indicate either something being strange or a number that has a remainder of one when divided by two. Additionally, individuals must learn to compute based on the order of operations rather than going left to right, as is done in reading (Yakubova et al., 2015). Limited working memory and cognitive inflexibility may hinder Autistic individuals from switching between contextual word meanings and differing rules between academic domains.

Despite the difficulties, Autistic people may face with advanced math concepts, this does not suggest an inability to understand advanced mathematical concepts. An estimated 3.8% of Autistic adults surveyed between 2001 and 2009 in the national longitudinal transition study-2 held a job in a computer, mathematical, architecture, or science field (Newman et al., 2011). Compared to students in other disability categories, Autistic students were most likely to pursue STEM majors (Wei et al., 2012). Of these students, there was an 80.68% persistence rate for STEM majors at a 2-year community college in contrast to 47.39% Autistic students in non-STEM majors (Wei et al., 2013). Persistence was defined by students continuing to pursue their major in STEM, graduation with a STEM degree, or switching their major to STEM (2014). Thus, Autistic college students may be drawn to STEM fields and be more likely to persist in this topic of study.

When examining the overall mathematic profile of Autistic children including number identification and production, calculation, counting, and word problem solving, 40% of the Autistic participants had learning difficulties in math and the other 60% possessed average math ability. Chen et al. (2018) note that the high percentage of Autistic children who struggle with math emphasizes a need to begin focusing educational interventions to support mathematical skill-building. In general, Autistic individuals have comparable math fact knowledge to neurotypical peers, though they struggle with application. Difficulty with math application may stem from a lack of understanding of math vocabulary, situational knowledge, and the need to discern which information is relevant.

Math Assessment

In addition to the three global achievement tests discussed in the *General Achievement Assessments* section, these are specific measures focused uniquely on math. The KeyMath-3 Diagnostic Assessment (KeyMath-3 DA) is a measure of math ability that assesses basic math concepts, computation, and application that is based on real-world context and appropriate for ages 4:6 to 21:11 (Connolly, 2007). Autistic individuals were included in the norm sample with other individuals with disabilities under "Other Health Impairment." Adaptions of the KeyMath-3 include no time limit and simplified language (Connolly, 2007). The Math Fluency and Calculation Tests (MFaCTS) and Comprehensive Math Abilities Test (CMAT) are assessments focused on math ability as well (Reynolds et al., 2015; Hresko et al., 2002). The MFaCTs and CMAT do not provide norming and standardization information for Autistic individuals (Reynolds et al., 2015; Hresko et al., 2002). Benefits of these assessments include providing a skill assessment based on what is taught in schools. MFaCTS assesses operational skills and math fluency for ages 6:0 to 18:11 with content based on curriculum standards and recommendations (Reynolds et al., 2015). The CMAT assesses computation, problem-solving ability, and math application for ages 7:0 to 18:11 using real-world application modeling math concepts taught in schools (Hresko et al., 2002).

Math Intervention

A lack of research on math interventions and low sample sizes limits the known generalizability of math interventions among Autistic individuals. Common themes among interventions that have demonstrated improvement in math ability include making math problem-solving more concrete and modeling the correct way to solve the problem. Similar to reading interventions, math interventions using explicit instruction were effective in improving ability.

Levingston et al. (2009) suggest that teaching the behaviors that need to occur to solve word problems may be useful among students who have the computational skills needed to solve the problem but struggle to identify the correct way to solve the problem. Because Autistic individuals often have computational skills above their math reasoning ability, this strategy may be of use in this population. Teaching specific steps to follow to complete word problems has improved scores in students aged 10 to 14 on math problems involving algebra, multiplication, and division (Levingston et al., 2009; Root et al., 2018; Schaefer Whitby, 2012). Root et al. (2018) assessed the effects of explicit instruction to teach an 8-step strategy and a graphic organizer to solve and discriminate word problems in three Autistic youth with intellectual disabilities. A large effect was seen in improving independent word-problem solving and the ability to discriminate problem types.

Explicit instruction on the steps to solve word problems is a core component to the instructional method *Solve It!,* which was developed to teach word-problem solving to Autistic students (Montague, 2003; Schaefer Whitby, 2012). Using the *Solve It!* approach, instructors teach concrete steps including how to read the problem; paraphrase the text's information; visually represent the problem using pictures, tables, graphs, and organizers; plan how to solve the problem; estimate; compute; and check. When one step is mastered, the next step is taught until each step is mastered. Using this strategy to support word problem-solving among three Autistic middle school boys aged 13 to 14 was found to help correct previous misconceived strategies they had been using to solve problems (Schaefer Whitby, 2012).

Video modeling is an intervention where modeled behavior is presented in a video to help teach the correct method of responding. Though research on the effect of video modeling on math skills and academic skills as a whole is limited, video modeling has a strong research backing in behavioral interventions for Autistic students (Acar & Diken, 2012; Domir & Wolfe, 2014; Hitchcock et al., 2003). This intervention has a basis in social learning theory, where modeling and reinforcement are thought to facilitate the learning process. In video modeling, the video is watched to help acquire the skill then the use of the video is faded out. Currently, two studies have investigated the use of video modeling to teach math among Autistic individuals. Video self-modeling has been used to teach how to calculate exact change and solve word problems with fractions among adolescents aged 13 to 19 (Burton et al., 2013; Yakubova et al. 2015). For the six Autistic participants assessed in both studies, a large effect size was found for each student.

Evaluations of math interventions with Autistic individuals found that decreasing the abstraction and complexity of math problems was beneficial. The computational ability of Autistic individuals may be supported through the use of visual supports, math reasoning instruction, and modeling and breaking down the steps toward solving a problem. Additional research is needed to compare these interventions, assess the strength of these results, and investigate other intervention possibilities.

Written Language

Successful writing involves a complex skillset including writing mechanics, spelling, constructing sentences, content, and organization (Finnegan & Accardo, 2017). Autistic individuals often struggle with written expression. Estimates as high as 60% have been found for comorbid specific learning disabilities in writing among Autistic children (Mayes & Calhoun, 2006). Specific writing disabilities are characterized by a difficulty in integrating oral and written language, cognition, and motor abilities. On average, Autistic youth struggle with handwriting and create a lower quality written product when compared to neurotypical peers.

Difficulty with writing among Autistic students may be linked to a lack of automaticity in handwriting or typing. When the production of letters and words is not an automatic skill, working memory space is dedicated to the mechanics of writing (Tindle, 2016). This leads to a lowered capacity to focus on the content of the writing and can be damaging to academic achievement (see Finnegan & Accardo, 2017 for a review). Specific to handwriting, school-aged Autistic students write less legibly than their typically developing peers and create larger letters, which may be related to fine motor, visual perception, or visual-motor integration impairments

(Finnegan & Accardo, 2017; Kushki et al., 2011). Avoidance may contribute to lower quality handwriting, as Autistic children have reported discomfort while writing, sensory sensitivity, and distress over imperfect handwriting (Ashburner et al., 2012). In the workplace and academic environment, poor handwriting can lead to lowered productivity, miscommunication, and lowered levels of achievement. Writing is a means of communicating thoughts, ideas, and understanding that is central in work and school. Consequently, poor writing ability can lead to long-term negative effects in school and beyond.

In addition to how challenged Autistic individuals can be in the process of writing, lower writing quality has been observed and may be related to deficits in executive function, processing ability, and language skills (Rosenblum et al., 2019; Brown et al., 2014). In general, writing quality among Autistic individuals tends to be lower than neurotypical peers. For example, during a persuasive writing task, the quality of writing among Autistic individuals was found to include less developed ideas, unclear statements, and lower cohesion compared to the writing of neurotypical peers (Brown et al., 2014). Grammar and writing conventions were a relative strength for Autistic individuals, with performance similar to neurotypical peers. According to Brown et al. (2014), lower persuasiveness of writing may be due to an Autistic person's focus on his perspective as opposed to writing for the audience. This lack of perspective-taking may be understood through theory of mind. When writing, neurotypical individuals tend to cater their writing to their reader, whereas Autistic individuals may not consider how the audience will perceive the text.

Lowered writing quality has been found in narrative and expository writing as well. In one study, Autistic adults were asked to type either a narrative where they wrote a personal story about a conflict or expository story where they wrote about problems between people (Brown & Klein, 2011). Quality was determined based on how enjoyable the text was to read, text complexity, text structure, text cohesiveness, and how often sentences referred to previous story content. Writing mechanics were also scored, with focus on the length of words, spelling, and grammar. For Autistic adults, compared to neurotypical adults, both narrative and expository writing was of significantly lower quality. Writing mechanics among Autistic individuals were also lower, though the difference was insignificant. Deficits in theory of mind were associated with a shorter text length and lower quality writing. Weak central coherence led to difficulty with text organization, simplistic writing, a lack of flow between ideas, and less developed characters. Therefore, theory of mind and weak central coherence may negatively impact the writing of individuals with ASD, resulting in text that is less developed and organized.

Similar results have been found for storytelling and retellings of movie clips and books. Autistic children and adults include basic story elements with an increased emphasis on story details in place of information about the big picture (Barnes & Baron-Cohen, 2011; Ferretti et al., 2018). For example, when describing the setting, Autistic adults are more likely to include specific details such as the background of a room as opposed to stating what the room is. While retelling story dialogue, Autistic children in kindergarten through third grade had less story parts representing one character's speech or thought (Stirling et al., 2009). No differences were observed in grades fourth through sixth on the quantity of dialogue or thought. However, atypical dialogue was observed, leading to reduced story coherence. Autistic children were more likely to have dialogue without a response from another character and character speech not clearly attributed to a specific character (Stirling et al., 2009). These results suggest that central coherence and theory of mind may influence the details Autistic people include in stories and how their story characters interact.

Overall, Autistic individuals tend to have intact writing mechanics, including spelling and grammar. Average ability in writing mechanics may be the result of an ability to memorize these concepts. Moreover, Autistic people tend to spend more time forming letters while writing by hand, which may lead to less cognitive space available to evaluate writing content. As a result, the writing quality of Autistic people tends to be more simplistic and lower in quality than that of typically developing individuals.

Writing Assessment

In addition to the three global achievement tests discussed in the *General Achievement Assessments* section, these are specific measures focused explicitly on writing. The Test of Written Language - Fourth Edition (TOWL-4) assesses writing ability in ages 9:0 to 17:11 through examining an individual's ability to create and combine sentences, knowledge of vocabulary and spelling, and skill in story composition (Hammill et al., 2009). Normative data for the TOWL-4 includes individuals with disabilities matched to US census data (Castro-Villarreal, 2017). This assessment may be useful in examining different writing skills, though separate norming and validity for Autistic individuals have not been reported. The NEPSY – Second Edition (NEPSY-II) has the benefit of allowing practitioners to compare mean performance and matched control groups for Autistic children (Korkman et al., 2007). The NEPSY-II contains subtests to assess graphomotor skills, sensorimotor ability, theory of mind, and language ability in students 3 to 16 years old. Suggestions for administration with Autistic individuals are included in the manual, as well (Korkman et al., 2007).

Writing Intervention

Accardo et al. (2019) provide a current research synthesis of interventions that support the written expression of Autistic students. Common themes among these interventions include providing visual supports, motivational support, modeling, and feedback. Of the interventions examined, those found to be highly effective were constant time delay, video modeling, graphic organizers, and self-regulated strategy development (Accardo et al., 2019). All interventions assessed, other than the self-regulated strategy development, have received minimal research focus, with small sample sizes and single studies investigating the intervention.

Allowing the use of a keyboard could be one way to improve writing in Autistic individuals. Ashburner et al. (2012) found that the majority of Autistic children report feeling more motivated write when using a keyboard than when writing by hand. Writing using a keyboard was also found to be a faster method of writing for most Autistic students. Furthermore, it is likely that typing would help improve the accuracy of spelling. Many tasks related to employment and college are adaptable and allow for Autistic individuals to type rather than to write by hand.

Self-regulated strategy development (SRSD) intervention was rated as an effective intervention for improving writing quality among school-aged and college-aged Autistic students. Accardo et al. (2019) identified 13 studies that assessed a total of 36 Autistic individuals aged 7 to 20 using the self-regulated strategy development method. Of those assessed, all showed improvements in quality of writing and/or writing production. This intervention combines strategies to address content with self-regulation strategies and also supports cognitive awareness, mindfulness, and self-efficacy. Stages involved in these strategies include increasing background knowledge, learning the strategy, having the strategy modeled and then memorizing it, practicing with support and collaboration, and finally practicing the strategy independently. While learning these steps, emphasis is placed on monitoring one's own writing, setting goals, and reinforcing desired behaviors.

Jackson et al. (2017) examined the use of SRSD and a mnemonic strategy among three Autistic college students aged 18 to 20 enrolled in college writing classes using a multiple baseline across participants design. Instruction began by building background knowledge to support strategy instruction. Participants were taught the DATE mnemonic provided on a cue card and practiced with feedback over the course of ten sessions. DATE stands for Develop, Add Supporting details, Tie it together, and Edit and revise with SCOPES. SCOPES refers to a checklist to facilitate writing revisions which stands for Sentences, Capitalization, Order, Punctuation, Edit, and Spelling. At the start of each session, students were instructed on the lesson's purpose. During strategy implementation, students were encouraged to use a graphic organizer to add details and use self-talk throughout. Essay quality was evaluated using a rubric used by the students' university. Each participant increased writing rubric scores and the amount of time spent planning their writing using graphic organizers during the intervention and at a 2-week follow-up. Following the intervention, each student increased their grades in college writing classes. In fact, one participant who had previously failed College Writing I was able to increase their grade to an "A-". This study provides preliminary support for the use of SRSD to improve the advanced writing skills of Autistic young adults.

To date, the greatest amount of evidence for promoting writing quality among Autistic individuals exists for the self-regulated strategy development intervention. Other writing interventions for Autistic individuals, including graphic organizers and video-modeling, show promise, though more research is needed to evaluate effectiveness.

Normative Assessment Adaptations

Adaptations to normative assessments may be used to ascertain the functioning of Autistic individuals unable to take traditional assessments. For students where standard assessment practices are not possible or do not provide valid assessment results, testing accommodations and modifications may provide information on achievement levels. Testing accommodations permit minor changes to the assessment being administered, which allow for the same score comparisons to be used. These may include, for example, providing additional time for responses and regular breaks from the assessment (Sattler, 2018). Suggestions for test administration among children with special needs include being "observant, sensitive, intuitive, and sometimes even creative to figure out what will work" (Sattler, 2018, p. 216). When assessing Autistic individuals using a norm-referenced assessment, it is important to evaluate their abilities and the difficulties they may have that are impacting the results of the assessment process to avoid an inaccurate representation of their abilities. Modifications to the test outside of standardization would result in the test results being invalid for normative comparison purposes but would provide important qualitative information on the individual. Examples include rewording assessment questions, clarifying questions through providing examples, and giving directions multiple times when not permitted by the assessment manual (Sattler, 2018). Alternatively, after fully administering a measure in a standardized manner, one can query further to discover if a misunderstanding of the directions or of the task contributed to the scores. If not able to develop a complete picture of the student's abilities using grade level tests, practitioners may consider using off-grade level testing or beginning the test at an earlier starting point than that recommended by the youth's age or grade. This can result in scores which are limited to qualitative interpretation but may allow practitioners to better understand the child's abilities. At times, depending on the individual's level of functioning, there may not be a test with a low enough floor that includes the individual's chronological age in the norming sample. In these cases, assessments developed and normed for younger children may be used to derive functional goals and academic goals for growth. Scores would not be reported, but descriptions of what the individual can do would assist in planning. Sattler (2018) notes that every modification and accommodation made should be recorded on the Record Form and explained in the report.

General Achievement Assessments

There are three main published batteries that are used to measure achievement in reading, math, writing, and language abilities: the Kaufman Test of Educational Achievement (KTEA), Woodcock Johnson Tests of Achievement (WJ ACH), and Wechsler Individual Achievement Test (WIAT; Kaufman & Kaufman, 2014; Mather et al., 2014; NCS Pearson, 2020). These measures may be useful in determining profiles of academic strengths and weaknesses, whether a specific learning disability is present, and for intervention planning. In a review of the technical manuals for the most recent versions of these achievement measures, KTEA-III, WJ IV ACH, and WIAT-IV, documentation of inclusion of Autistic individuals in the norming sample was not found.

The KTEA-III measures reading, math, writing, written language, and general academic skills for ages 4:0 to 25:11 (Kaufman & Kaufman, 2014). Standardization for the KTEA-III included individuals with exceptionalities (McCurdy, 2017). However, "individuals with a sensory, physical, or cognitive disability" who were unable to complete the assessment in a standardized way were excluded from the normative sample. According to Mackler (2017), studies with the KTEA-III and special populations suggest strong discriminant validity and clinical usefulness. Additionally, when using the online scoring platform, Q-Global, to score the KTEA-III, suggestions are provided for which interventions may be beneficial for students based on their scores. The generalizability of these interventions to Autistic individuals is uncertain, though this information may be useful in knowing the types of interventions used to target specific areas of weakness.

The WJ IV ACH is an achievement test battery in the WJ IV assessment system (Mather, et al., 2014). The achievement battery may be used to assess reading, math, writing, science, social studies, humanities, and spelling sounds for ages 2 through 90 (Mather et al., 2014). Group differences in the WJ IV ACH are included for small clinical samples of Autistic individuals in specific tests. This information may be useful for score comparisons among Autistic individuals, though more research is needed as the sample size is small and there is no comparison group (Canivez, 2017).

The WIAT-IV is an achievement test battery used to assess "listening, speaking, reading, writing, and mathematics skills" for children and adults aged 4:0 to 50:11 (Breaux, 2020, p. 1). The WIAT-IV may provide data to identify a pattern of academic strengths and weakness, make placement decisions, inform instruction or accommodations, complete progress monitoring, assess response to intervention, and screen for dyslexia (Breaux, 2020). According to the WIAT-IV technical manual, an estimated 8–10% of the normative sample included individuals with one or more special education classifications. However, this did not include Autistic individuals. Special education classifications included attention-deficit/hyperactivity disorder, developmental delay, gifted and talented, intellectual disability, specific learning disability, and speech/language impairment.

Commonly, Autistic students are also evaluated by a speech language pathologist (SLP) for functional language ability and related needs. Clinicians may wish to work with SLPs to determine if the student would benefit from services for a language impairment, listening or expression, and/or language impairment services. The SLP will also assess functional and pragmatic skills while developing an intervention for the setting.

Comorbid Specific Learning Disabilities

A specific learning disability is defined as "a disorder in one or more of the basic psychological processes involved in understanding or in using language, spoken or written, which may manifest itself in the imperfect ability to listen, think, speak, read, write, spell, or do mathematical calculations" (Individuals with Disabilities Education Act, §1401, 2004). Currently, no easily accessible and interpretable national data exists on the comorbidity of specific learning disabilities and ASD. However, studies assessing specific learning disabilities and autism suggest that co-occurring specific learning disabilities are common. For example, through assessing 124 children with autism spectrum disorder at their clinic, Mayes and Calhoun (2006) found that 67% of Autistic individuals had a reading, math, or written expression disability. Learning disabilities were identified through subtest scores that were significantly lower than what would be predicted based on Full-Scale IQ scores on the Weschler Individual Achievement Test - Third Edition. Comorbid specific learning disability prevalence in Autistic individuals has been estimated as ranging from 6 to 33% for reading, 7 to 23% for math, and 60 to 70% for written expression (Mayes & Calhoun, 2006, 2007).

Conclusions

Research on ASD and academic performance is still in infancy. Particularly in writing and math profiles, further research is needed to gain a complete sense of the abilities of Autistic adolescents. Additional research is needed to understand the validity of assessments for Autistic individuals and the effectiveness of interventions with this group. Given the heterogeneity of academic performance among Autistic people, one must assess the individual abilities across academic domains, in addition to the skills that underlie performance. Reading, math, and writing are important to consider, as these abilities are necessary for most professional work. Through implementation of interventions that are specific to the strengths and weaknesses of Autistic students, the potential exists to address areas of difficulty, ease transitions, and improve lifelong outcomes.

References

Abidoğlu, Ü. P., Ertuğruloğlu, O., & Büyükeğilmez, N. (2017). Importance of computer-aided education for children with autism spectrum disorder (ASD). *EURASIA Journal of Mathematics, Science and Technology Education, 13*(8). https://doi.org/10.12973/eurasia.2017.00975a

Accardo, A. L. (2015). Research synthesis: Effective practices for improving the reading comprehension of students with autism spectrum disorder. *Rowan Digital Works, 12*, 7–20.

Accardo, A. L., Finnegan, E. G., Kuder, S. J., & Bomgardner, E. M. (2019). Writing interventions for individuals with autism spectrum disorder: A research synthesis. *Journal of Autism and Developmental Disorders*. https://doi.org/10.1007/s10803-019-03955-9

Alfassi, M. (2006). Literacy learning in communities of discourse: Reading to learn and writing to communicate. In S. Hogan (Ed.), *Trends in learning research* (pp. 41–66). Nova Science Publishers, Inc.

American Psychiatric Association. (2013). *Diagnostic and statistical manual of mental disorders* (5th ed.). https://doi.org/10.1176/appi.books.9780890425596

Anderson, A. H., Stephenson, J., & Carter, M. (2017). A systematic literature review of the experiences and supports of students with autism spectrum disorder in post-secondary education. *Research in Autism Spectrum Disorders, 39*, 33–53. https://doi.org/10.1016/j.rasd.2017.04.002

Anderson, A. H., Stephenson, J., Carter, M., & Carlon, S. (2018). A systematic literature review of empirical research on postsecondary students with autism spectrum disorder. *Journal of Autism and Developmental Disorders, 49*(4), 1531–1558. https://doi.org/10.1007/s10803-018-3840-2

Anderson, C., & Butt, C. (2017). Young adults on the autism spectrum at college: Successes and stumbling blocks. *Journal of Autism and Developmental Disorders, 47*(10), 3029–3039. https://doi.org/10.1007/s10803-017-3218-x

Ashburner, J., Ziviani, J., & Pennington, A. (2012). The introduction of keyboarding to children with autism spectrum disorders with handwriting difficulties: A help or a hindrance? *Australasian Journal of Special Education, 36*(1), 32–61. https://doi.org/10.1017/jse.2012.6

Bae, Y. S., Chiang, H.-M., & Hickson, L. (2015). Mathematical word problem solving ability of children with autism spectrum disorder and their typically developing peers. *Journal of Autism and Developmental Disorders, 45*(7), 2200+. Retrieved from https://link-gale-com.proxy.bsu.edu/apps/doc/A436974841/HRCA?u=munc80314&sid=HRCA&xid=387f998e

Baio, J., Wiggins, L., Christensen, D. L., et al. (2018). Prevalence of autism spectrum disorder among children aged 8 years – Autism and developmental disabilities monitoring network, 11 sites, United States, 2014. *MMWR Surveillance Summaries, 67*(SS-6), 1–23. https://doi.org/10.15585/mmwr.ss6706a1

Barnes, J. L., & Baron-Cohen, S. (2011). The big picture: Storytelling ability in adults with autism spectrum conditions. *Journal of Autism and Developmental Disorders, 42*(8), 1557–1565. https://doi.org/10.1007/s10803-011-1388-5

Benz, M. R., Lindstrom, L., & Yovanoff, P. (2000). Improving graduation and employment outcomes of students with disabilities: Predictive factors and student perspectives. *Exceptional Children, 66*(4), 509–529. https://doi.org/10.1177/001440290006600405

Breaux, K. C. (2020). *Wechsler individual achievement test: Administration manual* (4th ed.). NCS Pearson.

Brown, H. M., Johnson, A. M., Smyth, R. E., & Cardy, J. O. (2014). Exploring the persuasive writing skills of students with high-functioning autism spectrum disorder. *Research in Autism Spectrum Disorders, 8*(11), 1482–1499. https://doi.org/10.1016/j.rasd.2014.07.017

Brown, H. M., & Klein, P. D. (2011). Writing, Asperger syndrome and theory of mind. *Journal of Autism and Developmental Disorders, 41*(11), 1464–1474. https://doi.org/10.1007/s10803-010-1168-7

Brown, H. M., Oram-Cardy, J., & Johnson, A. (2012). A meta-analysis of the reading comprehension skills of individuals on the autism spectrum. *Journal of Autism and Developmental Disorders, 43*(4), 932–955. https://doi.org/10.1007/s10803-012-1638-1

Brunsman, B. A. (2014). Test review of Woodcock reading mastery tests. In J. F. Carlson, K. F. Geisinger, & J. L. Jonson (Eds.), *The nineteenth mental measurements yearbook* (3rd ed.). Lincoln, NE.

Burgess, S., & Cimera, R. E. (2014). Employment outcomes of transition-aged adults with autism spectrum disorders: A state of the states report. *American Journal on Intellectual and Developmental Disabilities, 119*(1), 64–83. https://doi.org/10.1352/1944-7558-119.1.64

Burton, C. E., Anderson, D. H., Prater, M. A., & Dyches, T. T. (2013). Video self-modeling on an iPad to teach functional math skills to adolescents with autism and intellectual disability. *Focus on Autism and Other Developmental Disabilities, 28*(2), 67–77. https://doi.org/10.1177/1088357613478829

Canivez, G. L. (2017). Test review of Woodcock-Johnson IV. In J. F. Carlson, K. F. Geisinger, & J. L. Jonson (Eds.), *The twentieth mental measurements yearbook*. Buros Center for Testing.

Castro-Villarreal, F. (2017). Test review of test of written language. In J. F. Carlson, K. F. Geisinger, & J. L. Jonson (Eds.), *The twentieth mental measurements yearbook* (4th ed.). Buros Center for Testing.

Chen, L., Abrams, D. A., Rosenberg-Lee, M., Iuculano, T., Wakeman, H. N., Prathap, S., Chen, T., & Menon, V. (2018). Quantitative analysis of heterogeneity in academic achievement of children with autism. *Clinical Psychological Science, 7*(2), 362–380. https://doi.org/10.1177/2167702618809353

Chiang, H.-M., & Lin, Y.-H. (2007). Mathematical ability of students with Asperger syndrome and high-functioning autism. *Autism, 11*(6), 547–556. https://doi.org/10.1177/1362361307083259

Cimera, R. E., Burgess, S., & Wiley, A. (2013). Does providing transition services early enable students with ASD to achieve better vocational outcomes as adults? *Research and Practice for Persons with Severe Disabilities, 38*(2), 88–93. https://doi.org/10.2511/027494813807714474

Connolly, A. J. (2007). *KeyMath diagnostic assessment* (3rd ed.). Pearson Assessments.

Dementriou, E. A., Lampit, A., Quintana, D. S., Naismith, S. L., Song, Y. J. C., Pye, J. E., Hickle, I., & Guastella, A. J. (2018). Autism spectrum disorders: A meta-analysis of executive function. *Molecular Psychiatry, 23*, 1198–1204.

El Zein, F. E., Solis, M., Vaughn, S., & McCulley, L. (2014). Reading comprehension interventions for students with autism spectrum disorders: A synthesis of research. *Journal of Autism and Developmental Disorders, 44*(6), 1303–1322. https://doi.org/10.1007/s10803-013-1989-2

Estes, A., Rivera, V., Bryan, M., Cali, P., & Dawson, G. (2011). Discrepancies between academic achievement and intellectual ability in higher-functioning school-aged children with autism spectrum disorder. *Journal of Autism and Developmental Disorders, 41*, 1044–1052.

Ferretti, F., Adornetti, I., Chiera, A., Nicchiarelli, S., Valeri, G., Magni, R., Vicari, S., & Marini, A. (2018). Time and narrative: An investigation of storytelling abilities in children with autism spectrum disorder. *Frontiers in Psychology, 9*. https://doi.org/10.3389/fpsyg.2018.00944

Finnegan, E., & Accardo, A. L. (2017). Written expression in individuals with autism spectrum disorder: A meta-analysis. *Journal of Autism and Developmental Disorders, 48*, 868–882. https://doi.org/10.1007/s10803-017-3385-9

Finnegan, E., & Mazin, A. L. (2016). Strategies for increasing reading comprehension skills in students with autism spectrum disorder: A review of the literature. *Education and Treatment of Children, 39*(2), 187–219. https://doi.org/10.1353/etc.2016.0007

Frith, U. (1989). *Autism: Explaining the enigma*. Blackwell.

Goldstein, G., Minshew, N., & Siegel, D. (1994). Age differences in academic achievement in high-functioning autistic individuals. *Journal of Clinical and Experimental Neuropsychology, 16*, 671–680.

Gough, P., & Tunmer, W. (1986). Decoding, reading, and reading disability. *RASE: Remedial & Special Education, 7*(1), 6–10. https://doi.org/10.1177/074193258600700104

Gunning, T. G. (2020). *Creating literacy instruction for all students* (10th ed.). Pearson.

Hammill, D.D., Larsen, S.C., Hresko, W.P., and Williams, C. (2009). Test of written language third edition [measurement instrument] 4th ed. : Retrieved from Pro-Ed.

Happé, F., Cook, J. L., & Bird, G. (2017). The structure of social cognition: In(ter)dependence of sociocognitive processes. *Annual Review of Psychology, 68*(1), 243–267. https://doi.org/10.1146/annurev-psych-010416-044046

Happé, F., & Frith, U. (2006). The weak coherence account: Detail-focused cognitive style in autism spectrum disorders. *Journal of Autism and Developmental Disorders, 36*(1), 5–25. https://doi.org/10.1007/s10803-005-0039-0

Hedges, S. H., Odum, S. L., Hume, K., & Sam, A. (2018). Technology use as a support tool by secondary students with autism. *Autism, 22*(1), 70–79. https://doi.org/10.1177/1362313177717976

Hochhauser, M., & Engel-Yeger, B. (2010). Sensory processing abilities and their relation to participation in leisure activities among children with high-functioning autism spectrum disorder (HFASD). *Research in Autism Spectrum Disorders, 4*(4), 746–754. https://doi.org/10.1016/j.rasd.2010.01.015

Hresko, W. P., Schlieve, P. L., Herron, S. R., Swain, C., & Sherbenou, R. J. (2002). *Comprehensive mathematical abilities test*. PRO-ED.

Hunter, J., Runswick-Cole, K., Goodley, D., & Lawthom, R. (2019). Plans that work: Improving employment outcomes for young people with learning disabilities. *British Journal of Special Education, 47*(2), 134–151. https://doi.org/10.1111/1467-8578.12298

Individuals with Disabilities Education Act, 20 U.S.C. § 1401 (2004).

Iuculano, T., Rosenberg-Lee, M., Supekar, K., Lynch, C. J., Khouzam, A., Phillips, J., Uddin, L. Q., & Menon, V. (2014). Brain organization underlying superior mathematical abilities in children with autism. *Biological Psychiatry, 75*, 223–230. https://doi.org/10.1016/j.biopsych.2013.06.018

Jackson, L. G., Duffy, M. L., Brady, M. P., & Mccormick, J. (2017). Effects of learning strategy training on the writing performance of college students with Asperger's syndrome. *Journal of Autism and Developmental Disorders, 48*(3), 708–721. https://doi.org/10.1007/s10803-017-3170-9

Jacobs, D. W., & Richdale, A. L. (2013). Predicting literacy in children with a high-functioning autism spectrum disorder. *Research in Developmental Disabilities, 34*(8), 2379–2390. https://doi.org/10.1016/j.ridd.2013.04.007

Jones, C. R. G., Happé, F., Golden, H., Marsden, A. J. S., Tregay, J., Simonoff, E., Pickles, A., Baird, G., & Charman, T. (2009). Reading and arithmetic in adolescents with autism spectrum disorders: Peaks and dips in attainment. *Neuropsychology, 23*(6), 718–728. https://doi.org/10.1037/a0016360

Just, M. A., Cherkassky, V. L., Keller, T. A., & Minshew, N. J. (2004). Cortical activation and synchronization during sentence comprehension in high-functioning autism: Evidence of underconnectivity. *Brain, 127*(8), 1811–1821. https://doi.org/10.1093/brain/awh199

Kaufman, A. S., & Kaufman, N. L. (2014). *Kaufman test of educational achievement third edition [measurement instrument]*. Retrieved from Pearson: PsychCorp.

Kimhi, Y. (2014). Theory of mind abilities and deficits in autism spectrum disorders. *Topics in Language Disorders, 34*(4), 329–343. https://doi.org/10.1097/tld.0000000000000033

Kimhi, Y., Shoam-Kugelmas, D., Ben-Artzi, G. A., Ben-Moshe, I., & Bauminger-Zviely, N. (2014). Theory of mind and executive function in preschoolers with typical development versus intellectually able preschoolers with autism spectrum disorder. *Journal of Autism and Developmental Disorders, 44*(9), 2341–2354. https://doi.org/10.1007/s10803-014-2104-z

Korkman, M., Kirk, U., & Kemp, S. (2007). *NEPSY–II* (2nd ed.). The Psychological Corporation.

Kushki, A., Chau, T., & Anagnostou, E. (2011). Handwriting difficulties in children with autism spectrum disorders: A scoping review. *Journal of Autism and Developmental Disorders, 41*(12), 1706–1716. https://doi.org/10.1007/s10803-011-1206-0

Lee, C., Mathur, S. R., Zucker, S. H., & McCoy, K. M. (2014). ASD academic transitions: Trends in parental perspective. *Education and Training in Autism and Developmental Disabilities, 49*(4), 576–593.

Levingston, H. B., Neef, N. A., & Cihon, T. M. (2009). The effects of teaching precurrent behaviors on childrens' solution of multiplication and division word problems. *Journal of Applied Behavior Analysis, 42*(2), 361–367. https://doi.org/10.1901/jaba.2009.42-361

Livingston, L. A., Carr, B., & Shah, P. (2018). Recent advances and new directions in measuring theory of mind in autistic adults. *Journal of Autism and Developmental Disorders, 49*(4), 1738–1744. https://doi.org/10.1007/s10803-018-3823-3

Mackler, K. (2017). Test review of Kaufman test of educational achievement. In J. F. Carlson, K. F. Geisinger, & J. L. Jonson (Eds.), *The twentieth mental measurements yearbook* (3rd ed.). Lincoln, NE.

Mather, N., Wendling, B. J., McGrew, K. S., LaForte, E. M., & Schrank, F. A. (2014). *Woodcock Johnson IV [measurement instrument]*. Retrieved from Houghton Mifflin Harcourt.

Matthews, N. L., Smith, C. J., Pollard, E., Ober-Reynolds, S., Kirwan, J., & Malligo, A. (2015). Adaptive functioning in autism spectrum disorder during the transition to adulthood. *Journal of Autism and Developmental Disorders, 45*(8), 2349–2360. https://doi.org/10.1007/s10803-015-2400-2

Mayes, S. D., & Calhoun, S. L. (2006). Frequency of reading, math, and writing disabilities in children with clinical disorders. *Learning and Individual Differences, 16*(2), 145–157. https://doi.org/10.1016/j.lindif.2005.07.004

Mayes, S. D., & Calhoun, S. L. (2007). Learning, attention, writing, and processing speed in typical children and children with ADHD, autism, anxiety, depression, and oppositional defiant disorder. *The Child Neuropsychology, 13*(6), 469–493.

McCauley, R. (2017). Test review of test of word reading efficiency. In J. F. Carlson, K. F. Geisinger, & J. L. Jonson (Eds.), *The twentieth mental measurements yearbook* (2nd ed.). Buros Center for Testing.

McClain, M. B., Haverkamp, C. R., Benallie, K. J., Schartz, S. E., & Simonsmeier, V. (2021). How effective are reading comprehension interventions for children with ASD? A meta-analysis of single-case design studies. *School Psychology, 36*(2), 107–121. https://doi.org/10.1037/spq0000424

McCurdy, M. (2017). Test review of Kaufman test of educational achievement. In J. F. Carlson, K. F. Geisinger, & J. L. Jonson (Eds.), *The twentieth mental measurements yearbook* (3rd ed.). Buros Center for Testing.

McIntyre, N. S., Solari, E. J., Gonzales, J. E., Solomon, M., Lerro, L. E., Novotny, S., Oswald, T. M., & Mundy, P. C. (2017a). The scope and nature of reading comprehension impairments in school-aged children with higher-functioning autism spectrum disorder. *Journal of Autism and Developmental Disorders, 47*(9), 2838–2860. https://doi.org/10.1007/s10803-017-3209-y

McIntyre, N. S., Solari, E. J., Grimm, R. P., Lerro, L. E., Gonzales, J. E., & Mundy, P. C. (2017b). A comprehensive examination of reading heterogeneity in students with high functioning autism: Distinct reading profiles and their relation to autism symptom severity. *Journal of Autism and Developmental Disorders, 47*(4), 1086–1101.

Montague, M. (2003). *Solve it! A practical approach to teaching mathematical problem solving skills*. Exceptional Innovations.

Nasamran, A., Witmer, S. E., & Los, J. E. (2017). Exploring predictors of postsecondary outcomes for students with autism spectrum disorder. *Education and Training in Autism and Developmental Disabilities, 52*, 343–356.

NCS Pearson. (2020). *Wechsler individual achievement test* (4th ed.). NCS Pearson.

Newman, L. (2007). Facts from NLTS2: Secondary school experiences of students with autism. *PsycEXTRA Dataset*. https://doi.org/10.1037/e608592011-001

Newman, L., Wagner, M., Knokey, A.-M., Marder, C., Nagle, K., Shaver, D., Wei, X., with Cameto, R., Contreras, E., Ferguson, K., Greene, S., & Schwarting, M. (2011). *The post-high school outcomes of young adults with disabilities up to 8 years after high school* (A report from the national longitudinal transition study-2 (NLTS2) (NCSER 2011-3005)). SRI International.

Norbury, C., & Nation, K. (2011). Understanding variability in reading comprehension in adolescents with autism spectrum disorders: Interactions with language status and decoding skill. *Scientific Studies of Reading, 15*(3), 191–210.

Nuske, H. J., & Bavin, E. L. (2010). Narrative comprehension in 4–7-year-old children with autism: Testing the weak central coherence account. *International Journal of Language & Communication Disorders,* 100824014249025. https://doi.org/10.3109/13682822.2010.484847

Oswald, T. M., Beck, J. S., Iosif, A.-M., McCauley, J. B., Gilhooly, L. J., Matter, J. C., & Solomon, M. (2016). Clinical and cognitive characteristics associated with mathematics problem solving in adolescents with autism spectrum disorder. *Autism Research, 9*(4), 480–490. https://doi.org/10.1002/aur.1524

Pavlov, N. (2014). User interface for people with autism spectrum disorders. *Journal of Software Engineering and Applications, 7*(2), 128–134. https://doi.org/10.4236/jsea.2014.72014

Peklari, E. (2019). Mathematical skills in autism spectrum disorder. *Asian Journal of Applied Science and Technology (AJAST), 3*(1), 111–123.

Pellicano, E. (2007). Links between theory of mind and executive function in young children with autism: Clues to developmental primacy. *Developmental Psychology, 43*(4), 974–990. https://doi.org/10.1037/0012-1649.43.4.974

Pellicano, E. (2012). The development of executive function in autism. *Autism Research and Treatment, 2012,* 1–8. https://doi.org/10.1155/2012/146132

Peterson, C. C., Garnett, M., Kelly, A., & Attwood, T. (2008). Everyday social and conversation applications of theory-of-mind understanding by children with autism-spectrum disorders or typical development. *European Child & Adolescent Psychiatry, 18*(2), 105–115. https://doi.org/10.1007/s00787-008-0711-y

Premack, D., & Woodruff, G. (1978). Does the chimpanzee have a theory of mind? *Behavioral and Brain Sciences, 1*(4), 515–526. https://doi.org/10.1017/s0140525x00076512

Randi, J., Newman, T., & Grigorenko, E. L. (2010). Teaching children with autism to read for meaning: Challenges and possibilities. *Journal of Autism and Developmental Disorders, 40*(7), 890–902. https://doi.org/10.1007/s10803-010-0938-6

Reutebuch, C. K., Zein, F. E., Kim, M. K., Weinberg, A. N., & Vaughn, S. (2015). Investigating a reading comprehension intervention for high school students with autism spectrum disorder: A pilot study. *Research in Autism Spectrum Disorders, 9,* 96–111. https://doi.org/10.1016/j.rasd.2014.10.002

Reynolds, C. R., Voress, J. K., & Kamphaus, R. W. (2015). *Mathematics fluency and calculation tests examiners manual.* Pro-Ed.

Ricketts, J., Jones, C. R. G., Happé, F., & Charman, T. (2013). Reading comprehension in autism spectrum disorders: The role of oral language and social functioning. *Journal of Autism and Developmental Disorders, 43*(4), 807–816.

Roeyers, H., & Demurie, E. (2010). How impaired is mind-reading in high-functioning adolescents and adults with autism? *European Journal of Developmental Psychology, 7*(1), 123–134. https://doi.org/10.1080/17405620903425924

Root, J. R., Henning, B., & Boccumini, E. (2018). Teaching students with autism and intellectual disability to solve algebraic word problems. *Education and Training in Autism and Developmental Disabilities, 53,* 325–338.

Rosenblum, S., Ben-Simhon, H. A., Meyer, S., & Gal, E. (2019). Predictors of handwriting performance among children with autism spectrum disorder. *Research in Autism Spectrum Disorders, 60,* 16–24. https://doi.org/10.1016/j.rasd.2019.01.002

Rosenthal, M., Wallace, G. L., Lawson, R., Wills, M. C., Dixon, E., Yerys, B. E., & Kenworthy, L. (2013). Impairments in real world executive function increase from childhood to adolescence in autism spectrum disorder. *Neuropsychology, 27*(1), 13–18. https://doi.org/10.1037/a0031299

Roux, A. M., Shattuck, P. T., Rast, J. E., Rava, J. A., & Anderson, K. A. (2015). *National autism indicators report: Transition into young adulthood.* Life Course Outcomes Research Program, A.J. Drexel Autism Institute, Drexel University.

Rust, J. (1996). *Wechsler objective numerical dimensions manual.* The Psychological Corporation.

Samuels, W. E., Tournaki, N., Blackman, S., & Zilinski, C. (2016). Executive functioning predicts academic achievement in middle school: A four-year longitudinal study. *The Journal of Educational Research, 109*(5), 478–490. https://doi.org/10.1080/00220671.2014.979913

Sattler, J. M. (2018). *Assessment of children: Cognitive foundations and applications.* Jerome M. Sattler, Publisher, Inc.

Schaefer Whitby, P. J. (2012). The effects of solve it! On the mathematical word problem solving ability of adolescents with autism spectrum disorders. *Focus on Autism and Other Developmental Disabilities, 28*(2), 78–88. https://doi.org/10.1177/1088357612468764

Schaefer Whitby, P. J., & Richmond Mancil, G. (2009). Academic achievement profiles of children with high functioning autism and Asperger syndrome: A review of the literature. *Education and Training in Developmental Disabilities, 44*(4), 551–560.

Scheeren, A. M., de Rosnay, M., Koot, H. M., & Begeer, S. (2013). Rethinking theory of mind in high-functioning autism spectrum disorder. *Journal of Child Psychology and Psychiatry, 54*(6), 628–635. https://doi.org/10.1111/jcpp.12007

Solari, E. J., Grimm, R. P., Mcintyre, N. S., Zajic, M., & Mundy, P. C. (2019). Longitudinal stability of reading profiles in individuals with higher functioning autism. *Autism, 23*(8), 1911–1926. https://doi.org/10.1177/1362361318812423

Spek, A. A., Scholte, E. M., & Berckelaer-Onnes, I. A. (2009). Theory of mind in adults with HFA and Asperger syndrome. *Journal of Autism and Developmental Disorders, 40*(3), 280–289. https://doi.org/10.1007/s10803-009-0860-y

Stirling, L. F., Barrington, G., Douglas, S., & Delves, K. (2009). Analysis of perspective management and reported interaction in story retellings by children with ASD and typically developing children. *E-Journal of Applied Psychology, 5*(1), 31–38. https://doi.org/10.7790/ejap.v5i1.148

Taylor, J. L., & Seltzer, M. M. (2010). Employment and post-secondary educational activities for young adults with autism spectrum disorders during the transition to adulthood. *Journal of Autism and Developmental Disorders, 41*(5), 566–574. https://doi.org/10.1007/s10803-010-1070-3

Tindle, R. F. (2016). *Handwriting and working memory: The role of memory and other cognitive factors in the performance of psychomotor skills such as handwriting and drawing.* Southern Cross University. https://researchportal.scu.edu.au/discovery/fulldisplay/alma991012821039202368/61SCU_INST:ResearchRepository

Titeca, D., Roeyers, H., Josephy, H., Ceulemans, A., & Desoete, A. (2014). Preschool predictors of mathematics in first grade children with autism spectrum disorder. *Research in Developmental Disabilities, 35*(11), 2714–2727. https://doi.org/10.1016/j.ridd.2014.07.012

Titeca, D., Roeyers, H., Loeys, T., Ceulemans, A., & Desoete, A. (2015). Mathematical abilities in elementary school children with autism spectrum disorder. *Infant and Child Development, 24*(6), 606–623. https://doi.org/10.1002/icd.1909

Torgesen, J. K., Wagner, R. K., & Rashotte, C. A. (2012). *Test of word reading efficiency (TOWRE-2)* (2nd ed.). Pro-Ed.

VanBergeijk, E., Klin, A., & Volkmar, F. (2008). Supporting more able students on the autism spectrum: College and beyond. *Journal of Autism and Developmental Disorders, 38*(7), 1359–1370. https://doi.org/10.1007/s10803-007-0524-8

Wei, X., Christiano, E. R., Yu, J. W., Blackorby, J., Shattuck, P., & Newman, L. A. (2013). Postsecondary pathways and persistence for STEM versus non-STEM majors: Among college students with an autism spectrum disorder. *Journal of Autism and Developmental Disorders, 44*(5), 1159–1167. https://doi.org/10.1007/s10803-013-1978-5

Wei, X., Christiano, E. R., Yu, J. W., Wagner, M., & Spiker, D. (2014). Reading and math achievement profiles and longitudinal growth trajectories of children with an autism spectrum disorder. *Autism, 19*(2), 200–210. https://doi.org/10.1177/1362361313516549

Wei, X., Yu, J. W., Shattuck, P., McCracken, M., & Blackorby, J. (2012). Science, technology, engineering, and mathematics (STEM) participation among college students with autism spectrum disorder. *Journal of Autism and Developmental Disorders, 42*(11). https://doi.org/10.1007/s10803-012-1700-z

White, S., Hill, E., Happé, F., & Frith, U. (2009). Revisiting the strange stories: Revealing mentalizing impairments in autism. *Child Development, 80*(4), 1097–1117. https://doi.org/10.1111/j.1467-8624.2009.01319.x

Woodcock, R. W. (2011). *Woodcock reading mastery test* (3rd ed.). Pearson.

Yakubova, G., Hughes, E. M., & Hornberger, E. (2015). Video-based intervention in teaching fraction problem-solving to students with autism spectrum disorder. *Journal of Autism Developmental Disorders, 45*, 2865–2875.

Social Emotional and Behavioral Assessment and School-Based Intervention for Adolescents with High Functioning ASD

Brittany A. Dale, Maria B. Sciuchetti, and David E. McIntosh

Abstract Accurate assessment of behavioral, social, and emotional difficulties in adolescents with high-functioning autism spectrum disorder (HFASD) is a vital component of intervention planning and evaluation. Furthermore, understanding the needs of this population with accurate assessment will aid in the postsecondary transition process. The unique challenges faced by adolescents during this often confusing emotional and social period in development, coupled with the innate social difficulties that are the hallmark of autism spectrum disorder, complicate the assessment and intervention process. School psychologists must be familiar with the literature on behavioral, emotional, and social assessment and intervention for adolescents with HFASD to best serve this population. This chapter presents a summary of the social difficulties experienced by adolescents with HFASD and discusses the assessment of ASD-specific characteristics through various types of measurement tools. Specific social skills measures that can be used to evaluate intervention effectiveness and the assessment of comorbid disorders in adolescents with HFASD are described. This chapter concludes with a summary of various school-based interventions that can be implemented by school psychologists, school counselors, and behavioral therapists.

Keywords HFASD · Adolescents · Behavior assessment · Intervention planning · Social-emotional assessment

---

B. A. Dale (✉) · M. B. Sciuchetti · D. E. McIntosh
Department of Special Education, Ball State University, Muncie, IN, USA
e-mail: badale@bsu.edu

© Springer Nature Switzerland AG 2022
K. D. Viezel et al. (eds.), *Postsecondary Transition for College- or Career-Bound Autistic Students*, https://doi.org/10.1007/978-3-030-93947-2_5

Social Emotional and Behavioral Assessment and School-Based Intervention for Adolescents with High Functioning ASD

Assessments help drive intervention. Without appropriate measures to identify autism spectrum disorder (ASD) and its comorbid conditions, interventions and individualized education program (IEP) goals may not be tailored to the individual's strengths and areas in need of growth. With impairment in social functioning considered a hallmark of ASD, accurate assessment and intervention for the social, emotional, and behavioral needs of adolescents with high-functioning ASD (HFASD) is essential to enhancing the necessary skills required for adulthood. Research suggests IEPs fail to adequately address the postsecondary needs of students with HFASD (Ruble et al., 2019) and parents view the social tasks associated with independent living as one of the greatest needs for those who progress to college (Elias & White, 2018). Research indicates modest improvement in some of core features of ASD over the lifespan, especially for those with HFASD (Shattuck et al., 2007). Maladaptive behaviors such as withdrawal, socially offensive behavior, and repetitive behaviors improve over time with a greater change seen in those with HFASD compared to those with ASD and intellectual disability. With consistent intervention, these adolescents can function more and more like their peers who do not present with developmental disorders. However, not all characteristics of ASD improve at the same rate. Shattuck et al. (2007) suggest impairment in social reciprocity may be more central and persistent than other characteristics of ASD, further supporting the vital need for effective social interventions during the adolescent years.

In this chapter, we focus exclusively on assessment and school-based remediation of social, emotional, and behavioral difficulties in adolescents with high-functioning autism spectrum disorder (HFASD). Although the assessments that can be used with this population far exceed the space limitations of this chapter, we present an overview of common assessment instruments used to evaluate the social, emotional, and behavioral skills of adolescents with HFASD along with their psychometric properties. We then present an overview of school-based intervention strategies that can be implemented to address the social, emotional, and behavioral needs of this population.

Behavioral Presentation

According to the *Diagnostic and Statistical Manual of Mental Disorders, Fifth Edition* (American Psychological Association [APA], 2013), individuals with ASD exhibit persistent impairment in social communication and social interaction as well as restricted interests and repetitive behaviors. However, these symptoms manifest differently depending on the functioning of the individual, supporting the spectrum notion of the diagnosis. When describing ASD, the term "high functioning" generally refers to individuals with ASD who do not present with a co-occurring intellectual disability. Adaptive skills within this population are highly variable and typically are not commensurate with their cognitive abilities (Klin et al., 2007).

Description of Social Difficulties

Adolescents with HFASD experience difficulties with social communication, often to a lesser degree than individuals with more severe ASD (Seltzer et al., 2004), in three distinct areas: social-emotional reciprocity, non-verbal communication, and social relationships, including initiation and response (APA, 2013). Social-emotional reciprocity deficits refer to the ways in which the individual approaches and/or engages in social interactions and conversations. Difficulties with back and forth conversations, social approach and initiations, and sharing of interests and emotions are characteristic of social-emotional reciprocity deficits (APA, 2013). Nonverbal communication difficulties often stem from a misalignment between verbal and nonverbal communication and include deficits related to making and sustaining eye contact; recognizing, understanding, and using body language; and recognizing and understanding facial expressions (APA, 2013). Social relationship deficits pertain to difficulties developing and maintaining appropriate relationships and adjusting behavior(s) based on the social context. Difficulties with taking another person's perspective, understanding and responding to social cues (e.g., failure to notice a lack of interest, distress), and a lack of interest in others are characteristics of social relationship deficits (APA, 2013). Additionally, some adolescents with HFASD desire friendships but may be unsure of how to go about making friends. The social deficits characteristic of individuals with HFASD can impede effective communication and interactions with others. Such difficulties can be particularly problematic in school settings.

Adolescents with ASD, especially those who are high functioning, present with unique social difficulties due to the increased importance of social relationships during this developmental period. Additionally, adolescents with HFASD often become more aware of their unique traits and differences between themselves and their typically developing peers during this period (Tse et al., 2007). Adolescents with HFASD often experience deficits in understanding and communicating their needs. At school, these may manifest as difficulties in understanding classroom directions and instruction from teachers; navigating and participating in conversations; accurately interpreting and using body language and inflection; and self-expression. These social communication challenges can contribute to an adolescent with HFASD exhibiting disruptive behavior both at home and at school and increase the risk of developing an internalizing disorder such as depression. Effective communication in social situations may also be a challenge for individuals with ASD, which may disrupt the development of reciprocal relationships with adults and peers.

Management of social and emotional skills can be challenging for most adolescents, especially adolescents with HFASD (Winner & Crooke, 2011). In addition to negatively impacting the formation and maintenance of peer relationships, social deficits can lead to an increased risk for social isolation (Anderson et al., 2011). Adolescents with ASD have been found to engage in social activities less frequently than peers with other disabilities (e.g., learning disability, intellectual impairment) and rarely see or get calls from friends outside of school (Shattuck et al., 2007).

In addition to deficits in social communication, individuals with ASD present with various patterns of restricted behaviors. These patterns include adherence to routines, repetitive movements or vocalizations, restricted interests, and maladaptive responses to sensory input (APA, 2013). A review of the current research indicates that the restricted and repetitive behaviors of older individuals with HFASD are commonly characterized as insistence on sameness and attachment to specific objects (Jiujias et al., 2017). These may manifest as adherence to daily routines, requiring symmetry with the placement of objects, or making lists of facts about a favorite topic. The social deficits of ASD and restricted, repetitive behaviors may intertwine when adolescents attempt to utilize their restricted interest to engage a peer in conversation. Adolescents may limit their choice of peer to someone they know shares their interest causing them to cut out other peers completely (Scahill et al., 2015). Additionally, adolescents with HFASD may be stigmatized by their typically developing peers due to these interests leading to further social isolation (Scahill et al., 2015).

Assessment of ASD-Specific Symptomology

Best practices for the assessment of individuals with ASD, either for diagnostic clarification or assessment of behavioral comorbidity, support a multi-informant, multimethod strategy (Doepke et al., 2014). These strategies include interviews, administration of individualized assessments, rating scales, direct observations, and functional behavior assessments, which play key roles in developing the overall behavioral profile of the adolescent with HFASD. Specifically, despite the heterogeneity of the population, common patterns often emerge regarding the cognitive and behavioral profiles of adolescents with ASD. For example, impairment in adaptive skills despite intact cognitive ability is commonly seen in ASD (Klin et al., 2007). Cognitive profiles of individuals with ASD reveal markers for poor processing speed, low verbal comprehension (Oliveras-Rentas et al., 2012), and impaired verbal memory (Weschler, 2014). These differences in executive functioning of adolescents with HFASD may account for the heterogeneity of social dysfunction within this group (Scheeren et al., 2012). Social emotional patterns may also emerge with diagnostic evaluation of comorbid disorders. Adolescents with HFASD are more likely to be diagnosed with comorbid psychiatric disorders than their typically developing peers (Vuijk et al., 2018; Mannion & Leader, 2013), which may be a result of the social isolation that often occurs with the core social impairments of the disorder. Accurate assessment of all these constructs is necessary not only for diagnostic purposes but for helping interventionists tailor the interventions to match the individual's skills and abilities.

ASD Specific Assessments Autism-specific diagnostic measures provide clinicians and school psychologists with tools to assess ASD symptomology and behavioral profiles in adolescents diagnosed with or suspected of ASD. The *Autism Diagnostic Observation Schedule, Second Edition* (ADOS-2; Lord et al., 2012) is considered the "gold-standard" in diagnostic assessment of ASD and is frequently utilized as a direct observation tool in an evidence-based assessment (Aiello et al., 2017). To administer a valid ADOS-2, the developers of the ADOS-2 indicate training is required through in-person workshops or publisher-developed training videos (ADOS-2; Lord et al., 2012). Training alone, however, does not mean that a professional is considered a "trained examiner." Additional requirements include experience with ASD, practice and supervision of the ADOS-2 that are not part of a formal evaluation, and sufficient experience with psychometric testing. Training and experience improve the accuracy of ADOS administrations (Wiggins et al., 2015; Zander et al., 2016).

Administered by a trained examiner, the ADOS-2 provides observational data on the individual's severity level of the core features of autism spectrum disorder. An adolescent with HFASD would most likely be administered Module 3 for exhibiting fluent language or Module 4 for older adolescents (above age 16) who would consider the play scenarios childish. Module 3, however, has better psychometric properties due to the updated algorithm and would be the preferred module for adolescents (Lord, 2018). The ADOS-2 administration manual reports good inter-rater ($r = >0.90$) and test-retest ($r > 0.80$) reliability for Module 3 as well as good predictive validity (Lord et al., 2012). Literature supports the strong psychometric properties of the ADOS-2 and its predecessor for individuals displaying significant symptoms of ASD, but it has been criticized for its ability to distinguish milder cases (Zander et al., 2016). Zander et al. (2016) found that the ADOS-2, administered by less experienced clinicians, displayed less diagnostic agreement within a heterogeneous sample compared to a homogeneous sample (i.e., those who were lower functioning and displaying classic symptoms of ASD). Given the heterogeneity among adolescents with HFASD, a more experienced clinician should administer the ADOS-2 to ensure better diagnostic accuracy.

The *Autism Diagnostic Interview—Revised* (ADI-R; Rutter, Le Couteur, & Lord, 2003) is a structured interview utilized within a comprehensive assessment to provide categorical information on the individual suspected of having ASD. Developed by the same research team as the ADOS-2, the ADI-R explores characteristics of the core features of ASD as described in the *Diagnostic and Statistical Manual of Mental Disorder, Fourth Edition, Text Revision* (DSM-IV-TR; APA, 2000) through interview by a trained examiner. According to the test developers, this interview can take up to two and a half hours to complete, and at the time of this writing, no revised algorithms were available to align with the DSM-5. Given the length of the measure and the requirement of a trained examiner, the ADI-R has been criticized as impractical within a clinical setting and remains mostly utilized in research (Murray et al., 2011). As an alternative, the *Social Communication Questionnaire* (Rutter, Bailey & Lord, 2003) is available as a 40-item, parent rating scale containing the same content, with identically worded items, as the ADI-R. The test authors indicate the SCQ is a reliable, brief screening measure that can help clinicians or educators determine children in need of diagnostic evaluations for ASD. The SCQ includes scales measuring reciprocal social interaction, communication, and restricted, repetitive, and stereotype patterns of behavior. The *Lifetime Form* looks at the individual's symptoms over the entire life span whereas the *Current Form* instructs caregivers to refer to the last three months of the individual's life.

The *Social Responsiveness Scale, Second Edition* (SRS-2; Constantino, 2012) is another rating scale used in clinical practice, educational settings, and research to screen for and provide evidence of ASD. According to the test publishers (Constantino, 2012), the SRS-2 measures the level of social impairment in an individual suspected of ASD and can help differentiate the social impairment seen in ASD from that seen in other disorders. This scale identifies social impairments in the areas of social awareness and social information processing and can help identify severity of social anxiety and avoidance often seen in ASD. The measure is appropriate to use with individuals through the age of 18.

Several studies have investigated the reliability of the SRS in identifying ASD in children and adolescents. Murray et al. (2011) found the SRS had 90% diagnostic agreement with the ADI-R for a sample of adolescents suspected of having ASD, making it a useful, shorter tool for use in a diagnostic or school assessment. Although social skill–specific measures may be useful in the diagnostic process, research supports the recommendation of multidimensional assessment in diagnosing ASD. Specifically, Aldridge et al. (2012) found that utilizing the SRS in clinical settings (i.e., individuals referred because of ASD-like traits) yielded more false positives than the original validation studies completed with a community sample. This finding was especially true for parent report, and the authors argue that parents may deem their child's behavior as "Autistic-like" when referred to a specialty clinic for diagnosis due to the power of suggestion. Practitioners and educators are discouraged to make diagnostic or educational decisions on one measure alone (APA, AERA, NCME, 2014).

Adaptive Behavior Scales Adaptive skill measures are utilized in an evidence-based assessment of an individual suspected of having ASD and are often useful in helping determine differential diagnosis. Research has demonstrated individuals with ASD display a pattern of adaptive functioning on the *Vineland Adaptive Behavior Scales* (Sparrow et al., 1984) marked by deficits in socialization and communication (Kenworthy et al., 2010; Klin et al., 2007). Specifically, Klin et al. (2007) found a one to two standard deviation deficit in communication skills, and a two to three standard deviation deficit in a high-functioning sample of individuals with ASD aged 7 through 18. Furthermore, age was negatively correlated with skill level suggesting that individuals with ASD display more marked differences in socialization skills compared to similarly aged typically developing peers as they move into adolescence (Klin et al., 2007). Similarly, research utilizing the *Adaptive Behavior Assessment System, Second Edition* (Harrison & Oakland, 2000) found marked deficits in all areas of adaptive functioning across individuals with HFASD, with the lowest adaptive behavior scores in the social domain regardless of age (Kenworthy et al., 2010). With the majority of participants in this sample over the age of 12, these findings suggest that adaptive functioning, including social skills, plateau sometime in the pre-adolescent to early adolescent years. Given the marked differentiation in adaptive skills between typically developing adolescents and those with HFASD, adaptive scales can be a useful tool in identifying ASD in an adolescent population.

Additionally, including adaptive skill measures in the assessment of adolescents with HFASD can alert practitioners to individuals who may be at risk for comorbid psychiatric disorders such as anxiety and depression. Kraper et al. (2017) investigated a sample of adults with ASD and found that lower adaptive functioning was a risk factor for significant levels of anxiety, depression, and attention deficit hyperactivity disorder (ADHD). Furthermore, the greater the gap between IQ and adaptive functioning, the greater the level of anxiety, depression, and social impairment, suggesting adults with HFASD are at greater risk than their lower functioning counterparts to suffer from significant psychiatric impairment.

Behavior Rating Scales General measures of behavior problems are often used in the process of determining comorbid psychopathy in individuals with ASD (Deprey & Ozonoff, 2018), but may also be useful in identifying autism. Research suggests individuals with ASD may display specific behavioral patterns on these scales making them useful as a part of a comprehensive diagnostic assessment (Hass et al., 2012). Specifically, Hass and colleagues (2012) found the developmental social disorder, withdrawal, and functional communication scales from the *Behavior Assessment System for Children, Second Edition, Teacher Rating Scales* (Reynolds & Kamphaus, 2004) to be useful in distinguishing students with an educational label of ASD from their typically developing peers. For the adolescents in the study's sample, the withdrawal scale contributed to most discriminative power in differentiating autism from typically developing groups. However, the differences between both groups on the developmental social disorder and functional communication scales became less pronounced into adolescence suggesting some areas improve with age and intervention, but the core social deficits remain. With an updated edition available, assessment professionals will likely utilize the various parent, teacher, and self-report forms of the *Behavior Assessment System for Children, Third Edition* (BASC-3; Reynolds & Kamphaus, 2015) during an evaluation of ASD. Although research is needed on this most recent version, research results utilizing the BASC-2 will likely generalize to this newer version given the similarity of the behavioral scales included.

The *Achenbach System of Empirically Based Assessment* (Achenbach, 1991) is another common comprehensive behavioral system utilized in the assessment of individuals with ASD. Specifically, the *Youth Self-Report* (YSR) and *Child Behavior*

Checklist (CBCL; parent report) have been used to differentiate adolescents with ASD from their typically developing peers. Pisula et al. (2017) found youth with ASD self-reported more symptoms of withdrawal, anxiety/depression, social problems, and internalizing problems compared to a non-ASD control group. Parent report, on the other hand, indicated significant elevations on all behavioral scales of the CBCL compared to the non-ASD group. This research provides interesting insight into how adolescents with ASD view their problems compared to their typically developing peers. Findings indicated that adolescents with ASD viewed their problems as less severe than their parents whereas the opposite was true for the matched typical peers. These findings support the need for a multi-informant method as part of a comprehensive evaluation of individuals with ASD. Additionally, despite the lack of insight into their own symptoms displayed by adolescents with ASD, research consistently shows that individuals with HFASD and their parents endorse more clinically significant behavior problems compared to typically developing adolescent peers (Paul et al., 2015), making general behavior assessment a vital component of an ASD evaluation. As discussed later in this chapter, clinicians must be cognizant of how individuals with HFASD respond to these measures as to not over-diagnose psychopathology in this population.

Social Skills Assessment Although some measures of social skill functioning have been described already in this chapter, the central social deficit of ASD warrants a more in-depth discussion. Measurement of various social skills, such as reciprocity, in individuals diagnosed with or suspected of ASD typically occurs within a broader assessment of symptoms of ASD. For example, the ADOS-2 contains scoring codes and guidelines for reciprocal social interaction. To obtain the necessary data to score social reciprocity (as well as all other aspects of the scoring algorithm), the entire ADOS-2 must be administered, making it a lengthier assessment if the desire is to only assess one aspect of an individual's functioning. The availability of valid and reliable observational tools geared towards the assessment of social skills is scarce.

Given the comprehensive nature of psychometrically sound observational tools for social skills assessment, parent report of an adolescent's social functioning may present as a more time-effective measurement of social skills and reciprocity, and several measures of social functioning are available and validated with individuals with autism spectrum disorder. These scales, however, are often used as autism-specific measurement tools within comprehensive diagnostic evaluation. Limited research exists on the use of the measures discussed earlier in this chapter (e.g., ADOS-2 and SCQ) as tools to monitor the progress of skill acquisition during interventions. According to Freeman and Cronin (2017), the *Social Skills Improvement System Rating Scales* (SSIS; Gresham & Eliott, 2008) and the *Social Responsiveness Scale, Second Edition* (SRS-2; Constantino, 2012) are the only social skills–specific rating scales standardized for identifying social skills deficits in the ASD population that can lead to treatment planning. Researchers commonly utilize one or both of these measures when conducting social skills interventions with adolescents with HFASD (Matthews et al., 2018; Jamison & Schuttler, 2015; Van Hecke et al., 2015).

According to the test publishers (Constantino, 2012), the SRS-2 measures the level of social impairment in an individual suspected of ASD and can help differentiate the social impairment seen in ASD from that seen in other disorders. This scale identifies social impairments in the areas of social awareness and social information processing, and can help identify the level of social anxiety and avoidance often seen in ASD. It is appropriate to use with individuals through the age of 18 and is commonly used in research on social skills interventions. Research conducted by Van Hecke et al. (2015) indicated the SRS is a useful tool in measuring the effectiveness of the *Program for the Education and Enrichment of Relational Skills* (*PEERS®*). Specifically, adolescents in their sample displayed significantly fewer symptoms of ASD, as measured on the SRS, after 14 weeks of intervention.

The *Social Skills Improvement System Rating Scales* (SSIS; Gresham & Eliott, 2008) has also been utilized in research as a tool to measure the response of adolescents with HFASD to social skills programming (Jamison & Schuttler, 2015; Macintosh & Dissanayake, 2006). The SSIS allows for targeted assessment of social skills across various populations and contains scales related to social skills, related problem behaviors, and academic competence. Furthermore, its use has not been limited to a diagnostic screening measure, making it a valuable tool when assessing the effectiveness of interventions and change in social skills over the lifespan. Matthews et al. (2018) utilized the SSIS as a social skills–specific measurement tool to evaluate the effectiveness of the *PEERS®* intervention with a group of adolescents with HFASD. They found significant improvement in social skills, as measured by the SSIS, in the intervention groups compared to a waitlist control. Additionally, Jamison and Schuttler (2015) indicated that the SSIS was an effective tool in evaluating the social characteristics of adolescent females with ASD, a population often understudied. According to their research, adolescent females rated their social competence, self-worth, and quality of life significantly lower than their non-ASD female peers, suggesting poorer social-emotional heath. SSIS may be a reliable tool in identifying adolescent females at-risk for comorbid disorders.

Mood and Other Emotional Difficulties

The complexity of adolescence (i.e., puberty, changes in peer dynamics, etc.), coupled with the social challenges of ASD, makes adolescents with HFASD at greater risk than their typical peers for a host of comorbid psychiatric conditions including social anxiety disorder, generalized anxiety disorder (GAD), depression, and personality dysfunction (Vuijk et al., 2018; Rosenberg et al., 2011). Prevalence rates, however, vary based on the research study, population included, and how data was gathered, making an estimate of overall comorbidity difficult (Mannion & Leader, 2013). In a large-scale study of parent-reported comorbid diagnoses, 49.1% of individuals with ASD aged 5 to 18 had one or more comorbid psychiatric conditions (Rosenberg et al., 2011). Compared with toddlers and children, adolescents experienced the highest percentage of comorbid conditions across all diagnostic categories (e.g., any anxiety disorder, depression, ADHD, and bipolar disorder). Aside from ADHD, anxiety disorders (lumped as one group including panic disorder, posttraumatic stress disorder, GAD, social anxiety disorder, etc.) were the most common comorbid diagnosis (44.7% of adolescents with ASD included in the study). Overall, literature suggests anxiety and depression are common among adolescents with HFASD, with lifetime prevalence rates of comorbid mood disorders described as "high" (Mannion & Leader, 2013).

Within recent years, there has been an increasing amount of literature focusing on comorbid conditions in adolescents with ASD, and several patterns have emerged regarding the assessment of psychopathology. As the following section summarizes, clinicians have the difficult task of deciding when scale elevations or reported symptomology warrant an additional diagnosis or if the elevations are due to the core features of ASD.

Assessment of Internalizing Disorders

Prior to 2013 and the publication of the DSM-5, individuals could not be dually diagnosed with ASD and several psychiatric disorders including obsessive-compulsive disorder (OCD), ADHD, and GAD. This exclusion was in part due to the overlapping symptomology between ASD and these disorders. As reported previously in this chapter, research on general rating scales of behavior can be helpful within the comprehensive evaluation process in determining an ASD diagnosis due to the predictable patterns these individuals exhibit on these scales. The clinician must then interpret the measure to ensure the scale elevations warrant a dual diagnosis or are simply a result of how individuals with ASD present on a measure that was not normed with an ASD population.

Research suggests anxiety disorders are the most common internalizing disorders diagnosed in individuals with ASD (Rosenberg et al., 2011; van Steensel et al., 2011). Assessment of comorbid anxiety disorders is complicated in this population given the overlap of ASD-specific symptoms and anxiety. For example, avoidance of social situations, adherence to routines, and insistence on sameness may all lead to symptoms of anxiety but are also considered potential presentations of the core diagnostic features. Lefyer and colleagues (2006) found that adolescents with comorbid OCD often displayed compulsions involving having others do things in a certain way or communicating to others in a circumscribed manner. These compulsions exemplify the core social deficits of autism, yet according to the *Autism Comorbidity Interview-Present and Lifetime*, the scale utilized in the study, these individuals also met criteria for OCD. Accurate assessment tools that help differentiate clinical anxiety from ASD-specific symptomology in adolescents are essential to further our understanding of this comorbidity. For instance, recent research suggests individuals with ASD and comorbid OCD score higher on OCD-specific scales compared to individuals with ASD and no comorbid disorder and individuals with OCD without ASD (Happe & Murphy, 2015). More research on the differentiation in performance on assessments between adolescents with HFASD and comorbid disorders and those without is necessary.

Another common theme discussed within the comorbidity literature is the impact of a general lack of insight adolescents and adults with HFASD have into their own mental health. This can be problematic since assessment of internalizing disorders commonly occurs through structured interviews. Individual interviews with the adolescent with HFASD can be challenging due to the common communication deficits found in these individuals. Specifically, these adolescents may experience difficulty describing their internal mental states because of deficits in theory of mind (understanding the intentions, desires, and beliefs of others), central coherence (the ability to "see the big picture"), and other problems with executive functioning (Leyfer et al., 2006). Interviews can either be informal questions developed by the clinician or formal assessment tools with established validity and reliability linked to the diagnostic criteria of various disorders found within the DSM-5 (or earlier versions depending on the tool). Research is trending towards the adaptation of published structured interviews for use with individuals with ASD. However, research needs to be completed to establish validity and reliability for this population.

When personality assessment occurs with measures not standardized on individuals with HFASD, clinicians must be cautious when diagnosing significant psychiatric disorders. A meta-analysis completed by Vuijk et al. (2018) found that individuals with ASD aged 15 through 89 displayed more schizotypal and avoidant personality traits compared to a psychiatric population. One must be careful not to overinterpret these results to mean more significant psychopathology is present in adolescents and adults with HFASD. Lack of sound psychometric properties within assessment tools for given populations causes problems when generalizing the interpretation of these tools; however, clinicians and researchers still utilize these measures. To avoid over-diagnosis of significant psychiatric comorbidity, the assessment of social emotional functioning of adolescents with HFASD should be completed by trained clinicians who understand the psychometric properties of personality assessments.

School-Based Intervention

Generally speaking, school-based interventions are systematically administered procedures implemented within the school setting to target student-specific needs. Interventions can be implemented in a variety of delivery formats such as school-wide, whole-class, small group, peer-mediated, and individual administration. A strategy may be considered an intervention provided that it (a) has a set of prescribed implementation procedures, (b) is implemented to target student-specific needs, and (c) has been empirically validated. Although the terms *strategy* and *intervention* are often used interchangeably, there are notable distinctions between the two. Strategies involve instructional and behavioral practices that have been found effective, but implementation may not follow prescribed procedures or systematic implementation (e.g., cooperative learning, differentiated instruction). Strategies are often associated with "good instruction." Interventions are *targeted* instructional procedures implemented based on the needs of an individual or group. As such, interventions require prescriptive implementation procedures and have empirical support for effectiveness. Whereas school-based strategies are often implemented by teachers and educational assistants, interventions are often implemented by BCBAs; school behavior specialists, coaches, and/or consultants; general and special education teachers and educational assistants (e.g., classroom aide); or other school-based services providers (e.g., school psychologists, counselors, occupational therapists).

Accurate identification of social, emotional, and/or behavioral skills deficits is a critical step for intervention planning. As previously noted, one goal of assessment should be to produce an individually tailored training program for the adolescent with HFASD. Often in school-based settings, this results in developing and incorporating a behavior intervention plan (BIP) that may include implementing strategies and individual or group-based interventions. Current literature on school-based interventions for youth with ASD, and particularly adolescents with HFSAD, is limited (Laugeson et al., 2014). Most studies have focused almost exclusively on preschool populations and young children (Anderson et al., 2018). As a result, there is a paucity of research evaluating the effects of school-based interventions for adolescents with HFASD. In the following sections, we provide an overview of a number of empirically supported interventions for adolescents with ASD and those with HFASD. Space limitations preclude us from a comprehensive discussion of interventions; therefore, we do our best to highlight a number of research-based approaches and interventions that may be used with adolescents with HFASD.

Applied Behavior Analysis

Applied behavior analysis (ABA) therapy and ABA-based interventions draw heavily on the theory of operant conditioning (Skinner, 1938) which entails the process of systematic observation of antecedents, behaviors, and consequences. Also referred to as the ABCs of ABA, correctly identifying the antecedent (the prompt, situation, or trigger that leads to a behavior), behavior (the action or behavior demonstrated in response to the antecedent), and consequence (the response, or reinforcement mechanism, associated with the behavior which increases the likelihood that the individual will continue to engage in the "behavior" as a response the identified antecedent) drives ABA intervention. Ultimately, one of the primary functions of ABA is to systematically alter behavior through the manipulation of consequences over time. There are a number of interventions that may be applied to achieve this goal including, but not limited to, antecedent-based intervention, differential reinforcement, social skills training, and video modeling.

Antecedent-Based Intervention Antecedent interventions are designed to address the conditions, circumstances, and/or events that may trigger behavior. In a school or classroom setting, antecedent interventions may address classroom management, environmental factors (e.g., preferential seating, lighting, décor), planning and implementing instruction (e.g., activities, formative and summative assessment methods, grouping), and communication and collaboration between peers and teachers. Antecedent interventions may also include choice, prompting, priming (previewing), noncontingent reinforcement (delivering reinforcement via a fixed-schedule), and time delay (incorporating prompt fading with reinforcement), to name a few.

Differential Reinforcement Used to increase desired behavior while reducing undesired behavior, differential reinforcement occurs when reinforcement is provided for the desired behavior and the inappropriate behavior is ignored. This approach can be used to target (a) low rates of behavior, (b) incompatible behavior, and (c) alternative behavior. Differential reinforcement of low rates of behavior targets reducing overutilized, yet acceptable, behaviors by limiting the amount of reinforcement that is given. This overutilization makes the behavior inappropriate (e.g., limiting the number of questions asked during instruction to reduce interruptions to the class). During differential reinforcement of incompatible behavior, a reinforcer is provided when the student engages in an identified behavior that is incompatible with, or cannot occur at the same time as, the target behavior. For example, a student may earn access to an iPad after remaining on task for a certain period of time instead of daydreaming. Differential reinforcement of alternative behavior occurs when reinforcement is given when the student refrains from engaging in the target behavior. In this scenario, a student might earn time towards an iPad break for each interval during which they refrained from talking with a peer during instruction (Wong et al., 2014).

Social Skills Training As the name implies, social skills training is designed to improve social skills. Social skills training interventions can be implemented in school-based settings by general or special education teachers, school psychologists, and behavioral specialists. Social skills interventions may be implemented one-on-one, in pairs, or in group-based settings. Generally, the student participates in intervention one to two times per week. The core features of social skills interventions include instruction, generally in the form of modeling; role-playing; corrective feedback; positive reinforcement; skillstreaming; and weekly homework assignments designed to provide opportunities for the student to generalize newly acquired skills. Two common social skills training interventions are Social Stories® (Gray & Garand, 1993) and social scripts (Weiss & Harris, 2001). Peer-mediated and cognitive behavioral interventions may also be considered social skills interventions depending on the target skills and desired replacement behaviors.

Video Modeling Video modeling is a form of video-based intervention which, as the name suggests, uses video recordings as a model to teach the desired replacement behavior or skill. There are different types of video modeling such as basic video modeling, video self-modeling, point-of-view modeling, and video prompting (McCoy & Hermansen, 2007). Regardless of which type of video modeling is selected, the implementation steps remain the same and include: selecting the target behavior; having the necessary equipment; planning for the recording; collecting baseline data; making the video; arranging the environment for the student(s) to watch the video; showing the video; monitoring progress; troubleshooting if the student is not making progress; and fading the video and prompts (National Professional Development Center on Autism Spectrum Disorders, 2010). Video modeling has shown positive outcomes in the areas of communication, joint attention, vocational skills, academics, and social functioning (Wong et al., 2014).

Cognitive-Behavioral Interventions

Cognitive-behavioral interventions are interventions used to change behavior by teaching individuals to understand and monitor their thoughts and behaviors (Riccomini et al., 2005). Cognitive-behavioral interventions can be implemented by school psychologists, school social workers, or behavior specialists (e.g., registered behavior technicians, BCBAs) and can be delivered in individual or group-based formats. Instructional techniques include mentoring, modeling (teacher or peer), role-playing, and reversal (Riccomini et al., 2005). Cognitive-behavioral interventions target a range of skills including problem solving, tolerance, anger management, and self-instruction and interventions can be developed by the interventionist. These interventions have also been shown to be an effective treatment for alleviating symptoms of comorbid anxiety disorders in adolescents with HFASD (Storch et al., 2015).

Peer-Mediated Instruction and Intervention (PMII)

Peer-mediated instruction and interventions are evidence-based approaches that involve one-to-one matching of an older or same-aged peer without disabilities with the student with HFASD (Wong et al., 2014). Peer mentors/tutors are typically trained by teachers to serve in the mentorship or tutoring role based on the needs of their partner with HFASD. Once trained, the pair require minimal supervision. PMII can be used to improve social skills and communication of the individual with HFASD and can assist in helping them acquire new behaviors that may improve their functioning in the school environment. Peer mentoring/tutoring addresses a limitation of individualized interventions in that it provides the student with HFASD with the opportunity to engage with peers and practice newly learned skills and strategies in natural and authentic settings.

Research-Based Curricula and Programs

Several intervention strategies described earlier in this chapter have been incorporated into structured programs that can be utilized in the school setting. While not an exhaustive list, we provide an overview of some curricula and programs specifically geared towards middle and/or high school students with ASD, including those with HFASD. We encourage readers to carefully review any curricula or program prior to adoption and implementation to determine the appropriateness for use with the students they are serving. We focus on a description of each program rather than the extensive research support, and further encourage readers to evaluate the evidence base prior to selecting a program.

The *Adolescent Curriculum for Communication and Effective Social Skills (ACCESS) Program* (Walker et al., 1988) is designed to teach social skills to middle and high school students. The *ACCESS* program can be implemented by general or special education teachers in one-to-one, small-group, or large-group instruction formats. *ACCESS* is designed to teach 30 different social skills which are grouped into one of three categories: Relating to Peers, Relating to Adults, and Relating to Yourself. The program includes scripts for teaching each skill via an eight-step instructional procedure and a student study guide with role-play scripts, discrimination exercises, and student report forms for contracted practice.

Prepare Curriculum: Teaching Prosocial Competencies (PREPARE; Goldstein, 1999) designed to meet the needs of middle and high school students, *PREPARE* is comprised of 10 interventions that target three primary areas: aggression reduction, stress reduction, and prejudice reduction. Part 1 of the curriculum incorporates skillstreaming, situational perception training, anger management, and moral reasoning interventions to reduce aggression. Part 2 utilizes stress management, problem-solving, and recruitment interventions to target stress reduction. Part 3 addresses prejudice reduction through empathy training, cooperation training, and group-based understanding interventions. The curriculum includes 93 supplementary exercises that incorporate a variety of hands on strategies and activities (e.g., games, role-playing, drawing, relaxation, tape recordings, photography).

The *Program for the Education and Enrichment of Relational Skills Curriculum for School-based Professionals* (*PEERS®;* Laugeson, 2014) is a 16-week social skills training program for adolescents with ASD. Utilizing a structured learning approach in a group-based setting of up to 15 students, the curriculum is comprised of 16 weekly lessons, each containing five 30–60 min. Daily lessons. Lessons incorporate methods of cognitive behavior therapy instruction such as didactic learning, role-play demonstrations, perspective taking, and performance feedback, to name a few. Weekly foci include two-way conversations, appropriate use of humor, good sportsmanship, changing reputations, and handling cyber bullying. In addition to comprehensive lesson plans, the curriculum also includes homework assignments linked to the weekly lessons, socialization activities to promote practice of skills, and resources for parents and interventionists (e.g., handouts, lesson planning tips). School-based *PEERS®* has been found to improve social functioning in the areas of teacher-reported social awareness, cognition, communication, motivation, and responsiveness (Laugeson et al., 2014; Wyman & Claro, 2019). In addition, decreased social anxiety and mannerisms characteristic of individuals with autism have been noted following participation in the school-based *PEERS®* program (Laugeson et al., 2014; Schohl et al., 2014). Adolescent self-reports have indicated improvements in social skills knowledge (Laugeson et al., 2014) and social interactions such as get-togethers, both hosted and invited, with friends.

Skillstreaming the Adolescent, third Edition (McGinnis et al., 2011) utilizes modeling, role-playing, performance feedback, and generalization to teach prosocial skills. This intervention program, designed for middle and high school students, targets five skills groups (classroom survival skills, friendship-making skills, skills for dealing with feelings, skill alternatives to aggression, and skills for dealing with stress). The program includes 50 lessons, skills summaries, homework for skills practice outside of the intervention group, and intervention integrity checklists. A similar program, *Skillstreaming Children and Youth with High-Functioning Autism* (McGinnis & Simpson, 2016), incorporates the same four-part approach to teach prosocial skills to youth with HFASD. This program consists of 80 lessons organized into six skills groups (relationship skills, social comprehension skills, self-regulation skills, problem-solving skills, understanding emotions skills, and school-related skills).

The *Social Skills Intervention Guide* (Gresham & Eliott, 2008) consists of 20 instructional units addressing 7 social skills domains (communication, cooperation, assertion, responsibility, empathy, engagement, and self-control). In addition to providing optional strategies and resources to support instruction, the *Social Skills Intervention Guide* includes program evaluation forms, student progress monitoring tools, and form letters and notes to parents. The program was developed for students in Kindergarten through 12th grade.

Conclusion

Accurate identification of ASD in adolescents is the first step to ensuring their functional needs are met. Social, vocational, and transitional interventions can be tailored to the individual needs of the adolescent when accurate assessment of their skills occurs. Accuracy in assessment depends on selecting measures that have sound psychometric properties for use with adolescents with HFASD.

As summarized in this chapter, over-diagnosis of significant psychopathology could occur when assessment professionals over-interpret the findings of tests not normed with the ASD population. On the other hand, adolescents with comorbid diagnoses that warrant specific interventions could be missed if the results of assessment tools are attributed to the person's ASD rather than their underlying emotional needs. This balance between over-diagnosis and missed treatment opportunities can become difficult even for the most experienced clinicians. With a variety of evidence-based intervention packages available (Wong et al., 2014), school psychologists and other clinicians should focus on the social, emotional, and behavioral needs that emerge from assessments regardless of whether or not criteria for additional diagnoses are met.

Once these social, emotional, and behavioral characteristics are identified, we encourage school personnel to consult the literature on evidenced-based interventions, such as the report from the National Professional Development Center on Autism Spectrum Disorder, *Evidence-Based Practices for Children, Youth and Young Adults with Autism Spectrum Disorder* (Wong et al., 2014). The interventions described in this chapter are not an exhaustive list of the available interventions for use in the schools but represent a strong selection of evidence-based practices that have shown positive outcomes for the social, emotional, and behavioral needs of adolescents with HFASD.

References

Achenbach, T. M. (1991). *Manual for the child behavior checklist/4–18 and 1991 profile.* Department of Psychiatry, University of Vermont.

Aiello, R., Ruble, L., & Esler, A. (2017). National study of school psychologists' use of evidence-based assessment in autism spectrum disorder. *Journal of Applied School Psychology, 33*(1), 67–88. https://doi.org/10.1080/15377903.2016.1236307

Aldridge, F. J., Gibbs, V. M., Schmidhofer, K., & Williams, M. (2012). Investigating the clinical usefulness of the Social Responsiveness Scale (SRS) in a tertiary level, autism spectrum disorder specific assessment clinic. *Journal of Autism and Developmental Disorders, 42*, 294–300. https://doi.org/10.1007/s10803-011-1242-9

American Educational Research Association, American Psychological Association, National Council on Measurement in Education, Joint Committee on Standards for Educational and Psychological Testing (U.S.). (2014). *Standards for educational and psychological testing.* AERA.

American Psychiatric Association. (2000). *Diagnostic and statistical manual of mental disorders, fourth edition, text revision.* Author.

American Psychiatric Association. (2013). *Diagnostic and statistical manual of mental disorders, fifth edition.* Author.

Anderson, D. K., Maye, M. P., & Lord, C. (2011). Changes in maladaptive behaviors from mid-childhood to young adulthood in autism spectrum disorder. *American Journal on Intellectual and Developmental Disabilities, 116*(5), 381–397.

Anderson, C. M., Smith, T., & Wilczynski, S. M. (2018). School-based interventions for students with autism spectrum disorder: Introduction to the special issue. *Behavior Modification, 42*(1), 3–8. https://doi.org/10.1177/0145445517743582

Constantino, J. N. (2012). *Social responsiveness scale, second edition.* Western Psychological Services.

Deprey, L., & Ozonoff, S. (2018). Assessment of comorbid psychiatric condidtions in autism spectrum disorders. In S. Goldstein & S. Ozonoff (Eds.), *Assessment of autism spectrum disorders, second edition.* The Guilford Press.

Doepke, K. J., Banks, B. M., Mays, J. F., Toby, L. M., & Landau, S. (2014). Co-occurring emotional and behavioral problems. In L. A. Wilkinson (Ed.), *Autism Spectrum disorder in children and adolescents: Evidence-based assessment and intervention in schools.* American Psychological Association.

Elias, R., & White, S. W. (2018). Autism goes to college: Understanding the needs of a student population on the rise. *Journal of Autism and Developmental Disorders, 48*, 732–746. https://doi.org/10.1007/s10803-017-3075-7

Freeman, B. J., & Cronin, P. (2017). Standardized assessment of social skills in autism spectrum disorder. In J. B. Leaf (Ed.), *Handbook of social skills and autism Apectrum disorder,: Assessment, curricula, and intervention*. Springer.

Gray, C. A., & Garand, J. D. (1993). Social stories: Improving responses of students with autism with accurate social information. *Focus on Autism and Other Developmental Disabilities, 8*(1), 1–10.

Gresham, F. M., & Elliott, S. N. (2008). *Social skills intervention guide*. Pearson.

Goldstein, A. P. (1999). *The prepare curriculum: Teaching prosocial competencies*. Research Press.

Happe, F., & Murphy, D. (2015). Obsessive-compulsive disorder in adults with high-functioning autism spectrum disorder: What does self-report with the OCI-R tell us? *Autism Research, 8*(5), 477–485. https://doi.org/10.1002/aur.1461

Harrison, P., & Oakland, T. (2000). *Adaptive behavior assessment system, second edition, [Manual]*. Western Psychological Services.

Hass, M. R., Brown, R. S., Brady, J., Johnson, D. B., (2012). Validating the BASC-TRS for use with children and adolescents with an educational diagnosis of autism. *Remedial and Special Education, 33*(3):173–183. https://doi.org/10.1177/0741932510383160

Jamison, T. R., & Schuttler, J. O. (2015). Examining social competence, self-perception, quality of life, and internalizing and externalizing symptoms in adolescent females with and without autism spectrum disorder: A quantitative design including between-groups and correlational analysis. *Molecular Autism, 6*(53), 1–16. https://doi.org/10.1186/s13229-015-0044-x

Jiujias, M., Kelley, E., & Hall, L. (2017). Restricted, repetitive behaviors in autism spectrum disorder and obsessive-compulsive disorder: A comparative review. *Child Psychiatry and Human Development, 48*, 944–959. https://doi.org/10.1007/s10578-017-0717-0

Kenworthy, L., Case, L., Harms, M. B., Martin, A., & Wallace, G. L. (2010). Adaptive behavior ratings correlate with symptmatology and IQ among individuals with high-functioning autism spectrum disorders. *Journal of Autism and Develpmental Disorders, 40*(4), 416–423. https://doi.org/10.1007/s10803-009-0911-4

Klin, A., Saulmier, C. A., Sparrow, S. S., Cicchetti, D. V., Volkmar, F. R., & Lord, C. (2007). Social and communication abilities and disabilities in higher functioning individuals with autism spectrum disorder: The Vineland and the ADOS. *Journal of Autism and Developmental Disabilities, 37*, 748–759. https://doi.org/10.1007/s10803-006-0229-4

Kraper, C. K., Kenworthy, L., Popal, H., Martin, A., & Wallace, G. L. (2017). The gap between adaptive behavior and intelligence persists into young adulthood and is linked to psychiatric comorbidities. *Journal of Autism and Developmental Disorders, 47*, 3007–3017. https://doi.org/10.1007/s10803-017-3213-2

Laugeson, E. A., Ellingsen, R., Sanderson, J., Tucci, L., & Bates, S. (2014). The ABC's of teaching social skills to adolescents with autism spectrum disorder in the classroom: The UCLA PEERS program. *Journal of Autism and Developmental Disorders, 44*, 2244–2256. https://doi.org/10.1007/s10803-014-2108-8

Laugeson, E. A. (2014). *The PEERS curriculum for school-based professionals: Social skills training for adolescents with autism spectrum disorder*. Routledge.

Leyfer, O.T., Folstein, S.E., Bacalman, S., Davis, N.O., Dinh, E., Morgan, J., . . . Lainhart, J.E. (2006). Comorbid psychiatric disorders in children with autism: Interview development and rates of disorders. Journal of Autism & Developmental Disorders, 36(7), 849–861. doi:https://doi.org/10.1007/s10803-006-0123-0.

Lord, C. (2018, March). *Autism spectrum disorder: Update on diagnosis and treatment*. Presentation at the 41st annual Authur B. Richter Conference in Child Psychiatry, Carmel Indiana.

Lord, C., Rutter, M., DiLavore, P. C., Risi, S., Gotham, K., & Bishop, S. L. (2012). *Autism diagnostic observation schedule, second edition (ADOS-2) manual (part 1): Modules 1–4*. Western Psychological Services.

Macintosh, K., & Dissanayake, K. (2006). Social skills and problem behaviours in school aged children with high-functioning autism and Asperger's disorder. *Journal of Autism and Developmental Disabilities, 36*, 1065–1076. https://doi.org/10.1007/s10803-006-0139-5

Mannion, A., & Leader, G. (2013). Comorbidity in autism spectrum disorder: A literature review. *Research in Autism Spectrum Disorders, 7*, 1595–1616. https://doi.org/10.1016/j.rasd.2013.09.006

Matthews, N. L., Orr, B. C., Warriner, K., DeCarlo, M., Sorensen, M., Laflin, J., & Smith, C. J. (2018). Exploring the effectiveness of a peer-mediated model of the PEERS curriculum: A pilot randomized control trial. *Journal of Autism and Developmental Disorders, 48*, 2458–2475. https://doi.org/10.1007/s10803-018-3504-2

McCoy, K., & Hermansen, E. (2007). Video modeling for individuals with autism: A review of model types and effects. *Education and Treatment of Children, 30*, 183–213.

McGinnis, E., & Simpson, R. L. (2016). *Skillstreaming children and youth with high-functioning autism: A guide for teaching prosocial skills*. Research Press.

McGinnis, E., Sprafkin, R. P., Gershaw, N. J., & Klein, P. (2011). *Skillstreaming the adolescent: A guide for teaching prosocial skills* (3rd ed.). Research Press.

Murray, M. J., Mayes, S. D., & Smith, L. A. (2011). Brief report: Excellent agreement between two brief autism scales (checklist for autism Spectrum disorder and social responsiveness scale) completed independently by parents and the autism diagnostic interview—Revised. *Journal of Autism and Developmental Disorders, 41*, 1586–1590. https://doi.org/10.1007/s10803-011-1178-0

National Professional Development Center on Autism Spectrum Disorders. (2010). *Steps for implementation: Video modeling*. Retrieved from http://autismpdc.fgp.unc.edu/sites/autismpdc.fgp.unc.edu/files/VideoModeling_Steps_0.pdf

Oliveras-Rentas, R. E., Kenworthy, L., Roberson, R. B., Martin, A., & Wallace, G. L. (2012). WISC-IV profiles in high functioning autism spectrum disorders: Impaired processing speed is associated with increased autism communication symptoms and decreased adaptive communication abilities. *Journal of Autism and Developmental Disorders, 42*, 655–664. https://doi.org/10.1007/s10803-011-1289-7

Paul, A. R., McKechanie, A. G., Johnstone, E. C., Ownes, D. G. C., & Stanfield, A. C. (2015). Brief report: The association of autistic traits and behavioural patterns in adolescents receiving special educational assistance. *Journal of Autism and Developmental Disorders, 45*, 3055–3060. https://doi.org/10.1007/s10803-015-2445-2

Pisula, E., Pudlo, M., Slowinska, M., Kawa, R., Strazaska, M., Banasiak, A., & Wolanczyk, T. (2017). Behavioral and emotional problems in high-functioning girls and boys with autism spectrum disorder: Parents' reports and adolescent' self-reports. *Autism, 21*(6), 738–748. https://doi.org/10.1177/1362361316675119

Reynolds, C. R., & Kamphaus, R. W. (2004). *BASC-2: Behavior assessment system for children, second edition*. Pearson Clinical.

Reynolds, C. R., & Kamphaus, R. W. (2015). *BASC-3: Behavior assessment system for children, third edition*. Pearson Clinical.

Riccomini, P. J., Bost, L. W., Katsiyannis, A., & Zhang, D. (2005). Cognitive behavioral interventions: An effective approach to help students with disabilities stay in school. *Effective Interventions in Dropout Prevention: A Practice Brief for Educators, 1*(1), 1–8.

Rosenberg, R. E., Kaufmann, W. E., Law, J. K., & Law, P. A. (2011). Parent report of community psychiatric comorbid diagnoses in autism spectrum disorders, *Autism Research and Treatment*, 1–10. https://doi.org/10.1155/2011/405849

Ruble, L., McGrew, J. H., Wong, V., Adams, M., & Yu, Y. (2019). A preliminary study of parent activation, parent-teacher alliance, transition planning quality, and IEP and postsecondary goal attainment of students with ASD. *Journal of Autism and Developmental Disorders, 49*, 3231–3243. https://doi.org/10.1007/s10803-019-04047-4

Rutter, M., Bailey, A., & Lord, C. (2003). *The social communication questionnaire*. Western Psychological Services.

Rutter, M., Le Couteur, A., & Lord, C. (2003). *ADI-R: Autism Diagnostic Interview-Revised (ADI-R)*. Western Psychological Services.

Scahill, L., Aman, M. G., Lecavalier, L., Halladay, A. K., Bishop, S. L., Bodfish, J. W., … Dawson, G. (2015). Measuring repetitive behaviors as a treatment endpoint in youth with autism spectrum disorder. *Autism, 19*, 38–52. https://doi.org/10.1177/1362361313510069

Scheeren, A. M., Koot, H. M., & Begeer. (2012). Social interavtion style of children and adolescents with high-functioning autism spectrum disorder. *Journal of Autism and Developmental Disorders, 42*, 2046–2055. https://doi.org/10.1007/s10803-012-1451-x

Schohl, K. A., Van Hecke, A. V., Meyer Carson, A., Dolan, B., Karst, J., & Stevens, S. (2014). A replication and extension of the PEERS intervention examine efforts on social skills and social anxiety in adolescents with autism spectrum disorders. *Journal of Autism and Developmental Disorders, 44*, 532–545. https://doi.org/10.1007/s10803-013-1900-1

Seltzer, M. M., Shattuck, P., Abeduto, L., & Greenberg, J. S. (2004). Trajectory of development in adolescents and adults with autism. *Mental Retardation and Developmental Disabilities Research Reviews, 10*, 234–247.

Shattuck, P. T., Seltzer, M. M., Greensburg, J. S., Orsmond, G. I., Bolt, D., Kring, S., Lounds, J., & Lord, C. (2007). Change in autism symptoms and maladaptive behaviors in adolescents and adults with an autism spectrum disorder. *Journal of Autism and Developmental Disorders, 37*, 1735–1747. https://doi.org/10.1007/s10803-006-0307-7

Skinner, B. F. (1938). *The behavior of organisms: An experimental analysis.* Appleton-Century-Crofts.

Sparrow, S. S., Balla, D. A., & Cicchetti, D. (1984). *Vineland adaptive behavior scales.* American Guidance Service.

Storch, E. A., Lewin, A. B., Collier, A. B., Arnold, E., De Nadai, A. S., Dane, B. F., Nadeau, J. M., Mutch, P. J., & Murphy, T. K. (2015). A randomized controlled trial of cognitive-behavioral therapy versus treatment as usual for adolescents with autism spectrum disorders and comorbid anxiety. *Depression and Anxiety, 32*, 174–181. https://doi.org/10.1002/da.22332

Tse, J., Strulovitch, J., Tagalakis, V., Meng, L., & Frombonne, E. (2007). Social skills training for adolescents with Asperger syndrome and high-functioning autism. *Journal of Autism and Developmental Disorders, 37*, 1960–1968. https://doi.org/10.1007/s10803-006-0343-3

van Hecke, A. V., Stevens, S., Carson, A. M., Karst, J. S., Dolan, B., Schohl, K., McKindles, R. J., Remmel, R., & Brockman, S. (2015). Measuring the plasticity of social approach: A randomized controlled trial of the effects of the PEERS intervention on EEG asymmetry in adolescents with autism spectrum disorders. *Journal of Autism and Developmental Disorders, 45*, 316–335. https://doi.org/10.1007/s10803-013-1883-y

van Steensel, F. J., Bogels, S. M., & Perrin, S. (2011). Anxiety disorders in children and adolescents with autistic spectrum disorders: A meta-analysis. *Clinical Child and Family Psychology Review, 14*(3), 302–317. https://doi.org/10.1007/s10567-011-0097-0

Vuijk, R., Deen, M., Sizoo, B., & Arntz, A. (2018). Temperament, character, and personality disorders in adults with autism spectrum disorder: A systematic literature review and meta-analysis. *Review Journal of Autism and Developmental Disorders, 5*, 176–197. https://doi.org/10.1007/s40489-018-0131-y

Walker, H., Todis, B., Holmes, D., & Horton, G. (1988). *The Walker social skills curriculum: Adolescent curriculum for communication and effective social skills (ACCESS).* Pro-ed.

Weiss, M. J., & Harris, S. L. (2001). Teaching social skills to people with autism. *Behavior Modification, 25*(5), 785–802.

Weschler, D. (2014). *Weschler intelligence scale for children, fifth edition: Technical and interpretive manual.* NCS Pearson.

Wiggins, L., Reynolds, A., Rice, C., Moody, E., Bernal, P., Blaskey, L., … Levy, S. (2015). Using standardized diagnostic instruments to classify children with autism in the study to explore early development. *Journal of Autism & Developmental Disorders, 45*, 1271–1280. https://doi.org/10.1007/s10803-014-2287-3

Winner, M., G., & Crooke, P. J. (2011). Social communication strategies for adolescents with autism. *The ASHA Leader*, 1–8. https://doi.org/10.1044/leader.FTR1.16012011.8

Wong, C., Odom, S. L., Hume, K., Cox, A. W., Fettig, A., Kucharczyk, S., … Schultz, T. R. (2014). *Evidence-based practices for children, youth, and young adults with Autism Spectrum disorder.* The University of North Carolina, Frank Porter Graham Child Development Institute, Autism Evidence-Based Practice Review Group. Retrieved from http://autismpdc.fpg.unc.edu/sites/autismpdc.fpg.unc.edu/files/2014-EBP-Report.pdf

Wyman, J., & Claro, A. (2019). The UCLA PEERS school-based program: Treatment outcomes for improving social functioning in adolescents and young adults with autism spectrum disorder and those with cognitive deficits. *Journal of Autism and Developmental Disorders, 50.* https://doi.org/10.1007/s10803-019-03943-z

Zander, E., Willfors, C., Berggren, Choque-Olsson, N., Coco, C., Almund, A., Moretto, A. H., Holm, A., Jifalt, I., Kosieradzki, R., Linder, J., Nordin, V., Olasfottir, K., Poltrago, L., & Bolte, S. (2016). The objectivity of the autism diagnostic observation schedule (ADOS) in naturalistic clinical settings. *Journal of European Child and Adolescent Psychiatry, 25*, 769–780. https://doi.org/10.1007/s00787-015-0793-2

Self-Management for Transition-Aged College-Bound Autistic Students

Susan M. Wilczynski, Robin A. Snyder, Amanda J. Kazee, Shawnna Sundberg, Cori A. Conner, Brandon N. Miller, and Sam Johnson

Abstract This chapter explores the use of self-management within a self-determination model to address challenges unique to the transition experience of college-bound Autistic students. Self-management empowers individuals to both participate in and lead their behavior change programs through self-monitoring, evaluating, and recording, as well as self-delivering reinforcement so behaviors associated with valued goals can be used and generalized to relevant environments. Self-management allows Autistic adults to independently manage a multitude of their own behaviors in a manner that is consistent with their academic, social, and life goals. Specific self-management issues that should be considered by transition-aged and/or college-bound Autistic students include, but are not restricted to, effectively working with the Office of Disability Services, registering for classes, managing time appropriately, living independently, and engaging in community and social activities, including dating. Recommendations for how school psychologists and other secondary-level school personnel can assist Autistic students in developing and using self-management skills are provided.

Keywords Self-management · Autistic college students · Postsecondary education · Self-determination

---

S. M. Wilczynski (✉) · R. A. Snyder · S. Sundberg
Department of Special Education, Ball State University, Muncie, IN, USA
e-mail: smwilczynski@bsu.edu

A. J. Kazee
Department of Educational Psychology, Ball State University, Muncie, IN, USA

C. A. Conner
Department of Psychology, Ball State University, Muncie, IN, USA

B. N. Miller
Department of Counseling Psychology, Ball State University, Muncie, IN, USA

S. Johnson
Department of Educational Studies, Ball State University, Muncie, IN, USA

© Springer Nature Switzerland AG 2022
K. D. Viezel et al. (eds.), *Postsecondary Transition for College- or Career-Bound Autistic Students*, https://doi.org/10.1007/978-3-030-93947-2_6

Self-Management for Transition-Aged College-Bound Autistic Students

Colleges and universities provide students with the opportunity to expand their knowledge, build personal skills, meet new people, gain a new level of independence, and develop valuable skills such as time management and organization. College attendance also comes with unique challenges for students, such as choosing the right classes, navigating relationships, learning to become more independent, and initiating one's educational trajectory (Ashbaugh et al., 2017).

Initiating the college experience provides especially unique challenges for Autistic students when there is a mismatch between the skills they possess and those expected in university environments. Autism spectrum disorder (ASD) as defined by psychiatrists, psychologists, and other health professionals entails difficulties in social communication and interaction, as well as restricted, repetitive behaviors, interests, or activities (American Psychiatric Association, 2013). Communication difficulties are a common experience for Autistics and this is no different for Autistic college students, whose social engagement patterns may differ from those typically expected in university classrooms, dormitories, and social organizations. As a result, the everyday actions and motivations of Autistic college students may be misinterpreted by neurotypical (i.e., without a neurological disability) professors and classmates alike. Administrators, professors, and students who are insufficiently informed about autism may perceive restricted, repetitive behaviors demonstrated by Autistics, such as repetitive movements, fixated interests, stereotyped speech, and inflexible routines (American Psychiatric Association, 2013; Van Hees et al., 2015), as concerning or problematic.

Conversely, Autistic students are likely to have trouble interpreting the communication of their non-Autistic professors and classmates and learning to adapt their communication to address this disjuncture is a task inevitably undertaken by every Autistic individual (Harmsen, 2019). This mismatch between the expectations of Autistics and neurotypical people on a college campus can lead to minor problems (e.g., discomfort of one or both social partners) or major problems (e.g., a professor or classmate feeling threatened even though the Autistic student does not intend to intimidate or threaten others).

In the general population, college is often the first time students experience independence (Ashbaugh et al., 2017), as they may decide to live on campus and need to manage their daily living activities and school workload without parental support. Activities college students may find challenging as they enter a college environment include organizing schedules, managing time appropriately, participating in social activities, and gaining/managing independence without the support of parents, teachers, or direct support staff that may have been present while attending high school (Ashbaugh et al., 2017). Autistic college students may be particularly at risk of experiencing these transition difficulties when educators have not sufficiently supported the development of self-determination and self-management skills during middle and high school. Self-management is an evidence-based intervention that systemizes self-regulation strategies. Although self-management will be the primary focus of this chapter, value of self-management is best understood within the context of self-determination.

The Role of Self-Determination in Self-Management

The primary goal of self-determination is to increase independent control over large and small actions, setting control over one's own trajectory across important domains in life (Chao, 2018). Self-determination involves using a range of skills, such as decision-making, problem-solving, goal setting and attainment, self-advocacy, self-regulation, self-awareness, self-knowledge, and self-management. People develop plans for attaining their goals under the self-determination model based on their unique motivations or needs, and these goals are connected to decisions they make to shape their own destiny (Alamri et al., 2020).

Gaining independence and autonomy is a major goal for all young adults, including most people diagnosed with ASD. Independence in adulthood often includes gaining employment, living by oneself or with friends, and managing one's own finances. Self-determined Autistic adults become more independent because they have learned to focus on what unique goals they want to achieve and why those outcomes are important to them. In addition, self-determined Autistic adults identify areas in which they benefit from external support and access those resources in order to further attain goals that can lead to a high quality of life.

School psychologists and other school personnel can improve their approach to intervention for transition-aged Autistic students (i.e., middle and high school students) once they acknowledge that Autistic adults are more motivated to succeed when they choose both their goals and the processes used to achieve these goals (Chao, 2018). For example, school psychologists who actively promote self-management as an intervention as early as possible during the school years (but no later than middle school) are more likely to assist Autistic students in acquiring skills that will support their later transition to college campuses.

Overview of Self-Management

Autistic students who use self-management are often able to discriminate between behavior that is desired in a given environment and those that are more likely to lead to conflict. Autistic students can learn to accurately monitor and record their behavior against identified criteria and then reward themselves for desired behavior (Sam & AFIRM Team, 2016) that helps them achieve their life goals. We argue that self-management is most likely to be a useful strategy when developed within the context of self-determination. That is, middle- and high-school-aged students should receive support in developing self-management skills that support their goals.

The Self-Management Process

The self-management process consists of five steps (see Fig. 1). Self-management begins with determining the behavior(s) to be targeted for change (Step 1), which should result from a detailed conversation with the student about their goals and the strategies to help them achieve these goals. The target behavior should be clearly defined (Schulze, 2016), which ideally includes both examples and non-examples that delineate what behaviors fall within or outside of acceptable parameters. Given Autistics often have difficulty understanding the ways neurotypical people communicate with them (and vice versa), a clear and comprehensive operational definition is essential for decreasing the chances the goals of self-management are misunderstood (Schulze, 2016). For example, when nervous, an Autistic college student had difficulty remaining seated and attending to the professor during class, which caused the professor to become distracted and/or the Autistic student to miss valuable information. The Autistic college student had a conversation with a counselor at the university counseling center and determined how best to address this challenge. After a thorough discussion, the Autistic college student established a two-tiered goal. To begin, the Autistic college student determined they possessed the skill of approaching the professor to discuss the need to get out of their seat and stand in the back of the room or leave the classroom altogether when they are extremely distressed. They then developed a plan to bring bulleted points (e.g., self-disclosing they are Autistic, identifying that when extremely distressed they will not be able to pay attention while seated, etc.) when they went to the professor's posted office

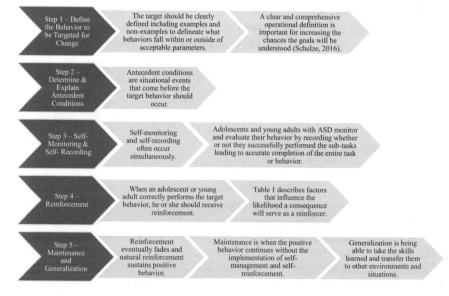

Fig. 1 Steps of the self-management process

hours so they could most effectively self-advocate for their need to get out of their seat when severely distressed.

The Autistic college student wanted to work on their ability to remain seated when facing lower levels of distress because they wanted to look more like other college students in their class. The counselor worked with the Autistic college student to identify cues to let them know which strategy to attempt. For example, remaining seated but being unable to attend to class while experiencing increasing levels of anxiety was deemed undesirable. If these conditions occurred, the Autistic college student was encouraged to stand in the back of class or leave the classroom based on the intensity of the experience. When distress did not reach this level, other self-management strategies would be used to achieve the student's goal of remaining seated and attending to the professor. At this point, the operational definition of remaining seated (e.g., the student's buttocks and back in contact with the chair) and attending (e.g., taking notes, asking content related questions) was developed by the student in collaboration with the university counselor. Non-examples of remaining seated included standing, walking around the classroom, kneeling on the chair, and laying with his or her head down on top of the desk. Non-examples of attending included checking their phone for non-course content, facing the professor but not taking notes, etc.

Once the target behavior(s) is chosen, antecedent conditions are determined and thoroughly described (Step 2; Aljadeff-Abergel et al., 2015). Antecedent conditions are situational events that exist before the target behavior is expected to occur. For instance, if the target behavior is remaining seated and attending to the professor, the antecedent condition for seated behavior may be the professor walking into the classroom, the professor making statements that class is being initiated (e.g., "let's begin"). These events may be identified as the cues for the Autistic college student to be seated and to attend to the professor.

Self-monitoring and self-recording often occur simultaneously (Step 3; Schulze, 2016). Autistic adults monitor and evaluate their behavior by recording whether they successfully performed the desired target behavior(s) to criterion (Aljadeff-Abergel et al., 2015). Continuing with our example, the Autistic college student had a phone (and eventually a watch) that was set to vibrate every 5 min. If the criteria for seated behavior and attending were met when the device vibrated, they recorded a '+' on a check sheet.

Early in the self-management process (ideally, prior to college attendance), a support person (e.g., direct care staff, teachers, parents) concurrently records and determines whether or not the behavior is being performed to the criterion. The purpose of both parties collecting data is to ensure that Autistic students know how to use a recording system, can accurately evaluate their performance, and establish how discrepant their current behavior is from the desired goal. Inquiries regarding the source of discrepancy should be made, and systematic errors should be addressed by changing the operational definition (e.g., clarifying) or providing additional training of accurate self-monitoring and self-recording. As accurate self-recording skills improve, supports must be faded so Autistic college students can independently manage and record their behavior successfully (Koegel et al., 2015). In our example, the student had been taught to use self-management strategies in high school and the system developed was consistent with their preferences.

Step 4 of self-management involves reinforcement. Reinforcement is the process of increasing a behavior based on the consequences that follow the behavior. A consequence is a reinforcer when the likelihood a student will perform a target behavior increases when it is delivered contingent on accurate performance of a task (Sam & AFIRM Team, 2015). For example, the Autistic college student who identified remaining in their seat during sociology class identified playing preferred video games (for a pre-determined amount of time) after class as a reinforcer they would like to access. They then monitored their remaining seated/attending and decided whether or not they got to play the video game if they meet a pre-specified criterion (e.g., remaining seated throughout the class unless extreme distress was experienced). Access to the video games increased this Autistic college student's level of remained seated and attended during class, so playing the video game was considered a reinforcer. See Fig. 2 for factors that influence whether or not a consequence will serve as a reinforcer. In addition to the identification of reinforcers, the schedule of reinforcement (i.e., how often reinforcers are accessed) influence the likelihood new behaviors will be developed and maintained over time.

External supports may be necessary to ensure self-management most effectively helps Autistic students achieve their goals. Transition-aged Autistic students should receive help in identifying potent reinforcers, which can be facilitated when school psychologists or other school personnel conduct preference assessments. However,

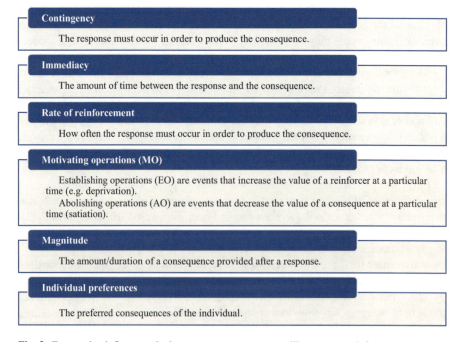

Fig. 2 Factors that influence whether or not a consequence will serve as a reinforcer

transition-aged Autistic students could be taught to graph and interpret their own data as a means of determining if an alternative reinforcer may be needed as they acquire self-management skills. For example, if progress toward meeting a self-determined goal has stagnated (i.e., the slope has flattened), it is likely time to select a different reinforcer as long as the goal is still valued by the student. Following this procedure during the transition years would mean Autistic college students might not require external supports to evaluate their own data and draw their own conclusions about reinforcer effectiveness. When analysis of their own data is not a skill that was taught during middle or secondary school years, Autistic college students should seek support from professionals who can assist in the development of these graphing and data analysis skills.

The final step of self-management is maintenance and generalization (Step 5). Maintenance occurs when a behavior continues in the formal absence of steps 1–4 (e.g., remaining seated/attending in sociology without self-monitoring or self-reinforcement; Dixon & McKeel, 2011). Ideally, programmed reinforcement eventually fades, and natural reinforcement (e.g., good grades) sustains positive behaviors (e.g., studying and doing homework; Schulze, 2016). However, it is important to recognize that many adults use self-management supports (e.g., app alerts, "to do" lists, calendar reminders, etc.) and ongoing use of these systems should be viewed as desirable when they continue to help Autistic college students succeed in meeting their goals. Generalization occurs when learned behavior(s) are appropriately used in other environments and situations (e.g., remaining seated/attending when in English class; Liu et al., 2015).

Self-Management Implementation Variants

Self-management is a multi-component intervention that incorporates numerous aspects of self-observation and regulation (see Table 1). As noted previously, self-determination begins with goal setting (Getzel, 2014), which is desirable before the implementation of self-management systems because goal setting (a) respects the dignity of Autistic students; (b) involves identifying and defining tasks to be completed (Step 1 of the self-management process); and (c) establishes the criteria associated with these tasks. Self-cueing (i.e., providing oneself external prompts, such as an alarm) and self-instruction (i.e., verbally discussing subcomponents prior to and/or during task completion) can be used at Steps 2 and 3 of the self-management process. Self-observation, monitoring, and recording are interrelated terms reflected in Step 3 of the self-management process. When combined, these self-observation and regulation skills yield self-management intervention.

Table 1 Self-management implementation variants

Self-Management Variants	Description of Strategy	Supporting Evidence	Uses
Goal setting	An Autistic student chooses a goal, chooses a criterion to meet in order to demonstrate completion, makes a plan to reach the goal, and reinforces the completion of the goal once criterion is reached.	Schulze, 2016	• Accessing accommodations relevant to coursework • Completion of coursework • Class attendance • Cleaning • Determining the need for assistance • Dating and sexuality • Dorm behavior • Emotional regulation • Fitness • Issues with roommates • Medication Usage/Following Medical Regimen • Meeting with professors/advisor • Navigating email • Nutrition/food choices • Personal care/hygiene • Organization and time management • Registering for classes • Time management • Sleep • Social interactions • Transitions between activities
Self-cueing	Signals, such as alarms that are used to indicate to a an Autistic student the need to switch from one activity to the next.	Ferguson et al., 2005	
Self-instruction	An Autistic student verbally states the steps to complete a task.	Schulze, 2016	
Self-observation, Self-recording, & Self-monitoring checklists **5-point scale**	An Autistic student assesses his or her behavior to determine if the desired behavior occurred (self-observation). He or she records whether or not the behavior occurred (self-recording). Self-monitoring entails marking if items on a list as items are completed until the class is completed. The 5-point scale is a unique self-monitoring tool that allows young adults with ASD to identify their emotional level and identify appropriate behaviors they can engage in to lessen their level of discomfort.	Bouck, Savage, Meyer, Taber-Doughty, & Hunley, 2014; Schulze, 2016; Parker & Kamps, 2011 Buron & Curtis, 2012; Buron, Brown, Curtis, & King, 2012; Burin & Curtis, 2004	
Self-reinforcement	An Autistic student recruits or secures reinforcers based on successful performance on a goal. Self-reinforcement often include all other forms of self-management but does not have to meet this criterion.	Beaver, B. N., Reeve, S. A., Reeve, K. F., & DeBar, R. M. (2017); Todd, T., Reid, G., & Butler-Kisber, L. (2010).	

Self-Management for Common Postsecondary Education Challenges

Individuals with disabilities, including Autistic students, are less likely than their neurotypical peers to pursue postsecondary education (Plotner & May, 2017). Given the completion of postsecondary education improves employment outcomes and overall quality of life for people (Mamiseishvili & Koch, 2011; National Council on Disability, 2003), school psychologists should endorse interventions that not only address the immediate needs of school-aged Autistic students, but also equip them with skills that support the independent completion of academic, social, and life tasks that increase the likelihood that college completion is manageable when it matches the identified goals of the student. Autistic students who are entering college have effectively increased verbal responding, developed appropriate nonverbal skills, and decreased problem behaviors as a result of self-management (Koegel et al., 2014; Gear et al., 2011; Carr, 2016). Despite these positive outcomes for Autistic college students, self-management should be introduced during the K-12 years (Briesch et al., 2018) and should ideally involve application across social, academic, and life domain to increase the likelihood postsecondary outcomes will be optimized (e.g., selecting college as an option, successful college completion, etc.).

Below we have identified a number of ways school psychologists can support transition-aged Autistic students as they consider entering college settings. For example, school psychologists can help college-bound Autistic students understand their choices from working with the office of disability services and registering for classes to independent living and social engagement. We underscore the value of adopting self-management as a means of preparing transition-aged Autistic students for a range of challenges some will face between matriculation and graduation. However, most of the challenges we describe are faced by many neurotypical college students and will not be faced by some Autistic college students. For this reason, we endorse using self-management across this range of areas for transition-aged neurotypical and Autistic college-bound students. School psychologists should consider offering self-management training for neurotypical and Autistic students in a group format not only because it is likely to be beneficial for all of these transition-aged students, but also because this format more closely approximates the conditions both will face on a college campus. Limited research has been conducted on self-management with transition-aged or college Autistic students. The recommendations that follow have largely been generated from the existing literature base for self-management with younger Autistic students and extended to college settings and/or challenges that are more likely to emerge during an Autistic student's years at a university.

Working with University and Office of Disability Services

Before selecting an institution of higher learning, transition-aged Autistic students should consider the accommodations available at each university they visit. Knowledge and use of available accommodations can dramatically alter academic outcomes (Anderson et al., 2018). School psychologists can support transition-aged Autistic students' goals for college attendance by assisting in the development of a list of questions to ask staff at the Office of Disability Services. The Office of Disability Services offers accommodations based on the student's individual needs. This "climate and accommodation use" self-management checklist (see Table 2) could not only help in the selection of a college that is the best match for a transition-aged Autistic student but also increase the likelihood accommodations will be accessed. The climate and accommodation use checklist should reflect both general concerns (i.e., concerns about general university supports for disabled students generally and Autistic students specifically) and individualized needs and interests (i.e., student-specific questions). Although the checklist provides an example of general and individualized questions, school psychologists should support transition-aged Autistic students in developing their own climate and accommodation checklists. The questions identified on this example climate and accommodation use checklist are not exhaustive, and even the general questions identified on Table 2 might not be

Table 2 Example climate accommodation use self-management checklist

Example general questions	Answer
What supports are available to students on this campus?	
What supports have people who have graduated used the most?	
What is the most common complaint Autistic students raise with you?	
What percentage of Autistic students report experiencing ableism on a regular basis?	
Is this university doing anything to address ableism on campus?	
Do you have enough staff at the Office of Disability Services?	
Do you ever have faculty unwilling to provide accommodations?	
Are there any groups on campus that focus on the needs of Autistic students?	
Have there been negative outcomes for students who have self-disclosed their ASD diagnosis to professors?	
Example individualized questions	**Answer**
What challenges have students with a major of _____ reported to you?	
What can I do to increase the chances of having a roommate who is supportive but respectful (e.g., will not view me as a "project").	
Is there anyone on campus who can help me select faculty who are sensitive to my need to wear noise-cancellation headphones (or other accommodation) during lectures?	
Will professors object if I use my cell phone to record lectures?	
What percentage of Autistic students on this campus developed intimate relationships with others?	
Do you believe the university counselors understand autism and reject ableism?	
What is the best way to address a misunderstanding between me and another student on campus?	

relevant for all students. School psychologists who understand transition-aged Autistic student's college goals are better positioned to support the generation of additional general and individual questions. Thus, an ongoing focus on self-determination during the transition years is highly beneficial.

School psychologists can help college-bound Autistic students to develop a number of self-management checklists that can support the transition to the campus environment. A "transition to college" checklist could be generated based on the student's goals for entering their college experience and the challenges in managing the university system they are likely to encounter. For example, the university cannot specify the supports that will be provided to any individual student until the Office of Disability Services is provided documentation of the disability. When developing a "transition to college" self-management checklist, school psychologists might suggest transition-aged Autistic students include the process of registering with the Office of Disability Services prior to starting their first semester. However, school psychologists must respect the transition-aged Autistic student's right to refuse self-disclosure. That is, some Autistic people prefer not to self-disclose their ASD diagnosis to the university and school psychologist will want to respect this decision (Organization for Autism Research, 2020).

Once the decision to register with the Office of Disability Services has been made, students may still benefit from using self-management as they engage with this university office. Some universities provide letters of accommodation via email, and this can represent a barrier for students with problems organizing and managing these materials. For example, although many schools send the request for accommodation directly to professors, others require students to find the email that documents their specific needs for accommodations and to share it with each of their professors (Hewitt, 2011). School psychologists and other school personnel can support transition-aged Autistic students by replicating this method in high school for students who agree this will be beneficial. Teachers will already know a student's disability status, but the process of self-disclosing and relying on documentation from the school as you interact with your teachers at the beginning of the term means generalization of the skill is more likely to occur. School psychologists can act as the "Office of Disability Services" representative and support transition-aged Autistic students in developing self-management regarding the use of computer skills, navigation of email, and/or the utilization of organizational systems for important electronic "paperwork." Students can be taught to use self-management (e.g., self-instruction) to evaluate email and determine whether or not to keep or delete it. In order for self-instruction to be effective, students must define the task, learn a self-instruction system, and receive reinforcement for using the system appropriately (Schulze, 2016). In this example, transition-aged Autistic students could be taught to ask themselves, "Does this have to do with my classes?" or "Is this relevant to my major?" (e.g., is the high school course related to their planned area of study in college?). If they answer "yes," the self-instruction system might direct them to place the email in a separate email folder unique to school-related emails related to their major. If it is relevant to school only, a general "school-related" email folder would be the appropriate repository.

Even when the Office of Disability Services directly contacts professors about disability status and required accommodations, deficits with social skills may still serve as a barrier to accessing these accommodations. Autistic students may need to remind professors with large numbers of students about their disability status after initial notification (e.g., before an examination to ensure additional time is offered) to prevent the situation in which the professor has temporarily forgotten and the student feels awkward about reminding them in front of other students. Self-advocacy involves the act of representing one's own needs, orally or in writing, as a means of asserting control over one's own destiny. Self-management for the purpose of self-advocacy can be addressed in middle and high school, but should also be combined with other interventions when skill development should precede governing one's own behavior.

An example of combining other interventions with self-management follows. However, school psychologists should select interventions that are most likely to produce skill acquisition based on student history and preferences, evidence in the empirical literature, and ongoing data collection (Wilczynski, 2017). That is, this example is only illustrative and not prescriptive. Transition-aged Autistic students should participate in their own individualized education plan (IEP; See Legal and Ethical chapter in this book). School psychologists can support transition-aged Autistic students by first clearly defining the purpose and process of an IEP and then explicating the student's role in the IEP meeting. At this point, goal setting is valuable and provides the transition-aged Autistic student to determine what they want to accomplish by attending the IEP meeting. Next, the school psychologist and student can role-play each step of the IEP meeting, with the school psychologist stopping to ask what choices for engagement the student wants to make at different parts of the mock IEP meeting (e.g., This is your chance to state what you think your strengths are. Do you want to tell the teachers, administrators, and your parents what strengths you have that they should think about before moving on to skills you will want to develop in school?). Once the student understands the basic purpose and process of the IEP meeting, the school psychologists can ask the student what aspects of the role-play were particularly challenging (e.g., sharing strengths, identifying skills that should appear on the IEP, etc.) and share their own point of view about where difficulties emerged. When discrepant viewpoints emerge, the school psychologists and the transition-aged Autistic student can resolve these differences through discussion, which can help students learn to self-advocate and engage in active listening simultaneously. Both self-advocacy and active listening will be extremely helpful in the IEP meeting. The length of time this process will take will vary considerably across transition-aged Autistic students, with some students demonstrating strong self-advocacy skills after one iteration of this process and others requiring considerable practice. Prior to the IEP meeting, the school psychologist should then collaborate with the student in developing self-management strategies that match the student's needs. For example, some students may need more self-cueing and others might require more self-instruction. As the meeting progresses, the student can place check marks next to their actions to determine if they demonstrated the skill they identified as important to them.

Registering for Classes

Registering for classes can be a complex and challenging task for all individuals transitioning to postsecondary education. Decisions regarding selecting required and elective coursework, how many credits to take in a given semester, or what time of day a course is offered (e.g., should they take a morning, afternoon, or night class) may be daunting. Universities offer all students advisement regarding coursework. Once a college is selected, the advisement process should be investigated, and a self-management system can be developed while the student is still in high school. Self-management could involve identifying the point during each semester that registration begins and ends, contacting the advisement office for support, selecting courses based on the number of required and elective courses needed to make progress toward degree completion, and problem-solving when obstacles emerge (e.g., needing permission to take a course). Each semester the student would check their performance of each step until they graduate.

Attendance, Class Engagement, and Study Habits

Attendance

Attendance policies are often set by and vary across professors. For example, some professors may require student attendance and lateness (e.g., more than 10 min) be counted as an absence. Conversely, other professors may not require students to attend classes as long as assignments are turned in and the final exam or project is completed. Autistic college students should review their syllabi and consult with their individual professors if they are confused about what attendance is expected. Developing a self-management system that supports course attendance and individual meetings with professors (e.g., attend office hours) can increase the likelihood Autistic college students complete work in a timely manner. For example, students can use self-monitoring (See Table 1) to track their classroom attendance and the number of times they meet their professor during office hours. Self-monitoring tools such as checklists, to-do lists, or calendars can be electronic (e.g., smartphone); or paper-pencil should be adopted while the Autistic student remains in high school. If self-reinforcement is needed, then this variant of self-management should be combined with self-monitoring.

Class Engagement

Autistic college students who have prioritized class engagement because it can help them understand more course materials can use self-management systems (Hart et al., 2010) that best match their needs. For example, the student may develop a "course engagement" self-instruction system asking questions such as "Do I understand the assignment?" "Can I repeat what the professor said in my own words?" or "Have I completed responsibilities for group assignments on time?" Some might utilize self-reinforcement systems when the answer is "yes," and others may decide the lower level of stress associated with knowing they are managing their courses effectively is sufficient reinforcement. "No" answers can be addressed (e.g., approaching the professor for additional help, seeking tutoring, apologizing for group work that was not completed on time, and making a plan to rectify the problem) and followed by self-reinforcement as well. School psychologists can engage transition-aged Autistic students in goal setting around "course engagement" and can help students develop self-management self-systems so potential problems can be addressed during the middle and high school years. For example, students may forget to use the self-management system or identify that the reinforcers are not valuable enough to change their behavior. School psychologists can collaborate with transition-aged Autistic students to problem-solve challenges. This process is not only useful for the transition to college but will likely produce benefit during middle and high school. The higher levels of engagement and understanding that occur during middle and high school increase the chances academic skills will be mastered, setting a foundation for college coursework.

Study Habits

The difference in academic workload from high school to college is typically substantial. Studying with classmates (e.g., peer-mediated instruction) may benefit transition-aged Autistic students by allowing them to gain different perspectives about the material and alternate ways to describe the information. Differences in social-communication strengths among transition-aged Autistic students means coaching may be necessary prior to self-assess about whether a study partner versus a study group would be more beneficial and less stressful. Transition-aged Autistic students can develop and use a self-management system to make sure they have read materials and taken notes before the meeting, generated questions regarding material, and then use self-cueing to ensure contributions to the group are made.

Self-management strategies may be needed to ensure self-regulation (e.g., relaxation strategies, time to engage in restricted and repetitive behaviors, etc.) occurs pre- and/or post-study group meetings, even when a study group is small. Collaborative discussion about class topics and note-sharing can be triggering, not only due to student-specific characteristics of ASD (e.g., the lighting or sounds in the environment can be painful or anxiety-producing), but also because members of study groups will unintentionally adopt views of our larger ableist culture (Wilczynski et al., 2021), which may result in patronizing comments (e.g., "Let me just do this algebra problem for you") or microaggressions (i.e., exclusions or less obvious statements of discrimination against a marginalized group; Kattari, 2020). For example, classmates may state microaggressions such as "Are you sure you really have autism? You are good at this." Or "It must be nice to get accommodations. I could get A's if I got more time on exams too." In addition, classmates might use colloquial terms common to same-aged "in groups," but to which some transition-aged Autistic students are not exposed. Should these occur during the middle or high school years, the school psychologist will want to collaborate with the student by engaging in goal-setting around how to manage these stressful conditions and follow the student's lead on what, how, and when to address any concerns (e.g., should they say something when microaggressions occur, would they like the school psychologists to explain microaggressions to the group, would the student prefer to work on their reaction to these microaggressions, etc.).

Time Management

Transition-aged and Autistic college students may have difficulty maintaining schedules and managing their time wisely (Van Hees et al., 2015). Any college student can feel overwhelmed by the amount of required information covered in a course or the number of assignments that may be due simultaneously or sequentially. Implementation of self-management skills can aid students in managing their time and arranging their day into useful "chunks." For example, students can use an electronic visual system (e.g., calendar or "app" on their smartphone) that allows them to plan their day and alarms can be used to signal it is time to switch from one activity to the next (Ferguson et al., 2005; Gentry et al., 2015). Smartphone apps have been found to be effective and highly motivating self-management tools for transition-aged Autistic students (Francis et al., 2018). These electronic visual systems should not be stigmatizing or require a decision about self-disclosure regarding a diagnosis given these apps are commonly used by college students. There are an ever-growing number of apps available that support students in tracking classes, assignments, and projects. Once dates are entered, the apps can help students see what work needs to be completed each day as well as provide reminders (cues/alarms) for when to attend class or complete course work (Francis et al., 2018). New time-management apps that support college students in different ways are being regularly developed. For example, some apps target how you spend your time (e.g., RescueTime) and others focus on all relevant tasks (e.g., Trello). The same app might be overwhelming to a freshman college student but helpful by their sophomore year. Similarly, some time-management apps might be more feasible or have more compatible use for one Autistic college student versus another. For this reason, we do not provide specific recommendations for time management apps. However, we recommend Autistic college students have conversations with current college students and then obtain supports from school psychologists, their teachers, and/or their parents as needed prior to selecting and trying out new apps. Also, parents and professionals need to give Autistic college students the space to reject apps they originally thought might be a good fit because most people download apps that they later decide were not exactly what they wanted. That is, Autistic students should not be held to a different standard than any other student.

Alternatively, students can utilize a paper-pencil planner to block off times in order to work on specific tasks. Utilizing this self-management strategy, students can independently create and follow a study schedule shifting from one activity or subject to the next (Newman et al., 1995). As with all applications of self-management, the components that best meet the needs of students should be adopted (e.g., Should a self-instruction component be added to the prompts an app provides? Is completing the tasks successfully a sufficient reinforcer or should the student deliver self-reinforcement in some other way?).

Independent Living

Independent living skills (e.g., eating, grooming, caring for personal health, cleaning, cooking, shopping, and managing finances) can pose challenges for anyone living on their own for the first time (Cullen & Alber-Morgan, 2015; Loyd & Brolin, 1997). Transition-aged Autistic students are often able to demonstrate these skills with the support of family members while living at home but may still struggle to perform them when living on their own at college. Difficulty executing independent living skills could lead to a decline in productivity and adversely impact the student's overall performance and success in higher education (Hume et al., 2009) as well as their social interactions with other college students. Prior to the transition to college, school psychologists can work with Autistic students to adopt self-management systems that will support their use of independent living skills (e.g., cooking or doing laundry). However, it is noteworthy that some daily living skills are less valued than other opportunities in college and families financially positioned to access additional supports (e.g., cleaning professionals, personal assistants) may choose to focus their funds on these resources if these daily living skills are not a high priority for the student, thus allowing the Autistic college student to focus on goals related to academics and social relationships.

Mental Health Independent living can be challenging when people experience mental health issues (Di Rezze et al., 2016). A large percentage of colleges students experience anxiety (60.7%) and depression (48.6%; LeViness et al., 2019). These psychiatric disorders are even more common for Autistics. A survey found that Autistic adults were 3.2 times more likely to have an anxiety disorder and 2.6 times more likely to have depression (Croen et al., 2015). Of particular concern on college campuses are self-harm and suicidal ideation among Autistic college students (Anderson et al., 2020a). These data strongly suggest Autistic college students should take advantage of counseling centers on most college campuses and utilize whatever outside mental health supports (e.g., psychologists, counselors, etc.) that have historically supported these symptoms; counselors should integrate self-management into their treatment plans.

Smartphone apps that involve some forms of self-management may play a useful role in addressing mental health needs. Smartphone apps requiring self-monitoring for mental health issues are only beginning to be investigated empirically, but the emerging data are promising. Although usability, acceptability, and feasibility will differ across apps, ratings for some of these apps are very high, suggesting they are more likely to be adopted and used by college students (*50 Highly Rated Self-Help Apps,* 2020). In addition, use of a self-management app (i.e., MoodPrism) was associated with lower levels of depression and anxiety and higher mental well-being for a community sample of adults using smartphone apps that addresses mental health (Bakker & Rickard, 2018). Additional research on smartphone self-management apps specific to Autistic college students is needed; however, if Autistic students find smartphone self-management apps useful for other skills (see examples below), extending the use of smart-phone apps to mental health needs is likely feasible.

Self-management apps may not be viable for every Autistic college student, or it may be limited in its application, so, paper-and-pencil systems still have a value. For example, a self-management app might provide cueing and allow for easy self-monitoring for an Autistic college student's prioritized behavior (e.g., eating in the residence hall) but it might not reflect the extent to which barriers (e.g., anxiety associated with social engagement or sensory issues) interfere with achieving this goal. In this case, an app might be helpful but it would need to be supplemented with notes regarding barriers to goal attainment. Autistic college students may find eating in a residence hall cafeteria triggering for a number of reasons. It is not uncommon for Autistic college students to have limited or specific food prefer-ences, which can be problematic when the cafeteria does not have those foods as options or does not offer those items at every meal. Availability of specific foods can be particularly anxiety-provoking when it is hard to predict when foods will or will not be available. Eating in the cafeteria can also lead to physical or emotional dys-regulation due to sensory issues such as noises, lighting, and smells (Adreon & Durocher, 2007; Kinnaird et al., 2019). Five-point (5-point) scales can be used to assist Autistic college students identify how they feel when problems are encoun-tered in the cafeteria (or other anxiety provoking situation) and provide examples of what should be done to cope and work through the problem (e.g., contact the Resident Assistant and the Office for Disability Services; Buron et al., 2012). When school psychologists utilize 5-point scales in a smaller setting that is common in middle and high school, they may help their transition-aged students develop not only awareness of problems and set the stage for problem-solving during transition years, but also increase the likelihood these students will successfully generalize these self-assessment and self-regulation skills to college.

Roommates

Roommate disagreements may require more frequent mediation by a dormitory's residential assistant when Autistic college students or their roommates lack the req-uisite social-communication skills to manage the challenge independently (Hendrickson et al., 2017). The 5-point scale is a self-management strategy (see

Table 1) that an Autistic college student can use to identify his or her feelings about a situation, likely outcomes, ideas about how to rethink a situation, and where to go for support. 5-point scales can be created to work through common roommate issues like coming in late and being loud, being messy, and taking personal items (Buron et al., 2012).

Sleep, Personal Care, Physical Activity, and Nutrition

Many college students struggle with going to sleep at a reasonable hour, getting enough sleep, and waking up to an alarm, which can adversely impact their college experience (Becker et al., 2018). Sleep problems are even more problematic for Autistics than their neurotypical peers (Jovevska et al., 2020). Smartphone apps may aid students in managing their time wisely and ensuring a sufficient quantity of sleep is obtained. The advantage of self-management apps is that they are ubiquitous on a college campus and therefore not stigmatizing. In addition, they are convenient, readily available, allow for self-cueing, and can involve interconnected electronic devices (e.g., the same cue might appear on a computer, a smartphone, and a watched), which increases the likelihood cues will be received irrespective of the activity in which students are engaged.

Self-management apps can be set not only to address sleep issues, but also to support adherence to medication schedules, complete hygiene tasks (e.g., showering, brushing teeth and doing laundry (Ferguson et al., 2005), address physical fitness goals (Molina & Sundar, 2018), or manage nutritional needs. Given academic performance is correlated with physical fitness (Santana et al., 2016) and nutritional status (Rahmatillah & Mulyono, 2019), supporting transition-aged Autistic students to use self-management apps to effectively support their overall quality of life is advisable.

Community Participation/Social Engagement

Making and maintaining new friendships, dating, and attending social activities such as campus sporting events or clubs are common college experiences. These social opportunities may be challenging for all college students (Wolf et al., 2017), but may be particularly difficult for Autistic college students because there is often a mismatch between the social-communication engagement patterns of neurotypical and Autistic college students. Professionals must avoid the ableist assumption that they can predict which social activities Autistic college students will or will not select. Like their neurotypical peers, Autistic college students are likely to seek different experiences at different points in their college careers. Social opportunities that were considered aversive upon college entry may be highly desirable only a semester or a year later. Regular assessment of evolving motivations for community participation and social engagement increases the chances for a more well-rounded college experience.

Social Interactions and Friendships

Due to differences in social interaction expectations between neurotypical and Autistic college students, Autistic college students may struggle more than their same-aged peers in making and maintaining friendships and may both become socially isolated on college campuses and experience anxiety and bullying (McLeod et al., 2019). However, people engaged in campus life (e.g., students, professors, staff) often have growing awareness of ASD (Tipton & Blacher, 2014), which should contribute to a more supportive university experience. Office of Disability Services on campuses should also be better prepared to offer support to Autistic college students than in years past. Although Autistic college students' report high rates of satisfaction with services they access, they are not consistently accessing these supports (Anderson et al., 2020a, b). Self-management is a strategy that can be initiated for transition-aged Autistic students so that the capacity for self-management for social relationships is well established before entering college campuses.

As with all self-management systems, students can establish their own social goals by identifying a behavior they seek to change (e.g., spending more time-sharing interests with others), utilizing self-observation (e.g., how many activities are planned with others), and monitoring whether or not the behavior occurred via self-recording (e.g., visual or checklist to monitor occurrence or non-occurrence; Schulze, 2016). Transition-aged and Autistic college students can determine if increasing specific skills will be helpful toward meeting their social goals. For example, Autistic students could use a social conversation framework to develop a self-recording system to record when the questions asked by others are answered, when new information is added to the conversation, and when follow-up questions are used (Koegel et al., 2014). The development of these self-management systems may be supported by psychologists or therapists who can help Autistic students generate their own goals and then problem-solve about the self-management system that best meets the unique needs of their students or clients. In addition, transition-aged Autistic college students should decide if they want input from other relevant people who share their lives. For example, evaluation of the number of social responses can be easily addressed with self-management, but the quality of responses is typically harder for all people to self-assess. Psychologists or therapists can discuss the benefits and challenges associated with self-disclosure (e.g., with a classmate or a college roommate) as well as help develop a comfortable and equitable method for obtaining external input (e.g., a roommate agreeing to identify statements made by Autistic students that were hard to understand, frustrating, or upsetting) while diminishing ableism (e.g., the roommate agrees to listen when the Autistic student shares what statements were made by the roommate that were hard to understand, frustrating, or upsetting). In this case, a self-management system should be combined with a second intervention (e.g., a contingency contract) to make sure the skills being developed are comprehensive and not one-sided. School psychologists can adopt this dual pronged approach to social interactions if they engage with transition-aged school groups who provide peer mentorship (e.g., one-to-one cross-age peer mentoring; Karcher & Berger, 2017) while supporting a goal-directed self-management system unique to each Autistic student.

Sexuality and Dating

Autistic adults express interest in sexuality and intimate relationships but often report having fewer sexual experiences and less sex education than neurotypical peers (Dewinter et al., 2017; Cheak-Zamora et al., 2019). We encourage readers to review Wilczynski et al. (2021) chapter in this book to better understand the topic of sexuality and intimate relationships for Autistic students. For the purposes of this chapter, we encourage school psychologists to consider the value of self-management systems for the purpose of self-advocacy in general and on the topic of sexuality and dating specifically. For example, stronger self-advocacy skills around gender identification and sexual orientation may unfortunately prove vital for Autistics in the face of the reluctance of many non-Autistics to trust Autistic individuals as capable of knowing their own sexual experiences (MacKenzie, 2018).

In conjunction with increasing access to sexual education for transition-aged Autistic students, school psychologists can encourage the use of self-management for the purpose of skill development and maintenance. A 5-point scale might be constructed to facilitate the understanding of essential components of dating by pairing levels of intimacy expected in different types of relationships, initiating friend or intimate relationships, or appropriate responses to various social cues (Buron et al., 2012). For example, a scale illustrating the attributes that characterize different relationships could involve pairing a casual acquaintanceship with the description "I see this person occasionally in my daily activities and may know his or her name, but we do not know each other well or socialize regularly." Examples and non-examples of behaviors for each level of familiarity can be generated together to support transition-aged and Autistic college students in discerning the difference between behaviors that are appropriate or inappropriate on the basis of the type of relationship that exists between two people. Constructing a 5-point scale could help with emotional responses associated with each level of the scale. However, school psychologists need to challenge their own assumptions about how static the nature of relationships can be. Relationships do change over time and someone who is an "acquaintance" today might be an "intimate partner" in the near future. Actively discouraging Autistic students from changing the status of the relationship should be avoided unless problems with stalking or other inappropriate sexual behavior occur (see Wilczynski et al.'s chapter).

Self-management can include cultivating specific social behaviors (e.g., asking someone on a date) that can increase the likelihood social efforts will be successful (e.g., the person asked will say "yes"). The psychologist or therapist should discuss the role of natural (e.g., someone you like goes out with you) and/or programmed reinforcers (e.g., I get to spend extra time playing my preferred video games when someone rejects my request for a date) with Autistic students and make certain the decisions about the value of these reinforcers are made by the student.

Although self-management can be used to address specific dating skills that may be needed, school psychologists and other therapists should avoid assuming their own experiences with dating and intimate relationships are relevant to any students because the current norms for these relationships among young adults may differ significantly from the norms applying to dating for the psychologist (currently or in the past). We provide a specific example below; however, this example may not be applicable for anyone (neurotypical or Autistic students) using self-management to improve their success with intimate or sexual relationships.

A transition-aged or Autistic college student who identifies dating as a goal could self-cue by entering the time of the date into their calendar/schedule and setting the alarm on their smartphones as a reminder to go on their date. They can use a checklist to dress both comfortably and appropriately to the planned event or to choose specific topics to discuss on a date, which will vary by occasion and as a relationship progresses. Adults supporting the development of self-management systems must again avoid the risk of imposing their own views about appropriate attire to generationally different people.

Participation in Social Activities

There are a variety of social activities available to all students at the postsecondary level including but not limited to athletics or social clubs and activities (e.g., debate team, foreign language club, attending college event). Engaging with these social clubs and activities is an individual choice for all college students, including Autistic students. There can be features of these social opportunities that could trigger a negative experience for Autistic college students or that can lead to bi-directional miscommunication, which can frustrate all parties. For example, if a social club meets in a setting with distracting visual or auditory stimuli, the Autistic student may not be able to fully participate because they are distracted as well as physically and emotionally uncomfortable or drained. Similarly, a "start of the year" party at a dormitory in which a lot of students do not know each other could quickly turn into social interactions around sexual activity. Rules around consent can be particularly murky around hooking up (i.e., causal sexual activity that may be recurring; Muehlenhard et al., 2016) and may be in direct opposition to those Autistic students have been learning from well-meaning adults. Many of these concerns can be reasonably anticipated and discussed with transition-aged students, and individualized self-management systems can be developed. Autistic students can learn to first identify their triggers and then to access and apply a self-management system that reflects their self-determined actions when they find themselves in that situation. There is no reason students should have to wait until their postsecondary years to develop these skills. In addition, Autistic students could use the 5-point scale to self-monitor, make decisions in difficult or hard to understand social situations, and manage their anxiety or other emotional responding that is painful (Jaime & Knowlton, 2007). School psychologists can recommend and guide the use of a 5-point scale to address these social activities at the high school level so that Autistic college students have already applied this self-management system across a range of situations prior to entering college.

Conclusion

Autistic college students have self-reported difficulties with organization and time-management as well as challenges with coping under distressing conditions as well as social skills (Anderson et al., 2020a). Self-management is highly adaptable and appropriate for all college-bound students, and there are available data to suggest self-management may be an effective strategy to employ across these areas of difficulty. However, it is important to recognize that the vast majority of the examples offered in this chapter are not born from the empirical literature. That is, we generated examples using anticipated challenges for transition-aged or Autistic college students based on the general self-management literature because there is extremely limited research specifically focusing on self-management for Autistic college students. Given self-management has been robust across populations (Dineen-Griffin et al., 2019) and has been effective with Autistic individuals who are not college-bound, we argue that our suggestions are reasonable and consistent with the scientist-practitioner model when limited data are available. It is clear that significantly more research is needed for Autistic college students across interventions, including self-management.

Self-management is likely a good fit for Autistic college students because it is consistent with the self-determination model. College students make more decisions for themselves than they had previously and Autistic college students should be no exception. By connecting their own values and goals to the actions they take, Autistic and neurotypical college students alike can set their own trajectories for their college experiences. We do not argue that any intervention is appropriate for all Autistic college students; however, self-management is highly adaptable to different behaviors and contexts and can involve technology that eliminates stigmatization (e.g., smartphone apps). Autistic college students who select self-management as a desirable intervention can experience greater independence, succeed academically, and explore new facets of themselves in a manner that is sufficiently consistent with local norms but does not require them to restrict their own choices or behaviors to perfectly reflect ableist societal views. School psychologists should advocate for the use of self-management in the elementary, junior high, and high school years to the maximum extent possible so that Autistic college students are experienced with this intervention and can self-select their goals and methods for self-management.

References

50 highly rated self-help apps. (2020, September 4). Retrieved February 10, 2021, from https://www.topcounselingschools.org/top-self-help-apps/

Adreon, D., & Durocher, J. S. (2007). Evaluating the college transition needs of individuals with high-functioning autism spectrum disorders. *Intervention in School and Clinic, 42*(5), 271–279.

Alamri, H., Lowell, V., Watson, W., & Watson, S. L. (2020). Using personalized learning as an instructional approach to motivate learners in online higher education: Learner self-determination and intrinsic motivation. *Journal of Research on Technology in Education, 52*(3), 322–352.

Aljadeff-Abergel, E., Schenk, Y., Walmsley, C., Peterson, S. M., Frieder, J. E., & Acker, N. (2015). The effectiveness of self-management interventions for children with autism – A literature review. *Research in Autism Spectrum Disorders, 18*, 34–50.

American Psychiatric Association. (2013). *Diagnostic and statistical manual for mental disorders* (5th ed.). American Psychiatric Publishing.

Anderson, A. H., Carter, M., & Stephenson, J. (2018). Perspectives of university students with autism spectrum disorder. *Journal of Autism and Developmental Disorders, 48*, 651–665.

Anderson, A. H., Carter, M., & Stephenson, J. (2020a). An on-line survey of university students with autism spectrum disorder in Australia and New Zealand: Characteristics, support satisfaction, and advocacy. *Journal of Autism and Developmental Disorders, 50*(2), 440–454.

Anderson, A. H., Stephenson, J., & Carter, M. (2020b). Perspectives of former students with ASD from Australia and New Zealand on their university experience. *Journal of Autism and Developmental Disorders, 50*, 2886–2901.

Ashbaugh, K., Koegel, R., & Koegel, L. (2017). Increasing social integration for college students with autism spectrum disorder. *Behavior Development Bulletin, 22*, 183–196.

Bakker, D., & Rickard, N. (2018). Engagement in mobile phone app for self-monitoring of emotional wellbeing predicts changes in mental health: MoodPrism. *Journal of Affective Disorders, 227*, 432–442.

Beaver, B. N., Reeve, S. A., Reeve, K. F., & DeBar, R. M. (2017). Self-reinforcement compared to teacher-delivered reinforcement during activity schdules on the iPod touch. *Education and Training in Autism and Developmental Disabilities, 52*(4), 393–404.

Becker, S. P., Jarrett, M. A., Luebbe, A. M., Garner, A. A., Bruns, G. L., & Kofler, M. J. (2018). Sleep in a large, multi-university sample of college students: Sleep problem prevalence, sex differences, and mental health correlates. *Sleep Health, 4*(2), 174–181.

Bouck, E. C., Savage, M., Meyer, N. K., Taber-Doughty, T., & Hunley, M. (2014). High-tech or low-tech? Comparing self-monitoring systems to increase task independence for students with autism. *Focus on Autism and Other Developmental Disabilities, 29*(3), 156–167.

Briesch, A. M., Daniels, B., & Beneville, M. (2018). Unpacking the term "self-management": Understanding intervention applications within the school-based literature. *Journal of Behavioral Education.* https://doi.org/10.1007/s10864-018-9303-1

Buron, K. D., & Curtis, M. (2004). *The incredible 5-point scale: Assisting students with autism spectrum disorders in understanding social interactions and controlling their emotional responses.* AAPC Publishing.

Buron, K. D., & Curtis, M. (2012). *The incredible 5-point scale: The significantly improved and expanded second edition: Assisting students in understanding social interactions and controlling their emotional responses.* AAPC Publishing.

Buron, K. D., Brown, J. T., Curtis, M., & King, L. (2012). *Social behaviour and self-management: 5-point scales for adolescents and adults.* AAPC Publishing.

Carr, M. E. (2016). Self-management of challenging behaviors associated with autism spectrum disorder: A meta-analysis. *Australian Psychologist, 51*, 316–333.

Chao, P. (2018). Using self-determination of senior college students with disabilities to predict their quality of life one year after graduation. *European Journal of Educational Research, 7*, 1–8.

Cheak-Zamora, N. C., Teti, M., Maurer-Batjer, A., O'Connor, K. V., & Randolph, J. K. (2019). Sexual and relationship interest, knowledge, and experiences among adolescents and young adults with autism spectrum disorder. *Archives of Sexual Behavior, 48*, 2605–2615.

Croen, L. A., Zerbo, O., Qian, Y., Massolo, M. L., Rich, S., Sidney, S., & Kripke, C. (2015). The health status of adults on the autism spectrum. *Autism, 19*(7), 814–823. https://doi.org/10.1177/1362361315577517

Cullen, J. M., & Alber-Morgan, S. R. (2015). Technology mediated self-prompting of daily living skills for adolescents and adults with disabilities: A review of the literature. *Education and Training in Autism and Developmental Disabilities, 50*, 43–55.

Dewinter, J., Graaf, H. D., & Begeer, S. (2017). Sexual orientation, gender identity, and romantic relationships in adolescents and adults with autism spectrum disorder. *Journal of Autism and Developmental Disorders, 47*, 2927–2934.

Di Rezze, B., Nguyen, T., Mulvale, G., Barr, N. G., Longo, C. J., & Randall, G. E. (2016). A scoping review of evaluated interventions addressing developmental transitions for youth with mental health disorders. *Child: Care, Health & Development, 42*(2), 176–187. https://doi.org/10.1111/cch.12306

Dineen-Griffin, S., Garcia-Cardenas, V., Williams, K., & Benrimoj, S. (2019). Helping patients help themselves: A systematic review of self-management support strategies in primary health care practice. *PLoS One, 14*(8), 1–29.

Dixon, M. R., & McKeel, A. N. (2011). *Self-management. Teaching and behavior support for children and adults with autism spectrum disorder: A practitioner's guide*. Oxford University Press.

Ferguson, H., Smith Myles, B., & Hagiwara, T. (2005). Using a personal digital assistant to enhance the independence of an adolescent with asperger syndrome. *Education and Training in Developmental Disabilities, 40*, 60–67.

Francis, G. L., Duke, J. M., Kliethermes, A., Demetro, K., & Graff, H. (2018). Apps to support a successful transition to college for students with ASD. *Teaching Exceptional Children, 48*(5), 225–231.

Gear, S., Bobzien, J., Judge, S., & Raver, S. A. (2011). Teaching social skills to enhance work performance in a child care setting. *Education and Training in Autism and Developmental Disabilities, 46*(1), 40–51.

Gentry, T., Kriner, R., Sima, A., McDonough, J., & Wehman, P. (2015). Reducing the need for personal supports among workers with autism using an ipod touch as an assistive technology: Delayed randomized control trial. *Journal of Autism and Developmental Disorders, 45*, 669–684.

Getzel, E. E. (2014). Fostering Self-Determination in Higher Education: Identifying Evidence-Based Practices. *Journal of Postsecondary Education and Disability, 27*(4), 381–386.

Harmsen, I. E. (2019). Empathy in autism spectrum disorder. *Journal of Autism and Developmental Disorders, 49*, 3939–3955.

Hart, D., Grigal, M., & Weir, C. (2010). Expanding the paradigm: Postsecondary education options for individuals with autism spectrum disorder and intellectual disabilities. *Focus on Autism and Other Developmental Disabilities, 25*(3), 134–150.

Hendrickson, J. M., Woods-Groves, S., Rodgers, D. B., & Datchuk, S. (2017). Perceptions of students with autism and their parents: The college experience. *Education and Treatment of Children, 40*(4), 571–596.

Hewitt, L. E. (2011). Perspectives on support needs of individuals with autism spectrum disorders. Transition to college. *Topics in Language Disorders, 31*(3), 273–285.

Hume, K., Loftin, R., & Lantz, J. (2009). Increasing independence in autism spectrum disorders: A review of three focused interventions. *Journal of Autism and Developmental Disorders, 39*(9), 1329–1338.

Jaime, K., & Knowlton, E. (2007). Visual supports for students with behavior and cognitive challenges. *Intervention in School and Clinic, 42*(5), 259–270.

Jovevska, S., Richdale, A. L., Lawson, L. P., Uljarevic, M., Arnold, S. R. C., & Trollor, J. N. (2020). Sleep quality in autism from adolescence to old age. *Autism in Adulthood, 2*(2), 152–162.

Karcher, M. J., & Berger, J. R. M. (2017). *One-to-one cross-aged peer mentoring; National mentoring resource center model review*. National Mentoring Resource Center. Retrieved from https://nationalmentoringresourcecenter.org/index.php/component/k2/item/432-one-to-one-cross-age-peer-mentoring.html

Kattari, S. (2020). Ableist microaggressions and the mental health of disabled adults. *Community Mental Health Journal, 56*, 1170–1179.

Kinnaird, E., Norton, C., Pimblett, C., Stewart, C., & Tchanturia, K. (2019). Eating as an autistic adult: An exploratory qualitative study. *PLoS One, 14*(8), e0221937. https://doi.org/10.1371/journal.pone.0221937

Koegel, L. K., Park, M. N., & Koegel, R. L. (2014). Using self-management to improve the reciprocal social conversation of children with autism spectrum disorder. *Journal of Autism and Developmental Disorders, 44*, 1055–1063.

Koegel, K., Ashbaugh, K., Navab, A., & Koegel, R. L. (2015). Improving empathic communication skills in adults with autism spectrum disorder. *Journal of Autism and Developmental Disorders, 51*(2), 111–124.

LeViness, P., Bershad, C., Gorman, K., Braun, L., & Murray, T. (2019). The Association for University and College Counseling Center directors annual survey 2018. Chicago.

Liu, Y., Moore, D. W., & Anderson, A. (2015). Improving social skills in a child with autism spectrum disorder through self-management training. *Behaviour Change*. Retrieved from http://journals.cambridge.org/abstract_S0813483915000145

Loyd, R. J., & Brolin, D. E. (1997). *Life centered career education: Modified curriculum for individuals with moderate disabilities*. Council for Exceptional Children.

MacKenzie, A. (2018). Prejudicial stereotypes and testimonial injustice: Autism, sexuality and sex education. *International Journal of Educational Research, 89*, 110–118. https://doi.org/10.1016/j.ijer.2017.10.007

Mamiseishvili, K., & Koch, L. C. (2011). First-to-second year persistence of students with disabilities in postsecondary institutions in the United States. *Rehabilitation Counseling Bulletin, 54*(2), 93–105.

McLeod, J. D., Meanwell, E., & Hawbaker, A. (2019). The experiences of college students on the autism spectrum disorder: A comparison to their neurotypical peers. *Journal of Autism and Developmental Disorders, 49*, 2320–2336.

Molina, M. D., & Sundar, S. (2018). Can mobile apps motivate fitness tracking? A study of technological affordances and workout behaviors. *Health Communications, 35*(1), 65–74.

Muehlenhard, C. L., Humphreys, T. P., Jozkowski, K. N., & Peterson, Z. D. (2016). The complexities of sexual consent among college students: A conceptual and empirical review. *The Journal of Sex Research, 53*(4–5), 457–487.

National Council on Disability. (2003). *People with disabilities and postsecondary education*. Retrieved August 13, 2018, from http://www.ncd.gov/newsroom/publications/2003/education.htm

Newman, B., Buffington, D. M., O'Grady, M. A., & McDonald, M. (1995). Self-management of schedule following in three teenagers with autism. *Behavioral Disorders, 20*(3), 190–196.

Organization for Autism Research. (2020). *Preparing your young adult for the transition to postsecondary education*. Retrieved February 9, 2020 from https://researchautism.org/postsecondary-education/

Parker, D., & Kamps, D. (2011). Effects of task analysis and self-monitoring for children with autism in multiple social settings. *Focus on Autism and Other Developmental Disabilities, 26*(3), 131–142.

Plotner, A. J., & May, S. (2017). A comparison of the college experience for students with and without disabilities. *Journal of Intellectual Disabilities, 23*(1), 57–77.

Rahmatillah, S. U., & Mulyono, S. (2019). The relationship between the nutritional status of school-age children and their academic achievement and physical fitness levels. *Comprehensive Child and Adolescent Nursing, 42*(sup1), 147–153.

Sam, A., & AFIRM Team. (2015). *Reinforcement*. National Professional Development Center on Autism Spectrum Disorder, FPG Child Development Center, University of North Carolina. Retrieved from http://afirm.fpg.unc.edu/reinforcement

Sam, A., & AFIRM Team. (2016). *Self-management*. National Professional Development Center on Autism Spectrum Disorder, FPG Child Development Center, University of North Carolina. Retrieved from http://afirm.fpg.unc.edu/self-management

Santana, C. A., Axevedo, L. B., Cattuzzo, M. T., Hill, J. O., Andrade, L. P., & Prado, W. L. (2016). Physical fitness and academic performance in youth: A systematic review. *Scandinavian Journal of Medicine and Science in Sports, 27*(6), 579–603.

Schulze, M. A. (2016). Self-management strategies to support students with ASD. *Teaching Exceptional Children, 48*(5), 225–231.

Tipton, L. A., & Blacher, J. (2014). Brief report: Autism awareness: Views from a campus community. *Journal of Autism and Developmental Disorders, 44*(2), 477–483.

Van Hees, V., Moyson, T., & Roeyers, H. (2015). Higher education experiences of students with autism spectrum disorder: Challenges, benefits and support needs. *Journal of Autism and Developmental Disorders, 45*(6), 1673–1688.

Wilczynski, S. M. (2017). *A practical guide to finding treatments that work for people with autism*. Academic Press.

Wilczynski, S. M., Kazee, A., & Sundberg, S. (2021). *Title*. [Manuscript submitted for publication]. Department of Special Educations, Ball State University.

Wolf, D. A. P. S., Perkins, J., Butler-Barnes, S. T., & Walker, T. A., Jr. (2017). Social belonging and college retention: Results from a quasi-experimental pilot study. *Journal of College Student Development, 58*(5), 777–782.

Understanding Autistic College Students

Kathleen D. Viezel and Elizabeth Froner

Abstract Autistic adolescents and adults are planning for and attending college in record numbers. The strengths of this population make them well-suited for college; however, the paucity of empirical inquiries examining their unique characteristics and needs presents a difficulty for high school and postsecondary practitioners. This chapter synthesizes current relevant literature on Autistic college students. Topics include prevalence and outcomes, strengths, areas of cognitive functioning, and challenges often faced by these students, including academic, social, emotional, and behavioral concerns. Practical strategies based on this literature are offered where appropriate. Knowledge of Autistic college students, as well as how the college community might receive and serve these students, will help all stakeholders engage in informed practice.

Keywords Autism · College · Postsecondary education · Transition planning

Understanding Autistic College Students

High school students with autism spectrum disorder (ASD) are increasingly including college in their postsecondary transition plans. Although this represents an appropriate broadening of options for these students, the dearth of literature on Autistic college students poses a challenge for school psychologists, educators, university faculty, support staff, and other stakeholders attempting to facilitate a smooth college transition. One recent literature review (Gelbar et al., 2014) found only 20 peer-reviewed journal articles examining firsthand experiences of and services for Autistic college students. Additionally, the average sample size of the included studies was less than 5, and the largest sample size was 12. Although the pool of research has increased somewhat in the few years following Gelbar et al.'s (2014) review, this area of inquiry is still emerging, and empirical investigations still typically include small samples and/or are limited to participants from one institution.

K. D. Viezel (✉) · E. Froner
School of Psychology and Counseling, Fairleigh Dickinson University, Teaneck, NJ, USA
e-mail: viezel@fdu.edu

© Springer Nature Switzerland AG 2022
K. D. Viezel et al. (eds.), *Postsecondary Transition for College- or Career-Bound Autistic Students*, https://doi.org/10.1007/978-3-030-93947-2_7

This chapter will review and synthesize the literature available on Autistic college students in order to help practitioners engage in informed practice. Knowledge of the actual characteristics and needs of Autistic college students is important for policy and intervention implementation, as those based on stereotypes or popular media representations of autism promote ableism and potentially harmful educational environments (Brown, 2017). Specifically, research supports that disabled students are more willing to utilize available accommodations when faculty members display positive attitudes towards disability (Hartman-Hall & Haaga, 2002). However, other research highlights that oftentimes college and university faculty are unaware of the accommodation process and disability support services in general (Bolt et al., 2011). Although the primary goal of this chapter is increased knowledge and understanding, practical tips for practitioners based on the literature available as well as the authors' clinical experience are offered to help address challenges Autistic college students may face.

Prevalence and Success of College Students with ASD

The rise in diagnoses of ASD is a well-known phenomenon. Currently, the Center for Disease Control (CDC)'s Autism and Developmental Disabilities Monitoring (ADDM) Network estimates 1 in 59 8-year-old children have ASD, with males four times as likely to carry the diagnosis as females (Baio et al., 2018). There are a handful of hypothesized reasons as to why ASD diagnoses have been on the rise. Most notably is the increase in sensitivity amongst diagnostic tools. This improvement in diagnostic tools may be attributed to the standardization of the diagnostic process following the 1987 publication of the DSM III-R and as a result those with high-functioning autism, previously known as Asperger's, are more easily identified (Zylstra et al., 2014). Less is known, however, about the number of Autistic older adolescents and young adults who are attending college. Prevalence rates are hard to estimate, a problem which is likely complicated by students' reluctance to disclose the disability (Cai & Richdale, 2016) and the institutions themselves (rightly) not asking current or potential students about disability status. Researchers do, however, tend to agree that this number is on the rise. This is unsurprising given the general increase in ASD diagnoses coupled with better understanding of the disorder and improved school-based interventions for younger children. Indeed, Autistic students represent one of the fastest-growing demographics on college campuses (Cox, 2017).

Despite the lack of a completely accurate prevalence rate, some data is useful when estimating the extent of the rise of Autistic college students. Extrapolation from prevalence data of autism diagnoses in children suggests that by 2020 there could be as many as 433,000 Autistic students in college (Cox, 2017). White et al. (2011) examined the prevalence of ASD symptomology in undergraduates at a large, public, southeastern university. Out of 667 participants, 13 (1.9%) met the cutoff criteria for clinically significant self-reported Autistic traits. A subset of eight students who met this initial cutoff participated in further diagnostic testing with a clinical psychologist, and five met full diagnostic criteria according to the *DSM-IV-TR*. Overall, the authors estimated between 0.7 and 1.9 percent of college students could meet criteria for ASD. This is not an insignificant proportion of college students, as it indicates between 1 in 130 to 1 in 53 students enrolled have ASD (White et al., 2011). This is fairly consistent with the CDC's recent 1 in 59 estimate. Interestingly, none of the five students identified as having ASD in White et al.'s (2011) study had been previously diagnosed, further evidencing that prevalence rates are likely underestimates, and suggests university support personnel, such as counseling center and disability services staff, should be familiar with intervention strategies effective for Autistic students regardless of whether a significant portion of the student body is formally diagnosed.

A discussion of the prevalence of ASD on college campuses should be conducted in the context of students with disabilities in general. Results from the National Longitudinal Transition Study-2 (NLTS2), funded by the US Department of Education, reveal that 60% of young adults with disabilities entered into postsecondary education within 8 years of leaving high school, with more entering community college than a traditional 4-year college. However, type of disability mattered. For Autistic students, 43.9% enrolled in some type of postsecondary school, which is less than any disability category with the exception of intellectual disability and multiple disabilities (Newman et al., 2011). Although this suggests Autistic students may be underrepresented in postsecondary settings, high school level practitioners working with Autistic students should be adequately prepared to help a sizable portion of their caseload transition to college. Up to 8 years after high school, 32.2% of Autistic students enrolled at a community or 2-year college, and 17.4% had matriculated in a traditional 4-year college. Additionally, 21% had enrolled in a vocational, business, or technical school (numbers total more than 100% due to some students experiencing multiple types of schools; Newman et al., 2011). This is consistent with estimates derived from surveys of postsecondary institutions; enrollment of students with documented ASD seems to be greatest at two-year public institutions, followed by four-year public institutions, followed by four-year private institutions (Brown, 2017).

Of course, enrollment does not guarantee graduation or other indicators of success. Indeed, some preliminary findings indicate that for Autistic students educational and vocational disruption in the years immediately following high school is common (Taylor & Dawalt, 2017). Students with disabilities complete postsecondary programs at a rate less than that of their similarly aged classmates (41% vs 52%), and Autistic students reported a completion rate of 38.8 (Newman et al., 2011), suggesting this growing population would benefit from increased understanding and support from postsecondary educational settings. Although reasons for withdrawal are not completely understood, failing classes and choosing to leave may be two common reasons, both of which may be due to inadequate supports (Taylor & Dawalt, 2017). Indeed, appropriate accommodations may be lacking; for example, although Autistic students are more likely to attend two-year than four-year colleges, these institutions generally do not provide a greater level of support to Autistic students (Brown, 2017). Additionally, practitioners may not include other stakeholders in the supports they do offer; specifically, many interventions focus solely on the student. In a study examining post-high school educational and employment stability, Taylor and Dawalt (2017) found no individual differences between Autistic students who remained in a postsecondary educational or vocational setting and those who experienced a disruption, including IQ, adaptive behavior, autism severity, behavior problems, or stress reactivity. However, there were differences in parent characteristics. Parents of the Autistic young adults who had an educational or vocational disruption had higher self-reported depression and anxiety and a lower quality of life while their child was in high school as compared to parents of children who maintained postsecondary stability. Although this study did not report any potential differences between individuals or families who elected educational versus vocational paths, these preliminary results suggest high school and college-level practitioners should be vigilant for transition-related difficulties, and consider family and other ecological factors when designing transition plans.

There is some emerging evidence that when provided with appropriate transitional support Autistic college students can achieve a graduation rate similar to that of the general population of their University (Viezel et al., 2017). Similarly, students who participated in a two-year full-time certificate program for individuals with developmental disabilities at a large University reported positive experiences and skills related to student life on campus, emotional adjustment, independent living skills, interpersonal relationships, and self-advocacy after their first and last semesters of their program, as did their parents (Hendrickson et al., 2017). However, due to small sample size and limited generalizability of both of these studies, success of Autistic students is an area of research which necessitates continuation.

Strengths of Autistic College Students

It is important to recognize that Autistic college students present with several strengths, and should not be conceptualized as a group of students solely comprising a host of difficulties. Additionally, when considering both strengths and areas of need, practitioners and administrations should remember Autistic students represent a heterogeneous population, and individuals should be considered as such, and not simply as a member of a group. There are, however, population trends recognized by emerging research which may assist support personnel working with Autistic students. Educating college stakeholders about strengths of Autistic students may help increase acceptance of and positive attitudes towards neurodiverse individuals in administration, faculty, and staff.

Some diagnostic features of ASD may indeed contribute to success in an academic environment. For some students, a desire for rules and routine could contribute to successful scholastic behaviors such as coming to class and appointments on time and meeting academic deadlines (Gobbo & Shmulsky,

2014). Notably, having heightened/focused areas of interest may be helpful for obtaining higher education and make classes enjoyable, particularly if graduate school is a goal. Adults with ASD who participated in college have reported enjoying exploring academic subjects, which sometimes developed into continued special interests (Wiorkowski, 2015). Faculty have observed that passionate areas of interest not only contribute to success in related academic areas, but this expertise can also contribute to ability to inform peers about interesting topics (Gobbo & Shmulsky, 2014). Unlike curriculum restrictions that are typically present in earlier education, college students have a higher level of autonomy when selecting a major and which classes to enroll in each semester. Many postsecondary educational institutions offer a wide variety of courses and areas of study, allowing students to focus their academic efforts on subjects that are of interest. Research examining the Special Interest Motivation Scale (SIMS), developed by Roth et al. in 2013, supports that special areas of interest motivate Autistic individuals to learn, engage in experiences, increase a sense of achievement, and are associated with increased confidence and a positive sense of self (Grove et al., 2015).

Additionally, some Autistic individuals present with a strong desire to be correct, which can be beneficial in the classroom via motivating students to seek answers and attend to details. In general, analyzing details with accuracy could be a strength for Autistic students, particularly in preliminary classes which require rote memorization (Gobbo & Shmulsky, 2014). Indeed, Autistic students often have the capacity to do quite well academically. White et al. (2011) found that in a large sample of undergraduate students, those with more self-reported symptoms of ASD s had better GPAs than students with fewer symptoms. Both parents and University personnel have recognized intelligence as a strength in this population (Dymond et al., 2017).

Another strength Autistic college students bring to postsecondary settings is a desire for socialization, which is coupled with improved social abilities (Wiorkowski, 2015). College may present opportunities for higher-quality social interaction compared to those available in earlier education. Autistic students have reported they felt more accepted in college than in high school, and social interactions were generally better, likely due to increased maturity level of their peers and greater acceptance of diversity in general (Wiorkowski, 2015). Autistic college students attributed some of their social growth to opportunities and demands of the college environment, such as completing group projects (Wiorkowski, 2015). This suggests that, in at least some cases, students should be supported in completing class exercises which require socialization, rather than these requirements being waived altogether. For example, when assigning group projects, college professors may use strategies to assist in forming groups as opposed to letting students self-select group members, such as predetermining groups or forming groups based on seating arrangements.

Cognitive Abilities

School psychologists and other educational personnel may be interested in the cognitive abilities of transition-aged Autistic students, and understanding the strengths and weaknesses of this population can help with postsecondary transition planning. There are a few facets of cognitive abilities particularly relevant to Autistic students, including intelligence, executive functioning, and theory of mind.

Intelligence A significant proportion of Autistic students have the intellectual capacity for college. Studies have indicated over half of those with ASD present without intellectual disability (e.g., Matthews et al., 2015a, b) and approximately 44% of those with ASD have IQs above 85 (Baio et al., 2018). Although such prevalence rates are commonly derived from a pediatric sample, there is some suggestion that individuals with "high-functioning" ASD (e.g., Asperger Syndrome) have a full-scale IQ (FSIQ) which is stable from adolescence to adulthood (Cederlund et al., 2010). To date, there are no peer-reviewed published studies examining the cognitive abilities of Autistic college students.

Practitioners, and school psychologists in particular, may be interested in looking beyond FSIQ when considering the needs of college (or college-seeking) Autistic students. Full assessment recommendations are offered elsewhere in this volume; however, selected results from relevant studies examining the cognitive profiles of Autistic individuals are offered here. Particularly relevant for this chapter, cognitive profiles of those with ASD may differ by overall ability level; in other words, those without intellectual disability may have different ipsative strengths and weaknesses than those who have intellectual disabilities (Matthews et al., 2015a, b). There are conflicting results regarding whether those with ASD but without intellectual delay have better verbal or nonverbal abilities. One analysis of 100 Swedish males with Asperger Syndrome (AS) and an IQ above 70 found that more than half had significantly higher (15 or more points) verbal than nonverbal IQs at the time of diagnosis in adolescence. However, upon repeat testing in adulthood, this proportion had reduced to fewer than 20% (Cederlund et al., 2010). This conflicts with findings of a younger sample of children and adolescents with ASD, which found youth both with and without intellectual disability had stronger performance on nonverbal rather than verbal tasks (Matthews et al., 2015a, b). These divergent findings may be due to age, changes in diagnoses (e.g., collapsing Asperger Disorder into ASD), different measurement tools, or simply the heterogenic nature of ASD. However, results from the Matthews, Pollard, et al. (2015a, b) study (which replicated and expanded upon the work of Coolican et al., [2008]) offers some practical information for those working with students for whom college is a goal. Notably, the personal nonverbal visual-spatial reasoning strengths many practitioners may expect to see in a student with autism may not appear in those without intellectual disability. Additionally, abbreviated IQ scores may be higher than an FSIQ, at least on the Stanford-Binet Intelligence Scales (Roid, 2003). Finally, if practitioners are interested in further examining the research on cognitive profiles of those with ASD, analyzing results by groups of individuals with similar overall intellectual ability may be more useful than by groups determined by the presence or absence of a language delay.

Executive Functioning Executive functions are those cognitive abilities required for metacognitive control and direction of mental actions, and allow an individual to pursue self-serving behavior (Lezak et al., 2004). Autistic individuals frequently display difficulties with executive functioning, including planning, flexibility, and inhibition (Hill, 2004). The link between executive functioning and social functioning in school-age children with ASD is also notable. This research suggests that the ability to switch inhibitions is associated with social functioning, indicating youth who are better able to control themselves and self-regulate have more opportunities to engage with peers (Freeman et al., 2017).

The scant literature available about the executive functions of Autistic college students is primarily focused on stakeholder reports (rather than direct assessment), and students, parents, and college personnel consistently report problems with executive functioning in this population (Cai & Richdale, 2016; Dymond et al., 2017; White et al., 2016). These difficulties include organization, time management, and problem-solving. Factors that lead to disorganization could include lack of interest in subject matter, distractibility, and difficulty multitasking. Autistic students might also take more time to process new information, making completing classwork on time difficult (Cai & Richdale, 2016). Because many college students have less daily support from teachers and family members than they did in high school, executive functioning difficulties may be more apparent, emphasizing the need for students to participate in interventions designed to teach them to self-manage and remediate skill deficits. For example, students may need to be taught how to schedule their time on a daily basis, organize class work, and self-monitor attention to lectures.

Theory of Mind The term "theory of mind" was first used by Premack and Woodruff (1978) and refers to an individual's ability to attribute a mental state to themselves or others. Theory of mind is typically assessed via asking subjects to identify the thoughts and feelings of other people (Richman & Bidshahri, 2018), and is often noted as a potential deficit in Autistic individuals, based largely on the works of Simon Baron-Cohen and colleagues. Youth and young adults with high-functioning ASD also have difficulty with theory of mind tasks, especially when these tasks are advanced and require understanding of indirect or nonliteral communication (e.g., Mathersul et al., 2013; Pedreño et al., 2017). It should be noted some individuals with high-functioning ASD may not demonstrate difficulty with the theoretical principals of theories of mind, although they may encounter problems in real-world scenarios (Scheeren et al., 2013).

Impairments in theory of mind have specific connotations for college students. Difficulty with perspective-taking may, for instance, negatively affect student–professor interactions. A hypothetical example (based on the clinical experiences of the first author) offers an illustration. Unlike in high school, college professors may not confront a late student, although such lateness may impact participation grades or their perception of the motivation or commitment of the student. A student with ASD who arrives late due to an unexpected difficulty may not realize the professor might attribute negative student characteristics to the lateness and not offer an explanation when one is not requested.

Theory of mind may also explain difficulty with peer interactions. Autistic college students may have difficulty with physical boundaries, such as coming too close in conversation (Gobbo & Shmulsky, 2014). The propensity to speak or walk too closely to peers could spark feelings of discomfort or even fear in the other student, while the Autistic student may not consider this perspective. Finally, theory of mind could explain some academic difficulties in college, such as difficulty understanding the perspective of literary characters or writing for a hypothetical audience (e.g., not themselves or the professor [Gobbo & Shmulsky, 2014]). This is consistent with preliminary research that suggests theory of mind deficits (e.g., difficulties with perspective-taking, anticipating the reader's needs, understanding social environments, and pragmatic difficulties) may explain the propensity for adults with high-functioning autism to write shorter, lower-quality narrative and expository passages than neurotypical peers (Brown & Klein, 2011).

Social, Emotional, and Behavioral Challenges

Faculty and staff in high schools and colleges may underestimate the effects of potential social, emotional, and behavioral challenges of college-seeking Autistic students. At the high school level, transition plans may be overly focused on the academic readiness of high-functioning students with ASD, while social and mental health needs are not adequately addressed. If students get good grades, these other areas of need might be overlooked, resulting in overconfidence in the student's ability to succeed in college (Anderson & Butt, 2017). This trend often continues when students matriculate into postsecondary programs, as colleges may be less prepared to deal with the social/emotional than academic challenges of this population (Vanbergeijk et al., 2008). In one study analyzing the experiences of Australian Autistic college students, it was reported that their academic needs were met; however, their social needs were neglected (Cai & Richdale, 2016). These needs could be significant; ASD symptomology in college students is positively correlated with feelings of social anxiety, depression, and feelings of anger/aggression (White et al., 2011). Lack of appropriate prevention and intervention services can have significant consequences. Although their sample size was somewhat small (18 students), Anderson & Butt (2017) found a sizable proportion (28%) of Autistic students who attempted 2- or 4-year college experienced a significant mental health crisis while enrolled. The following sections detail the potential social, emotional, and behavioral challenges of Autistic college students so as to better inform transition plans and other services for both high school and college-level students.

Social Challenges As deficits in social skills are a hallmark of ASD (American Psychiatric Association, 2013), it is unsurprising that social difficulties are common for Autistic college students. Indeed, social challenges of college and college-seeking Autistic students are reported by parents, school personnel, and students themselves (White et al., 2016), although in some cases, family may be more aware of and concerned about social needs than the student is (Cai & Richdale, 2016). In one small study, parents of Autistic male college students and university personnel indicated deficits in social skills led to difficulties in initiating and maintaining friendships (Dymond et al., 2017). Specific skill deficits of this population may include problems with listening, communicating, and cooperating effectively, following too closely, or bringing up topics inappropriate to the situation in an effort to make friends (Miele et al., 2018; White et al., 2016). College students who display rigidity, preference for sameness, and a high attention to detail may have fewer friendships, and friendships they do form may not be lasting. They may also be less likely to have a best friend (Jobe & White, 2007).

Whether or not Autistic college students desire to meet new people depends on the individual (Cullen, 2015), but those working with this population should not assume Autistic students do not want interpersonal attachments (Faso et al., 2016). White et al. (2011) found most college students with significant ASD symptomology reported a desire for social relationships; indeed, this desire was no different from a matched comparison group without ASD traits. Autistic college students who do want social connections, but have difficulty doing so, may encounter communication and social barriers, need assistance with finding places to meet others with similar interests, or be fearful of being taken advantage of or not being accepted (Cullen, 2015; Wiorkowski, 2015). Students may also feel they need to choose to focus on academic success instead of exploring social opportunities (Wiorkowski, 2015). Some Autistic college students have reported their social needs were often met through family, classmates, and school activities, and social media. (Cullen, 2015).

College represents a time period for a young adult to expand social relationships, not only with friendships, but with roommates or romantic partnerships. A few studies have examined these relationship dynamics in undergraduate students who display a broad autism phenotype (BAP), meaning that although they may not have autism diagnoses, they have characteristics similar to those who do. Faso et al. (2016) examined the effects of BAP on newly formed college roommate relationships. Although rigid personality and pragmatic language abnormalities had little effect, level of aloofness of the individuals was important. Interestingly, the presence of aloofness itself was not predictive of relationship satisfaction, but match on this character trait was. In other words, when both members of the dyad were aloof (or not aloof), the roommates could be satisfied with the relationship. However, if one was aloof and one was not, there was increased relationship dissatisfaction.

Autistic college students may or may not want a roommate, and sometimes report that rather than causing isolation having a single room can provide a place of "retreat," allowing the student to better engage socially in other settings (Wiorkowski,

2015). If the student does have a roommate, it seems that personality type match may be important. Discussions about the pros and cons of having a roommate should be part of transition planning for college-bound Autistic students. The clinical experience of the first author suggests that, if possible, having a single room within a suite can provide Autistic college students with a desired private space yet prevent isolation due to interaction with suitemates. Given the research on the importance of personality matches, college-level residence life departments may wish to consider these variables (e.g., levels of desire for social interaction) when making roommate assignments.

Lamport and Turner (2014) examined romantic relationships, and found a positive correlation between BAP (particularly pragmatic language difficulties) and attachment anxiety and avoidance in a sample of undergraduate students. In the case of attachment avoidance, but not anxious attachment, this relationship was mediated by empathy. Overall, college students with Autistic traits were less likely to have secure romantic attachments. Jobe and White (2007) found that students with higher autism characteristics had longer romantic partnerships, perhaps due to preference for sameness and routine. However, only sustained friendships (not romances) was a protective factor against loneliness (Jobe & White, 2007), perhaps due to low romantic relationship quality or satisfaction, which was not directly investigated. College-level practitioners are urged to avoid shying away from romantic and sexual psychoeducation for Autistic clients. The reader is further directed to *The Need for Relationship and Sexuality Education & Transition Aged Youth with ASD* (this volume).

Emotional Challenges Autistic individuals have unique emotional challenges, perhaps caused by high levels of emotional arousal, a lack of emotional control, and/or a lack of effective coping strategies (Zantinge et al., 2017). High-functioning adolescents and adults with ASD may have high frequencies of depression, as well as significant Attention-Deficit/Hyperactivity Disorder symptomology, particularly inattention (Cederlund et al., 2010; Hofvander et al., 2009). Indeed, depression and feelings of loneliness and isolation seem to be common amongst Autistic college students (Gelbar et al., 2014), as well as challenges with emotional regulation (White et al., 2016). Postsecondary personnel have also observed that Autistic students have difficulty with emotional independence; in other words, they may be more reliant on family than their neurotypical peers (White et al., 2016). In addition to these challenges, anxiety is a significant concern.

Anxiety Transitioning to college can be a stressful time for any student, regardless of disability status. There are, however, special considerations for Autistic students. In a study of 122 Swedish and Parisian adults with high-functioning autism, anxiety disorders, particularly OCD, were common comorbidities (Hofvander et al., 2009). Indeed, anxiety is an overwhelmingly common reported experience of Autistic college students, and is perhaps the most prevalent emotional difficulty of this population (Gelbar et al., 2014). Feelings of stress and anxiety in Autistic students are reported by students themselves and are observed by their parents and university faculty and staff (Cai & Richdale, 2016; Dymond et al., 2017; Gobbo & Shmulsky, 2014; White et al., 2016).

Some diagnostic features of ASD could be contributing factors to anxiety in college or college-seeking students. Difficulties with transitions is diagnostic of ASD (American Psychiatric Association, 2013), and interviews with students and parents suggest the upcoming transition to college can manifest in significant increases in anxiety (Anderson & Butt, 2017). The future-oriented mindset of the college environment (e.g., picking a major, postcollege planning), while exciting for some, can also cause anxiety for Autistic students (Wiorkowski, 2015). Similarly, changes in routine presented by examinations can exacerbate normal test anxiety in Autistic college students (Vanbergeijk et al., 2008). Stress also may be magnified by an inadequate social network, which could serve as a protective factor for neurotypical students. For Autistic students, their social needs might have been primarily met through family interaction, which may decrease when students enroll in college (Glennon, 2001).

Gobbo and Shmulsky (2014) conducted and analyzed focus groups of faculty who taught Autistic students at a small New England liberal arts college focused on students with special needs. Results shed light on the potential impact anxiety experienced by Autistic students has on classroom and academic functioning. Faculty reported that student anxiety interfered with class work and increased when classroom social demands were present. Additionally, anxiety seemed to increase other ASD symptomology that can interfere with successful performance; for example, perseveration, rigidity, and social withdrawal (Gobbo & Shmulsky, 2014). The interaction between anxiety and academics is further highlighted by the finding that self-reported symptoms of anxiety are greatly reduced when appropriate academic supports are in place (Cai & Richdale, 2016).

Given the prevalence of anxiety among Autistic college students, and its impact on social, emotional, and academic functioning, college-level support personnel (e.g., those working in counseling centers or for an ASD support program) should be prepared to deliver appropriate anxiety-reducing interventions for both occasional and chronic anxiety. These could range from development and promotion of quiet relaxation areas, college-wide psychoeducation about stress and anxiety, to individual therapy for students. Similarly, those working with transition-aged students should inquire about these supports in colleges they are considering, even if the individual student has not previously had significant difficulty with anxiety.

Behavioral Challenges Uninformed members of the college community may be fearful that Autistic students will present with significant, or even violent, behavioral problems. However, it is important to remember that those with psychological disabilities, including autism, are more likely to be victims, not perpetrators, of violence (e.g., Autistic Self Advocacy Network, n.d.). In one study, White et al. (2011) found no differences between undergraduates with either high or low ASD symptomology in self-reported victimization nor aggressive behavior towards others. Of particular interest to those working in a college setting, Autistic adolescents and adults with typical intelligence may also be no more likely to abuse substances than the general population (Hofvander et al., 2009). Overall, behavioral problems are rarely a prominent theme in the literature examining the self- or other (e.g., parent, educators) -reported experiences of Autistic college students. There are, however, some considerations worth noting. If student codes of conduct are not concrete or specific, Autistic students may have some difficulty following rules. Additionally, if a student with ASD violates a code of conduct, either knowingly or unknowingly, their disability status may not protect them from disciplinary actions due to the Americans with Disabilities Act's (ADA) "otherwise qualified" standard (Miele et al., 2018). Some protections may be possible. Specifically, if an Autistic student is facing conduct proceedings, they could have an advocate familiar with ASD, and if they receive university-granted accommodations, such as a notetaker or extra breaks, these accommodations should be honored during the hearing process (Miele et al., 2018).

Self-Care When considering the behavioral skills of Autistic college students, those involving self-care or self-advocacy may be most relevant for intervention planning. Research has demonstrated that age is negatively correlated with adaptive behavior standard scores in Autistic individuals. In other words, as these students get older, the adaptive skills gap between them and their neurotypical peers widen, and this phenomenon is particularly observed in higher-functioning individuals (e.g., Kanne et al., 2011; Matthews et al., 2015a, b). The scant research in the daily living skills of Autistic students supports this concern. Students have reported difficulty with daily living skills, including functional skills and prioritizing daily tasks (Cullen, 2015). Students may also struggle with independent living skills such as getting ready in the morning and taking medications without prompts or reminders (Dymond et al., 2017).

Self-advocacy skills are well-summarized in another chapter in this volume (see *Self-Management for Transition-Aged College-Bound Autistic Students*), but some information particularly relevant to Autistic college students will be briefly highlighted here. Both self-advocacy and self-determination may be areas of difficulty for college and college-bound Autistic students, including setting and working towards goals and knowing how and when to ask for help (Dymond et al., 2017; White et al., 2016). These students are generally aware of the problems they experience, but may have difficulty accessing the accommodations and services designed to help them. Further complicating this problem, students may respond to stress with internalizing coping mechanisms such as daydreaming or demonstrating a flat affect, making it difficult for stakeholders to know when help is needed (Glennon, 2001).

Students often need to disclose a disability in order to access intervention services. College students may, however, be hesitant to disclose and may do so only under parent influence and/or only after a crisis (Cai & Richdale, 2016). Alternatively, high-functioning individuals may experience a lack of understanding and empathy from the college community due to the perception that their disability is not severe enough to be taken seriously (Wiorkowski, 2015). Students also report institutional barriers. For example, they may recognize accommodations are necessary, but obtaining them may be perceived as tedious or inconvenient. In general, Autistic college students may feel frustrated because of lack of assistance from the University with certain administrative tasks, such as procedures required to obtain help or select a major (Wiorkowski, 2015). At times, these students may not use accommodations and supports, even when they are available (Dymond et al., 2017).

Academic Needs

Students on the spectrum often possess a set of academic needs that differ from their neurotypical peers, but also have many scholastic strengths, including good word recognition skills, strong rote memory (Randi et al., 2010), and cognitive abilities comparable to neurotypical students (Barnhill et al., 2000). However, high school may not adequately prepare Autistic students for the academic demands of college. A small sample of Autistic adults who participated in college consistently reported different skills were needed for learning in college versus high school, and they frequently felt behind academically (Wiorkowski, 2015). Specifically, recognizing personal learning style preferences and learning in various ways (abstract discussions versus experiential learning) were cited. Other samples of Autistic college students have also reported difficulty managing a college workload (Cai & Richdale, 2016; White et al., 2016). For some students, their special education classes in high school did not adequately prepare them for college-level work, including in essential basic subjects such as math, English, and science. This resulted in students having to work harder or change their major based on their skills rather than area of interest (Wiorkowski, 2015). Those working in high schools may want to carefully examine whether college-bound Autistic students are being exposed to college-level demands at a level similar to those of neurotypical peers. Support teams should also consider whether to fade supports that would likely not be available at a traditional college (e.g., a 1:1 aide, significantly reduced workload), assuming there is evidence the student may be able to succeed without them.

Both students and faculty have reported Autistic students may have difficulty with abstract thinking and concepts, for example, symbolism in literature (Gobbo & Shmulsky, 2014; Wiorkowski, 2015). Faculty also have indicated problems with generalizing details, and with converging details into an overarching concept, lending support to the theory that Autistic college students may have weak central coherence. In other words, they might be better at processing details ("bottom up") than seeing overarching ideas and themes ("top down"; Gobbo & Shmulsky). Other academic deficits observed by college personnel and parents of Autistic students included staying focused in class, effective study skills, and turning things in by the deadline (Dymond et al., 2017).

There is a paucity of peer-reviewed literature examining the specific academic skills of Autistic college students. Indeed, almost all of the peer-reviewed literature focuses on younger students. A full review of the academic skills of Autistic individuals in general is beyond the scope of this chapter; however, below we offer a brief summary of the potential reading, writing, and math needs of Autistic college students, often generalizing and extrapolating from the research done with younger students. In addition, Autistic students face some nonacademic challenges in the classroom setting.

Reading According to O'Connor and Klein (2004), a majority of students with high-functioning autism present a mild deficit in reading comprehension. Problems in reading comprehension become most evident when Autistic students are tasked not with single word comprehension, but with more abstract pieces of writing and when grammatical complexity increases (O'Connor & Klein, 2004.) Reading comprehension is a necessary skill for success in academia, specifically higher education. Without this foundational skill, Autistic students will struggle to understand contextual information discussed in class (Flores & Ganz, 2007).

A lack of interpersonal knowledge, or the ability to understand social behavior and the social world, may negatively impact reading comprehension of Autistic students (Brown et al., 2013). Autistic individuals may not have relevant knowledge about social contexts, the mental states of themselves or others, or the general rules of society that can be used to understand text. Without this knowledge, Autistic college students may struggle to relate the material they are reading to a larger social context, which can lead to surface-level comprehension of text rather than deep, big picture thinking and understanding.

Writing As described above, deficits in theory of mind can impact writing ability for Autistic students. This is well-illustrated by a study conducted by Brown and Klein (2011), who investigated writing quality of adults with high-functioning autism. Autistic participants produced lesser quality narrative text than their neurotypical peers. One of the areas in which they struggled the most was text structure, which is an indication that Autistic individuals have difficulty successfully organizing their writing. It was also found that participants in the study had a hard time thinking globally; the stories they created did not show their ability to fit stories together as a cohesive whole. Individuals with high-functioning ASD also did not incorporate an appropriate amount of background information into their works, leaving the reader with a lack of cohesiveness (Brown & Klein, 2011). The findings from Brown and Klein's (2011) study support Tager-Flusberg's (2007) theory that those with high-functioning ASD may have writing deficits because they lack an understanding on the social world, have difficulties taking the perspective of others, and struggle with pragmatics. Autistic college students have also reported handwriting difficulties (Cai & Richdale, 2016). This is consistent with studies which have found a high prevalence of coordination difficulties in Autistic individuals. For example, Bhat (2020) reported that more than 85% of Autistic participants in their study were at risk for developmental coordination disorder (DCD), a developmental disorder that impacts individuals' motor abilities throughout their lifespan.

Mathematics Research has shown that Autistic individuals commonly do not show deficits in early mathematic skills, but may begin to struggle as math problems become more complex and require more steps to reach the answer (Kurth & Mastergeorge, 2010). Math achievement for Autistic children is highly variable, but research has shown that Autistic individuals typically perform worse on calculation and applied mathematics problems than those diagnosed with unspecified learning disabilities (King et al., 2016; Wei, Lenz, & Blackorby, 2012). There is some suggestion that when Autistic individuals attend college they are more likely to choose majors involving mathematics (Migliore et al., 2012). However, other students are not particularly drawn to hard sciences and have more interest in social science and business (Wiorkowski, 2015). Overall, even when difficulties in math persist, it does not appear to stop Autistic individuals from studying mathematics in higher education. It has also been shown that a diagnosis of autism does not automatically mean a deficit in math achievement. Almost one fourth of children in Wei et al.'s (2014) study had average or above average achievement in mathematics, despite other deficits.

Classroom Demands There are some nonacademic challenges Autistic students face in the college classroom. Due to social pragmatic difficulties inherent in autism, it is no surprise that group work is consistently cited as a challenge by students and other stakeholders (e.g., Cai & Richdale, 2016; Cullen, 2015; Gobbo & Shmulsky, 2014). Even when academically capable of the group work, students often feel they need assistance with the social interactions (Cullen, 2015), and group work can cause frustrations for both Autistic students and their neurotypical peers (Gobbo & Shmulsky, 2014). In addition to group projects, other classroom-based social interactions may be problematic. Autistic students may miss nonverbal classroom social cues or unstated social rules that result in violating academic social norms; for example, when to use computers and how to appropriately participate in a class discussion (Cai & Richdale, 2016; Gobbo & Shmulsky, 2014).

Autistic students may also experience difficulty with sensory stimuli, or struggle with the less structured nature of a college classroom (as compared to high school; Cai & Richdale, 2016). Indeed, professors have indicated that Autistic students benefit from instructional styles that are structured and provide clear expectations (Gobbo & Shmulsky, 2014), which is consistent with the first author's clinical experience. Instructors may provide specially designed instructional methods for these students, and are especially likely to do so when there is institutional support. However, if the classroom has a generally tolerant climate that is accepting of varying levels of need, there is less need for specialized techniques (Ponomaryova et al., 2018).

The College Community

There is an emerging body of research examining the knowledge of and attitudes about autism in various members of the college environment. One study primarily focusing on the college community as a whole (inclusive of undergraduates, graduate students, faculty, and staff) found promising results, with overall reasonably high knowledge of ASD (Tipton & Blacher, 2014). There were, however, still some areas of concern. For example, those who correctly acknowledged that autism diagnoses were on the rise tended to incorrectly attribute the rise in ASD to vaccinations (Tipton & Blacher, 2014). The following sections will address how peers and faculty might view Autistic students, and provide some suggestions on how various members of the campus community might contribute to improving the experience of Autistic students.

Peers Although neurotypical undergraduates may not have direct personal experience with an Autistic individual, initial evidence suggests they can be reasonably knowledgeable about and accepting of autism (Gardiner & Iarocci, 2014). When reading about a hypothetical person with ASD characteristics, undergraduates indicated the character did not cause them fear or discomfort, they would not mind living with them, would like them as a person, and viewed them as equally smart as themselves. However, less than half indicated they would choose to spend free time with the person (Gardiner & Iarocci, 2014).

The emerging literature is inconsistent regarding whether there is a difference by gender; however, when taken as a whole, it appears that male undergraduate students may be slightly more accepting of Autistic peers. For example, males have displayed more positive affective, behavioral, and cognitive attitudes towards vignette characters with ASD characteristics (Matthews, Ly, & Goldberg, 2015a). Although Nevill and White (2011) found no gender difference with regard to overall openness towards Autistic peers, males were more likely to self-report feelings of comfort and likeliness to spend free time with an Autistic person. Brosnan and Mills (2016) found males to be slightly less negative (but no more positive) than females towards students with Autistic characteristics. It is possible that male students tend to be more introverted and therefore perhaps less affected by atypical social behaviors, or that the social transgressions exhibited by vignette characters are more typical of males in general (Brosnan & Mills, 2016; Matthews, Ly, & Goldberg, 2015a). It should be noted the research is far from conclusive. Gardiner and Iarocci (2014) found no gender difference for overall acceptance of a hypothetical Autistic student. Further, female undergraduate students may have less stigma against Autistic peers (Obeid et al., 2015), and may be more likely to volunteer with an ASD-related organization (Gardiner & Iarocci, 2014). The tendency for female undergraduate students to be more likely to volunteer is consistent with the first author's clinical experience overseeing an undergraduate peer mentorship program designed to assist Autistic students. This can be problematic if same-sex pairings are desired by the Autistic student given the gender imbalance of the diagnosis. However, the literature demonstrating male students can be accepting of Autistic peers suggests recruitment strategies targeting males may be effective.

Researchers have also investigated if an undergraduate's personal experience with ASD influences acceptance of others with the disorder. Studies have fairly consistently shown that those with higher ASD symptomology themselves either have no difference in attitudes towards individuals with Autistic characteristics (Gardiner & Iarocci, 2014; Neville & White, 2011) or have less positive views (Matthews, Ly, & Goldberg, 2015a; Obeid et al., 2015). It is possible that the social and empathetic difficulties experienced by many Autistic individuals makes them less open to peers in general, and this includes those who may have similar social difficulties as themselves. Regarding an undergraduate's personal experience with another Autistic person (e.g., a friend or family member), there is some suggestion that individuals with a first-degree relative with autism demonstrate more openness than matched gender comparison group (Nevill & White, 2011), but having a family or friend with ASD may not necessarily reduce stigma (Brosnan & Mills, 2016). It seems that quality of previous contact (versus quantity) is most influential in promoting feelings of acceptance. Enjoyable interactions with an Autistic peer are important, and it is promising that most undergraduates who have had direct (e.g., not just media) exposure to a person with ASD found the experience to be positive (Gardiner & Iarocci, 2014). College practitioners could work to foster integrated social events on campus. Although online training to undergraduates can increase knowledge of ASD and lower autism-related stigma (Obeid et al., 2015), in general, it seems as if knowledge by itself is not related to actual acceptance or positive attitude (Gardiner & Iarocci, 2014; Matthews, Ly, & Goldberg, 2015a).

Autistic students may be unsure whether to disclose their diagnosis to peers. There are few studies investigating this issue directly, but the information available suggests disclosure may be beneficial. The hidden nature of the disability in high-functioning individuals may exacerbate social difficulties, as the other person may not understand why the peculiarities exist, contributing to potentially critical reactions (Glennon, 2001). Matthews, Ly, & Goldberg (2015a) presented undergraduate students with a vignette describing a person exhibiting autism characteristics. There were three conditions: the character was labeled as having high-functioning autism, as a typical college student, or had no label. When the character had the autism label, peers reported a more positive behavioral and cognitive disposition towards them than when there was no label. There was also no difference in attitudes towards the high-functioning autism label and typical label (Matthews, Ly, & Goldberg, 2015a). Similarly, Brosnan and Mills (2016) presented college students with read vignettes about a person displaying social interactions illustrative of a person with ASD. The character in the story was either described as a typical college student, a student with autism, a student with ASD, or with schizophrenia. There were no differences in positive or negative affective responses towards any of the diagnostic groups. This indicates the diagnostic label assigned to the person may not matter to undergraduates in terms of attitude towards peers. However, the responses to the person without a diagnostic label were more negative and less positive (Brosnan & Mills, 2016). Overall, it appears that students in general may be more accepting of a peer with atypical social behavior if they are aware of their diagnosis. However, it should be noted that some students may still experience direct prejudice (Wiorkowski, 2015).

Instructors There is limited research on faculty knowledge and attitudes of Autistic students. This is unfortunate, as positive relationships with instructors can help postsecondary Autistic students achieve success (Ponomaryova et al., 2018). One study found that faculty know more about autism than undergraduate students, yet had about the same level of knowledge as graduate students (Tipton & Blancher, 2014). There is some evidence that faculty are able to recognize strengths of Autistic students (Gobbo & Shmulsky, 2014; Dymond et al., 2017). Despite the fact that faculty likely have limited personal contact with Autistic individuals (Gibbons et al., 2015) and may be unaware about some issues, such as the prognosis of persons with autism, they recognize the importance of learning more about how to work with this population (White et al., 2016). More research is needed on faculty attitudes towards Autistic students. One study attempting to investigate this issue (Gibbons et al., 2015) grouped Autistic students with students with intellectual disability, limiting the utility of results for those working with college or college-bound students with high-functioning autism.

Overall, faculty training on pedagogical issues for Autistic college students is recommended. Faculty may also benefit from direct training on classroom management techniques to address some common behavioral difficulties expressed by Autistic and neurotypical students alike (i.e., inattention, conforming to classroom expectations around participation, etc.). Faculty could also participate in workshops around knowledge of disability supports in general, including their role in implementing approved accommodations.

Other College Staff A thorough review of accessing college resources and accommodations are beyond the scope of this chapter, and the reader is directed to the *Obtaining Appropriate Services in College* chapter in this volume. However, it should be noted that myriad other college staff will interface with Autistic students, including those in recruitment/admissions offices, residence life, campus security, counseling and academic service centers, and disability support. Autistic college students should be familiar with the purposes of these departments, and the associated staff may benefit from strength-based training about ASD. The chapter *Considerations for School Psychology University Faculty: Developing and Implementing Services for Students with ASD* (this volume) would be a useful resource for those interested in fostering professional development and consultation services for faculty and staff in the college community.

Conclusions

College and college-ready Autistic students present with many strengths and have the potential to be an asset to the campus community. These students are often bright, focused, and academically capable. Exposure to neurodiverse individuals could also enrich the experience of neurotypical college peers. It is unsurprising that college enrollment for Autistic students is on the rise, and both high school and college-level practitioners need to be prepared to assist this traditionally under-served population. Autistic college students present with challenges that could interfere with successful college completion and/or enjoying the college experience even if they are cognitively and academically high-functioning. Indeed, ASD symptomology is associated with an overall dissatisfaction with college (White et al., 2011). The emerging literature, while relatively scant and often dependent on small sample sizes, offers at least one consistent recommendation: effective postsecondary transition plans (e.g., Adreon, & Durocher, 2007; Anderson & Butt, 2017; Cai & Richdale, 2016; Dymond et al., 2017; Vanbergeijk et al., 2008). We encourage the reader to review other chapters in this book, including *Transition Preparation: Providing Building-Level Supports in Middle and High Schools* to assist with developing high-quality transition plans. We echo the recommendation of previous researchers that transition plans should address all needs of the student, and not focus entirely on academic readiness. Transition planning work should be shared by college, as well as high school, personnel. Finally, we encourage college personnel to carefully consider how recognizing the strengths and addressing the needs of Autistic students described in this chapter might help them not only succeed in college, but to obtain high-quality employment after degree obtainment.

References

Adreon, D., & Durocher, J. S. (2007). Evaluating the college transition needs of individuals with high-functioning autism spectrum disorders. *Intervention in School and Clinic, 42*(5), 271–279. https://doi.org/10.1177/10534512070420050201

American Psychiatric Association. (2013). *Diagnostic and statistical manual of mental disorders* (5th ed.). Author.

Anderson, C., & Butt, C. (2017). Young adults on the autism spectrum at college: Successes and stumbling blocks. *Journal of Autism and Developmental Disorders, 47*(10), 3029–3039.

Autistic Self Advocacy Network. (n.d.). *Make real change on gun violence: Stop scapegoating people with mental health disabilities.* Retrieved from: https://autisticadvocacy.org/policy/briefs/gunviolence/

Baio, J., Wiggins, L., Christensen, D. L., et al. (2018). Prevalence of autism spectrum disorder among children aged 8 years – Autism and developmental disabilities monitoring network, 11 sites, United States, 2014. *MMWR Surveill Summ 2018, 67*(SS-6), 1–23.

Barnhill, G., Hagiwara, T., Myles, B. S., & Simpson, R. (2000). Asperger syndrome: A study of the cognitive profiles of 37 children and adolescents. *Focus on Autism and Other Developmental Disabilities, 15*(3), 146–153.

Bhat, A. N. (2020). Is motor impairment in autism spectrum disorder distinct from developmental coordination disorder? A report from the SPARK study. *Physical Therapy, 100*(4), 633–644. https://doi.org/10.1093/ptj/pzz190

Bolt, S. E., Decker, D. M., Lloyd, M., & Morlock, L. (2011). Students' perceptions of accommodations in high school and college. *Career Development for Exceptional Individuals, 34*(3), 165–175. https://doi.org/10.1177/0885728811141509

Brosnan, M., & Mills, E. (2016). The effect of diagnostic labels on the affective responses of college students towards peers with 'Asperger's syndrome' and 'autism spectrum disorder.'. *Autism, 20*(4), 388–394.

Brown, K. R. (2017). Accommodations and support services for students with autism spectrum disorder (ASD): A national survey of disability resource providers. *Journal of Postsecondary Education and Disability, 30*(2), 141–156.

Brown, H. M., & Klein, P. D. (2011). Writing, Asperger syndrome and theory of mind. *Journal of Autism and Developmental Disorders, 41*, 1464–1474.

Brown, H. M., Oram-Cardy, J., & Johnson, A. (2013). A meta-analysis of the reading comprehension skills of individuals on the autism spectrum. *Journal of Autism and Developmental Disorders, 43*(4), 932–955.

Cai, R., & Richdale, A. (2016). Educational experiences and needs of higher education students with autism spectrum disorder. *Journal of Autism and Developmental Disorders, 46*(1), 31–41.

Cederlund, M., Hagberg, B., & Gillberg, C. (2010). Asperger syndrome in adolescent and young adult males. Interview, self - and parent assessment of social, emotional, and cognitive problems. *Research in Developmental Disabilities, 31*(2), 287–298.

Coolican, J., Bryson, S. E., & Zwaigenbaum, L. (2008). Brief report: Data on the Stanford-Binet intelligence scales (5th ed.) in children with autism spectrum disorder. *Journal of Autism and Developmental Disorders, 38*, 190–197.

Cox, B. E. (2017). *Autism coming to college (issue brief)*. Center for Postsecondary Success.

Cullen, J. A. (2015). The needs of college students with autism spectrum disorders and Asperger's syndrome. *Journal of Postsecondary Education and Disability, 28*(1), 89–101.

Dymond, S. K., Meadan, H., & Pickens, J. L. (2017). Postsecondary education and students with autism spectrum disorders: Experiences of parents and university personnel. *Journal of Developmental and Physical Disabilities, 29*(5), 809–825.

Faso, D. J., Corretti, C. A., Ackerman, R. A., & Sasson, N. J. (2016). The broad autism phenotype predicts relationship outcomes in newly formed college roommates. *Autism, 20*(4), 412–424.

Flores, M. M., & Ganz, J. B. (2007). Effectiveness of direct instruction for teaching statement inference, use of facts, and analogies to students with developmental disabilities and reading delays. *Focus on Autism and Other Developmental Disabilities, 22*(4), 244–251.

Freeman, L. M., Locke, J., Rotheram-Fuller, E., & Mandell, D. (2017). Brief report: Examining executive and social functioning in elementary-aged children with autism. *Journal of Autism and Developmental Disorders, 47*(6), 1890–1895.

Gardiner, E., & Iarocci, G. (2014). Students with autism spectrum disorder in the university context: Peer acceptance predicts intention to volunteer. *Journal of Autism and Developmental Disorders, 44*(5), 1008–1017.

Gelbar, N. W., Smith, I., & Reichow, B. (2014). Systematic review of articles describing experience and supports of individuals with autism enrolled in college and university programs. *Journal of Autism and Developmental Disorders, 44*, 593–2601.

Gibbons, M. M., Cihak, D. F., Mynatt, B., & Wilhoit, B. E. (2015). Faculty and student attitudes toward postsecondary education for students with intellectual disabilities and autism. *Journal of Postsecondary Education and Disability, 28*, 149–162.

Glennon, T. J. (2001). The stress of the university experience with students with Asperger syndrome. *Work: Journal of Prevention, Assessment & Rehabilitation, 17*(3), 183–190.

Gobbo, K., & Shmulsky, S. (2014). Faculty experience with college students with autism spectrum disorders: A qualitative study of challenges and solutions. *Focus on Autism & Other Developmental Disabilities, 29*(1), 13–22.

Grove, R., Roth, I., & Hoekstra, R. A. (2015). The motivation for special interests in individuals with autism and controls: Development and validation of the special interest motivation scale. *Autism Research, 9*(6), 677–688. https://doi.org/10.1002/aur.1560

Hartman-Hall, H. M., & Haaga, D. A. F. (2002). College students' willingness to seek help for their learning disabilities. *Learning Disability Quarterly, 25*, 263–274. https://doi.org/10.2307/1511357

Hendrickson, J. M., Woods-Groves, S., Rodgers, D. B., & Datchuk, S. (2017). Perceptions of students with autism and their parents: The college experience. *Education and Treatment of Children, 40*(4), 571–596.

Hill, E. L. (2004). Executive dysfunction in autism. *Trends in Cognitive Science, 8*, 1–13.

Hofvander, B., Delorme, R., Chaste, P., Nydén, A., Wentz, E., Ståhlberg, O., ... Leboyer, M. (2009). Psychiatric and psychosocial problems in adults with normal-intelligence autism spectrum disorders. *BMC Psychiatry, 9*(1). https://doi.org/10.1186/1471-244x-9-35

Jobe, L. E., & White, S. W. (2007). Loneliness, social relationships, and a broader autism phenotype in college students. *Personality and Individual Differences, 42*(8), 1479–1489.

Kanne, S. M., Gerber, A. J., Quirmbach, L. M., Sparrow, S. S., Cicchetti, D. V., & Saulnier, C. A. (2011). The role of adaptive behavior in autism spectrum disorders: Implications for functional outcome. *Journal of Autism and Developmental Disorders, 41*, 1007–1018.

King, S. A., Lemons, C. J., & Davidson, K. A. (2016). Math interventions for students with autism spectrum disorder. *Exceptional Children, 82*(4), 443–462.

Kurth, J. A., & Mastergeorge, A. M. (2010). Academic and cognitive profiles of students with autism: Implications for classroom practice and placement. *International Journal of Special Education, 25*(2), 8–14.

Lamport, D., & Turner, L. A. (2014). Romantic attachment, empathy, and the broader autism phenotype among college students. *The Journal of Genetic Psychology: Research and Theory on Human Development, 175*(3), 202–213.

Lezak, M. D., Howieson, D. B., Loring, D. W., Hannay, H. J., & Fischer, J. S. (2004). *Neuropsychological assessment* (4th ed.). Oxford University Press.

Mathersul, D., McDonald, S., & Rushby, J. A. (2013). Understanding advanced theory of mind and empathy in high-functioning adults with autism spectrum disorder. *Journal of Clinical and Experimental Neuropsychology, 35*(6), 655–668.

Matthews, N. L., Ly, A. R., & Goldberg, W. A. (2015a). College students' perceptions of peers with autism spectrum disorder. *Journal of Autism and Developmental Disorders, 45*(1), 90–99.

Matthews, N., Pollard, E., Ober-Reynolds, S., Kirwan, J., Malligo, A., & Smith, C. (2015b). Revisiting cognitive and adaptive functioning in children and adolescents with autism spectrum disorder. *Journal of Autism and Developmental Disorders, 45*(1), 138–156.

Miele, A. N., Hamrick, F. A., & Kelley, J. W. (2018). Different is not deficient: Addressing student conduct concerns among residential college students with autism spectrum disorder. *The Journal of College and University Student Housing, 44*(3), 30–45.

Migliore, A., Timmons, J., Butterworth, J., & Lugas, J. (2012). Predictors of employment and postsecondary education of youth and autism. *Rehabilitation Counseling Bulletin, 55*, 176–184. https://doi.org/10.1177/0034355212438943

Nevill, R. E. A., & White, S. W. (2011). College students' openness toward autism spectrum disorders: Improving peer acceptance. *Journal of Autism and Developmental Disorders, 41*(12), 1619–1628.

Newman, L., Wagner, M., Knokey, A.-M., Marder, C., Nagle, K., Shaver, D., Wei, X., Cameto, R., Contreras, E., Ferguson, K., Greene, S., & Schwarting, M. (2011). *The post-high school outcomes of young adults with disabilities up to 8 years after high school. A report from the National Longitudinal Transition Study-2 (NLTS2) (NCSER 2011–3005)*. SRI International.

O'Connor, I. M., & Klein, P. D. (2004). Exploration of strategies for facilitating the reading comprehension of high-functioning students with autism spectrum disorders. *Journal of Autism and Developmental Disorders, 34*(2), 115–127. https://doi.org/10.1023/b:jadd.0000022603.44077.6b

Obeid, R., Daou, N., DeNigris, D., Shane-Simpson, C., Brooks, P. J., & Gillespie-Lynch, K. (2015). A cross-cultural comparison of knowledge and stigma associated with autism spectrum disorder among college students in Lebanon and the United States. *Journal of Autism and Developmental Disorders, 45*(11), 3520–3536.

Pedreño, C., Pousa, E., Navarro, J. B., Pàmias, M., & Obiols, J. E. (2017). Exploring the components of advanced theory of mind in autism spectrum disorder. *Journal of Autism and Developmental Disorders, 47*(8), 2401–2409.

Ponomaryova, E., Guterman, H. G., Davidovitch, N., & Shapira, Y. (2018). Should lecturers be willing to teach high-functioning autistic students: What do they need to know? *Higher Education Studies, 8*(4), 35–45.

Premack, D., & Woodruff, G. (1978). Does the chimpanzee have a theory of mind? *Behavioral and Brain Sciences, 4*, 581–590.

Randi, J., Newman, T., & Grigorenko, E. L. (2010). Teaching children with autism to read for meaning: Challenges and possibilities. *Journal of Autism and Developmental Disorders, 40*(7), 890–902. https://doi.org/10.1007/s10803-010-0938-6

Richman, K. A., & Bidshahri, R. (2018). Autism, theory of mind, and the reactive attitudes. *Bioethics, 32*(1), 43–49.

Roid, G. H. (2003). *Stanford-Binet intelligence scales* (5th ed.). Riverside Publishing.

Scheeren, A. M., de Rosnay, M., Koot, H. M., & Begeer, S. (2013). Rethinking theory of mind in high-functioning autism spectrum disorder. *Journal of Child Psychology and Psychiatry, 54*(6), 628–635.

Tager-Flusberg, H. (2007). Evaluating the theory-of-mind hypothesis of autism. *Current Directions in Psychological Science, 16*, 311–315.

Taylor, J. L., & Dawalt, L. S. (2017). Brief report: Postsecondary work and educational disruptions for youth on the autism spectrum. *Journal of Autism and Developmental Disorders, 47*(12), 4025–4031.

Tipton, L. A., & Blacher, J. (2014). Brief report: Autism awareness: Views from a campus community. *Journal of Autism and Developmental Disorders, 44*(2), 477–483.

Vanbergeijk, E., Klin, A., & Volkmar, F. (2008). Supporting more able students on the autism spectrum: College and beyond. *Journal of Autism and Developmental Disorders, 38*(7), 1359–1370. https://doi.org/10.1007/s10803-007-0524-8

Viezel, K. D., Williams, E., Todd, L. E., & Cleveland, J. (2017). Supporting college students with autism. *The School Psychologist, 71*(3), 36–44.

Wei, X., Lenz, K. B., & Blackorby, J. (2012). Math growth trajectories of students with disabilities: Disability category, gender, racial, and socioeconomic status differences from ages 7 to 17. *Remedial and Special Education, 34*, 154–165.

Wei, X., Christiano, E. R. A., Yu, J. W., Wagner, M., & Spiker, D. (2014). Reading and math achievement profiles and longitudinal growth trajectories of children with an autism spectrum disorder. *Autism: The International Journal of Research and Practice, 19*, 200–210. https://doi.org/10.1177/1362361313516549

White, S. W., Ollendrick, T. H., & Bray, B. C. (2011). College students on the autism spectrum: Prevalence and associated problems. *Sage Publications and the National Autistic Society, 15*(6), 683–701.

White, S. W., Elias, R., Salinas, C. E., Capriola, N., Conner, C. M., Asselin, S. B., … Getzel, E. E. (2016). Students with autism spectrum disorder in college: Results from a preliminary mixed methods needs analysis. *Research in Developmental Disabilities, 56*, 29–40.

Wiorkowski, F. (2015). The experiences of students with autism spectrum disorders in college: A heuristic exploration. *The Qualitative Report, 20*(6), 847–863.

Zantinge, G., van Rijn, S., Stockmann, L., & Swaab, H. (2017). Physiological arousal and emotion regulation strategies in young children with autism Spectrum disorders. *Journal of Autism and Developmental Disorders, 47*(9), 2648–2657.

Zylstra, R. G., Prater, C. D., Walthour, A. E., & Feliciano Aponte, A. (2014). Autism why the rise in rates? *The Journal of Family Practice, 63*(6), 316–320.

Considering College Alternatives

Beth A. Trammell, Amanda Kazee, Susan M. Wilczynski, Evette Simmons-Reed, Anita Kraft, and Shawnna Sundberg

Abstract Many alternatives to four-year college may prove optimal for students with high-functioning autism (HFA). Alternative options include but are not restricted to entering the workforce, attending a two-year program or community college, or choosing a technical (i.e., trade or vocational) school. Limited supports are available across all postsecondary options for individuals with autism spectrum disorder (ASD), irrespective of the alternative selected. School psychologists and other education professionals better support students when they teach them to select and prepare for their postsecondary options. To best support students, school psychologists should be aware of the barriers to employment faced by individuals with ASD and the factors that undermine sustained employment. In addition, school psychologists may need to incorporate a range of career inventories throughout the transition to adulthood process to support students entering the workplace and to help identify areas of study for technical school or community college attendance. This chapter reviews strategies school psychologists and other education professionals can implement to help students with HFA achieve success when entering the workforce or attending a two-year program or technical school. Research on the supports most commonly utilized in each of these environments are also addressed.

Keywords College alternatives · Autism spectrum disorder · High-functioning autism · Workforce · Community college · Technical school

---

B. A. Trammell (✉) · A. Kraft
Department of Psychology, Indiana University East, Richmond, IN, USA
e-mail: batramme@iue.edu; amkraft@iu.edu

A. Kazee · S. M. Wilczynski · E. Simmons-Reed · S. Sundberg
Department of Special Education, Ball State University, Muncie, IN, USA
e-mail: Amanda.Kazee@choa.org; smwilczynski@bsu.edu; easimmonsree@bsu.edu; slsundberg@bsu.edu

© Springer Nature Switzerland AG 2022
K. D. Viezel et al. (eds.), *Postsecondary Transition for College- or Career-Bound Autistic Students*, https://doi.org/10.1007/978-3-030-93947-2_8

Although a four-year college degree is seen as an ideal goalpost for students in some communities, it is not the ideal outcome for all high school students. A sound understanding of alternatives to a university experience begins with an analysis of the National Longitudinal Transition Study-2 (NLTS2), a 10-year study examining the experiences and achievements of individuals with disabilities in different domains during secondary school years and into young adulthood (Wagner et al., 2005). Following secondary school, students may seek (a) employment opportunities (e.g., competitive, supported, or sheltered employment), (b) postsecondary education (e.g., vocational/technical school, community college, or four-year college), or (c) job training (e.g., on the job training for specific job skills; Wagner et al., 2005). Students' trajectories following secondary education will look vastly different depending on their overall goals. For example, students entering the workforce should consider their interests, as well as strengths and weaknesses, related to their overall career path. In contrast, students considering postsecondary education may focus on identifying their college major and determine how college life may differ from the high school experience.

College may be an appropriate option for many high school students with high-functioning autism (HFA) and other chapters in this book dedicated to this topic. In contrast, this chapter focuses on transition planning for students with HFA who seek alternatives to the traditional four-year college path. Helping students give serious consideration to all potential options by developing a postsecondary transition plan within the first two years of high school may result in better overall outcomes (Shattuck et al., 2012). This chapter was written to help school psychologists and related professionals effectively engage in consultation with students, parents, and teachers about the noncollege postsecondary options available. Although different options may exist based on student preference and community opportunities; we discuss three of the most common alternatives to the traditional four-year college path: entering the workforce, community college (i.e., two-year college), and technical schools. Path-specific factors to be considered by students with HFA and the transition planning team are described below.

Transition Planning into Young Adulthood

Although awareness and visibility of autism spectrum disorder (ASD) has increased over the last two decades, limited research is available to inform professionals supporting students transitioning to the life of a young adult (Anderson et al., 2018; Hendricks & Wehman, 2009; Wehman et al., 2014). Vocational rehabilitation (VR) is a well-known community-based support for young adult transitions. VR is a federally funded program that supports individuals with disabilities to secure employment (McDonough & Revell, 2010). In 2010, 58% of individuals with ASD received VR services (Migliore et al., 2014). Eligibility for VR services requires impairment that has a known cause (e.g., autism, intellectual disability, epilepsy, TBI; Roux et al., 2016). However, consistent determination of impairment, particularly within the HFA population, is lacking (Nye-Lengerman, 2015). Recent research has suggested variability among the access to VR services for transition-aged youth across different states (Roux et al., 2018). As a result, students in some states do not have the same options for support and are likely to face a more daunting transition. Therefore, school psychologists are encouraged to explore their specific state requirements for VR services to share with students and their families.

The Individuals with Disabilities Education Act (IDEA) mandates that students have an individualized transition plan including a coordinated set of activities supporting the student's movement from high school to the postsecondary environment (IDEA, 2004). Transition plans should have goals designed to increase independence, obtain gainful employment, attend postsecondary education, and increase social connections (Wehman, 2006). Best practice in postsecondary transition planning includes the active involvement of students with HFA and transition plans focusing on functional skills that lead to independence (e.g., daily living skills, self-advocacy skills, and communication should be developed as early as possible; Kuo et al., 2018).

Helping each student with HFA determines their best postsecondary option can pose a challenge for educators guiding the transition process due to the incongruency between the student's specific abilities and the supports available in the postsecondary environment. Both parents and students have identified the painful lack of supports in postsecondary environments and the need for more supports to facilitate a smoother transition (Anderson et al., 2018). For example, high school students are often supported by teachers, counselors, administrators, and parents, whereas these supports are not automatically included in the postsecondary environment, regardless of the path. Additional research is needed on methods for structuring the postsecondary path to yield successful outcomes for young adults with HFA.

Although some ASD symptoms can be strengths in the transition to adulthood (e.g., protracted interest in a topic central to a job position), other symptoms can interfere with long-term success. For example, students who develop fewer functional independence skills (e.g., telling time, counting money, understanding signage in public, using public transportation) can be expected to experience greater difficulty functioning independently as an adult (Shattuck et al., 2012). One of the greatest service needs for students with HFA is to increase social competence (Rosenblatt, 2008). Therefore, school psychologists should conduct assessments that identify specific strengths and needs related to functional independence and social competence to inform a well-built transition plan that will maximize the potential for success, for example, creating a student profile of strengths and weaknesses related to social, cognitive, and emotional ability (Fast, 2004) or evaluating decision-making skills (Sampson et al., 2004).

Identifying the algorithm for success for each individual student with ASD may seem daunting, but researchers have identified several predictive factors that can guide the development, implementation, and evaluation of transition services that may be relevant across postsecondary paths. Aggregating across the school-to-work and vocational rehabilitation literature, researchers highlight the importance of: (a) advocacy in the areas of skill development related to employment opportunities, (b) social inclusion with neurotypical peers, (c) incorporation of more naturalistic teaching opportunities in the K-12 environment, (d) coordination of multiagency support teams, (e) peer mentoring, (f) educational coaching, and (g) specific instruction of skills can provide a framework as postsecondary plans are being considered (Fleury et al., 2014; Hart et al., 2010; Lee & Carter, 2012; Wehman et al., 2014). Although it goes beyond the scope of this chapter to discuss each of these at length, we incorporate these areas within our discussion of the three alternative paths. School psychologists should keep in mind that some support services may not be available to students with HFA or students with more severe impairment; however, we include them here as a reference point for starting the process.

Entering the Workforce

Students with ASD are still far more likely to transition into the workforce than to attend postsecondary education settings (Burgess & Cimera, 2014). Individuals with ASD have the lowest postsecondary employment rate of any group of people with disabilities, with only 63.2% securing any form of postgraduation employment (Burgess & Cimera, 2014; Lee & Carter, 2012). Students with ASD may be unemployed altogether or they experience underemployment (i.e., employees hold jobs in which they are overqualified), or malemployment (i.e., strengths and interests of employees do not match their job placement) when sufficient preparation for transitioning to the workforce is absent. Not only is unemployment too common, students with ASD often experience low engagement in other social activities after leaving high school (Neary et al., 2015). Underemployment also makes it challenging for individuals with HFA to have enough income to support independent living, making supports for employment even more necessary. Information about obtaining additional supports for employment is also discussed in another chapter. Here we explore how school psychologists can facilitate students' and parents' understanding of obtaining employment by addressing key outcomes early in the transition process. By actively and gradually addressing career development skills, barriers to employment, social competence and engagement, as well as maintaining employment with both students and parents directly and early in the transition process, negative outcomes are more likely to be avoided.

Career Development Students' participation in early work experiences affords them valuable opportunities in short- and long-term career development, such as job-shadowing programs, career exploration courses, interviewing, and resume-writing practice. Approximately half of students with ASD participate in school-sponsored work experiences during secondary education (Lee & Carter, 2012; Wagner et al., 2003). School psychologists can advocate for all students, especially those with ASD, to participate in career development programs to build job skills and facilitate student determination of interests before pursuing postsecondary education or employment.

Considering College Alternatives

Career Inventories Career inventories assess a student's strengths, weaknesses, and interests, which can be useful in identifying a good career fit for students with ASD. Students with ASD may interact with professionals or other students who view disability solely or primarily in terms of the limitations (i.e., deficit model of disability), rather than the insights, skills, or perspectives unique to each person with ASD and, unfortunately, this can limit their views about themselves (Jones, 2012). By focusing on strengths, the positive qualities each student brings to the postsecondary experience can be affirmed. In addition, the best match between interest and skills may also be optimized because of the strength-focused nature of career inventories. For example, a student with a restricted interest in health data might be taught to develop skills and acquire experience to perform a range of jobs in a community health setting, hold positions in medical billing and coding, or work as an actuarial assistant.

Self-Directed Search (SDS) The SDS (Holland, 1985) assesses a student's career-related personality and interests (Barak & Cohen, 2002) and is grounded in the personal career theory, which includes student achievement, life history, beliefs, and future aspirations. Four areas (i.e., activities, competencies, occupations, and self-ratings) are assessed using a like/dislike rating scale. The self-ratings evaluate six unique dimensions (e.g., realistic, investigative, artistic, social, enterprising, and conventional) that are classified in both individuals and work environments to maximize job fit (Holland, 1985). The SDS identifies an overall personality type and career interest that can then be used to direct future career aspirations (Barak & Cohen, 2002). Although evidence of using the SDS with students with non-ASD learning or cognitive disabilities exists (Mattie, 2000), the SDS may be particularly useful as a career planning tool for students with HFA because it captures information from the student's perspective that may otherwise be hard to verbally articulate.

Myers-Briggs Type Indicator (MBTI) The MBTI is one of the most widely used self-report career inventories for identifying ways in which students experience the world, as connected to their values, needs, and motivations (Capraro & Capraro, 2002). The 93 forced-choice items (i.e., students are given two statements and are required to choose one of two options) are scored and placed on one of the four scales: extraversion/introversion (EI), sensing/intuition (SN), thinking/feeling (TF), and judgement/perception (JP). The resulting four-letter personality type can be used by school psychologists to connect the student's personality to matched work-related variables. For example, individuals with the INTJ type are most closely aligned with careers such as engineering, computer science, and mathematics. Additional career planning tools (e.g., *YES Jobsearch Program*, *Career Maturity Inventory Revised*, *My Vocational Skills*, etc.) may also be worth considering (Murray et al., 2016), but research as to their clinical utility with the ASD population is still forthcoming.

Barriers to Employment

Approximately 19% of individuals with a disability were employed in 2017, compared to roughly 66% of individuals without a disability during the same time period (Bureau of Labor Statistics, 2018). School psychologists working alongside students with ASD can decrease the common barriers to employment (e.g., completing job applications and interviewing for jobs). See Table 1 for a list of common barriers to both securing and maintaining employment as well as potential solutions for school psychologists to implement.

School professionals should initiate conversations about future career options and help students search for relevant jobs based on completed career inventories that provide a well-rounded picture of the student's strengths, weaknesses, and potential career paths. Students can learn to use common job search engines (e.g., *Indeed* [https://www.indeed.com/] or *Monster* [https://www.monster.com]) to identify relevant job matches in their area. In addition, students should learn that jobs may only be listed on a company's website, requiring more intensive efforts to find the best job opening. Students should also be taught about the barriers the job application process may involve. For example, school psychologists or other school personnel can teach students how to navigate the job-search websites, generate appropriate and comprehensive responses to job application questions, and anticipate "wait times" prior to follow-up (i.e., when and how applicants should call to check on the status of an application).

Table 1 Barriers to securing and maintaining employment

	Challenging barriers	Potential solutions
Securing employment	Identifying career interests	Career assessments
	Identifying career-readiness skills	Career/workplace assessments
	Resume preparation	Review and give feedback
	Job applications	Review and give feedback
	Job interviews	Practice with trusted mentor
Maintaining employment	[a]Interacting with colleagues	Sharing information and education about the diagnosis
	[a]Communication	[a]Proactively approach colleagues or supervisors
	[a]Customers and supervisors	Job coach/video modeling
	[a]Work setting/sensory influences	[a]Acceptance/perseverance
	[a]Cognitive skills' deficits	Job coach/video modeling, [a]using strengths to compensate
	[a]Stress	[a]Reduction of work time
	Fit between workplace and student	Clear assessment of career goals and skills

[a] Identified as problem or solution (Lorenz et al., 2016)

Students may be asked to complete in-person or video conference interviews after they have submitted job applications. School professionals should build students' interview skills in preparation for both interview options well in advance, as the job interview is often the first obstacle to securing employment (Strickland et al., 2013). Many employers tailor questions that challenge an interviewee's problem-solving and teamwork skills during job interviews. Unprepared students with ASD can be at a distinct disadvantage during job interviews as a result of their qualitative impairments in social communication. For this reason, school psychologists can support employment interviewing skill repertoires by providing practice with similar questions prior to the interview (e.g., conduct mock interviews in which students dress professionally and ask questions similar to those asked at a job interview). Although this training is applicable to all students, school professionals should also provide supports for the acquisition of nonverbal interview skills (e.g., eye contact, posture, work attire, etc.) for students with ASD as social pragmatic aspects of communication are often impaired even in high-functioning individuals with ASD (Strickland et al., 2013).

Supported Employment The discussion to this point has centered on competitive employment opportunities (i.e., paid at least minimum wage and functioning independently in their roles; Schall et al., 2012). However, alternative employment arrangements may be necessary for students who require more supports to join the workforce based on their present levels of skill development.

Supported employment can be a stepping stone for students with disabilities to acquire and maintain competitive employment. A quality supported employment program includes four components: (1) completion of job-seeker profile and assessment, (2) job development and career search, (3) job-site training and support, and (4) long-term support and job retention (Schall et al., 2012). Employment services such as supported employment have effectively increased employment rates for individuals with ASD as compared to other disability populations (Burgess & Cimera, 2014). However, school psychologists must be careful about advocating for supportive employment because it has rightly been criticized for its lack of consistency in producing long-term employment (Kregel & Dean, 2002).

Sheltered workshops are more restrictive than supported employment (Cimera et al., 2012). Skills training, prevocational services, and group work placements are some of the diverse services sheltered workshops provide for individuals with disabilities, with the long-term goal of positioning people with disabilities to gain competitive employment in the future. Sheltered workshops have been justly criticized for being segregated from other employment settings (i.e., they are not provided in the general community where people without disabilities are employed; Kregel & Dean, 2002). Students with HFA are far less likely to benefit from sheltered workshops because they have a stronger array of skills within their repertoire than individuals with significant intellectual disabilities. School psychologists should not rule out sheltered workshops, but should ensure they are a temporary solution only in more extreme cases with students with HFA. Finally, school psychologists must guard against the temptation to select supported employment or sheltered workshops simply on the basis of local availability of these resources; instead, they must match the supports with the needs of their students with ASD.

Maintaining Employment Maintaining competitive employment once a position has been secured is a challenge facing many students with ASD (Schall et al., 2015). Like symptoms along the autism spectrum, skill sets vary considerably, and some students need more intensive supports for a range of employment activities. School psychologists training students with ASD should assess workplace supports at the beginning of employment (Lee & Carter, 2012), because a collaborative and supportive work environment is key for employment success (Hendricks, 2010).

Once students with ASD have secured a job, school psychologists should turn their attention to training and interventions that could help students maintain employment. Individuals with HFA may experience more difficulty maintaining employment than securing a job (Higgins et al., 2008). The sustained social-communication demands required in most jobs can tax the communication skills of individuals with HFA. The continual self-assessment of social communication with coworkers and superiors that may be required to maintain employment can be exhausting and anxiety-provoking. In addition, problems in the workplace resulting from social communication may be confusing when performance in other aspects of the job are exemplary (Baldwin et al., 2014; Muller et al., 2003). Workplace assessments and training will now be discussed as methods school psychologists can employ.

Workplace Assessments Workplace assessments identifying job-specific challenges and students' overall work performance can enhance effective communication and problem-solving for both employees and employers. The *Autism Work Skills Questionnaire* (AWSQ) identifies challenges in the workplace, general abilities, and work performance (Hedley et al., 2016). The AWSQ was recently developed to fill the gap in career planning inventories specific to the ASD population (Gal et al., 2013). This 78-item questionnaire uses a 5-point Likert-type scale for each of the nine subscales; three pertaining to personal and educational data, and the other six subscales identifying work habits, working style, independence in work and studying, sensory responses and needs, routine daily activities, and interpersonal skills. Preliminary validity and reliability are moderate to high (i.e., Cronbach's alpha = 0.65–0.90; Gal et al., 2013). The AWSQ includes both a self-report and parent report, which may identify discrepancies between a student's perception and their actual work performance. The AWSQ report can serve as the foundation of a well-rounded employment profile (Gal et al., 2013; Hedley et al., 2016).

Workplace Training School psychologists can draw from a number of research-supported interventions to improve workplace skills, including the "soft skills" often reflecting the social-communication domain. Despite the lack of large-scale randomized clinical trials on workplace training for individuals with ASD, video modeling, behavioral skills training, and having a peer mentor or job coach represent three treatment options that enjoy sufficient research support to encourage their use. Of these alternatives, video modeling is the least intrusive form of intervention and peer mentoring or job coaching are the most intrusive. The ideal workplace training method for each individual minimizes intrusion and stigmatization while improving workplace skills and behavior.

Video Modeling Video modeling involves the video presentation of workplace tasks being performed in the correct sequence and to criterion (Allen et al., 2010; Burke et al., 2013; Gentry et al., 2015). Video modeling has the advantage of task presentation occurring in an invariant manner, so individuals with ASD are unlikely to become distracted by minor differences in presentations that may emerge across live models. Yet many empirical questions remain about the use of video modeling for employment skill development. For example, it seems probable that some students could experience difficulty generalizing from video models when environmental conditions are different from those presented in the video. In addition, tasks may be difficult to remember and perform, particularly with complex activities in which sequential replication of the model influences the accuracy of outcomes. Emerging literature suggests that in these cases school psychologists should select video prompting, which still has the advantage of presenting the video model but involves stopping the video at critical points to ensure each step of the task is completed in the correct order (Cullen et al., 2017). The National Professional Development Center on Autism Spectrum Disorders has an evidence-based practice brief about video modeling (2010) that includes steps for implementation and implementation checklists for school psychologists who may be looking for a template to get started.

Behavioral Skills Training Behavioral skills training (BST) is an effective strategy for teaching a wide range of skills. BST includes six steps: (1) generate a clear description of the target skill, (2) provide a written description of the skill, (3) model the target skill for the learner, (4) have the learner practice the target skill, (5) provide feedback during practice, and (6) repeat practice and feedback until mastery is achieved (Parsons et al., 2012). BST can effectively teach simple to complex skills for all populations, including individuals with ASD and it has effectively targeted conversation skills in nonwork settings (Nuernberger et al., 2013) and decreasing off-task behavior on the job (Palmen & Didden, 2012). School psychologists should individualize BST based on the skill profile of their students with ASD, the tasks, and the tone of the workplace. For example, if students will be greeting customers, school psychologists could clearly describe a greeting, write out a script for the students, model that scripted greeting, have students practice, and continue to provide feedback. In addition, encouraging multiple school personnel (e.g., librarian, administrative assistant, etc.) to participate in the practice of these same steps in different school settings could further benefit students by increasing the repetition and variation in delivery of the skill with untrained staff members. Thus, the probability that unexpected difficulties (e.g., distractions occurring mid-greeting) increases and can be problem-solved while supports are available.

Peer Mentor/Job Coach Peer mentors and/or job coaches can support every aspect of the new job, ranging from appropriate social interactions with coworkers to complex job requirements (Dipeolu et al., 2015). Prompts should be based on the unique needs of the employee and should be faded to decrease dependency on a peer mentor or job coach. Once individuals with ASD can perform their job to criterion with prompting, technology (e.g., mobile phone apps or reminders) can facilitate independence in a non-stigmatizing way.

Community College

The most common postsecondary path for students with disabilities is the two-year college or community college, compared to other types of schools (Wagner et al., 2005). A two-year community college opens the path for students to either get an Associate's degree and then enter the workforce or transition to a four-year university. Approximately 81% of one recent sample of transition-aged students with ASD who attended college attended a two-year college only or used the community college as an introduction to a four-year institution (Roux et al., 2015). Students with HFA may be more than intellectually capable of completing college coursework (Baio, 2014), but decide that the social demands of a four-year college are greater than they wish to manage immediately out of high school. A recent study suggested a two-year college may be a good stepping stone for students with ASD, as the authors found students who attend two-year colleges were more likely to persist in a four-year institution later (Wei et al., 2014). A two-year program at a community college has a variety of additional benefits including: giving students with ASD the opportunity to live the young adult life with less risk than the four-year college, as well as increasing social connections due to smaller class sizes and a shared community prior to college attendance. Moreover, students who are less confident in their independent living skills may find this a less threatening next step. Students with HFA who determine their executive functioning skills require further refinement may find it easier to stay organized, manage unexpected events, and plan social or academic tasks on a smaller campus, such as most community colleges.

Community college might produce a smoother transition to adulthood because the proximity to the student's home, smaller class sizes, and open enrollment likely mean better supports compared to a four-year university (Ankeny & Lehmann, 2010). With student consent, parents may anticipate or respond in a timely manner to problems when students live closer to home. Particularly, when students with ASD seek additional supports, parents may be involved in both big and small decisions, including navigating the social nuances of college life, as well as coaching students to become more independent (Morrison et al., 2009). School psychologists will want to help parents come to terms with the need for independence and growth for all college-aged students, so some previous supports may need to be carefully faded. For example, giving parents suggestions for ways they can increase the student's daily living skills for better preparation of young adult life.

Community college can be a good way to give students with HFA the valued social role of being college students (Hart et al., 2010), as well as additional social and educational opportunities to improve life after high school. Having at least some level of college coursework also makes students more marketable in the job force (Roux et al., 2015). Compared to a four-year university, community colleges have lower tuition costs, smaller class sizes, and reduced costs for things like fees and textbooks. According to the American Association of Community Colleges (2018), the annual cost of community college is approximately one third the cost, on average, of four-year universities, which makes this choice considerably less financially burdensome.

Upwards of 70% of community colleges have enrolled students with ASD on their campuses (Roux et al., 2015) and the majority of students (approximately 75%) attend classes full time (Wagner et al., 2005). Despite wide attendance at universities, some community colleges may be better prepared to address the needs of students on the spectrum (Roux et al., 2015). Faculty members at community colleges may be more accustomed to individualizing classroom management strategies (e.g., students with HFA who may ruminate on classroom discussions or ask off-topic questions during lectures that are consistent with their specific interest) because of smaller classroom sizes and the likelihood instructors can share effective strategies with each other. Students with ASD may be enabled to develop and generalize effective coping skills and self-management skills in a more understanding environment than they might encounter in a larger four-year university.

Many community colleges have dual-enrollment programs with local high schools, effectively providing students with ASD the opportunity to experience college coursework while in high school when more supports are available. Dual enrollment programs may reduce anxiety over the transition to community college and help students adapt to the rigors of college courses because teachers, parents, and counselors can provide supports (Adreon & Durocher, 2007). Community colleges also frequently partner with vocational schools or offer technical courses that focus on job-specific training and skills, unlike the interdisciplinary approach of a four-year university (Zeedyk et al., 2014). School psychologists should provide information on these programs if students are interested because dual enrollment programs are helpful supports regardless of a students' postsecondary goals (i.e., college or career track).

Developing independent living skills at community colleges may be a more manageable setting for students, as they generally offer more support services (Zeedyk et al., 2014). A recent poll from the American Association of Community Colleges (2018) indicated that 28% of community colleges report on-campus housing options for students, a number that has increased over the last decade. Some community colleges now offer a scaffolding-based plan including real-life experiences with independent living skills within a campus environment so that students can gradually adjust to living on campus (Roux et al., 2015). Being aware of students' needs and matching those needs with an appropriate postsecondary experience can make the difference between college success (i.e., receiving a college degree) and considering alternatives (i.e., leaving community college, entering the workforce). School psychologists should prepare students for potential difficulties with roommates, adapting to living with new people, and knowing how to handle common college-life issues (e.g., illnesses, arguments, and disagreements).

Transition Planning into Community College Fewer supports are available at all levels of college experience (i.e., community or a four-year college) as compared to support provided through IDEA or a 504 plan during the high school years. Approximately 66% of postsecondary students with disabilities do not receive any accommodations due to a lack of disclosure regarding disability status (i.e., college personnel are unaware of their disability; Wagner et al., 2005). More recently, one study indicated a greater percentage of students with ASD who disclosed their disability (69%), yet less than half of those who disclosed received any services or accommodations (48.6%; Roux et al., 2015). Similar to four-year colleges, parental access to information at a community college is barred by Family Educational Rights and Privacy Act (FERPA) laws, unless students sign a release of information. Thus, school psychologists should prepare students for the self-advocacy needs they will encounter in a community college to receive academic supports. Specifically, school psychologists should describe the importance of disclosing the students' disability with the college's Office of Disability Services. A recent guide to the post-secondary path was published through the U.S. Department of Education that would be a great resource for students and parents with HFA (Transition Planning Guide; U.S. Department of Education, 2017), including rights and responsibilities, tips for success, and specific resources across the country.

Postsecondary graduation rates among those with ASD still fall well behind the national average by almost 20% at community colleges and 8% at technical college (Newman et al., 2011), so developing a strong plan is necessary. First, students with HFA who have a rigorous and individualized general curriculum in secondary school achieve better post-school outcomes (Baer, 2003; Kucharczyk et al., 2015; Test et al., 2014). Inclusion in general education classes and equal expectations from educators in secondary school set students up for the high demands that college educators will have (Newman et al., 2011). School psychologists may remind secondary school educators about the postsecondary plans of students on the spectrum so that high academic standards are maintained from the point of entry into high school.

The student-college fit is an important factor for student success (Adreon & Durocher, 2007). If the student-college fit is not successful, students may miss out on opportunities such as living in a dorm or experiencing the traditional college "feel." School psychologists should work closely with guidance counselors to maximize student-college fit as they are often knowledgeable of many specific colleges due to their college planning role. Some students may prefer a smaller campus (i.e., community college; VanBergeijk, et al., 2008); however, one study suggested some students with ASD may prefer a larger campus where they can have additional opportunities for anonymity and fitting in with a diverse student body (Hendrickson et al., 2017). In general, the students' sense of belonging may not be as high on a community college campus, as opposed to a traditional college, which has been noted to be an important factor in student success for neurotypical young adults (Freeman et al., 2007). School psychologists should consider students' sense of belonging and social relationships as these factors may be important for some individuals with HFA. Social relationships should be considered in the initial planning stages of the community college path. Developing a circle of social support for students with ASD may be an additional way to advocate for students' social deficits that may be more evident in a smaller, community college setting. Creating a "circle of friends" has been identified as an effective intervention for K-12 students whereby individuals with ASD are surrounded by peers who are strategically placed in the same courses to be an ally for them (Frederickson & Turner, 2003; Kalyva & Ayramidis, 2005; Schlieder et al., 2014). Although there is limited research on the effectiveness of a "circle of friends" with postsecondary students, this intervention may be a potential intervention for students choosing a community college where social connections may be harder to form compared to a traditional college campus.

Students on the autism spectrum must understand what services or accommodations they need to be successful in college. Being actively involved in transition planning during high school can help students advocate for what services or accommodations may be useful in the college setting. For example, students with executive functioning deficits may advocate for class notes prior to the lecture in order to review the concepts. Reviewing the student's IEP and other documentation can assist counselors in advising students on what types of supports may be useful in the college setting. Because laws greatly reduce the amount of assistance postsecondary schools are required to provide, the range of support is expansive from school to school. The secondary transition planning team can look for information on college websites and seek out regional programs that go beyond the American with Disabilities Act (ADA) requirements. Additionally, school psychologists and students can investigate whether student organizations specific to the ASD population are available. For instance, at one university, the Students on the Spectrum Club (SOS), now in its tenth year, meets weekly to support students learning to engage with peers, develop self-advocacy skills, and manage their emotions (Indiana Resource Center for Autism). A successful student organization can be indicative of an active support network at the college. School psychologists could also recommend other common accommodations for ASD including: exam accommodations, help with note-taking, tutoring for specific courses, periodic or continuing "check-in" meetings with faculty or staff, and organizational skills' training (Dallas et al., 2018). For additional best practices and supports for students with ASD considering community college, see Brown and Coomes (2016) and Gelbar, Smith, and Reichow (2014).

Trade or Vocational School

Trade or vocational school (i.e., technical college) is another potential alternative to the four-year college. This option may be of particular interest to students with HFA who have especially honed skills in a specific area. For instance, some technical schools offer specialized training in computer sciences that may be particularly interesting for students with HFA. Other fields that offer trade or vocational training include but are not limited to health care, automotive, culinary, cosmetology, and animal care. A technical college offers many of the same advantages to students on the spectrum as community colleges, including smaller campuses and class sizes, and more focus on the needs of individual students.

Deciding to attend a technical college can offer many advantages to students on the spectrum. Technical colleges design programs with the local or regional market in mind resulting in higher employment rates for students than those who earn an academic degree (Institute of Education Sciences, 2009; Newman et al., 2011). Taking classes outside their area of interest may present motivational difficulties for some students with HFA. Technical colleges may be an appropriate choice for students as these colleges do not require an abundance of general education classes, such as English or History. Further, more hands-on and focused training in a student's area of interest can be applied (Adreon & Durocher, 2007).

Additional advantages of attending a technical college include reduced cost for a degree, as well as lower costs for textbooks and academic-related fees (Institute of Education Sciences, 2009). Furthermore, technical colleges are often commuter campuses allowing students to remain at home, reducing stressors such as living in a dorm, money management, shopping, roommate issues, and handling illnesses (Adreon & Durocher, 2007; Jekel & Loo, 2002).

Transition Planning into Technical College

The literature surrounding ASD and technical college is sparse, but a growing need considering the growth in students likely interested in this postsecondary career path. School psychologists should give due consideration to a student's specific goals and abilities, the possibility of dual credit for their trade of interest (e.g., electrician), and the cost of the technical college. The benefits of attending a technical college include hands-on training plus the needed skills for job placement in that specific trade for students with HFA. Students also can connect with a mentor or engage in an apprenticeship-type opportunity in their field of interest. Hands-on training may be more fitting for students with HFA who are visual learners, and may be less dependent on executive functioning skills. As school psychologists assist families with options for technical schools, they may wish to consider connecting students with specific mentors that could provide support for students upon leaving high school. Further, this mentorship may allow them a foot in the door for later employment.

Conclusion

Entering the workplace or attending a community or technical college may be the best option for those students who are not socially or academically prepared for a four-year college transition, or who do not desire to do so. School psychologists are uniquely situated to help with transition planning for these alternative paths. School psychologists may assist with career planning and exploration, behavioral skills training to teach necessary skills for employment, and/or modeling advocacy skills for appropriate accommodations for academic or employment success. Although opportunities for students with HFA at colleges and in the workplace are growing, many institutions are still not prepared to provide the support students require. It is imperative for student success that the transition process be a joint effort between secondary school counselors, parents, or guardians, and most importantly, the students. Identifying student needs for a postsecondary path, and beginning the transition process early in the student's education, can help ensure success at any postsecondary environment.

References

Adreon, D., & Durocher, J. S. (2007). Evaluating the college transition needs of individuals with high-functioning autism spectrum disorders. *Intervention in School and Clinic, 42*(5), 271–279.

Allen, K. D., Wallace, D. P., Renes, D., Bowen, S. L., & Burke, R. V. (2010). Use of video modeling to teach vocational skills to adolescents and young adults with autism spectrum disorders. *Education and Treatment of Children, 33*(3), 339–349.

American Association of Community Colleges. (2018). *Fast facts.* Retrieved from: https://www.aacc.nche.edu/research-trends/fast-facts/

Anderson, K. A., Sosnowy, C., Kuo, A. A., & Shattuck, P. T. (2018). Transition of individuals with autism to adulthood: A review of qualitative studies. *Pediatrics, 141*(Supplement 4), S318–S327.

Ankeny, E. M., & Lehmann, J. P. (2010). The transition lynchpin: The voices of individuals with disabilities who attended a community college transition program. *Community College Journal of Research and Practice, 34*(6), 477–496. https://doi.org/10.1080/10668920701382773

Baer, R. M. (2003). A collaborative follow-up study on transition service utilization and post-school outcomes. *Career Development for Exceptional Individuals, 26*, 7–25.

Baio, J. (2014). *Prevalence of autism spectrum disorder among children aged 8 years-autism and developmental disabilities monitoring network, 11 sites, United States, 2010.* Retrieved from: https://stacks.cdc.gov/view/cdc/22182

Baldwin, S., Costley, D., & Warren, A. (2014). Employment activities and experiences of adults with high-functioning autism and Asperger's disorder. *Journal of Autism and Developmental Disorders, 44*(10), 2440–2449.

Barak, A., & Cohen, L. (2002). Empirical examination of an online version of the self-directed search. *Journal of Career Assessment, 10*(4), 387–400. https://doi.org/10.1177/1069072702238402

Brown, K. R., & Coomes, M. D. (2016). A spectrum of support: Current and best practices for students with autism spectrum disorder (ASD) at community colleges. *Community College Journal of Research and Practice, 40*(6), 465–479.

Bureau of Labor Statistics (2018). Persons with a disability: Labor force characteristics summary. Retrieved from https://www.bls.gov

Burgess, S., & Cimera, R. E. (2014). Employment outcomes of transition-aged adults with autism spectrum disorders: A state of the states report. *American Journal on Intellectual and Developmental Disabilities, 119*(1), 64–83.

Burke, R. V., Allen, K. D., Howard, M. R., Downey, D., Matz, M. G., & Bowen, S. L. (2013). Tablet-based video modeling and prompting in the workplace for individuals with autism. *Journal of Vocational Rehabilitation, 38*(1), 1–14.

Capraro, R. M., & Capraro, M. M. (2002). Myers-Briggs type indicator score reliability across studies: A meta-analytic reliability generalization study. *Educational and Psychological Measurement, 62*(4), 590–602.

Cimera, R. E., Wehman, P., West, M., & Burgess, S. (2012). Do sheltered workshops enhance employment outcomes for adults with autism spectrum disorder? *Autism, 16*(1), 87–94.

Cullen, J. M., Alber-Morgan, S. R., Simmons-Reed, E. A., & Izzo, M. V. (2017). Effects of self-directed video prompting using iPads on the vocational task completion of young adults with intellectual and developmental disabilities. *Journal of Vocational Rehabilitation, 46*, 361–375.

Dallas, B., Ramisch, J., & Ashmore, A. (2018). How involved should they be? Students with ASD in post-secondary settings and their family members. *The Qualitative Report, 23*(5), 1208–1222. Retrieved from https://nsuworks.nova.edu/tqr/vol23/iss5/13

Dipeolu, A. O., Storlie, C., & Johnson, C. (2015). College students with high-functioning autism spectrum disorder: Best practices for successful transition to the world of work. *Journal of College Counseling, 18*(2), 175–190.

Fast, Y. (2004). *Employment for individuals with Asperger syndrome or non-verbal learning disability*. Jessica Kingsley Publishers.

Fleury, V., Hedges, S., Hume, K., Browder, D. M., Thompson, J. L., Fallin, K., … Vaughn, S. (2014). Addressing the academic needs of adolescents with autism spectrum disorder in secondary education. *Remedial and Special Education, 35*(2), 68–79.

Frederickson, N., & Turner, J. (2003). Utilizing the classroom peer group to address children's social needs: An evaluation of the circle of friends intervention approach. *The Journal of Special Education, 36*(4), 234–245.

Freeman, T. M., Anderman, L. H., & Jensen, J. M. (2007). Sense of belonging in college freshmen at the classroom and campus levels. *The Journal of Experimental Education, 75*(3), 203–220.

Gal, E., Meir, A. B., & Katz, N. (2013). Developmental and reliability of the autism work skills questionnaire (AWSQ). *The American Journal of Occupational Therapy, 67*, 1–5.

Gelbar, N. W., Smith, I., & Reichow, B. (2014). Systematic review of articles describing experience and supports of individuals with autism enrolled in college and university programs. *Journal of Autism and Developmental Disorders, 44*(10), 2593–2601.

Gentry, T., Kriner, R., Sima, A., McDonough, J., & Wehman, P. (2015). Reducing the need for personal supports among workers with autism using an iPod touch as an assistive technology: Delayed randomized control trial. *Journal of Autism and Developmental Disorders, 45*(3), 669–684.

Hart, D., Grigal, M., & Weir, C. (2010). Expanding the paradigm: Post-secondary education options for individuals with autism spectrum disorder and intellectual disabilities. *Focus on Autism and Other Developmental Disabilities, 25*, 134–150.

Hedley, D., Uljarevic, M., Cameron, L., Halder, S., Richdale, A., & Dissanayake, C. (2016). Employment programmes and interventions targeting adults with autism spectrum disorder: A systematic review of the literature. *Autism, 21*(8), 929–941.

Hendricks, D. (2010). Employment and adults with autism spectrum disorders: Challenges and strategies for success. *Journal of Vocational Rehabilitation, 32*(2), 125–134.

Hendricks, D. R., & Wehman, P. (2009). Transition from school to adulthood for youth with autism spectrum disorders: Review and recommendations. *Focus on Autism and Other Developmental Disabilities, 24*(2), 77–88.

Hendrickson, J. M., Woods-Groves, S., Rodgers, D. B., & Datchuk, S. (2017). Perceptions of students with autism and their parents: The college experience. *Education and Treatment of Children, 40*(4), 571–596.

Higgins, K. K., Koch, L. C., Boughfman, E. M., & Vierstra, C. (2008). School-to-work transition and Asperger syndrome. *Work, 31*(3), 291–298.

Holland, J. L. (1985). *Professional manual for the self-directed search*. Psychological Assessment Resources.

Indiana Resource Center for Autism. (n.d.) *Students on the Spectrum Club at Indiana University*. Retrieved from: https://www.iidc.indiana.edu/pages/students-on-the-spectrum-club

Individuals with Disabilities Education Act, 20 U.S.C. § 1400 (2004).

Institute of Education Sciences. (2009). *Beginning post-secondary students longitudinal study, second follow-up (BPS:04/09)*. Washington D.C.: United States Department of Education, National Center for Education Statistics. Retrieved from https://nces.ed.gov/surveys/ctes/figures/fig_2016107-2.asp

Jekel, D., & Loo, S. (2002). *So you want to go to college: Recommendations, helpful tips, and suggestions for success at college*. Asperger's Association of New England.

Jones, J. (2012). Factors associated with self-concept: Adolescents with intellectual and developmental disabilities share their perspectives. *Intellectual and Developmental Disabilities, 50*, 31–40.

Kalyva, E., & Avramidis, E. (2005). Improving communication between children with autism and their peers through the 'circle of friends': A small-scale intervention study. *Journal of Applied Research in Intellectual Disabilities, 18*(3), 253–261.

Kregel, J., & Dean, D. H. (2002). Sheltered vs. supported employment: A direct comparison of long-term earnings outcomes for individuals with cognitive disabilities. In J. Kregel, D. Dean, & P. Wehman (Eds.), *Achievements and challenges in employment services for people with disabilities: The longitudinal impact of workplace supports*. Virginia Commonwealth University, Rehabilitation Research and Training Center on Workplace Supports.

Kucharczyk, S., Reutebuch, C. K., Carter, E. W., Hedges, S., El Zein, F., Fan, H., & Gustafson, J. R. (2015). Addressing the needs of adolescents with autism spectrum disorder: Considerations and complexities for high school interventions. *Exceptional Children, 81*(3), 329–349.

Kuo, A. A., Crapnell, T., Lau, L., Anderson, K. A., & Shattuck, P. (2018). Stakeholder perspectives on research and practice in autism and transition. *Pediatrics, 141*(Supplement 4), S293–S299.

Lee, G., & Carter, E. (2012). Preparing transition-age students with high functioning autism spectrum disorder for meaningful work. *Psychology in the Schools, 49*(10), 988–1000.

Lorenz, T., Frischling, C., Cuadros, R., & Heinitz, K. (2016). Autism and overcoming job barriers: Comparing job-related barriers and possible solutions in and outside of autism-specific employment. *PLoS One, 11*(1), e0147040.

Mattie, H. D. (2000). The suitability of Holland's self-directed search for non-readers with learning disabilities or mild mental retardation. *Career Development for Exceptional Individuals, 23*(1), 57–72.

McDonough, J. T., & Revell, G. (2010). Accessing employment supports in the adult system for transitioning youth with autism spectrum disorders. *Journal of Vocational Rehabilitation, 32*(2), 89–100.

Migliore, A., Butterworth, J., & Zalewska, A. (2014). Trends in vocational rehabilitation services and outcomes of youth with autism: 2006–2010. *Rehabilitation Counseling Bulletin, 57*(2), 80–89.

Morrison, J. Q., Sansosti, F. J., & Hadley, W. M. (2009). Parent perceptions of the anticipated needs and expectations for support for their college-bound students with Asperger's syndrome. *Journal of Post-secondary Education and Disability, 22*(2), 78–87.

Muller, E., Schuler, A., Burton, B. A., & Yates, G. B. (2003). Meeting the vocational support needs of individuals with Asperger syndrome and other autism spectrum disabilities. *Journal of Vocational Rehabilitation, 18*(3), 163–175.

Murray, N., Hatfield, M., Falkmer, M., & Falkmer, T. (2016). Evaluation of career planning tools for use with individuals with autism spectrum disorder: A systematic review. *Research in Autism Spectrum Disorders, 23*, 188–202.

Neary, P., Gilmore, L., & Ashburner, J. (2015). Post-school needs of young people with high-functioning autism spectrum disorder. *Research in Autism Spectrum Disorders, 18*, 1–11.

Newman, L., Wagner, M., Huang, T., Shaver, D., Knokey, A.-M., Yu, J., ... Cameto, R. (2011). *Secondary school programs and performance of students with disabilities: A special topic report of findings from the National Longitudinal Transition Study-2 (NLTS2). (NCSER 2012–3000)*. U.S. Department of Education, National Center for Special Education Research.

Nuernberger, J. E., Ringdahl, J. E., Vargo, K. K., Crumpecker, A. C., & Gunnarsson, K. F. (2013). Using a behavioral skills training package to teach conversation skills to young adults with autism spectrum disorders. *Research in Autism Spectrum Disorders, 7*(2), 411–417.

Nye-Lengerman, K.M. (2015). *Predicting vocational rehabilitation employment outcomes for individuals with autism spectrum disorder*. (Doctoral dissertation). Retrieved from ProQuest. (3733258).

Office of Special Education and Rehabilitative Services. (2017). *A transition guide to postsecondary education and employment for students and youth with disabilities*. U.S. Department of Education, The Office of Special Education and Rehabilitative Services.

Palmen, A., & Didden, R. (2012). Task engagement in young adults with high-functioning autism spectrum disorders: Generalization effects of behavioral skills training. *Research in Autism Spectrum Disorders, 6*(4), 1377–1388.

Parsons, M. B., Rollyson, J. H., & Reid, D. H. (2012). Evidence-based staff training: A guide for practitioners. *Behavior Analysis in Practice, 5*(2), 2–11.

Rosenblatt, M. (2008). *I exist: The message from adults with autism in England*. The National Autistic Society.

Roux, A., Shattuck, P., Rast, J., Rava, J., Edwards, A., Wei, X., ... Yu, J. (2015). Characteristics of two-year college students on the autism spectrum and their support services experience. *Autism Research and Treatment*, 1–10.

Roux, A. M., Rast, J. E., Anderson, K. A., & Shattuck, P. T. (2016). *National Autism Indicators Report: Vocational rehabilitation*. Life Course Outcomes Research Program, A.J. Drexel Autism Institute, Drexel University.

Roux, A. M., Rast, J. E., & Shattuck, P. T. (2018). State-level variation in vocational rehabilitation service use and related outcomes among transition-age youth on the autism spectrum. *Journal of Autism and Developmental Disorders*, 1–13.

Sampson, J. P., Reardon, R. C., Peterson, G. W., & Lenz, J. G. (2004). *Career counseling and services: A cognitive information processing approach*. Brooks/Cole.

Schall, C., Wehman, P., & McDonough, J. L. (2012). Transition from school to work for students with autism spectrum disorders: Understanding the process and achieving better outcomes. *Pediatric Clinics, 59*(1), 189–202.

Schall, C. M., Wehman, P., Brooke, V., Graham, C., McDonough, J., Brooke, A., ... Allen, J. (2015). Employment interventions for individuals with ASD: The relative efficacy of supported employment with or without prior project SEARCH training. *Journal of Autism and Developmental Disorders, 45*(12), 3990–4001.

Schlieder, M., Maldonado, N., & Baltes, B. (2014). An investigation of "circle of friends" peer-mediated intervention for students with autism. *The Journal of Social Change, 6*(1), 27–40.

Shattuck, P. T., Narendorf, S. C., Cooper, B., Sterzing, P. R., Wagner, M., & Taylor, J. L. (2012). Post-secondary education and employment among youth with an autism spectrum disorder. *Pediatrics, 129*(6), 1042–1049.

Strickland, D. C., Coles, C. D., & Southern, L. B. (2013). JobTIPS: A transition to employment programs for individuals with autism spectrum disorders. *Journal of Autism and Developmental Disorders, 43*(10), 2472–2483.

Test, D. W., Smith, L. E., & Carter, E. W. (2014). Equipping youth with autism spectrum disorders for adulthood: Promoting rigor, relevance, and relationships. *Remedial and Special Education, 35*(2), 80–90.

U.S. Department of Education. (2017). *Office of Special Education and Rehabilitative Services*. A Transition Guide to Postsecondary Education and Employment for Students and Youth with

Disabilities. Retrieved from: https://sites.ed.gov/idea/files/postsecondary-transition-guide-may-2017.pdf

Van Bergeijk, E., Klin, A., & Volkmar, F. (2008). Supporting more able students on the autism spectrum: College and beyond. *Journal of Autism and Developmental Disorders, 38*(7), 1359–1370. https://doi.org/10.1007/s10803-007-0524-8

Wagner, M., Newman, L., Cameto, R., Levine, P., & Marder, C. (2003). *Going to school: Instructional contexts, programs, and participation of secondary school students with disabilities.* SRI International.

Wagner, M., Newman, L., Cameto, R., Garza, N., & Levine, P. (2005). *After high school: A first look at the postschool experiences of youth with disabilities. A report from the National Longitudinal Transition Study-2 (NLTS2).* SRI International.

Wehman, P. (2006). *Life beyond the classroom: Transition strategies for young people with disabilities* (4th ed.). Paul H Brookes Publishing.

Wehman, P., Schall, C., Carr, S., Targett, P., West, M., & Cifu, G. (2014). Transition from school to adulthood for youth with autism spectrum disorder: What we know and what we need to know. *Journal of Disability Policy Studies, 25*(1), 30–40.

Wei, X., Christiano, E. R. A., Yu, J. W. et al. (2014). Postsecondary pathways and persistence for STEM versus Non-STEM majors among college students with an autism spectrum disorder. *Journal of Autism Developmental Disorders, 44*, 1159–1167. https://doi.org/10.1007/s10803-013-1978-5

Zeedyk, S., Tipton, L., & Blacher, J. (2014). Educational supports for high functioning youth with ASD: The post-secondary pathway to college. *Focus on Autism and Other Developmental Disabilities, 31*(1), 37–48.

Addressing Transition Preparation in Middle and High Schools

Erik W. Carter and Michele A. Schutz

Abstract A primary purpose of special education and secondary education is to equip students with autism spectrum disorder (ASD) with the skills, experiences, supports, and linkages they need to transition successfully to life after graduation. Middle and high school programs have a central role in the design and delivery of transition services that prepare students for college, career, and community outcomes. This chapter focuses on the transition principles, planning, practices, personnel, and partnerships that can place students with ASD on a strong pathway toward their flourishing in adulthood. Across these areas, we highlight best practices and emphasize ways that school psychologists can be key players and partners in the delivery of high-quality transition services within their schools and districts.

Keywords Transition programs · Middle school · High school

Most young people hold high hopes for life after graduation. Enrolling in college or postsecondary training, obtaining meaningful work, participating in the community, moving out of their home, forging new relationships, experiencing new levels of independence, helping to meet the needs of others, and finding a place to belong—these represent just a sampling of the myriad possibilities that may await. Although adulthood introduces a host of exciting pathways for most young people, many students with autism spectrum disorder (ASD) still lack the opportunities, preparation, or supports needed to pursue these ordinary experiences. Nearly every longitudinal or follow-along study indicates that the post-school outcomes of transition-age individuals with ASD can be highly uneven and often disappointing (e.g., Chiang et al., 2012; Nasamran et al., 2017). Up to eight years after leaving high school, Newman et al. (2011) reported that only 37% of young adults with ASD in the United States were currently employed, only 44% had ever enrolled in any type of postsecondary education, only 61% were involved in a variety of community

---

E. W. Carter (✉) · M. A. Schutz
Department of Special Education, Peabody College, Vanderbilt University,
Nashville, TN, USA
e-mail: erik.carter@vanderbilt.edu

© Springer Nature Switzerland AG 2022
K. D. Viezel et al. (eds.), *Postsecondary Transition for College- or Career-Bound Autistic Students*, https://doi.org/10.1007/978-3-030-93947-2_9

activities (e.g., community groups, volunteering), and only 20% lived independently or semi-independently. The aspirations adolescents with ASD hold do not always materialize; the future they imagine is too often elusive.

Schools can play a powerful role in changing the current trajectories of students with ASD. By equipping students with the right combination of skills, supports, experiences, and linkages, educators can prepare students to successfully navigate the transition to adulthood in ways that lead to elevated outcomes. In other words, middle and high school provide a critical period of preparation for, exploration of, and connection to adult roles and responsibilities. This chapter addresses the ways in which secondary school programs can be designed and delivered to promote successful transitions, and it highlights the important roles of school psychologists within this essential work. We begin by emphasizing core principles that should undergird the investments of school teams in the area of transition. Next, we address the high-quality planning as the foundation for individualized transition programming. We then highlight recommended practices related to preparing students for postsecondary education, integrated employment, independent living, social relationships, and self-determination. Recognizing the importance of a team-based approach to transition, we describe the contributions different school staff (e.g., school psychologists, special educators, school administrators) might bring to this work. We then provide an overview of community partnership that can be drawn upon to support the work of schools and the transitions of students. In short, this chapter addresses the principles, planning, practices, personnel, and partnerships that comprise high-quality transition education in middle and high schools.

Core Principles in Transition

Although an investment in effective practices should always characterize the work of secondary school teams, adherence to a number of core principles should also undergird their practices. A series of reflection questions that highlights some of the commitments school teams should adopt is listed below. In this section, we highlight a few of these principles—emerging from research, policy, legislation, and advocacy efforts—considered to be especially important when serving students with ASD. Core principles of effective transition

Are we beginning the transition planning process early in middle school?
Are we adopting person-centered practices that lead to individualization?
Are we identifying and building upon students' strengths and positive qualities?
Are we raising the aspirations of students and building their self-determination?
Are we holding high expectations and elevating the expectations of others?
Are we promoting inclusive experiences throughout our school and community?
Are we developing strong partnerships within and beyond the school?
Are we focusing on and documenting the outcomes of students?
Are we data-driven in our instruction, programming, and supports?

Are we reflecting best practices and moving beyond minimal compliance?
Are our practices, programs, and partnerships leading to a better quality of life for
students with ASD? Adapted from Carter (2017).

First, school teams should design transition experiences that have the very best chance of improving the post-school outcomes of students with ASD. In other words, transition programs must remain focused on results. The Individuals with Disabilities Education Improvement Act (IDEA, 2004) defines transition as "a coordinated set of activities that...is designed to be within a results-oriented process, focused on improving the academic and functional achievement of the child with a disability to facilitate the child's movement from school to postschool activities, including post-secondary education, vocational education, integrated employment (including supported employment), continuing and adult education, adult services, independent living, or community participation..." (IDEA, 2004, §602.34). In other words, the effectiveness of transition programing is not determined by the intentions of educators, by the plans they craft, by the partnerships they form, or even by the services they deliver. Ultimately, the best barometer for evaluating success is the extent to which the transition goals of students with ASD are achieved in early adulthood.

Second, individualization must be a hallmark of transition programming. Students with ASD are quite diverse in their needs, strengths, preferences, and interests. Indeed, no two students are likely to pursue the very same post-school pathways, experience the same challenges and needs, possess the same talents and strengths, require the same supports and assistance, or hold the same dreams for adulthood (Carter, 2018). As a result, transition cannot be conceptualized as a one-size-fits-all endeavor or approached from a categorical perspective (i.e., all students with ASD need [fill in the blank]). Instead, careful assessment and person-centered planning are needed to ensure the instruction and experiences students receive are tailored in ways that address their individualized needs.

Third, emphasis should be placed on supporting students with ASD to access the ordinary experiences and opportunities available to any other student attending the same school. Most schools already offer a range of courses, career development programming, extracurricular activities, service experiences, and mentorship opportunities designed to prepare students for adulthood. Before creating specialized experiences just for students with disabilities, schools should build capacity and commitment across existing programs to include students with ASD in meaningful ways. Early inclusion in school is predictive of later inclusion in workplaces, on college campus, and in community settings (Haber et al., 2016). Therefore, school teams should seek to include students with ASD in general education classes—both for core academics and elective studies of interest—to the greatest extent appropriate. Moreover, teams should support students in extracurricular clubs, field trips, and career development assessments and activities alongside their peers without disabilities. Establishing a pattern of full participation in typical activities throughout middle and high school can help establish a trajectory of inclusion into adulthood.

Fourth, high expectations should be fostered among professionals and parents alike. Decisions regarding programs of study, degree pathways, vocational experiences, and instructional emphases are all driven by the expectations that the adults who surround and serve students with ASD hold. When these individuals adopt high expectations for future employment or college enrollment, they pursue services and supports that aim in those directions; when expectations are low, such pursuits are rare. Indeed, longitudinal studies find that the expectations parents and school staff hold are among the strongest predictors of early post-school outcomes for students with ASD (Carter et al., 2012; Kirby et al., 2016). Likewise, schools and families should also take steps to raise the expectations of students with ASD so that they too catch a personal vision of future college, career, and community participation.

High-Quality Transition Planning

The transition experiences of each student with ASD should be unique and tailored in ways that reflect "the individual child's needs, taking into account the child's strengths, preferences, and interests" (IDEA, 2004, §602.34). The transition assessment and planning process provides the primary pathway through which this individualization takes place.

Age-Appropriate Assessment

Several other chapters in this book have described the types of assessments that address the domains of academics, social skills, behavior, emotional regulation, self-determination, and cognitive functioning. Current transition mandates require that the individualized education programs (IEPs) of students with disabilities include "appropriate measurable postsecondary goals *based on age-appropriate transition assessments* related to training, education, employment, and, where appropriate, independent living skills" (§300.320(b), italics added). In other words, transition assessment provides a primary avenue for identifying which educational practices and programs are most essential for a particular student with ASD. Rather than relying on anecdotes and assumptions, transition teams should gather and reflect upon good data when designing a compelling transition plan.

Transition assessment is often conceptualized as a process of "collecting information on the student's strengths, needs, preferences, and interests as they relate to the demands of current and future living, learning, and working environments" (Sitlington et al., 1997, p. 70). This understanding of assessment affirms the importance of gathering relevant information across a range of domains that may be related to a student's present experiences and anticipated post-school pathways. For example, a transition team might assemble information related to the areas of employment, postsecondary education, community participation, independent living, recreation and leisure activities, financial literacy, technology use, health, self-determination, social relationships, and transportation (Carter et al., 2014a). In each of these areas, teams would gather information related to a student's strengths, talents, and positive personal qualities; their instructional and support needs; their current preferences; and their present interests. This information is then evaluated in light of the expectations that will characterize the particular college, career, and community experiences the student is pursuing. In other words, teams work to discern the extent to which a student's present capacities align with anticipated demands; strong transition programs aim to bridge the gap between the two. The inclusion of "strengths" in this definition also means that assessment should emphasize the identification of the various positive qualities, skills, and talents that students with ASD possess. During the transition period, connections to jobs, community activities, and social relationships are often made on the basis of the personal strengths and contributions. In other words, it may be more important to know what students with ASD can do than what they struggle to do.

Effective implementation of transition assessment requires (a) a combination of diverse assessment approaches and (b) input from a variety of voices. For example, teams may incorporate information gathered using curriculum-based assessments, situational assessments, ecological inventories, direct observations, interest inventories, preference assessments, checklists, rating scales, questionnaires, interviews, and/or person-centered planning approaches (National Technical Assistance Center on Transition, 2016). School psychologists can be especially helpful in identifying appropriate and accessible assessment approaches. Unlike some other areas of education practice, transition assessment often integrates both formal (i.e., standardized instruments with adequate reliability and validity) and informal (i.e., tools that are individualized, flexibly applied, or staff-created) assessment to create a clear picture of the student's needs, strengths, interests, and preferences. However, developing such a comprehensive portrait requires the involvement of multiple people who know the student well, have spent time with the student in different settings, and are familiar with demands of the contexts in which the student will participate after graduation. Soliciting the perspectives of individuals who have different vantage points—such as school psychologists, special educators, general educators, guidance counselors, employers, extracurricular program leaders, paraprofessionals, parents, and other family members—can be instrumental in developing this portrait. Such a multi-informant approach is widely advocated because any given person will have an incomplete view and multiple people can diverge in their views (Carter et al., 2014a).

Team-Based Transition Planning

A well-crafted transition plan identifies a student's personal goals for life after high school and outlines the instruction, experiences, services, and supports the student will receive in preparation for these post-school goals. Although current federal legislation requires that transition planning begin no later than the first IEP to be in effect when a student is 16 years old, many states require that this planning begin no later than age 14. These early plans are considered more flexible than fixed, as it is rare that students in middle school or early on in high school will know exactly what they want to do after graduation. Instead, plans are revisited annually and revised as students continue to gain a clearer sense of what they want to do after graduation. As students accrue new experiences, develop new skills, and meet new people, their plans for the future typically evolve over time. So too should their written transition plans.

The National Technical Assistance Center on Transition (2012) developed a set of eight reflection questions that can be used to evaluate the extent to which essential elements of a high-quality transition plan are apparent. These include:

Are there appropriate measurable postsecondary goals in the areas of training, education, employment, and, where appropriate, independent living skills?
Are the postsecondary goals updated annually?
Is there evidence the measurable postsecondary goals were based on age-appropriate transition assessment(s)?
Are there transition services in the IEP that will reasonably enable the student to meet his or her postsecondary goals?
Do the transition services include courses of study that will reasonably enable the student to meet his or her postsecondary goals?
Is (are) there annual IEP goal(s) related to the student's transition service needs?
Is there evidence the student was invited to the IEP team meeting where transition services were discussed?
If appropriate, is there evidence a representative of any participating agency was invited to the IEP team meeting with the prior consent of the parent or student who has reached the age of majority?

Such questions are also used to evaluate the extent to which schools are meeting Indicator 13, one of twenty indicators established by the U.S. Department of Education. Specifically, Indicator 13 addresses the percentage of youth with an IEP that includes coordinated, measurable, annual goals and transition services that will reasonably enable the students to meet postsecondary goals.

It is especially important to encourage and support students with ASD to play an active role in their own transition planning (Chandroo et al., 2018). Such meetings introduce authentic opportunities for students to learn about and demonstrate self-awareness, self-advocacy, decision-making, goal-setting, and other self-determination qualities. Moreover, the presence and active contributions of a student at his or her own planning meeting can substantially change how others view and talk about the student. For example, students with ASD can learn to lead aspects of this meeting by introducing others who are in attendance; describing their personal goals for life after high school; sharing about their strengths, interests, preferences, and needs; asking for feedback on their recent progress over the past year; and suggesting potential school or community experiences of interest. Such student-led transition planning meetings are considered best practice, but still remain rare. Findings from a nationally representative study of students with ASD found that although 85.5% of youth (ages 17 and older) were reported to have been invited to their transition planning meeting, only 40.5% of youth with ASD were reported by their parents to provide at least some input during the transition planning meeting and only 59.5% self-reported that they provided at least some input (Lipscomb et al., 2017).

Recommended Transition Practices

The Individuals with Disabilities Education Improvement Act describes the primary purpose of special education as preparing students with disabilities "for further education, employment, and independent living" (2004). Although every person's transition program will be different, students with ASD are likely to benefit from instructional and other experiences focused on the areas of academics, employment, independent living, social relationships, and self-determination. We provide an overview of the types of preparation schools and districts might offer in these areas that align toward this central purpose of special education services. School psychologists can advocate within their schools and districts to ensure each of these areas are addressed and well supported.

Academics

Access to the general curriculum and attainment of a regular diploma are both predictive of entry into postsecondary education and a host of improved post-school outcomes (Chiang et al., 2012; Haber et al., 2016). In recent years, increasing numbers of students with ASD are receiving the majority of instruction in general education classrooms alongside their peers without disabilities. Participating in core academic, related arts, and other elective courses can expose students with ASD to rigorous instruction delivered by highly qualified teachers and addressing a wide range of interesting curricular topics. To maximize these inclusive learning opportunities, many students with ASD will benefit individualized instruction and supports. For example, Fleury et al. (2014) identified a number of interventions that may be helpful for adolescents with ASD, such as the introduction of routines and written schedules that structure students' academic day and priming (i.e., exposing students to assignments or experiences prior to their instruction in the classroom). Likewise, explicit strategy instruction, visual supports (e.g., graphic organizers, video modeling), and peer-mediated instruction may also help students with ASD in areas such as reading, writing, and math (e.g., Delano, 2007; Olson et al., 2015). To support generalization of learning, students with ASD may also benefit from receiving multiple opportunities to practice new skills across contexts and learning strategies for self-managing their own behavior (Fleury et al., 2014).

The courses of study students with ASD pursue also influence their preparation for postsecondary education and employment. The specific classes and credits students accrue determine the type of diploma students receive, which opens or closes the post-school opportunities available to them. For example, attainment of a regular high school diploma is closely connected with access to both college and career outcomes for students with ASD (Newman et al., 2011). Moreover, access to and success within rigorous coursework can be a requisite for admission to more selective colleges and universities. In addition to required courses, students should be encouraged to enroll in elective, related arts, career/technical education, and other courses that help them encounter a variety of career possibilities, deepen their existing interests, or expose them to new possibilities they had never considered. An ideal high school course of study provides opportunities both for focused preparation and fortuitous exploration as students develop a vision for their futures.

Employment

In addition to accessing the general curriculum, students with ASD can benefit from instruction, exposure, and support in the area of career development. A striking 94.9% of youth with ASD expect to have a paid job in early adulthood (Lipscomb et al., 2017). Yet, nearly one third of young adults with ASD do not participate in paid employment within 8 years of exiting high school. Among those who do find work, many earn wages that are well below average and hold jobs that offer few benefits (Newman et al., 2011; Chiang et al., 2013). Such findings emphasize the importance of having school staff and parents who view competitive employment as a real possibility and who provide students with opportunities to develop the skills, experiences, and goals that will prepare them to find future success in the workplace (Blustein et al., 2016). Moreover, students will need help identifying ambitious, but realistic, career goals that align with their interests, strengths, and needs.

A number of instruction strategies have been found to be effective for teaching employment skills to students with ASD (e.g., Bennett & Dukes, 2013; Gilson et al., 2017b). For example, video modeling, self-management strategies, audio coaching, peer-delivered instruction, picture prompts, and direct instruction have all been used to teach a variety of vocational skills and work-related social behaviors among students with disabilities. In addition, students may benefit from supplemental instruction related to their specific career interests, disability disclosure, appropriate workplace behaviors, and accessing community-based employment services (Lee & Carter, 2012). In addition to focused instruction, schools can promote career awareness and exposure by having students with ASD take career interest surveys, attend career fairs, participate in job shadowing, connect with mentorships, join vocational-related student organizations (e.g., BPA, DECA, FBLA, FFA), take career and technical education courses, or access career counseling. Most secondary schools already offer a constellation of career-related preparatory experiences for any student; yet students with ASD are infrequently encouraged or supported to participate (Carter et al., 2010b).

Although employment preparation is important, real-life practice may be even more powerful. Involvement in paid work experiences before leaving high school is a consistent predictor of better post-school employment outcomes for individuals with ASD (Chiang et al., 2012; Haber et al., 2016). For example, Carter et al. (2012) reported that students with autism and intellectual disability who exited school with at least one paid work experience were 2.5 times more likely to obtain integrated employment in the first few years after leaving high school students compared to students who lacked such experiences. Other avenues for providing hands-on work experiences can also be considered, including school-based enterprises, school-sponsored jobs, internships, apprenticeships, and after-school or summer jobs. Developing strong partnerships with local businesses and organizations can be critical to ensuring students with ASD are able to make connections to employers in areas aligned with students' career interests.

Independent Living

Preparation for life in the community is also an important aspect of transition education for many students with disabilities. According to a national study by Lipscomb et al. (2017), 80.1% youth with ASD expect to be living on their own by age 30; just under half (48.8%) of parents shared this same expectation. However, only 17% of young adults with ASD report living independently up to 8 years after exiting high school; less than half expressed high satisfaction with their current living arrangement. To address this gap between expectations and outcomes, schools can connect students with ASD to instruction, experiences, and supports that prepare them for future independent living. Some independent living skills—such as time management, financial literacy, functional skills, nutrition, personal safety, appropriate hygiene, and personal management strategies—are covered in elective courses or can be addressed through supplemental instruction that takes place in resource settings. Others skills—such as shopping, cooking, navigating one's community, and maintaining one's residence—are better taught using community-based instruction that takes place beyond school grounds. Extracurricular activities, service-learning, and volunteer experiences can provide additional opportunities for students with ASD to learn and apply skills that will have relevance to their everyday lives (Carter et al., 2010a).

Social Skills and Relationships

The social dimensions of secondary schooling also have particular relevance during the transition to adulthood. The development of appropriate social skills can impact the success with which individuals find and maintain employment, as well as the extent to which they are able to make and sustain satisfying relationships (Carter et al., 2014b; Nasamran et al., 2017). Moreover, middle and high school is a period during which peer relationships take on increasing importance yet become increasingly challenging for adolescents to navigate successfully. Because social and communication challenges are defining characteristics within the autism diagnoses, schools should pursue practices that strengthen the social skills and knowledge of students with ASD. A number of approaches exist for providing individualized or group-based social skills instruction to adolescents with ASD (e.g., Gates et al., 2017; Ke et al., 2018). These interventions have addressed a breadth of social-related behaviors related to initiating conversations, reciprocity, maintaining eye contact, social cognition, appropriate affect, perspective taking, navigating social scenarios, and employment "soft skills." Although the impact of social skills instruction alone tends to be modest, interventions may be made more effective by tailoring them to address the individualized needs of students, implementing instruction with high levels of fidelity, and offering instruction over time and across settings (Bellini & Peters, 2008). Embedding and extending instruction beyond the classroom and school campus can help promote the generalization of new social skills to a variety of employment and community settings.

Although efforts to strengthen the social competence of students with ASD are important, schools should also establish regular, well-supported opportunities for these adolescents to develop and deepen relationships with same-age peers. Such friendships and supportive relationships provide rich contexts for students with ASD to acquire and practice new social skills, learn prevailing social norms, access a range of emotional and practical supports, develop a deeper sense of self, form new friendships, and experience a sense of belonging and membership (Carter et al., 2014b). Schools should adopt a comprehensive approach to promoting relationship formation that focuses on (a) building the social competencies of students with ASD; (b) improving the attitudes and intentions of peers, (c) expanding social supports and opportunities, and (d) enhancing the overall school climate and culture (Carter & Biggs, 2019). Peer-mediated interventions comprise an especially effective strategy for addressing each of these elements. For example, peer support arrangements can be used to promote shared learning within general education classrooms (Carter et al., 2016), peer networks can be established outside of the classroom to build social connections (Asmus et al., 2017), and peer partner programs can provide group-based opportunities for students to establish new friendships and promote schoolwide changes (Carter & Hughes, 2013). In addition to focusing on friendships, students with ASD may benefit from instruction—whether addressed in school, by families, or through community programs—related to navigating

Addressing Transition Preparation in Middle and High Schools

intimate relationships and topics related to healthy and safe sexual expression (Pecora et al., 2016). This latter area has received only scant attention in the professional literature.

Self-Determination

An additional area of practice for students with ASD surrounds efforts to build students' capacities and opportunities for self-determination. Self-determination involves having the skills, knowledge, opportunities, and supports needed to steer one's own life in valued ways that lead to personally satisfying outcomes (Field et al., 1998). Becoming more self-determined is a developmental task for every adolescent, but it is especially important for students with ASD who often receive few opportunities to act in self-determined ways and who sometimes struggle to act in self-directed and empowered ways (Carter et al., 2013; Chou et al., 2017). Schools can provide instruction in areas known to contribute to self-determination, such as self-awareness and self-knowledge, choice-making, decision-making, problem-solving, self-management, self-advocacy and leadership, and goal-setting and attainment. Although these skills are often addressed incidentally throughout the school day, students with ASD may benefit from more explicit and extended opportunities for instruction and practice in order to apply them meaningfully within their own lives.

Personnel Roles and Responsibilities

As emphasized throughout this book, transition education is a collaborative endeavor. An interdisciplinary approach is essential at the level of the IEP team, but is also strongly recommended when establishing a school- or community-level transition team (Povenmire-Kirk et al., 2015). In this section, we describe the ways in which different school staff can support transition from their particular professional roles. Families—who also play a critical role on this interdisciplinary team—are discussed in a later section. Such information can be drawn upon by school psychologists as they help spur a collaborative investment in transition services in their schools.

School Psychologists

The general roles of school psychologists regard ongoing psychological and academic assessment that can inform educational planning. Within the context of transition planning, these professionals can support a transition team in understanding a student's particular strengths and needs to help identify supports that are necessary to facilitate the meeting of future goals. More specifically, they can collect data that includes standardized assessments, observations of behavior, teacher reports, samples of student work, interviews with students, and curriculum-based measures and actively use this information to inform transition goals (Talapatra et al., 2018). They provide consultation and dissemination of resources regarding the instructional implications of a student's postsecondary goals and planning for a student's program evaluation by assessing the effectiveness of interventions and student progress toward post-school objectives (Lillenstein et al., 2006). They communicate assessment results to students with ASD and their families and provide them with documentation necessary to access accommodations and services in postsecondary education and employment settings. School psychologists may also provide direct services to students with ASD, such as social skills training and behavior management. Given the crucial roles these professionals can play in the transition process, they should receive training that is directly geared toward increasing their knowledge of students with ASD and other disabilities they serve.

Special Educators

The general roles of special educators concentrate upon the planning and delivery of special education services, including instruction and transition services, for students with ASD. These professionals take lead responsibility for developing, implementing, and evaluating transition goals and services. Within the context of transition planning, they often work the most closely with students and are aware of their strengths, challenges, and postsecondary goals. They may assess student skills, collect data across settings, and coordinate transition-related instruction, experiences, and supports. Other roles may include supporting general education teachers in meeting the needs of students with ASD within inclusive classrooms, training those paraprofessionals and job coaches who work directly with students, fostering access to general education and inclusive opportunities for extracurricular and community activities, and ongoing communication with families in regard to transition. At transition planning meetings, special educators often share assessment data and use it to inform transition goals. They connect families with outside supports that can facilitate their student's postsecondary goals.

General Educators

As content area experts, the typical roles of general educators pertain to high-quality instruction for all students, including those with ASD. They promote inclusive culture in their classroom so that students with ASD and other disabilities are active members of the learning community. Within the context of transition planning, general educators may embed transition instruction and career development within academic coursework and work closely with paraprofessionals to foster the academic success of students with ASD (Morningstar & Clavenna-Deane, 2018). They may support the student in developing goals specific to the content areas they teach, as well as share their own experiences and passion in ways that further the career interests of students with ASD. At transition planning meetings, general educators provide perspective on how students are functioning in general education classrooms, reference work samples, and provide feedback regarding accommodations and modifications that could also be helpful to students in future postsecondary educational settings. Finally, general educators who lead extracurricular activities or community programs can also actively promote the inclusion of students with ASD in these opportunities.

Career Technical Educators

The general roles of career technical educators (CTE) regard rigorous instruction that supports students with and without ASD develop skills and competencies expected by future employers. CTE educators are tasked with creating opportunities and real-world experiences for students to gain exposure and awareness of various career fields, particularly those with which they may not otherwise be familiar. They are often involved in developing partnerships with local businesses, developing internship and apprenticeship opportunities for students, and using vocational assessments to inform career planning. Within the context of transition planning, these professionals can help inform the team about career-related opportunities and address how students with ASD can gain access to instruction and skill-building aligned with their career goals. CTE educators can support students in identifying employment interests and preparing for postsecondary degrees and certificates in technical fields that match their aptitudes and preferences. Moreover, CTE educators can draw upon their own expertise and experiences to help students with ASD develop their passions into future careers.

Related Services

Related services personnel further support the transitions of students with ASD by reducing potential barriers to postsecondary success and helping the team to consider strategies that should be implemented to meet student needs for transition. The general roles of speech-language pathologists focus upon instruction and support related to social and communication skills that can be so critical to success in the workplace or in community settings. Within the context of transition planning, these specialists design accommodations and modifications that can support students in postsecondary settings. Similarly, the general roles of social workers relate to supporting the emotional and mental health of students. This support is especially crucial throughout the transition process, during which social workers can facilitate the development of self-advocacy and build student self-determination in both secondary and postsecondary settings. Behavior analysts bring expertise on teaching positive behaviors, and within the context of transition planning, they can address behaviors that facilitate a student's access to employment, college, and community participation. Physical therapists and occupational therapists generally bring expertise on supports and technology that promote physical access to inclusive instructional settings, and within the context of transition planning, these include job sites. All of these related service personnel contribute to the development and implementation of transition goals, augment the transition assessment process, and help support students with ASD connect to similar services when they exit high school.

Guidance Counselors

Building-level initiatives for transition are often best implemented by professionals with daily responsibilities that involve transition coordination (Morningstar & Clavenna-Deane, 2018). The general role of guidance counselors is to coordinate opportunities that can ensure all students gain awareness, exposure, and connections with colleges, trade schools, businesses, and adult agencies. Among school staff, they are typically most aware of the collection of courses, extracurricular activities, and job opportunities available to students. Guidance counselors are responsible for steering students toward rigorous and relevant courses that prepare them for graduation, for college admission, and for the attainment of their postsecondary goals. They often use career interest inventories to inform postsecondary goal-setting with all students, connect families with community resources, and host events (e.g., college and career nights) that connect the school with the community. Within the context of transition planning, guidance counselors can ensure their schoolwide efforts also reach students with ASD and they can share their deep knowledge of those college and career options that align with a particular student's interests and goals.

Transition Specialists

Transition specialists coordinate transition services and experiences specifically for students with disabilities. Although not every school or district allocates these responsibilities to a single person, transition specialists are typically responsible for building connections with outside agencies and organizations, collaborating with vocational rehabilitative services, and meeting with families (Noonan et al., 2008). They may also support other school staff in creating opportunities for students with ASD to explore their career interests, plan for postsecondary education, or acquire functional and community skills. Transition specialists may coordinate community-based instruction experiences and connect families with specific adult and community agencies through transition fairs. They may collaborate with special educators to develop transition goals and work with guidance counselors to consider the needs of students with ASD when establishing schoolwide college and career preparatory experiences.

School Administrators

The general roles of school administrators involve supporting staff to deliver high-quality services and supports that meet the needs of all students. Within the context of transition planning, they are responsible for setting a vision for transition and communicating high expectations for all students. Administrators support transitions for students with ASD by allocating funding and staffing toward community-based instruction, work-based training, job coaching, and other areas that comprise a comprehensive transition program. They can also ensure that school staff have access to professional development addressing evidence-based practices in the area of transition. During transition planning meetings, administrators, such as special education directors and principals, can ensure that effective communication leads to decisions that best meet the needs of individual students and help resolve divergent opinions amongst team members. Finally, school administrators should strive to ensure their schools meet both the letter and spirit of prevailing transition mandates, as well as ensure that students with ASD and other disabilities are not left out of schoolwide initiatives and programs that could support their successful transitions.

Strong Partnerships

Strong building-level teams should be coupled with compelling community partnerships. Although public schools are explicitly charged with providing transition services to students with ASD, they simply cannot provide all of the opportunities, resources, and assistance that students might need. Collaborations with adult agencies and community partners are critical to improving the outcomes of transition-age youth (Noonan et al., 2008; Povenmire-Kirk et al., 2015).

Adult Agencies and Service Providers

As students with ASD and their families transition from the familiarities of their local school system to the complexities of the adult service system, they need guidance on the types of programs and supports that can facilitate career, college, and community participation. Although students with ASD are entitled to transition services through their local school, they must be found eligible for services after exiting high school. Connecting students with ASD and their families to adult agencies and disability service providers *before* graduation can help promote a more seamless transition between these two critical systems. For example, vocational rehabilitation (VR) programs provide a variety of services (e.g., vocational counseling, skill training, college training, transportation, assistive technology, job coaching) to facilitate initial entrance into—or return to—work among adults with ASD. Area employment agencies can assist young adults with ASD in finding and maintaining employment through job development, job carving, on-the-job supports, and job retention strategies. Local residential providers can help support goals related to independent or semi-independent living. Centers for Independent Living (CILs) can provide information and referral, peer support, advocacy services, independent living skills training, and transition services. Staff from Social Security Administration can provide information about programs and benefits that facilitate employment. School teams should develop working partnerships with these different entities, become familiar with their eligibility requirements and available supports, and be ready to share this information in accessible ways with students with ASD and their families. Moreover, the IDEA (2004) requires schools to "invite to the IEP meeting a representative of any participating agency that is likely to be responsible for providing or paying for transition services" [34 CFR §300.321(b)(3)].

Employers

Obtaining employment is a primary goal for nearly all young people with ASD—whether after attending postsecondary education or in lieu of it. Strong partnerships with a diverse array of local businesses are essential to ensuring students with ASD can participate in internships, apprenticeships, work-based learning, or other hands-on experiences that will prepare them well for the world of work. Schools or districts might designate a staff person to serve in the role of "community connector" or "employer liaison" which involves identifying local employment opportunities that align with the vocational interests of students with disabilities, reaching out to local employers about job openings and partnerships, assisting students in applying for these jobs, and arranging needed on-the-job supports (Carter et al., 2009). Schools can also collaborate with local employer networks—such as an area Chamber of Commerce or other association of businesses—that represent a broad range of local industry sectors. Such networks can help support the career development of students with ASD by sharing job and internship opportunities, advocating for member businesses to hire students with disabilities, inviting schools to share about transition needs at network meetings, and sharing important economic forecast information.

Postsecondary Education Programs

A growing number of students with ASD are pursuing postsecondary educational pathways such as two- and four-year colleges, technical and trade schools, and other vocational training programs. Indeed, 74.5% of youth with ASD expect to obtain some type of postsecondary education (Lipscomb et al., 2017). Key school and district staff should be familiar with the full range of postsecondary programs available to their graduates—locally and beyond—including their entry requirements and application deadlines, available programs and majors, and the availability of financial supports. To support students with ASD, it is also important to understand issues related to campus accessibility, the quality of disability and other support services, and the documentation requirements to obtain services. To familiarize students with postsecondary options and supports, schools can arrange tours of area college campus, host college nights at their school, invite college representatives as guest speakers, arrange panel discussions led by college students with ASD, and launch mentorship programs that connect high school and college students with ASD. In addition, several disability-focused postsecondary initiatives are gaining momentum, such as the U.S. Department of Education's *Transition and Postsecondary Programs for Students with Intellectual Disability,* which supports college access for students with ASD who also have a cognitive impairment (www.thinkcollege.net); the *Project Search* (www.projectsearch.us) program, which helps prepare individuals with ASD for competitive employment; and the *College Autism Network* (www.collegeautismnetwork.org), which seeks to improve access, experiences, and outcomes for college students with ASD.

Civic and Community Groups

Schools and districts should also consider cultivating relationships with other "informal" or "generic" programs that have a presence in their local community. For example, most communities are home to a number of service, civic, leadership, fraternal, and charitable groups that are committed to supporting community initiatives, that involve a variety of community leaders, and whose members have connections to nearly every corner of the community. Examples include community foundations, Exchange, Lions, Kiwanis, Knights of Columbus, Moose, Optimists, Rotary, United Way, and many others. These groups can be instrumental in helping schools identify volunteer opportunities, mentors, internships, transportation, and other resources that could be helpful to transition-age students with ASD. Similarly, some local faith communities have supported transition programming by connecting youth with ASD to jobs by drawing upon the personal networks of fellow congregation members, identifying mentors willing to come alongside others through the job search, encouraging members to be advocates for inclusion in their own workplaces, providing community-based job training sites, and even hiring people within the congregation (Carter et al., 2016). Finally, communities often have local chapters of disability organizations (e.g., Arcs, autism societies), disability-focused grant projects, or university programs (e.g., University Centers for Excellence in Developmental Disabilities [UCEDDs]) in their region or state that can serve as key sources of information, training, and advocacy related to transition.

Families

Parents, siblings, and other relatives can be the most enduring sources of guidance, advocacy, and support for students with ASD. Although the extent to which each will participate directly in the transition process will vary, family engagement is essential to effective transition education. Inviting parents to transition planning meetings is a requirement of IDEA, but developing a strong working partnership that extends throughout the school year is considered best practice. Many parents of students with ASD also report great difficulty finding relevant and accessible information related to their child's needs and post-school interests (Gilson et al., 2017a). Providing them to reliable information about the agencies, organizations, and programs described throughout this book can ensure they have the tools they need to support their child's transition well. Likewise, they may need help connecting to the array of formal and informal programs that might assist them and their family members with disabilities during the transition years. For example, only 54.0% of parents indicated their children with ASD were given information on education, careers, and community living options when they leave high school at their transition planning meeting (Lipscomb et al., 2017).

Connecting Schools and Communities

Stitching together this breadth of formal and informal partners can be challenging. Several approaches have been used by schools to identify and engage these key stakeholders. First, "community resource mapping" provides a systematic way of determining what already exists in the community that might align with the interests, goals, and needs of students with disabilities at the school; and compiling this information into an accessible document that is made available to students with ASD, their families, and the educators who support them (Tindle et al., 2005). Second, "community conversation" events provide a structured approach for bringing together a cross section of local stakeholders (e.g., agency representatives, civic leaders, community programs, disability professionals, employers, parents, school staff, youth with disabilities) to identify solutions and partners that could be drawn upon to improve the in- and post-school outcomes of transition-age youth with disabilities (Carter & Bumble, 2018). Third, many districts establish community transition teams that meet regularly to address critical surrounding access to services and supports for students with disabilities within the community (Flowers et al., 2018). School psychologists can be leaders or contributors within all three of these efforts.

Conclusion

Like any young person, students with ASD hold dreams for a future of flourishing after graduation. Supporting their successful transitions to college, career, and community life is a primary purpose of special education and secondary education. Middle and high school represents a critical juncture during which the right combination of principles, planning, practices, personnel, and partnerships can dramatically elevate the trajectories of students with ASD. School psychologists are important partners within these efforts and potential catalysts for school- and district-level change. With the right combination of services and supports throughout the transition years, young people with ASD can attain their aspirations for adulthood and achieve their post-school goals.

References

Asmus, J., Carter, E. W., Moss, C. K., Biggs, E. E., Bolt, D., ... Wier, K. (2017). Efficacy and social validity of peer network interventions for high school students with severe disabilities. *American Journal on Intellectual and Developmental Disabilities, 122*, 118–137. https://doi.org/10.1352/1944-7558-122.2.118

Bellini, S., & Peters, J. K. (2008). Social skills training for youth with autism spectrum disorders. *Child and Adolescent Psychiatric Clinics of North America, 17*, 857–873. https://doi.org/10.1016/j.chc.2008.06.008

Bennett, K. D., & Dukes, C. (2013). Employment instruction for secondary students with autism spectrum disorder: A systematic review of the literature. *Education and Training in Autism and Developmental Disabilities, 48*, 67–75. https://doi.org/10.1002/jaba.196

Blustein, C. L., Carter, E. W., & McMillan, E. (2016). The voices of parents post–high school expectations, priorities, and concerns for children with intellectual and developmental disabilities. *The Journal of Special Education, 50*, 164–177. https://doi.org/10.1177/0022466916641381

Carter, E. W. (2017). *Toward a future of flourishing: Promoting rigor, relevance, and relationships foryouth with disabilities.* Keynote presentation at the Texas Transition Conference. Houston, Texas.

Carter, E. W. (2018). Supporting strong transitions for students with autism spectrum disorder. In N. Gelbar (Ed.), *Adolescents with autism spectrum disorder: A clinical handbook* (pp. 171–195). Oxford University Press. https://doi.org/10.1093/med-psych/9780190624828.001.0001

Carter, E. W., Austin, D., & Trainor, A. A. (2012). Predictors of postschool employment outcomes for young adults with severe disabilities. *Journal of Disability Policy Studies, 23*, 50–63. https://doi.org/10.1177/1044207311414680

Carter, E. W., & Biggs, E. E. (2019). Evidence-based practices for adolescents and adults with autism spectrum disorder and complex communication needs. In J. B. Ganz & R. L. Simpson (Eds.), *Interventions for individuals with autism spectrum disorder and complex communication needs* (pp. 225–247). Paul H. Brookes Publishing.

Carter, E. W., Brock, M. E., & Trainor, A. A. (2014a). Transition assessment and planning for youth with severe intellectual and developmental disabilities. *The Journal of Special Education, 47*, 245–255. https://doi.org/10.1177/0022466912456241

Carter, E. W., & Bumble, J. L. (2018). The promise and possibilities of community conversations: Expanding employment opportunities for people with disabilities. *Journal of Disability Policy Studies, 28*, 195–202. https://doi.org/10.1177/1044207317739408

Carter, E. W., Commons, E. A., Sreckovic, M. A., Huber, H. B., Bottema-Beutel, K., Gustafson, J. R., Dykstra, J., & Hume, K. (2014b). Promoting social competence and peer relationships for adolescents with ASD. *Remedial and Special Education, 35*, 27–37. https://journals.sagepub.com/doi/10.1177/0741932513514618

Carter, E. W., Endress, T., Gustafson, J., Shouse, J., Taylor, C., Utley, A., … Allen, W. (2016). *Putting faith to work: A guide for congregations and communities on connecting job seekers with disabilities to meaningful work.* Collaborative on Faith and Disability.

Carter, E. W., & Hughes, C. (2013). Teaching social skills and promoting supportive relationships. In P. Wehman (Ed.), *Life beyond the classroom* (5th ed., pp. 249–268). Brookes Publishing.

Carter, E. W., Lane, K. L., Cooney, M., Weir, K., Moss, C. K., & Machalicek, W. (2013). Parent assessments of self-determination importance and performance for students with autism or intellectual disability. *American Journal on Intellectual and Developmental Disabilities, 88*, 16–31. https://doi.org/10.1352/1944-7558-118.1.16

Carter, E. W., Swedeen, B., Moss, C. K., & Pesko, M. J. (2010a). "What are you doing after school?" Promoting extracurricular involvement for transition-age youth with disabilities. *Intervention in School and Clinic, 45*, 275–283. https://doi.org/10.1177/1053451209359077

Carter, E. W., Trainor, A. A., Cakiroglu, O., Swedeen, B., & Owens, L. (2010b). Availability of and access to career development activities for transition-age youth with disabilities. *Career Development for Exceptional Individuals, 33*, 13–24. https://doi.org/10.1177/0885728809344332

Carter, E. W., Trainor, A. A., Ditchman, N., Swedeen, B., & Owens, L. (2009). Evaluation of a multi-component intervention package to increase summer work experiences for transition-age youth with severe disabilities. *Research and Practice for Persons with Severe Disabilities, 34*, 1–12. https://doi.org/10.2511/rpsd.34.2.1

Chandroo, R., Strnadova, I., & Cumming, T. M. (2018). A systematic review of the involvement of students with autism spectrum disorder in the transition planning process: Need for voice and empowerment. *Research in Developmental Disabilities, 83*, 8–17. https://doi.org/10.1016/j.ridd.2018.07.011

Chiang, H., Cheung, Y. K., Hickson, L., Xiang, R., & Tsai, L. Y. (2012). Predictive factors of participation in postsecondary education for high school leavers with autism. *Journal of Autism and Developmental Disorders, 42*, 685–696. https://doi.org/10.1007/s10803-011-1297-7

Chiang, H., Cheung, Y., Li, H., & Tsai, L. (2013). Factors associated with participation in employment for high school leavers with autism. *Journal of Autism and Developmental Disorders, 43*, 1832–1842. https://doi.org/10.1007/s10803-012-1734-2

Chou, Y., Wehmeyer, M. L., Palmer, S. B., & Lee, J. (2017). Comparisons of self-determination among students with autism, intellectual disability, and learning disabilities: A multivariate analysis. *Focus on Autism and Other Developmental Disabilities, 32*, 124–132. https://doi.org/10.1177/1088357615625059

Delano, M. E. (2007). Video modeling interventions for individuals with autism. *Remedial and Special Education, 28*, 33–42. https://doi.org/10.1177/07419325070280010401

Field, S. S., Martin, J. E., Miller, R. J., Ward, M., & Wehmeyer, M. L. (1998). Self-determination for persons with disabilities: A position statement of the division on career development and transition. *Career Development for Exceptional Individuals, 21*, 113–128. https://doi.org/10.1177/088572889802100202

Fleury, V. P., Hedges, S., Hume, K., Browder, D. M., Thompson, J. L., … Vaughn, S. (2014). Addressing the academic needs of adolescents with autism spectrum disorder in secondary education. *Remedial and Special Education, 35*, 68–79. https://doi.org/10.1177/0741932513518823

Flowers, C., Test, D. W., Povenmire-Kirk, T. C., Diegelmann, K. M., Bunch-Crump, K. R., Kemp-Inman, A., & Goodnight, C. I. (2018). A demonstration of interagency collaboration for students with disabilities: A multi-level approach. *The Journal of Special Education, 51*, 211–222. https://doi.org/10.1177/0022466917720764

Gates, J. A., Kang, E., & Lerner, M. D. (2017). Efficacy of group social skills interventions for youth with autism spectrum disorder: A systematic review and meta-analysis. *Clinical Psychology Review, 52*, 164–181. https://doi.org/10.1016/j.cpr.2017.01.006

Gilson, C. B., Bethune, L., Carter, E. W., & McMillan, E. (2017a). Informing and equipping parents of people with intellectual and developmental disabilities. *Intellectual and Developmental Disabilities, 43*, 20–37. https://doi.org/10.1352/1934-9556-55.5.347

Gilson, C. B., Carter, E. W., & Biggs, E. E. (2017b). Systematic review of instructional methods to teach employment skills to secondary students with intellectual and developmental disabilities. *Research and Practice for Persons with Severe Disabilities, 42*, 89–107. https://doi.org/10.1177/1540796917698831

Haber, M. G., Mazzotti, V. L., Mustian, A. L., Rowe, D. A., Bartholomew, A. L., Test, D. W., & Fowler, C. H. (2016). What works, when, for whom, and with whom: A meta-analytic review of predictors of postsecondary success for students with disabilities. *Review of Educational Research, 86*, 123–162. https://doi.org/10.3102/0034654315583135

Individuals with Disabilities Education Improvement Act of 2004. PL 108–446. (2004).

Ke, F., Whalon, K., & Yun, J. (2018). Social skill interventions for youth and adults with autism spectrum disorder: A systematic review. *Review of Educational Research, 88*, 3–42. https://doi.org/10.3102/0034654317740334

Kirby, A. V., Baranek, G. T., & Fox, L. (2016). Longitudinal predictors of outcomes for adults with autism spectrum disorders: Systematic review. *Occupation, Participation and Health, 35*, 55–64. https://doi.org/10.1177/1539449216650182

Lee, G. K., & Carter, E. W. (2012). Preparing transition-age students with high-functioning autism spectrum disorders for meaningful work. *Psychology in the Schools, 49*, 988–1000. https://doi.org/10.1002/pits.21651

Lillenstein, D. J., Levinson, E. M., Sylvester, C. A., & Brady, E. E. (2006). School psychologist involvement in transition planning: A comparison of attitudes and perceptions of school psychologists and transition coordinators. *Journal for Vocational Special Needs Education, 29*, 4–16.

Lipscomb, S., Haimson, J., Liu, A. Y., Burghardt, J., Johnson, D. R., & Thurlow, M. L. (2017). *Preparing for life after high school: The characteristics and experiences of youth in special education* (Vol. 2). U. S. Department of Education.

Morningstar, M. E., & Clavenna-Deane. (2018). *Your complete guide to transition planning and services*. Paul H. Brookes.

Nasamran, A., Witmer, S. E., & Los, J. E. (2017). Exploring predictors of postsecondary outcomes for students with autism spectrum disorder. *Education and Training in Autism and Developmental Disabilities, 52*, 343–356. https://psycnet.apa.org/doi/10.1037/e603852013-001

National Technical Assistance Center on Transition. (2012). *NSTTAC indicator 13 checklist form A*. Author. https://transitionta.org/sites/default/files/transitionplanning/NSTTAC_ChecklistFormA.pdf

National Technical Assistance Center on Transition. (2016). *Age appropriate transition assessment toolkit* (4th ed.). University of North Carolina at Charlotte. https://transitionta.org/system/files/toolkitassessment/AgeAppropriateTransitionAssessmentToolkit2016_COMPLETE_11_21_16.pdf

Newman, L., Wagner, M., Knokey, A. M., Marder, C., Nagle, K., … Wei, X. (2011). *The post-high school outcomes of young adults with disabilities up to 8 years after high school*. SRI International. IES: https://ies.ed.gov/ncser/pubs/20113005/pdf/20113005.pdf

Noonan, P. M., Morningstar, M. E., & Erickson, A. G. (2008). Improving interagency collaboration: Effective strategies used by high-performing local districts and communities. *Career Development for Exceptional Individuals, 31*, 132–143. https://doi.org/10.1177/0885728808327149

Olson, A. J., Roberts, C. A., & Leko, M. M. (2015). Teacher-, student-, and peer-directed strategies to access the general education curriculum for students with autism. *Intervention in School and Clinic, 51*, 37–44. https://doi.org/10.1177/1053451214546406

Pecora, L. A., Mesibov, G. B., & Stokes, M. A. (2016). Sexuality in high-functioning autism: A systematic review and meta analysis. *Journal of Autism and Developmental Disorders, 46*, 3519–3556. https://doi.org/10.1007/s10803-016-2892-4

Povenmire-Kirk, T., Diegelmann, K., Crump, K., Schnorr, C., Test, D., … Aspel, N. (2015). Implementing CIRCLES: A new model for interagency collaboration in transition planning. *Journal of Vocational Rehabilitation, 42*, 51–65. https://doi.org/10.3233/JVR-140723

Sitlington, P. L., Neubert, D. A., & Leconte, P. J. (1997). Transition assessment: The position of the division on career development and transition. *Career Development for Exceptional Individuals, 20*, 69–79. https://doi.org/10.1177/088572288970200106

Talapatra, D., Roach, A., Varjas, K., Houchins, D., & Crimmins, D. (2018). Transition services for students with intellectual disabilities: School psychologists' perceptions. *Psychology in the Schools, 1-23*. https://doi.org/10.1002/pits.22189

Tindle, K., Leconte, P., Buchanan, L., & Taymans, J. M. (2005). Transition planning: Community mapping as a tool for teachers and students. *Research to Practice Brief, 4*, 1–6. NCSET: http://www.ncset.org/publications/viewdesc.asp?id=2128

Obtaining Appropriate Services in College

Elizabeth Williams

Abstract School psychologists play a unique professional role in supporting the academic, social, emotional, and executive functioning in students with disabilities. For Autistic students, this role is of particular importance due to the achievement gap in college graduation rates between Autistic students and their neurotypical peers as well as the graduation rates of students from other disability categories (Baio et al., MMWR Surveill Summ 67(SS-6):1–23, 2018). School psychologists' knowledge about the college selection process as well as the application procedures for university accommodations under the Americans with Disabilities Act (42 U.S.C. § 12101, 1990) is critically important in order to support successful student outcomes. Of additional importance is highlighting the gap between legally mandated disability accommodations and the full profile of needs of Autistic students. College-based specialty programs are designed to equip Autistic students with a full spectrum of support services in order to promote academic and social-emotional success during the college transition. By using this information to support students and families, high school psychologists can continue to advocate for students with disabilities, including Autistic individuals.

Keywords College · Autism · Autistic · College specialty programs · College transition programs · College support services · College disability accommodations

Obtaining Appropriate Services in College

School psychologists are allies to all students and have a unique professional focus that blends students' social-emotional well-being and their educational progress. This requires specialized knowledge of a variety of special needs, including expertise in the areas of attention-deficit/hyperactivity disorder, anxiety, Down

---

E. Williams (✉)
Darien Public Schools, Special Education and Student Services Department,
Darien, CT, USA

© Springer Nature Switzerland AG 2022
K. D. Viezel et al. (eds.), *Postsecondary Transition for College- or Career-Bound Autistic Students*, https://doi.org/10.1007/978-3-030-93947-2_10

201

syndrome, and autism spectrum disorder (ASD), just to name a few. Due to the increase in prevalence rates of ASD (Baio et al., 2018), school psychologists should be prepared to provide supportive services to this subset of students. One of these support services involves legally mandated postsecondary transition planning for students receiving Special Education services as required by the Individuals with Disabilities Education Act (IDEA). Although college is only one of the many types of postsecondary options, it is likely that more Autistic students will be seeking college admission in the future as 46% of Autistic individuals have average or above average intelligence (Christensen et al., 2016). Presently, there are more Autistic students than ever attending college (Cox, 2017). School psychologists should be prepared to support Autistic individuals with college transition planning.

In order to advocate for students' postsecondary goals as well as abide by the legal mandate for transition planning, it is important for school psychologists to be well-versed in the many variables contributing to a successful college transition, especially for students with disabilities. This includes selecting an appropriate college and applying for accommodations through campus disability offices as well as educating families about the change in disability laws. It is also critically important for school psychologists to be aware of the commonly granted accommodations by university disability offices. However, it is equally important to understand the areas of students' unique needs that will likely *not* be met through these accommodations. In turn, school psychologists should be a resource for additional support options, including college-based specialty programs providing intervention services to Autistic students. The following information provides an overview of the important details in the college planning process for Autistic students and ways school psychologists can support students and families in advocating for successful student outcomes.

Choosing a College

The decision to pursue college may feel a combination of daunting and exciting for all students; however, there are additional elements of college planning that are unique to students with disabilities. This can make the college search more complicated and stressful. School psychologists are a valuable resource in helping students and families with this transition planning process, including selecting a college and ensuring that the institution has the appropriate services required to support students with unique needs. The college selection process is a multifaceted decision that requires consideration of a number of important factors stemming from university location to types of disability services offered. Other specific variables to consider include: academic programs offered, location, cost, and campus activities. Details about each of these important components of college planning are discussed below.

Academic Programs and Majors

Selecting a college major is an exciting decision for students to make when applying to universities. It is important for students to ensure their area of interest is available as a college major at their desired postsecondary institution. While selecting a college major may be a challenging task for many college-bound students, this may be an area of the college transition process that is easier for Autistic students. A feature of ASD involves a restricted area of interest (American Psychiatric Association [APA], 2013), which may easily translate into an area of study. For example, students who have a focused interest in video games may only consider universities offering video game design as an academic major. Other skill sets and specific areas of strength (e.g., mathematical skills, curiosity about science, proficiency with computers, passion for art, musical talent) may guide a student in their decision to select an academic program. Researching universities that have a particular major is a way to narrow down what may otherwise be a large list of potential schools. While selecting an academic major, school psychologists should also discuss the availability of both 2- and 4-year college programs in order to ensure that community college vs. 4-year traditional college attendance is aligned with students' postsecondary educational and career goals.

When researching academic majors, school psychologists should help Autistic students navigate the admission requirements for a chosen university and academic program. The admission requirements (e.g., high school grade point average or standardized test scores) vary from one college to the next. School psychologists should consider all of the ways in which their students' strengths and weaknesses are aligned with the admission requirements for their desired colleges. For example, certain academic programs (e.g., Nursing, Education) may require a minimum grade point average for admission and continuation in the program. School psychologists should support students and families in seeking out a program with attainable academic rigor without being overwhelming. It is important for students to apply to programs with admission requirements that are consistent with their past performance in order to ensure that an academic program is appropriately challenging.

Cost

University attendance may be the first time students and families are tasked with paying for education. Throughout K-12 schooling, students with disabilities are ensured a free and appropriate education (FAPE) under the Individuals with Disabilities Education Act (IDEA, 2004). However, upon the transition into college, FAPE no longer applies and students are responsible for their own tuition costs. This can be an overwhelming responsibility as the average 4-year college tuition in the United States costs approximately $US 28,000 per year (United States

Department of Education, 2019). School psychologists should direct families to the financial aid department of their desired university for information on tuition support, funding opportunities, and the process for applying for student loans. This should also include providing families with a recommendation for completing a Free Application for Federal Student Aid (FAFSA) form. School psychologists may also wish to research scholarship opportunities to reduce the tuition costs. In addition to exploring financial aid and scholarship opportunities, school psychologists are encouraged to guide families in contacting their respective state vocational rehabilitation offices (University of Washington, 2017). College funding may be granted to qualifying students. In order to qualify, students must be eligible to receive vocational rehabilitation services and their college programming must be specific and necessary to obtain employment.

Location

A significant factor in students' college selection choices often involves the location of the university. Students must decide how far away from home they are comfortable with attending college. A particular consideration that may be of focus when making the determination about university location is a student's adaptive behavior profile. Attending school further from home increases the necessity to use on-campus housing, and therefore independent living skills, while students attending school closer to home may rely on family for continued living arrangements while they attend college (as family resources allow). School psychologists may wish to use an adaptive behavior measure, such as the Vineland Adaptive Behavior Scales, Third Edition (Vineland-3; Sparrow et al., 2016) or the Adaptive Behavior Assessment System, Third Edition (ABAS-3; Harrison & Oakland, 2017) to evaluate students' strengths and weaknesses with regard to adaptive behaviors. This may help make the determination about the preparedness for students to live independently in a dorm setting or whether additional time and focus at home is needed to expand upon adaptive behaviors and independent living skills (e.g., setting and responding to alarm clocks, doing laundry, maintaining personal hygiene). Information about student's adaptive behavior is important as many Autistic individuals have adaptive behavior deficits, regardless of a comorbid intellectual disability. While this information is important for college preparation, these areas can also be targeted for effective intervention at the college level (Engstrom, 2019).

Campus Activities

When deciding on which universities to apply, students may also consider activities and organizations that are available within the university community. This includes the presence of extracurricular activities such as sports, intermural, and clubs.

Autistic college students are at risk for loneliness, depression, and anxiety (Gelbar et al., 2014; Jobe & White, 2007), making participation in preferred activities an essential component to help protect against social isolation. School psychologists should support students with ways to blend their current interests and activities into recreational programs on campus. It may be helpful for school psychologists to provide students with a list of campus organizations, clubs, and sports in order to select at least one extracurricular activity that supports their areas of interest. For example, a student with a particular and focused passion in video games may look for a student-led gaming club while another student interested in frisbee may choose to participate in an intermural frisbee team. If a student's area of interest is not represented on a university's list of extracurricular opportunities, many universities allow students to create their own organization; however, this involves navigating campus procedures for starting an official organization for which a student with social communication and executive functioning challenges may need guidance.

Disability Supports

An additional component for transition planning involves educating students and families about the ways in which students with disabilities are accommodated at the college level. While universities are required to have a disability office in which students can request accommodations under the Americans with Disabilities Act ([ADA],1990), it is important for school psychologists to be aware of the important difference between K-12 disability laws and postsecondary disability laws.

Change in Disability Laws Entering College

K-12 school psychologists' roles rely heavily upon knowledge of disability laws, including the identification and support of students with disabilities. In accordance with IDEA, students are identified for Special Education programming if an identified disability is impacting their academic progress. K-12 schools are legally mandated to ensure that students with special needs receive a free and appropriate education, and districts are required to monitor academic progress in order to make individualized recommendations (e.g., access to paraprofessional, altered curriculum, modified worksheets). When students enter college, IDEA is no longer the governing disability law serving those with unique learning needs. However, students' needs do not disappear upon high school graduation and require continued support and accommodation when entering college. Instead, students with disabilities are protected under ADA and Section 504 of the Rehabilitation Act of 1973. ADA requires that postsecondary institutions provide students with equal access to educational environments and educational materials; however, they are not required to provide a free and appropriate education as was mandated during K-12 education under IDEA. As such, universities are not required to significantly modify course materials/graduation requirements or provide accommodations that would result in undue administrative or financial burden on the university (United States Department of Education - Office for Civil Rights, 2011). It is important for K-12 school psychologists to be knowledgeable about the process for obtaining college-level accommodations in order to prepare students and families for this switch in disability laws.

Applying for College-Level Accommodations

Given the aforementioned switch in disability law from high school to college, students should be proactive in applying for disability accommodations. In order to do so, a student must self-disclose their disability status to their institution's disability office as universities are prohibited from asking about the presence of a disability during the admission process. Colleges are also are not required to identify specific students as having a disability following their admission to the university. The process for requesting accommodations through the campus disability office varies from one college to another. School psychologists are encouraged to educate students and families on the specifics for applying for these accommodations by contacting the university's disability services center for detailed instructions.

While specific procedures vary from one university to another, there are many common requirements. Disability offices ask that students submit evidence of a disability requiring accommodations. The disability office will ask for the specific diagnosis or disability as well as how that disability impacts a major life activity and/or academic functioning. The disability office may also request information about the date of the assigned diagnosis as well as how this disability status was determined. Section 504 Plans and IEP paperwork are likely not sufficient documentation to access college-level accommodations (United States Department of Education Office for Civil Rights, 2011). The type of information requested by disability offices is often presented in the form of a recent evaluation (e.g., within 3 years) completed by a medical doctor, psychologist, or other appropriately qualified professional.

School psychologists should support families in obtaining an evaluation prior to the college application process in order to prepare students to apply for accommodations in a timely manner and not delay the receipt of any granted accommodations. School psychologists should also discuss resources for families in accessing this type of evaluation. Importantly, universities and high schools are *not* required to fund evaluations for postsecondary accommodations (United States Department of Education Office for Civil Rights, 2011). However, it may be beneficial for school psychologists to ensure that students with Special Education support services received a comprehension evaluation during their most recent triennial review. This should include the clear identification of a specific disability (e.g., autism) as well as the impact that the disability has on daily life activities and academic functioning. The evaluation should also include recommendations for accommodations and supports to address the identified areas of deficit. School psychologists should refer students who are not eligible for Special Education, and therefore are not entitled to school-based evaluations, to their child's pediatrician for a recommendation and referral for an evaluation with a qualified provider covered through their insurance, if applicable. Other avenues for obtaining an evaluation include consulting with local community mental health clinics that may provide evaluations with costs on a sliding scale based on income.

School psychologists should support students in preparing their materials to apply for college-based accommodations with the disability office. For example, it may be helpful for Autistic students to be involved in their IEP meetings in order to fully understand their high school accommodations and why these specific supports are helpful to them. School psychologists should focus on providing students with psychoeducation about their disability status. Psychoeducation should include information about personal strengths and areas for growth as is specific to their disability. Interestingly, 55% of students who were previously identified by K-12 schools as having a disability did not consider themselves to have a disability upon entrance into postsecondary education (Newman et al., 2009). Appropriate psychoeducation will be important as attending college comes with an increased need for self-advocacy skills (Adreon & Durocher, 2007) and an understanding of their current level of needs.

Types of College Accommodations

Specific accommodations are contingent on disability type and documented evidence of a need for said accommodations; however, there are particular accommodations that are commonly granted by university disability offices. These common types of accommodations include: extra time on tests, access to assistive technology, and tutoring services (Baio et al., 2018). Additional accommodations that may be granted by college disability offices involve accessing priority course registration and reducing the number of required course credits per semester (United States Department of Education Office for Civil Rights, 2011). Accommodations that may have been granted in high school that are *not* commonly provided at the postsecondary level may include: paraprofessional support, modified worksheets, and modified exams. It is important to note that these examples of uncommon accommodations are based on clinical experience and references to types of commonly granted accommodations (Accardo et al., 2019; Baio et al., 2018). School psychologists are encouraged to consult with specific universities for more details pertaining to their students' needs and available accommodations. As a function of these significant changes in accommodations, it is also helpful for school psychologists to be aware of the gap between what students will realistically receive from disability accommodations and the larger spectrum of required support.

School psychologists should help families in researching on-campus services that ensure all areas of a student's needs are met through other supplementary services that are not provided through the university's disability office. For example, most universities provide services to all students that is not contingent on disability status. On-campus services in the areas of tutoring and mental health counseling are available at no cost to students. It is also important to recognize that not all areas of Autistic students' needs may be met through disability accommodations under ADA. The hallmark deficits of social communication and executive functioning may be areas left unsupported upon entrance into college that were previously targeted in high school under IDEA. In order to bridge this gap, college-based specialty programs are a non-required element of college disability services designed to assist Autistic students with the transition from high school to college as well as provide intervention in a variety of known deficits (e.g., executive functioning, mental health, social skills). More information about these types of programs will be discussed in the upcoming section of this chapter. School psychologists may wish to work with families in narrowing down their college selection options by eliminating universities without this type of hands-on specialty program. Two helpful resources to use when searching for universities with these types of on-campus ASD specialty programs are the College Autism Network (https://collegeautismnetwork.org/institutional-initiatives/) and the College Autism Spectrum (http://collegeautismspectrum.com/collegeprograms/).

Specialty Programs for Autistic College Students

Despite the availability of accommodations through university disability offices, there are aspects of an ASD diagnosis that are not appropriately met by these common accommodations (Chiang et al., 2012). As mentioned previously, the accommodations provided through the disability offices are in place in order to give students equal access to an education and educational materials. While necessary for some Autistic students, these accommodations may not meet their full profile of needs. For example, extra time on tests, access to assistive technology, and availability of tutoring services (Baio et al., 2018) do not support the social communication deficits which can manifest in challenges with interactions in both the classroom and the college dorm settings (Gelbar et al., 2014). Importantly, Autistic students confirm the sentiments that the legally mandated accommodations are not sufficient in meeting their actual needs and do not provide an appropriate amount of support (Newman et al., 2009). Notably, Autistic students are falling behind their peers in college graduation rates (United States Department of Education, 2015) as well as the graduation rates of students from other disability categories (Baio et al., 2018).

One growing area of postsecondary supports for Autistic students are college-based specialty programs specifically designed for this population of students.

These types of programs may be commonly referred to as "support programs" or "transition programs." As such, many college specialty programs are in place to scaffold support such that by the end of college students are able to function with only the supports that are available to all college students. Other programs are designed to provide the services to students for their entire time at a university. It is important to note that the information provided in this chapter focuses on specialty programs for students accepted to and enrolled in degree-granting programs within postsecondary institutions. Information about specialty programs is discussed below.

Features of Specialty Programs

Specialty support programs provide supplemental services to students and families that target areas of social, emotional, academic, and executive functioning. The structure of the programs and types of services offered vary from one program to another, and school psychologists are encouraged to research specific programs in order to locate one that fits students' unique needs. Systematic reviews of college-based support programs for Autistic students yield information about the type and frequency of specific program services as well as the application process and required materials for admission (Barnhill, 2016; Viezel et al., 2020). The following includes an overview of the admission requirements and types of services offered through these college-based specialty programs.

Admission Requirements and Materials

Students seeking enrollment with a college-based specialty program are first and foremost students of their degree-seeking institution. Admission into a specialty program is contingent on general university acceptance and participation in a support program is secondary and not a required component of university enrollment nor is acceptance into a support program a guarantee that a student will receive general admission into the university. Another important distinction includes the difference between accommodations provided by the university's disability office and the services given through specialty programs. While the administrative home of some specialty programs may be housed within the disability office (Viezel et al., 2020), applying for disability accommodations does not guarantee application or acceptance into a specialty program and vice versa. University admissions offices are prohibited from inquiring about students' disability status (ADA, 1990) and as such, support programs usually have an application process that is separate from general university admissions. Students apply for general university admission and specialty program admission simultaneously and independently from one another.

Just as universities have varying application processes from one institution to another, applications to specialty programs are also unique. School psychologists are encouraged to work with students in locating the application process for desired programs, typically found on programs' website or by contacting program staff directly. Commonly required application materials include: application form, high school transcripts, IEP document/504 Plan (when applicable), psychological evaluation with an ASD diagnosis, writing sample, letter of recommendation, and an application fee (Viezel et al., 2020). An additional component of application materials may include a letter of acceptance from the university. It is an important consideration for school psychologists to support students with the completion of these application materials so that students have an active role in gathering materials as well as completing the program application. Doing so reflects students' independence and desire to pursue a personal goal of attending college.

The aforementioned application materials serve as a means for program staff to evaluate students' functioning and determine if they are a good fit for the program. When submitting a student's IEP or 504 Plan, it is important for school psychologists to ensure that the document is up-to-date and reflective of the student's true level of functioning. During high school, it is also important to consider removing any unnecessary services and accommodations. This may involve using early years of high school to pull back on supports that prevent the student from functioning independently (as is appropriate). For example, the utilization of one-to-one paraprofessional support may show that students require more support than college settings are able to provide. It may be an indication that students require more intervention in adaptive behaviors and executive functioning before pursuing college as a postsecondary goal.

An additional application component often (48.4%) required by programs includes a recent psychological evaluation. Many programs (67.5%) also require a documented ASD diagnosis to be included in this evaluation (Viezel et al., 2020). School psychologists can support students in this area by providing families with the aforementioned recommendations for obtaining a psychological evaluation for their child. For students receiving Special Education, school psychologists should ensure that a student's most recent triennial evaluation reflects testing in the area of autism as well as an assigned primary disability classification of autism (where appropriate). Additional information about the assessment of ASD can be found in Chap. 3 of this text.

In addition to the previously mentioned application materials, 33.3% of programs also require an interview as a component of their admission process (Viezel et al., 2020). The interview serves as a point of contact with the student in order to assess their goals for attending postsecondary education. The interview process also allows program staff to observe students' level of functioning in order to determine their goodness of fit with the program (such that the program is not too supportive or too restrictive). The interview process also allows students and families to meet program staff and ask questions.

Specialty Program Support Services

The exact services provided to students varies from one specialty program to another. The frequency and duration of these supports also differ between programs. School psychologists should be mindful of the amount of support students require (e.g., number of contact points per week, number of hours per week) and encourage students to apply to programs that meet their unique needs. The types of support services can be grouped into five overarching categories: executive functioning/academic coaching, mental health counseling, social skills support, vocational support, and consultation. Details about each type of support service are provided below.

Executive Functioning/Academic Coaching Autistic individuals often have challenges with executive functioning (Kenworthy et al., 2008). These concerns with executive functions can include weaknesses with cognitive flexibility, organization, time management, shifting, and self-monitoring. The structure of high school may externalize much of students' goal-directed behavior. For example, teachers may create interim deadlines for long-term assignments and provide reinforcement and incentive systems for desired behavior. Students also live with their parents/guardians who likely monitor behavior and academic progress. As students transition into college, the demands for independence increase significantly, which requires the application of their executive functions from waking up for class on time to submitting assignments by assigned deadlines.

Autistic college students (who likely received high school supports to navigate these goal-directed behaviors) may require additional scaffolding with regard to their executive functions. Many ASD specialty programs (68.2%) provide direct intervention in this area (Viezel et al., 2020). This type of support service may be called "academic coaching" or "executive functioning coaching" referring to explicit instruction and intervention with regard to time management, organization, self-monitoring, problem-solving, and cognitive flexibility. This type of executive function training at the postsecondary level also guides students through recognition of their own goals (Nachman, 2020; White et al., 2017). Academic coaching is an important distinction from tutoring such that direct instruction is not provided in a given subject area (e.g., Algebra or Economics). Instead, this service time involves check-ins with a student to monitor progress with regard to their course grades, assignment completion, and time management. When tutoring is needed, students are guided in recognizing when they need tutoring as well as the process for accessing this type of campus service. Not only does academic/executive functioning coaching directly target areas of deficit, Autistic students also report that this type of service is highly preferable (Accardo et al., 2019). Targeted intervention in this area is not only preferred by students, but has also shown to be effective in improving student GPAs (Rando et al., 2016).

Mental Health and Social Skills Support While not a diagnostic qualifier for ASD, Autistic college students experience anxiety, depression, and loneliness

(Gelbar et al., 2014; Jobe & White, 2007; Anderson & Butt, 2017). These challenges with mental health may be particularly difficult for Autistic individuals first entering college. The college transition process can be hard for students due to substantial changes in academic demands, social structures, and routines. In order to address these concerns related to social and emotional functioning, many programs provide group (47.0%) and/or individual (50.0%) counseling support as well as social skills intervention (54.0%; Viezel et al., 2020; Nachman, 2020). While most universities have an on-campus student counseling center, the providers within the specialty program likely have unique training with regard to the social-emotional wellness of Autistic students. For example, a key feature of ASD often involves deficits in social communication (APA, 2013). Due to the substantial change in social structure in college because of the differences in classroom settings/expectations as well as new dorm living experiences, social skills intervention is an important component to ASD specialty programs. The service providers in specialty programs have unique insight into college life both inside and outside of the classroom. Therefore, feedback and instruction can be provided to support students with interpreting and responding to these new social norms.

Peer Mentoring One additional component of social-emotional support for Autistic students is peer mentoring. This service is seen in most specialty programs (Viezel et al., 2020; Nachman, 2020) and is also a type of support that is preferred by Autistic students (Accardo et al., 2019). Peer mentoring involves pairing an Autistic student along with a neurotypical peer enrolled at the same university. The peer is pre-selected and is usually chosen on a voluntary basis from an interested pool of qualified candidates. The student and the peer mentor attend campus social functions together (e.g., club meetings) of which the peer mentor serves as a comfortable base for the student while also having some knowledge of strategies to support Autistic individuals. Many specialty programs (44.7%; Viezel et al., 2020) also sponsor social events to aid in the initiation and integration of social interactions of program members and the rest of the campus community. It is important to keep in mind that peer mentors are usually fellow undergraduate students and are not clinical service providers. As such, peer mentors are not trained to provide specific clinical interventions; however, they are important figures in supporting the social functioning of Autistic students.

Vocational Support While attending college is a large postsecondary goal for students, an overarching goal behind college attendance is obtaining employment after graduation. This may be an overwhelming task for most college students; however, the job search may feel even more stressful for Autistic students as only 37.2% of individuals with ASD are employed (Baio et al., 2018). While receiving a college education, many specialty programs (68.4%) are also providing their enrolled students with vocational supports in order to prepare them for the job market (Viezel et al., 2020). This includes equipping students with skills and experience in the areas of resumé and interview preparation. Specialty programs frequently partner with on-campus career services and state vocational agencies in order to provide expert instruction in internship and job applications.

Consultation In addition to providing direct services for students, support programs may also offer consultation to the other figures playing an important role in the educational career of Autistic students. This may include communication with students' professors and parents/guardians. Consultation may also extend to training opportunities for campus members with frequent contact with Autistic students (e.g., college orientation leaders, resident advisers, public safety officers). Program staff can provide global strategies that are effective when working with Autistic individuals and may also be available as a point of contact for consultation on specific cases. Program staff may also check in with students' professors in order to receive more detailed information about their academic progress and behavior in the classroom that can later be addressed in academic coaching or individual counseling.

Specialty programs may also extend their service delivery to include parent support. While offered in about one-third of programs (Viezel et al., 2020), this type of support provides families with strategies and tools needed in order to manage having a new college student. Families of students with special needs are likely used to being in frequent involvement in their child's education; however, the Family Education Rights and Privacy Act (FERPA; 1974) prevents universities from communicating with students' parents/guardians with regard to their academic performance. This is likely new territory for families and specialty program providers can provide guidance to support this transition.

Program Cost

In order to access the aforementioned support services and interventions as described above, these specialty programs may have an additional cost alongside general university tuition. Specialty programs cost an average of US $3,338.44 per semester (Viezel et al., 2020). There are, however, reported instances of scholarship opportunities to cover the cost of the specialty program. A recent study reported that 40.6% of programs offer some type of financial assistance for families with many more programs holding the expectation that they will have similar funding opportunities in the future (Viezel et al., 2020). Students and families may also wish to contact the financial aid department of the given university to discuss other financial options when cost is a barrier to program accessibility. Families and school psychologists are also encouraged to explore university options for support services that do not require formal enrollment and participation in a fee-based specialty program while also ensuring Autistic students have applied for accommodations through the university's disability office. For example, tutoring services and counseling services are offered at most universities and are available at no cost to the entire student body without specific participation in a specialty support program.

Final Thoughts

School psychologists play a unique professional role to support students with disabilities' academic, social, emotional, and executive functioning. For Autistic students, this role is of particular importance due to the gap in graduation rates between Autistic students and their general peers (Baio et al., 2018). K-12 school psychologists can impact student outcomes beyond high school graduation by supporting students and families through the college planning process. While transition planning is required under IDEA, detailed knowledge of college-based disability supports and programs is important due to changes in disability law after entering college. Understanding the discrepancy between typically granted accommodations and the actual needs of Autistic college students highlights the importance of additional university support. During post-high school transition planning, school psychologists can support students in identifying and selecting a college for which to apply, submitting documentation to request accommodations, as well as reviewing the features of ASD specialty programs designed to provide additional support and intervention beyond legally mandated accommodations. With this important information, high school psychologists, university-based school psychologists, as well as other important clinical service providers can work together to continue to close the achievement gap for Autistic students.

References

Accardo, A. L., Kuder, S. J., & Woodruff, J. (2019). Accommodations and support services preferred by college students with autism spectrum disorder. *Autism, 23*(3), 574–583.

Adreon, D., & Durocher, J. S. (2007). Evaluating the college transition needs of individuals with high-functioning autism spectrum disorders. *Intervention in School and Clinic, 42*(5), 271–279.

Anderson, C., & Butt, C. (2017). Young adults on the autism spectrum at college: Successes and stumbling blocks. *Journal of Autism and Developmental Disorders, 47*(10), 3029–3039.

American Psychiatric Association. (2013). *Diagnostic and statistical manual of mental disorders: DSM-5*. American Psychiatric Association.

Americans with Disabilities Act of 1990, 42 U.S.C. § 12101 (1990).

Baio, J., Wiggins, L., Christensen, D. L., et al. (2018). Prevalence of autism Spectrum disorder among children aged 8 years- autism and developmental disabilities monitoring network, 11 sites, United States, 2014. *MMWR Surveill Summ, 67*(SS-6), 1–23.

Barnhill, G. P. (2016). Supporting students with Asperger syndrome on college campuses: Current practices. *Focus on Autism and Other Developmental Disabilities, 31*(1), 3–15.

Chiang, H. M., Cheung, Y. K., Hickson, L., et al. (2012). Predictive factors of participation in postsecondary education for high school leavers with autism. *Journal of Autism and Developmental Disorders, 42*, 685–696.

Christensen, D. L., Baio, J., Braun, K. V., Bilder, D., Charles, J., Constantino, J. N., & Zahorodny, W. (2016). Prevalence and characteristics of autism Spectrum disorder among children aged 8 years — Autism and developmental disabilities monitoring network, 11 sites, United States, 2012. *MMWR. Surveillance Summaries, 65*(SS-3), 1–23.

Cox, B. E. (2017). *Autism coming to college (Issue brief)*. Center for Postsecondary Success.

Engstrom, E. (2019). *Improving daily living skills in college students with autism Spectrum disorder using a peer-mediated daily living checklist intervention.*

Family Educational Rights and Privacy Act of 1974, 20 U.S.C. § 1232g (1974).

Gelbar, N. W., Smith, I., & Reichow, B. (2014). Systematic review of articles describing experience and supports of individuals with autism enrolled in college and university programs. *Journal of Autism Developmental Disorders, 44*, 593–2601.

Harrison, P., & Oakland, T. (2017). *Adaptive behavior assessment system: Third edition.* WPS.

Individuals with Disabilities Education Improvement Act of 2004, 20 U.S.C. § 1400 (2004).

Jobe, L. E., & White, S. W. (2007). Loneliness, social relationships, and a broader autism phenotype in college students. *Personality and Individual Differences, 42*(8), 1479–1489.

Kenworthy, L., Yerys, B. E., Anthony, L. G., & Wallace, G. L. (2008). Understanding executive control in autism spectrum disorders in the lab and in the real world. *Neuropsychology Review, 18*(4), 320–338.

Nachman, B. R. (2020). Enhancing transition programming for college students with Autism: A systematic literature review. *Journal of Postsecondary Education and Disability, 33*(1), 81–95.

Newman, L., Wagner, M., Cameto, R., & Knokey, A. M. (2009). *The post-high school outcomes of youth with disabilities up to 4 years after high school. A report of Findings from National Longitudinal Transition Study-2* (NLTS) (NCSER 2009–3017). SRI International. Available at www.nlts2.org/reports/2009_04/nlts2_report_2009_04_complete.pdf

Rando, H., Huber, M. J., & Oswald, G. R. (2016). An academic coaching model intervention for college students on the Autism Spectrum. *Journal of Postsecondary Education and Disability, 29*, 257–262.

Section 504 of the Rehabilitation Act of 1973, 34 C.F.R. Part 104.

Sparrow, S. S., Cicchetti, D. V., & Saulnier, C. A. (2016). *Vineland adaptive behavior scales, third edition.* NCS Pearson, Inc.

United States Department of Education. (2015). *Protecting students with disabilities.* Available at: https://www2.ed.gov/about/offices/list/ocr/504faq.html

United States Department of Education, National Center for Education Statistics. (2019). *Digest of education statistics, 2018* (NCES 2020-009).

United States Department of Education, Office for Civil Rights. (2011). *Students with disabilities preparing for postsecondary education: Know your rights and responsibilities.* Available at: https://www2.ed.gov/about/offices/list/ocr/transition.html

University of Washington. (2017). *College funding for students with disabilities.* Available at: from:https://www.washington.edu/doit/sites/default/files/atoms/files/College_Funding_Strategies_0.pdf

Viezel, K. D., Williams, E., & Dotson, W. (2020). College-based support programs for students with autism. *Focus on Autism and Other Developmental Disabilities, 35*(4), 234–245.

White, S. W., Elias, R., Capriola-Hall, N. N., Smith, I. C., Conner, C. M., Asselin, S. B., & Mazefsky, C. A. (2017). Development of a college transition and support program for students with Autism Spectrum Disorder. *Journal of Autism and Developmental Disorders, 47*, 3072–3078.

Preparation for Successful Employment

Jennifer M. Cullen

Abstract Decades of outcomes research have found that individuals with autism spectrum disorder (ASD) have lifelong challenges attaining and maintaining employment. Understanding the employment challenges of individuals with ASD requires understanding historical data related to the employment of individuals with ASD, specific factors that have been found to be associated with employment outcomes, and services that have been provided to achieve those outcomes. The likelihood of accessing available services and developing skills that improve employment outcomes are directly related to access of appropriate planning and supports during the high school years. This chapter will discuss issues related to individuals with ASD and employment, services that have been provided in high school settings, and how these services can be improved to better support students with ASD in preparation for and success in the workplace.

Keywords Employment · Autism · Transition planning · Accommodations · Self-advocacy

Obtaining Appropriate Services for the Workplace

Public policy including educational legislation such as the Individuals with Disabilities Education Improvement Act (2004) and workforce initiatives such as Employment First has mandated transition planning and services to promote community employment for individuals with disabilities, including autism spectrum disorder (ASD) (Kiernan et al., 2011). Yet, individuals with ASD continue to have lifelong employment difficulties. More than 50% of young adults with ASD did not

---

J. M. Cullen (✉)
Teacher's College, Department of Special Education, Ball State University, Muncie, IN, USA
e-mail: jmcullen@bsu.edu

© Springer Nature Switzerland AG 2022
K. D. Viezel et al. (eds.), *Postsecondary Transition for College- or Career-Bound Autistic Students*, https://doi.org/10.1007/978-3-030-93947-2_11

participate in employment or education during their first two years after high school (Shattuck et al., 2012). According to the 2011 National Longitudinal Transition Study-2 (NLTS-2), only 37% of young adults with ASD were employed, which is lower than those without disabilities (66%) and most other disability categories including learning disabilities (67%), other health impairment (64%), speech/language impairment (64%), and traumatic brain injury (51%) (Newman et al., 2011). When considering whether individuals had ever been employed up to 8 years after high school, the NLTS-2 found that 63% of individuals with ASD had been employed, compared to 97% of those without disabilities, and among other disability categories of learning disabilities (95%), other health impairment (95%), speech/language impairment (94%), and traumatic brain injury (81%). These challenges may persist into adulthood, with less than 25% obtaining any improvement in employment and only 6% of individuals with ASD becoming competitively employed, which is defined as occurring in integrated settings, with wages at or above the minimum wage (Lawer et al., 2009; Taylor & Mailick, 2014). In this chapter, the provision of services to address these staggering statistics for youth and young adults with ASD will be discussed by first identifying the benefits of employment, briefly identifying the factors that impact employment, and the services to address those factors.

Benefits of Employment

To fully understand what services are needed by individuals with ASD to prepare them for success in the workplace, the benefits of employment must be considered. Employment has been found to have both financial and personal benefits for individuals. Competitive employment also has financial benefit for individuals with disabilities and society, due to the increase in salary for the individual, reduced societal costs for medical benefits, and an increase in revenue for local, state, and federal governments based on taxes paid through employment (Cimera, 2010). Employment has personal benefit including increased self-determination, improved quality of life, a reduction in problem behavior, and an improvement in social skills (Dunn et al., 2015).

Employment can provide a setting in which one has to engage in social interaction with coworkers, customers, supervisors, and others on a routine basis. These employment settings become a microenvironment where an individual becomes part of a team, and learns the daily routines associated with the workplace, as well as slowly being exposed to the inner workings of the workplace. These daily routines and many social interactions within them can be navigated by following basic scripts that can in some cases be directly taught as part of introduction to employment settings, which can facilitate early successes in socially interacting with others. For example, individuals may also have to engage in social interactions focused on tasks that also require problem-solving in order to accomplish assigned tasks. People with employment are more likely to report feelings of accomplishment and maintain higher cognitive performance than those who are not employed. Maintaining skills often requires practice, so those individuals with ASD who are employed are more likely to maintain skills, because of the increased opportunities for practice compared to those remaining at home. Employment provides a venue where one can have a role or purpose that leads to feeling valued.

Employment is highly correlated with Quality of Life (QOL). QOL is a complex construct that involves an individual's perception about their position in life in relation to others, in context of the culture in which they live and in relation to their goals, expectations, standards, and concerns (Kuyken, 1995). QOL includes satisfaction, competence/productivity, empowerment/independence, and social/community integration (Renty & Roeyers, 2006). Individuals with ASD have consistently rated employment components of QOL low, indicating that employment is an area that reduces their QOL (Burgess & Gutstein, 2007). QOL is also influenced by self-determination, which is "a combination of skills, knowledge, and beliefs that enable a person to engage in goal-directed, self-regulated, and autonomous behaviors" (Field et al., 1998, p. 2). QOL is likely to be maximized when an intervention uses a self-determined approach to improve employment outcomes.

Predictor Factors for Success in Employment

In order to understand the scope of the challenges individuals with ASD face to obtain appropriate services for the workplace, it is important to consider predictor factors related to the individual, family, and transition services provided and how these correlate with employment outcomes (Chiang et al., 2013). Identifying what these predictor factors are can help guide services needed to create successful outcomes. However, no single factor has been found that is universally successful in obtaining employment, but rather it is a combination of factors (Bennett et al., 2018).

Individual Factors For individual-level factors, the most significant predictors of employment are graduation from high school, social skills, independence in daily living skills, executive functioning, work experience in high school, and ability to manage impulses (see Table 1 for intervention ideas and roles for school psychologists) (Bennett et al., 2018; Chiang et al., 2013; Nicholas et al., 2018). In a secondary analysis of NLTS data on transition age youth with ASD, Chiang et al. (2013) identified the individual factors that contribute to future employment factors and found that graduating from high school is a predictor factor of employment at seven times more likely than those without a diploma. Another consideration related to graduating high school is the complexity of graduation requirements and diploma options for students. Graduating with a more rigorous diploma is also impactful on acquiring employment. However, nonacademic skills such as social skills, communication, ability to collaborate, daily living skills, and problem-solving are often more relevant than academic skills in post-school employment success (Gothberg et al., 2015).

Table 1 Ways for school psychologists to support employment skills in transition

Area	Key tasks and processes	Tools or resources	NASP domains[a]
Assessment	Collaborate with other professionals (counseling, special education, related services) to develop a bank of assessments related to employment to be used in transition planning Use a variety of assessments and methods to help students identify career interests (Carter et al., 2013) Collaborate with other school personnel to assess students in a variety of areas such as strengths, career interests, skill deficits, personality, adaptive behavior, and employability (Kellems et al., 2016) Ensure students have current assessment data related to their disability to support accommodations in employment and eligibility for community services such as Vocational Rehabilitation Communicate to students, school personnel, and families results of assessments and ensuring they understand what they mean	See Kellems et al. (2016) for a list of assessments	1, 2, 5
Services planning	Identify relevant transition goals Identify services needed to meet those goals Provide individualized counseling and instruction to help students identify own interests, strengths, and accommodation needs (Carter et al., 2013)	Triangulated GAP analysis Transition Goal Generator	2, 3, 4
Academic planning	Know diploma track options for the state you practice in and ramifications of each level Help advocate for students to participate in options that meet their ability and skills levels such as postsecondary dual programs, AP classes, gifted/talented programs Know available post-school options including colleges with good support programs for students with autism, career development programs, and internships	Project Search	1, 2, 3
Social and independent living skills	Identify needed skills and skill deficits through a variety of assessments that are both formal and informal. Help advocate and collaborate to develop opportunities for the school and district that will allow for development of social and independent living skills Ensure students with autism participate in options to help develop these skills available to all students (Finance courses, Home Economics Classes, etc.) Share information about school and community extracurricular options for students, especially as it relates to interests that may have career implications (e.g., clubs related to STEAM fields) Share information about social skills groups or other community resources that may provide direct instruction of these skills	Peer mentoring	1, 2, 4, 5

Self- determination	Ensure students can talk about their diagnosis, what it means, and what accommodations or supports they may need	Self-Determined Learning Model of Instruction (Wehmeyer et al., 2000) Self-Determined Career Development Model (Mazzotti et al., 2012) Strengths-based selection of career opportunities	2, 3, 5, 7
	Help develop processes at the school and district levels to involve students in actively participating (or leading) their evaluation, IEP, or transition planning meetings		
	Ensure students have opportunity through a variety of methods to state their goals for employment		
	Collaborate to create flexible opportunities to discover what strengths students have and provide career exploration to explore careers that match those strengths and interests		
	Help connect students to self-advocacy organizations and resources to promote self-determination such as Autistic Self-Advocacy Network		

(continued)

Table 1 (continued)

Area	Key tasks and processes	Tools or resources	NASP domains[a]
Technology	Help identify a variety of universal and specialized online tools, apps, and devices that can be used as accommodations Attend assistive technology fairs or conferences to learn about new technologies that may benefit students Read relevant special education, disability, technology, or vocational rehabilitation journals and newsletters to learn about new products or applications of existing products to meet the needs of students	Smartphones and tablets Boost-A Transition program (Hatfield et al., 2016) Video modeling or prompting Career OneStop MyNextMove Virtual job shadowing (Kellems et al., 2015) Virtual job interview practice	5, 7, 9

| Collaboration and connection to community supports | Work to build collaboration within the school and district to create interdisciplinary teams to address transition planning
Participate in regional, statewide, or national organizations related to autism or disability and get involved in their activities related to transition or advocate that they develop things related to transition if they do not have them
Attend district, regional, or state transition events to increase your own knowledge of transition and become aware of what resources are available to students, families, and school personnel
Help identify what resources are in the community and how to access those resources
Advocate for collaborative processes in transition that involve community partners such as person-centered planning, connection to Vocational Rehabilitation, coordination with local and state developmental disabilities boards, and involvement of healthcare providers
Know about community career development opportunities within the community to develop employability skills | Person-centered planning (Hagner et al., 2014) Pre-Employment Transition Services (Neary et al., 2015) Project Search (Wehman et al., 2017) | 5, 7, 10 |
| Workplace supports | Understand relevant laws related to employment and accommodations
Help advocate for connection of the school and district to local business advisory councils or employer groups to involve them in transition activities such as mock job interviews, internships, learning about their processes for hiring, and creation of job shadowing opportunities
Collaborate to create and provide information handouts and/or short video clips about ASD, core features, strengths, common challenges, and some tips on working with individuals with ASD to be used in career development activities of the school and district to help increase success of individuals with ASD
Collaborate with school personnel, community providers, and employers to create recommended practices for adapting hiring processes, acclimation to the workplace, request and use of accommodations, involvement of job coaches, and ongoing formal and informal supports | ADA | 5, 7, 10 |

[a] NASP Domains=1: Data-Based Decision-Making, 2: Consultation and Collaboration, 3: Academic Interventions and Instructional Supports, 4: Mental and Behavioral Health Services and Interventions, 5: School-Wide Practices to Promote Learning, 7: Family, School, and Community Collaborations, 9: Research and Evidence-Based Practice, 10: Legal, Ethical, and Professional Practice

Social skills are also associated with increased probability of successful employment outcomes. Individuals with more highly developed social skills according to parental rating scales are 5.40 more times likely to obtain employment after high school (Chiang et al., 2013). Social skills relevant for employment include interviewing skills, relationships with coworkers and supervisors, and learning and modifying social skills after feedback. General work skill behaviors are also critical for success in employment including accuracy, productivity, and punctuality. Promoting self-awareness, specifically in the areas of personal occupational strengths, individual interests, and career planning has been found to be a critical component of effective transition services in high school correlated with positive post-school employment. Independence in daily living activities has also been correlated with post-school employment (Scott et al., 2019). Closely related factors to independent living skills are an individual's executive functions (Nicholas et al., 2018). Having employment in high school and participation in other work-based learning experiences is strongly associated with post-school employment (Cease-Cook et al., 2015). Additionally, individuals with ASD who have a driver's license are five times more likely to be employed than those who do not have a license (Zalewska et al., 2016). It is likely that those with driver's licenses are able to have greater flexibility in where and when they obtain employment. In addition, they are not reliant on someone to transport them to apply for jobs. It may also be that those who obtain a driver's license had more independent living skills or were more likely to be in inclusive settings while in high school and that these were also impactful in the improved results.

Family Factors For family-level factors, the most significant predictors were annual household salary, parental education level, and parental involvement in transition planning (Bennett et al., 2018). Those from higher income families were more likely to be employed (Chan et al., 2018). Additionally, when there is a direct emphasis on employment by the family with supports they can provide, such as transportation or assistance with planning, an individual is more likely to acquire and maintain a job (Bennett et al., 2018).

Transition Services Provided Other predictor factors are having ongoing supports in employment settings, and involvement with vocational rehabilitation (Nicholas et al., 2018). Receiving career development and counseling while in high school has also been found to increase the odds for obtaining and maintaining employment after high school (Anderson et al., 2021). Participation in programs designed to bridge the transition between secondary settings and employment have also been effective at improving employment outcomes (Anderson et al., 2021).

Services Considerations

The road to employment begins with transition planning while still in high school. Effective transition planning will include opportunities for learning skills that relate to the factors associated with successful employment, specifically social skills, daily living skills, and self-determination (See Table 1 for ideas for school psychologists to support employment skills in Transition). Services in transition planning in high school should also include the use of tools and experiences that will help facilitate future success in employment, including the use of technology and career development opportunities within high school. Services for transition should implement collaboration between individuals, schools, and community service agencies, and have a focus on processes and accommodations to obtain and maintain employment both in the short- and long-term for individuals with ASD.

High School Services and Employment Supports Provided by School Staff

High school services and employment supports by school staff should include transition planning, academic planning, promotion of self-determination, social skills development, and career development opportunities. One of the main considerations for service delivery is the socioeconomic status of the individual being serviced. Given the known association of socioeconomic status to post-school employment, transition services for lower income individuals should focus on resources and supports needed that may be typically provided by families from higher socioeconomic levels such as access to resources, networking, and transportation (Chiang et al., 2013).

Transition Planning and School Counseling The Individuals with Disabilities Education Improvement Act of 2004 (IDEA, 2004) is the primary law governing special education services in the United States and covers more than 7.5 million children ages 0–21 (Hussar et al., 2020). The law covers key created mandates for special education students to include transition plans for ages 14 and up with measurable annual goals in the areas of training, education, employment, and independent living skills with appropriate services to meet those goals (Yell et al., 2006). Some high-functioning students may be serviced under 504 plans rather than IEPs, so it is important to also consider transition services in 504 plans, in addition to also assisting individuals who are not on an IEP or 504 Plan. A 504 plan includes such components as placement, services, and evaluation and is provided under the Rehabilitation Act of 1973 and covers a broader range of students with disabilities than IDEA (Katsiyannis & Reid, 1999). The primary difference is that services and accommodations are generally provided through general education, rather than special education personnel. Many high-functioning students with ASD may be in advanced classes such as AP or dual enrollment in college, so provision of services to meet transition goals may need to be flexible in its delivery to ensure that they are able to adequately take advantage of them (Kucharczyk et al., 2015).

Transition planning should utilize a variety of transition tools that assess academic achievement, self-determination, career interests, and independent living skills (Gothberg et al., 2015; Rowe et al., 2015). Transition assessments related to employment should be used to plan academic instruction, transition services needed, community employment experiences throughout high school, and future planning needed to meet the student's post-school goals (Rowe et al., 2015). It is crucial for methods of assessment, instruction, and services to address both academic and nonacademic areas, as well as the student's goals because nonacademic areas are highly correlated with employment by individuals with ASD (Gothberg et al., 2015; Rowe et al., 2015; Scott et al., 2019). Transition planning should involve collaboration between special education, general education personnel, and school psychologists (Kellems et al., 2016). Areas of assessment can consider adaptive behavior, daily living skills, aptitude testing, achievement testing, personality inventories, career and employability scales, self-determination assessments, transition planning inventories, observational assessments, and curriculum-based assessments (Kellems et al., 2016).

A variety of innovative tools and methods exist that can help facilitate transition planning for both academic and nonacademic areas such as the Transition Goal Generator (Gothberg et al., 2015), Triangulated Gap Analysis (Rowe et al., 2015), embedding special interest areas into transition planning (Bross & Travers, 2017), and utilizing online transition planning (Hatfield et al., 2016). In Triangulated Gap Analysis, a postsecondary goal is identified, and the goal is triangulated with the academic content and industry standards related to that goal. Then, the gap between student's current performance, knowledge, and standards is identified, steps to meet that gap are identified, and a plan to implement instruction and evaluate progress towards filling the gap is developed (Gothberg et al., 2015).

The Transition Goal Generator utilizes parent, teacher, and student forms to identify student strengths and limitations and identify the most relevant specific goals and behaviors for an individual student for transition planning (Burnes et al., 2018). In utilizing special interest areas in transition planning, the restricted interests often associated with ASD that have been traditionally seen as problematic are utilized for academic achievement, career development, and transition planning (Bross & Travers, 2017). For example, a student with a special interest in comic books may create a comic book for the student's future goals rather than writing a narrative of the goals. Also, the student's work-based learning experiences may include a job shadow with a professional at a comic book company, working at a comic bookstore, and volunteering to teach third-grade students about characters in comic books. Social skills instruction practice for this student may include participating in an after-school comic book club.

Utilizing assessment and transition strategies can ensure that all students are ready for life after high school, whether it is postsecondary education or employment and increase "buy-in" from individuals with ASD by not singling them out (Cease-Cook et al., 2015; Rowe et al., 2015). For example, utilizing freshman seminars where all students, regardless of whether they have disabilities learn life skills such as financial planning, soft skills for employment, or senior career portfolio creation (Kucharczyk et al., 2015). Also, the key to provision of services is the cooperation of the general education teacher in meeting the needs of individuals with ASD (Kucharczyk et al., 2015).

Academic planning in the form of advisors who help students with course scheduling and diploma tracks should be part of the services provided in high school. Given the complexity of diploma requirements and options, parents and students with autism need to be educated about the different plans and potential ramifications of each diploma. For example, some states have certificates of attendance that do not carry the same weight as a diploma when seeking employment (McDonough & Revell, 2010). Some diploma types may also limit postsecondary education and vocational training program eligibility (Chiang et al., 2013). For students who are struggling to complete their high school diploma, alternative programs could be considered such as community career services, Job Corps, or other community program. Additionally, final year programs such as Project Search where students with ASD participate in a year-long program with career development, social and work skills training, and internships can serve as a transition from school into employment (Wehman et al., 2017).

Social and Independent Living Skills Development Instruction in high school must also be balanced to meet the broad needs of students with ASD beyond just academics to include nonacademic areas such as social skills and independent living (Gothberg et al., 2015; Kucharczyk et al., 2015). Social skills development should include both social skills instruction and promoting opportunities for socialization. These social skills should be targeted towards skills needed for job interviews or in job settings (Dipeolu et al., 2015). In addition, other relevant communication and social skills training could include interaction with people in a supervisory role as well as peers, interpreting hidden social rules, working independently, and adapting to changes in the environment. Utilizing peers to assist with social skills instruction can allow greater generalization of skills than simply instruction alone, because it allows for a natural support to be provided in the environment that is more readily available (Carter et al., 2014). Extracurricular activities can be used to allow for practice of social skills and explore possible careers (Dunn et al., 2015). For example, utilizing a technology software extracurricular activity allows exploration of computer programming as a career, but this experience also allows social interaction with peers (Dunn et al., 2015).

Self-Determination and Selection of Career Opportunities An understanding of one's strengths and limitations together with belief in oneself as capable and effective is essential for self-determination. A self-determined process for matching services to the individual and the contexts in which they function is important because self-determination allows an individual to make decisions over their own life and ultimately contributes to an overall improved quality of life (Schalock, 1996). Specifically, individuals who score higher on measures of self-determination have more positive adult outcomes including better employment and better contexts for living situations (Wehmeyer & Schwartz, 1997). Models for teaching self-determination include the Self-Determined Learning Model of Instruction (SDLMI) (Wehmeyer et al., 2000) and the Self-Determined Career Development Model (SDCDM) (Mazzotti et al., 2012; Wehmeyer et al., 2009). The SDCDM and SDLMI teach the component elements of self-determination and promote the development of self-regulated problem-solving skills and participant-directed learning in academic or employment settings (Mazzotti et al., 2012). The SDLMI and the SDCDM consists of three phases: set a goal, take action, and adjust plan. Multiple single subject and quasi-experimental studies have linked the SDLMI and SDCDM to several positive outcomes including academic performance, increased employment, and transition goal achievement (Mazzotti et al., 2012).

Some self-determination practices particularly important for use in high school settings to promote employment are being able to identify strengths and interests and share them (Dipeolu et al., 2015; Scott et al., 2019). Individuals with ASD also have important strengths to contribute to employment settings such as thinking outside of the box and being focused, diligent, and detail-oriented (Kopelson, 2015; Markel & Elia, 2016). In addition, utilizing client interests and strengths to help drive career planning has been successful with high-functioning youth with ASD (Hagner et al., 2014; McLaren et al., 2017). Specifically, utilizing individualized job searches and supports based on strengths and interests have been associated with improved outcomes, rather than generic recommendations such as all students apply to fast food or grocery stores (McLaren et al., 2017; Wehman et al., 2017).

A variety of studies have also noted that capitalizing on strengths associated with autism such as propensity for technology use or being detail-oriented have also been associated with increased retention in employment settings (Dipeolu et al., 2015). To help ensure that individuals engage in self-determined career planning during transition and into adulthood, it is essential to consider services be provided by high school staff, what content transition planning related to employment and other relevant areas should include, and how it should be delivered.

Work-Based Learning Experiences Opportunities for workforce development should be considered in academic planning, such as work studies, internships, or career planning classes. These experiences are strongly associated with post-school success in employment, so a greater emphasis and accommodations within should be provided (Carter et al., 2011; Cease-Cook et al., 2015). Work-based learning experiences including career interests and exploration, job shadowing and sampling, service learning, and employment experiences including internships, apprenticeships, and paid employment have been found to also aid in employment for individuals with ASD (Cease-Cook et al., 2015; McDonough & Revell, 2010). Additionally, career counseling should be part of transition services provided in high school. However, these services need to be meaningful, and the relevance explained to individuals with ASD to increase the likelihood of individuals with ASD participating in them, as well as increase their effectiveness (Kucharczyk et al., 2015).

Technology Supports to Bridge Transition from School to Employment

Technology has become an integral part of providing support and interventions for individuals with ASD. Case studies have shown the utility of technology in helping students with ASD access the general education curriculum, increase motivation, build communication skills, increase independence and reduce dependence on parents/guardians, learn and practice essential life skills, reduce reliance on job coaches in vocational settings, and engage in online transition planning (Cullen et al., 2017; Hatfield et al., 2016; Kellems et al., 2015). Given the numerous benefits of adopting technology and the likelihood that these benefits will only increase as more research is conducted and technology improves, assistive technology assessment should be viewed as an integral part of transition assessment for all students with disabilities, particularly those with ASD, who have shown especially advantageous results from the use of technology in interventions and supports. Yet caution must also be exercised because of the potential for technology to be a distraction, to provide less opportunity for social interaction with others, and for there to be less opportunity for a natural support to be developed in vocational settings.

The use of technology to assist with transition and daily living supports for adults with autism is supported across occupation, with support in the literature from members of the medical field, educational specialists, and more (Bargeron et al., 2015; Nicolaidis et al., 2014). In a literature review of employment factors for individuals with ASD, Scott et al (2019) concluded that the utilization of technology as a tool by job coaches led to improvements in task management, problem-solving and organizational skills, self-regulation of workplace behaviors, and improved productivity. Technology has many applications for improving employment outcomes for individuals with ASD. For instance, technology can be used as a tool to improve access to information and text, as accommodations for writing, organization, self-management, prompting to acquire new tasks, and to allow for participation in career development experiences (Kellems et al., 2015).

Online Transition Planning Online transition planning can be used to improve self-determination as well as allow for future planning in a way that is accessible to students with ASD (Hatfield et al., 2016). The Boost-A program (Hatfield et al., 2016) systematically takes students through modules to help them understand what life after high school will be like with a greater purpose of (a) understanding the importance of transition planning, (b) identifying interests, work preferences, learning styles, and goals, (c) identifying teams to help them reach their goals, (d) leading a team meeting for transition planning, and (e) systematically evaluating progress.

Prompting to Acquire New Tasks and Skills Evidence has shown that video modeling and prompting can be used in conjunction with iPads to teach complex, novel skills (Cullen et al., 2017; Richter, 2011). Video modeling and prompting can also be used to teach general workplace and social skills and promote their maintenance and generalization (Walsh et al., 2018).

Career Development One application for technology related to career development is the use of virtual experiences. Virtual experiences can be helpful for a variety of activities in career development including development of prevocational skills, opportunities to practice social skills needed in employment, career exploration, practice interviews, virtual job shadowing, and simulations that mirror employment tasks (Kellems et al., 2015). Virtual environments allow individuals with ASD to practice prevocational and social skills in controlled online environments and provide data on individual acquisition of skills (Tsiopela & Jimoyiannis, 2017). Utilizing online virtual experience sites for career exploration sites such as Career One Stop or MyNextMove allows students with ASD to search careers to identify careers of interests, network with professionals in that career, and experience the profession firsthand (Kellems et al., 2015).

Job shadowing utilizing technology can provide an opportunity for career exploration by allowing students with ASD to experience the job by following a professional in that career for a day. This shadowing can be accomplished through synchronous, individualized opportunities set up for that student or asynchronous more generic and commercial experiences (Kellems et al., 2015). The value of these career exploration activities can open a wide array of doors for students. For example, if a student lives in the landlocked Midwest, but is interested in marine biology working with ocean animals, it would be difficult to allow authentic career exploration in that area. However, utilizing virtual technology, they may be able to do a practice interview with a marine biologist working with orcas in Iceland or a marine biologist doing environmental studies in the Gulf Coast.

Another application of technology for career development is software for virtual job interview training and practice (Smith et al., 2015). In virtual interview practice, students with ASD practice job interviewing through a simulation software or online site and receive feedback on their performance (Smith et al., 2015). Virtual job interviews have been associated with increased acquisition and retention in jobs by individuals with ASD (Smith et al., 2015). Viewing video job interviews as part of virtual job interview training helps facilitate learning of important communication and social skills needed for successful interviewing (Hayes et al., 2015). Another way to teach job skills utilizing technology is web coaching. Web coaching can be done through written chat or virtual meeting. Web coaching can be used to check-in daily with individuals with ASD or to problem-solve issues in employment settings (Nilsson & Lodestad, 2014).

Cross-Agency Collaboration to Employment After School

Collaboration is central to achieving successful post-school outcomes in employment and is particularly important as students transition from school systems to postsecondary settings (Test et al., 2009). Job training programs that integrate multiple agencies and services into one program have had promising results for individuals with ASD (Hagner et al., 2014; McLaren et al., 2017; Wehman et al., 2017). This collaboration should include joint decision-making on assessments, goals, services, and metrics for success (Hagner et al., 2014). Successful employment outcomes and services for individuals with ASD will come from multiple agencies and community entities collaborating together (McDonough & Revell, 2010).

Processes for Collaboration

Utilizing processes that involve key stakeholders in transition planning has been associated with improved employment outcomes (Lee & Carter, 2012; Test et al., 2009; Wong et al., 2020). One such process that has had positive outcomes is person-centered planning (Hagner et al., 2014). In person-centered planning, individuals with ASD help coordinate meetings through observation and coaching introductions and personal history, career profiles, visioning for the future, resources needed, possible barriers to reach future goals, transition and career goals, and then career exploration and action steps (Hagner et al., 2014). Another form of collaboration is programming cosponsored by multiple agencies. Project Search, a collaboration between vocational rehabilitation, the school system, a university, and a local community rehabilitation provider, has been associated with increased employment (Wehman et al., 2017). Differences in employment by individuals in the Project Search collaborative employment at 12 months postgraduation were approximately 87% employed compared to approximately 12% in the control group employed. Successful collaborations require clear communication and identifying primary case manager (McDonough & Revell, 2010).

Key Stakeholders in Collaboration

Vocational Rehabilitation Vocational rehabilitation (VR) services have been associated with increased success in employment for individuals with ASD (Nicholas et al., 2018). VR services are available in all 50 states and is an agency funded with state and federal funds to help people with disabilities obtain or retain employment (Kaya et al., 2018). However, the costs associated with servicing individuals with ASD has been prohibitive to wider implementation, especially when consideration of the high costs in relation to successful outcomes (Burgess & Cimera, 2014). Individuals with ASD have less successful outcomes associated with receipt of VR services than many other individuals with different disability types (Nicholas et al., 2018). Helpful VR practices include assessment of appropriateness, training, job placement, job coaching, customized employment, and helping employers develop environments that support individuals with ASD (Nicholas et al., 2018). Other services VR provide can include personal assistance services and assistive technology. Individuals with ASD often face challenges in accessing VR when compared to other disability types in several areas including referral and connection to VR, eligibility processes, and participation in early connection programs to VR, such as preemployment transition services (Neary et al., 2015; Roux et al., 2020). Even when they qualify, less than two thirds access the services for which they qualified (Nye-Lengerman, 2017). Another challenge related to utilization of vocational rehabilitation services is that the types of services required for successful closures, which is generally accomplished by successful employment for a specified number of weeks, may differ from those typically offered to individuals with other disabilities (Neary et al., 2015). Providing on-the-job services after obtaining successful employment has been associated with better long-term retention of employment, when compared to traditional VR practices focused on preemployment processes such as help navigating administrative processes related to benefits, exploring careers, and applying for jobs (Nye-Lengerman, 2017).

One tool that has been identified as effective at identifying career interests and obtaining and maintaining employment by VR is person-centered planning. Person-centered planning is a method in which key stakeholders can collaborate with the individual at the core of decision-making. Person-centered planning includes the individual themselves as well as others such as parents, friends, extended family, community members such as a coach or clergy, teachers, school transition staff, providers, and rehabilitation counselors in a multi-meeting process that works to identify strengths, goals, and an emphasis on less formal and more naturalistic assessments to determine career interests (Hagner et al., 2014). For example, flexible processes that allow individuals to participate on their own terms is likely to be more successful than following strict procedures for planning future directions (Hagner et al., 2014). One strategy would be allowing individuals to create a video, PowerPoint, or website that expresses interests and goals rather than requiring them to share that information verbally in a meeting. Other strategies may include giving written responses rather than verbal in a meeting or allowing think time for participants before jumping in to talk for them.

Community Career Services Utilizing community career centers and community rehabilitation services as part of collaborative planning can create a network of support that can be valuable in teaching job search skills, as well as accessing supports available to all residents of the community versus specialized services that individuals with high-functioning ASD may not be eligible for (McDonough & Revell, 2010). Many of these agencies offer opportunities for high schoolers with ASD with experiences such as semester-long job clubs or week-long trainings on soft skills, which are skills outside of learning work-related tasks that are essential for employment success (Connor et al., 2020). They include communication, attitude and cooperation, critical thinking, ability to cooperate with others and work within a team, quality of work, staying on task, punctuality and reliability, and personal hygiene and appearance (Clark et al., 2019; Connor et al., 2020). Other components may include summer work learning experiences and career exploration events. Community rehabilitation providers can provide career development, help with job searches, post-employment services, and development of independent living skills needed for employment (McDonough & Revell, 2010).

Community Mental Health and Other Providers

Mental health supports and managing stress are also critical services that can enable success in employment (Nicholas et al., 2018). Over 70% of transition age individuals with ASD have been estimated to have coexisting mental health conditions such as depression, anxiety, obsessive compulsive disorder, and ADHD, but more than half are not receiving services in this area (Neary et al., 2015). School psychologists can play critical roles in helping develop communication between systems of care for mental health and schools to ensure that students achieve the best outcomes. In addition, planning for adult systems of care is critical to future employment success.

Workplace Considerations and Supports

Workplace considerations and supports include the accommodations and processes that will facilitate success in employment. While primarily this will focus on permanent employment, the same principles can also be applied to work-based learning experiences within high school. The Americans with Disabilities Act (ADA) requires that employers provide jobs to individuals with disabilities who are equally qualified for the position. ADA also requires employers to provide any reasonable accommodations needed for that individual for them to accomplish the job they are hired to do (ADA, 1990). Successful employment outcomes generally have been associated with multiple types of accommodations across varying components of getting and keeping a job (McLaren et al., 2017). Accommodations for individuals with disabilities can vary greatly between workplaces but should begin with the hiring process.

Hiring Process

Some simple adaptations could be made to help individuals with ASD successfully navigate the hiring process. For example, human resources can make a minor change to job application forms by including space that is dedicated to listing accommodations that will be needed (Hill et al., 2011). In this way, the prospective employee with ASD (and other disabilities) has a simple way of broaching this topic and they will know the business is interested in how they can be supported to perform a job in the workplace. In addition, job descriptions can contain general characteristics that are not related to the actual job tasks that may hinder an applicant with ASD from applying, such as good communicator or works well with others. Adapting job descriptions to better contain relevant information will help individuals with ASD understand what is relevant and not as relevant in a job description to help them be more open to applying to these types of jobs (Scott et al., 2019).

Accommodations can also be addressed during the interview process. Arranging the format of the interview so that it is accessible to individuals with ASD is also a way to ensure they can be successful (Richards, 2012). For example, asking specific questions like, "Tell me about what tasks you did in your last job or work experience," is specific and allows the individual with ASD to focus on relevant materials. In contrast, asking, "Tell me about yourself" could be interpreted as a question about their favorite topic of interest. In addition, employers can avoid asking "what if" scenario questions. By asking for specific examples from the applicant's history, employers can address the same topic but avoid the confusion associated with nebulous questions. For example, employers can say, "Tell me about a time you had a conflict with a coworker and how you resolved it." The employer can also help guide the applicant to a similar scenario that would be relevant by providing verbal direction, if needed. If the applicant said, "I haven't worked before," then the employer can ask them about when they worked in a group for a project and conflict that may have occurred or if they volunteered or were on a team. One exception to adapting open-ended questions would be if the job position would require extensive interpersonal conversational interchange, then either later in the initial interview or at another time the ability for the candidate to answer similar questions they would encounter in the job could be evaluated.

In addition, employers can be direct by telling the applicant with ASD when they have answered a question by moving on to the next question. In this way, the individual with ASD will not stay fixed on one question. The employer will also be able to see that the job applicant with ASD can shift topics with minimal guidance from the employer. Finally, human resources can train employers to be aware that individuals with ASD may exhibit different body language or eye contact, and this does not represent a lack of interest or untrustworthiness on the part of the applicant. Employers who are not judgmental about these differences can help the individual with ASD in navigating the interview (Hill et al., 2011; Markel & Elia, 2016).

Acclimation to the Workplace

Acclimation to the workplace can be an important accommodation to help employees with ASD begin the job on a positive note. For example, a first day at work could begin with an orientation to the workplace, including visual cues such as a map of the office, a list of names of other employees (possibly with pictures), and a schedule for the first week (Hill et al., 2011). Providing an opportunity to go to the workplace before anyone else is there may also help to ease anxiety related to the first day. The employee with ASD will likely acclimate more quickly to the workplace when provided with a clear set of job assignments for the week and direct instruction when those assignments are modified. Additionally, identifying a person that the employee can ask for assistance is key to a successful acclimation (Markel & Elia, 2016). Although these recommendations are offered for employees with ASD, most employees will benefit from a similar acclimation process.

Ongoing Accommodations

For individuals with ASD, ongoing accommodations may need to be instituted in the workplace for them to be successful. For example, due to their social and communication deficits, they may need interventions that teach and train them on appropriate social responses in the workplace (Dipeolu et al., 2015). Although these accommodations would be helpful, coworkers may view these accommodations as preferential treatment. It is the responsibility of the business to provide accommodations for the individuals with disabilities (ADA, 1990) and the supervisor may need assistance in handling situations in which coworkers question the accommodations. Psychoeducation may be necessary by each institution that will be potentially working with the potential employees in this program.

One form of support for individuals in this program is the use of a job coach. A job coach provides on-the-job training so that individuals in the program can become successful in performing their jobs (McCabe & Wu, 2009; Wehman et al., 2017). Job coaches work with individuals with ASD as they begin new employment activities and then fade their support when it is no longer needed. The job coach will assist with teaching and ensuring understanding of rules and acceptable behaviors within the workplace (McCabe & Wu, 2009). As the individual with ASD gains success and independence from the job coach, the services will be reduced from direct supervision while natural supports are arranged for implementation (Wehman et al., 2017).

Other sources of assistance may be needed for the individual with ASD to be successful in the workplace once the job coach has faded support. Ongoing social skills training will be necessary to help clients navigate everyday social exchanges. If the employee with ASD can better understand the expectations of social interaction within the workplace, they may be better prepared and participate in this aspect of the workplace. Social skills training can include but should not be restricted to: greeting coworkers, asking for help, engaging in conversations, interrupting conversations appropriately when needing information from a supervisor or coworker to continue working, learning what is appropriate and inappropriate in the workplace, and nonverbal communication. Learning to "read" nonverbal cues could be taught through video modeling or direct role play (Chappel & Somers, 2010). This goes hand in hand with learning the social rules of the workplace. Many of these skills do not come naturally to all individuals with ASD and must be taught using direct training, role-play, the use of scripts, and performance feedback (Chappel & Somers, 2010). Ideally, many of these skills have been addressed in school and vocational rehabilitation settings prior to employment. But even when they have been taught, generalization of these social skills from one setting to another may be difficult. Thus, some level of training should be considered.

Self-advocacy is also a way that individuals with ASD can generally become more successful in the workplace. If individuals with disabilities disclose their limitations and accommodations needed as part of advocating for themselves, they are more likely to have a positive outcome (Chappel & Somers, 2010). Self-advocacy, disability disclosure, and making requests for appropriate accommodations in the workplace are important skills for the individuals with ASD to acquire. These skills, once learned and practiced, will assist with getting the accommodations needed to be successful in the workplace while educating peers and supervisors (Lee & Carter, 2012). Additionally, having a method of communication between supervisors and individuals with ASD that allows for questions and feedback to be communicated in a way that is open and not perceived as threatening can further the likelihood that individuals with ASD will retain a job. The feedback process should focus on a way that is effective for the individual with ASD. For example, some individuals with ASD may prefer written communication rather than verbal, because they may need additional time to process what is being said which may make verbal feedback difficult to process and fully implement (Scott et al., 2019). In a study of factors important to successful employment outcomes for individuals with ASD, both individuals and employers were surveyed to identify what factors they considered relevant to success. Consensus between employers and employees with ASD included having job expectations that are comprehensive, having knowledge of productivity expectations, supports that are available, and how to communicate with supervisors (Scott et al., 2019)

Implications for Practice

School psychologists can play a key role in ensuring that the student leaves school with appropriate proof of diagnosis and accommodations that can be utilized in the workplace. In addition, they can be involved in transition processes throughout high school to ensure they are ready for transition to employment. The National Association of School Psychologists (NASP, 2020) has established an updated version of their professional standards that can be related to these transition processes (See Table 1).

Accommodations for the hiring and employment process requires eligibility determinations. Often this is established in the K-12 system with the implementation of an IEP or 504 plans. Thus, even for high-functioning students with ASD who excel academically, it is essential to ensure they have supporting documentation of their disability and accommodations needed to ensure these can continue into the workplace.

The key to promoting successful employment outcomes for individuals with ASD begins with quality transition planning. This transition planning must address factors related to the individual, family, or previous services that may help or hinder the possibility of employment. Transition planning must be collaborative and include the individual with ASD, the family, community service agencies such as vocational rehabilitation. Transition planning must include appropriate services that address career development, provide work-based learning experiences, and are flexible. Transition planning is used to reach individuals with ASD serviced exclusively in general education as well as those who also receive special education services. Ensuring that individuals with ASD are prepared to enter the workforce requires promoting self-determination and communication skills needed to identify and access accommodations. Focusing exclusively on academics in high school may limit future employment by ignoring the importance of social skills, completing independent activities of daily living, and getting and maintaining a job. School psychologists can help IEP teams incorporate these into transition planning services. With appropriate skills developed through these critical services, we can ensure that individuals with ASD are ready for the workforce and can acquire the needed supports to attain, maintain, and succeed in the workforce.

References

Americans With Disabilities Act of 1990, 42 U.S.C.A. § 12101 *et seq.*

Anderson, C., Butt, C., & Sarsony, C. (2021). Young adults on the autism spectrum and early employment-related experiences: Aspirations and obstacles. *Journal of autism and developmental disorders, 51*, 88–105.

Bargeron, J., Contri, D., Gibbons, L. J., Ruch-Ross, H. S., & Sanabria, K. (2015). Transition planning for youth with special health care needs (YSHCN) in Illinois schools. *The Journal of School Nursing, 31*, 253–260.

Bennett, A. E., Miller, J. S., Stollon, N., Prasad, R., & Blum, N. J. (2018). Autism spectrum disorder and transition-aged youth. *Current Psychiatry Reports, 20*, 102–111.

Bross, L. A., & Travers, J. C. (2017). Special interest areas and employment skills programming for secondary students with autism. *TEACHING Exceptional Children, 50*, 74–83.

Burgess, S., & Cimera, R. E. (2014). Employment outcomes of transition-aged adults with autism spectrum disorders: A state of the states report. *American Journal on Intellectual and Developmental Disabilities, 119*, 64–83.

Burgess, A. F., & Gutstein, S. E. (2007). Quality of life for people with autism: Raising the standard for evaluating successful outcomes. *Child and Adolescent Mental Health, 12*, 80–86.

Burnes, J. J., Martin, J. E., Terry, R., McConnell, A. E., & Hennessey, M. N. (2018). Predicting postsecondary education and employment outcomes using results from the transition assessment and goal generator. *Career Development and Transition for Exceptional Individuals, 41*, 111–121.

Career One Stop. https://www.careeronestop.org

Carter, E., Austin, D., & Trainor, A. A. (2011). Factors associated with the early work experiences of adolescents with severe disabilities. *Intellectual and Developmental Disabilities, 49*, 233–247.

Carter, E. W., Common, E., Sreckovic, M. A., Huber, H., Bottema-Beutel, K., Gustafson, J., ... Hume, K. (2014). Promoting social competence and peer relationships for adolescents with autism spectrum disorders. *Remedial and Special Education, 35*, 91–101.

Cease-Cook, J., Fowler, C., & Test, D. W. (2015). Strategies for creating work-based learning experiences in schools for secondary students with disabilities. *Teaching Exceptional Children, 47*, 352–358.

Chan, W., Smith, L. E., Hong, J., Greenberg, J. S., Lounds Taylor, J., & Mailick, M. R. (2018). Factors associated with sustained community employment among adults with autism and co-occurring intellectual disability. *Autism, 22*, 794–803.

Chappel, S. L., & Somers, B. C. (2010). Employing persons with autism spectrum disorders: A collaborative effort. *Journal of Vocational Rehabilitation, 32*, 117–124.

Chiang, H. M., Cheung, Y. K., Li, H., & Tsai, L. Y. (2013). Factors associated with participation in employment for high school leavers with autism. *Journal of Autism and Developmental Disorders, 43*, 1832–1842.

Cimera, R. E. (2010). National cost efficiency of supported employees with intellectual disabilities: 2002 to 2007. *American Journal on Intellectual and Developmental Disabilities, 115*, 19–29.

Clark, K. A., Konrad, M., & Test, D. W. (2019). Teaching soft skills to students with disabilities with upgrade your performance. *Education and Training in Autism and Developmental Disabilities, 54*, 41–56.

Connor, A., Sung, C., Strain, A., Zeng, S., & Fabrizi, S. (2020). Building skills, confidence, and wellness: Psychosocial effects of soft skills training for young adults with autism. *Journal of autism and developmental disorders, 50*(6), 2064–2076.

Cullen, J. M., Simmons-Reed, E. A., & Weaver, L. (2017). Using 21st century video prompting technology to facilitate the independence of individuals with intellectual and developmental disabilities. *Psychology in the Schools, 54*, 965–978.

Dipeolu, A. O., Storlie, C., & Johnson, C. (2015). College students with high-functioning autism spectrum disorder: Best practices for successful transition to the world of work. *Journal of College Counseling, 18*, 175–190.

Dunn, L., Diener, M., Wright, C., Wright, S., & Narumanchi, A. (2015). Vocational exploration in an extracurricular technology program for youth with autism. *Work, 52*, 457–468.

Field, S., Martin, J., Miller, R., Ward, M., & Wehmeyer, M. (1998). *A practical guide for teaching self-determination*. Council for Exceptional Children.

Gothberg, J. E., Peterson, L. Y., Peak, M., & Sedaghat, J. M. (2015). Successful transition of students with disabilities to 21st-century college and careers: Using triangulation and gap analysis to address nonacademic skills. *Teaching Exceptional Children, 47*, 344–351.

Preparation for Successful Employment 239

Hagner, D., Kurtz, A., May, J., & Cloutier, H. (2014). Person-centered planning for transition-aged youth with autism spectrum disorders. *Journal of Rehabilitation, 80*, 4–10.

Hatfield, M., Falkmer, M., Falkmer, T., & Ciccarelli, M. (2016). Evaluation of the effectiveness of an online transition planning program for adolescents on the autism spectrum: trial protocol. *Child and Adolescent Psychiatry and Mental Health, 10*, 48–59.

Hayes, G. R., Custodio, V. E., Haimson, O. L., Nguyen, K., Ringland, K. E., Ulgado, R. R., … Weiner, R. (2015). Mobile video modeling for employment interviews for individuals with autism. *Journal of Vocational Rehabilitation, 43*, 275–287.

Hill, E. L., Dockery, L., Perkins, D., & McIntosh, B. (2011). *ASD, employment and mental health.* [Printed Ephemera]: Goldsmiths Research Online.

Hussar, B., Zhang, J., Hein, S., Wang, K., Roberts, A., Cui, J., ..., & Dilig, R. (2020). The condition of education 2020. NCES 2020-144. *National Center for Education Statistics.*

Individuals with Disabilities Education Improvement Act, H.R. 1350, 108th Congress (2004).

Katsiyannis, A., & Reid, R. (1999). Autism and Section 504: Rights and responsibilities. *Focus on Autism and Other Developmental Disabilities, 14*, 66–72.

Kellems, R. O., Grigal, M., Unger, D. D., Simmons, T. J., Bauder, D., & Williams, C. (2015). Technology and transition in the 21st century. *Teaching Exceptional Children, 47*, 336–343.

Kellems, R. O., Springer, B., Wilkins, M. K., & Anderson, C. (2016). Collaboration in transition assessment: School psychologists and special educators working together to improve outcomes for students with disabilities. *Preventing School Failure: Alternative Education for Children and Youth, 60*(3), 215–221.

Kiernan, W. E., Hoff, D., Freeze, S., & Mank, D. M. (2011). Employment first: A beginning not an end. *Intellectual and Developmental Disabilities, 49*, 300–304.

Kopelson, K. (2015). " Know thy work and do it": The rhetorical-pedagogical work of employment and workplace guides for adults with "high-functioning" autism. *College English, 77*, 553–576.

Kucharczyk, S., Reutebuch, C. K., Carter, E. W., Hedges, S., El Zein, F., Fan, H., & Gustafson, J. R. (2015). Addressing the needs of adolescents with autism spectrum disorder: Considerations and complexities for high school interventions. *Exceptional Children, 81*, 329–349.

Kuyken, W. (1995). The world health organization quality of life assessment (WHOQOL): Position paper from the world health organization. *Social and Science & Medicine, 41*, 1403–1409.

Lawer, L., Brusilovskiy, E., Salzer, M., & Mandell, D. (2009). Use of vocational rehabilitation services among adults with autism. *Journal of Developmental Disorders, 39*, 487–494.

Lee, G. K., & Carter, E. W. (2012). Preparing transition-age students with high-functioning autism spectrum disorders for meaningful work. *Psychology in the Schools, 49*, 988–1000.

Markel, K. S., & Elia, B. (2016). How human resource management can best support employees with autism: Future directions for research and practice. *Journal of Business and Management, 22*, 71–85.

Mazzotti, V. L., Wood, C. L., Test, D. W., & Fowler, C. H. (2012). Effects of computer-assisted instruction on students' knowledge of the self-determined learning model of instruction and disruptive behavior. *The Journal of Special Education, 45*, 216–226.

McCabe, H., & Wu, S. (2009). Helping each other, helping ourselves: A case of employment for an adult with autism in Nanjing, China. *Journal of Vocational Rehabilitation, 30*, 57–66.

McDonough, J. T., & Revell, G. (2010). Accessing employment supports in the adult system for transitioning youth with autism spectrum disorders. *Journal of Vocational Rehabilitation, 32*, 89–100.

McLaren, J., Lichtenstein, J. D., Lynch, D., Becker, D., & Drake, R. (2017). Individual placement and support for people with autism spectrum disorders: A pilot program. *Administration and Policy in Mental Health and Mental Health Services Research, 44*, 365–373.

My Next Move. https://www.mynextmove.org

National Association of School Psychologists. (2020). *The professional standards of the national association of school psychologists.* https://www.nasponline.org/standards-and-certification/nasp-2020-professional-standards-adopted

Neary, P., Gilmore, L., & Ashburner, J. (2015). Post-school needs of young people with high-functioning autism spectrum disorder. *Research in Autism Spectrum Disorders, 18,* 1–11.

Newman, L., Wagner, M., Knokey, A.-M., Marder, C., Nagle, K., Shaver, D., . . . Schwarting, M. (2011). The post-high school outcomes of young adults with disabilities up to 8 years after high school: A report from the national longitudinal transition study-2 (NLTS2) (NCSER 2011-3005). : SRI International.

Nicholas, D. B., Mitchell, W., Dudley, C., Clarke, M., & Zulla, R. (2018). An ecosystem approach to employment and autism spectrum disorder. *Journal of Autism and Developmental Disorders, 48,* 264–275.

Nicolaidis, C., Kripke, C. C., & Raymaker, D. (2014). Primary care for adults on the autism spectrum. *Medical Clinics, 98,* 1169–1191.

Nilsson, E., & Lodestad, S. (2014). Web coaching: An alternative and complementary form of meeting. *Journal of Vocational Rehabilitation, 41,* 59–66.

Nye-Lengerman, K. (2017). Vocational rehabilitation service usage and outcomes for individuals with autism spectrum disorder. *Research in Autism Spectrum Disorders, 41,* 39–50.

Project Search. https://www.projectsearch.us

Renty, J. O., & Roeyers, H. (2006). Quality of life in high-functioning adults with autism spectrum disorder: The predictive value of disability and support characteristics. *Autism, 10,* 511–524.

Richards, J. (2012). Examining the exclusion of employees with Asperger syndrome from the workplace. *Personnel Review, 42,* 630–646.

Roux, A. M., Rast, J. E., & Shattuck, P. T. (2020). State-level variation in vocational rehabilitation service use and related outcomes among transition-age youth on the autism spectrum. *Journal of Autism and Developmental Disorders, 50,* 2449–2461.

Rowe, D. A., Mazzotti, V. L., Hirano, K., & Alverson, C. Y. (2015). Assessing transition skills in the 21st century. *Teaching Exceptional Children, 47,* 301–309.

Scott, M., Milbourn, B., Falkmer, M., Black, M., Bölte, S., Halladay, A., … Girdler, S. (2019). Factors impacting employment for people with autism spectrum disorder: A scoping review. *Autism, 23,* 869–901.

Schalock, R. L. (Ed.). (1996). *Quality of life: Application to persons with disabilities* (Vol. 2). Aamr.

Shattuck, P. T., Narendorf, S. C., Cooper, B. P., Sterzing, P., Wagner, M., & Taylor, J. L. (2012). Postsecondary education and employment among youth with an autism spectrum disorder. *Pediatrics, 129,* 1042–1049.

Smith, M. J., Fleming, M. F., Wright, M. A., Losh, M., Humm, L. B., Olsen, D., & Bell, M. D. (2015). Brief report: Vocational outcomes for young adults with autism spectrum disorders at six months after virtual reality job interview training. *Journal of Autism and Developmental Disorders, 45,* 3364–3369.

Taylor, J. L., & Mailick, M. R. (2014). A longitudinal examination of 10-year change in vocational and educational activities for adults with autism spectrum disorders. *Developmental Psychology, 50,* 699–708.

Test, D. W., Fowler, C. H., Richter, S. M., White, J., Mazzotti, V., Walker, A. R., … Kortering, L. (2009). Evidence-based practices in secondary transition. *Career Development for Exceptional Individuals, 32,* 115–128.

Tsiopela, D., & Jimoyiannis, A. (2017). Pre-vocational skills laboratory: designing interventions to improve employment skills for students with autism spectrum disorders. *Universal Access in the Information Society, 16,* 609–627.

Walsh, E., Holloway, J., & Lydon, H. (2018). An evaluation of a social skills intervention for adults with autism spectrum disorder and intellectual disabilities preparing for employment in Ireland: A pilot study. *Journal of Autism and Developmental Disorders, 48,* 1727–1741.

Wehmeyer, M. L., Palmer, S. B., Agran, M., Mithaug, D. E., & Martin, J. E. (2000). Promoting causal agency: The self-determined learning model of instruction. *Exceptional Children, 66*(4), 439–453.

Wehman, P., Schall, C. M., McDonough, J., Graham, C., Brooke, V., Riehle, J. E., … Avellone, L. (2017). Effects of an employer-based intervention on employment outcomes for youth with significant support needs due to autism. *Autism, 21*, 276–290.

Wehmeyer, M. L., Parent, W., Lattimore, J., Obremski, S., Poston, D., & Rousso, H. (2009). Promoting self-determination and self-directed employment planning for young women with disabilities. *Journal of Social Work in Disability & Rehabilitation, 8*, 117–131.

Wehmeyer, M., & Schwartz, M. (1997). Self-determination and positive adult outcomes: A follow-up study of youth with mental retardation or learning disabilities. *Exceptional children, 63*, 245–255.

Wong, J., Cohn, E. S., Coster, W. J., & Orsmond, G. I. (2020). "Success Doesn't Happen in a Traditional Way": Experiences of school personnel who provide employment preparation for youth with autism spectrum disorder. *Research in autism spectrum disorders, 77*, 101631.

Yell, M. L., Shriner, J. G., & Katsiyannis, A. (2006). Individuals with disabilities education improvement act of 2004 and IDEA regulations of 2006: Implications for educators, administrators, and teacher trainers. *Focus on Exceptional Children, 39*, 1–24.

Zalewska, A., Migliore, A., & Butterworth, J. (2016). Self-determination, social skills, job search, and transportation: Is there a relationship with employment of young adults with autism? *Journal of Vocational Rehabilitation, 45*, 225–239.

Considerations for School Psychology University Faculty: Developing and Implementing Services for Students with ASD

Jennifer Cleveland and Elizabeth Williams

Abstract A growing number of students with autism spectrum disorder (ASD) are attending colleges nationwide. School psychology university faculty possess a unique set of clinical skills that lend themselves well to the supervision and provision of college-based support services for students with autism spectrum disorder (ASD). The present chapter will review the development and implementation of college-based services for students with ASD utilizing program theory as a framework. The authors also highlight ways to improve university culture for successfully teaching students with ASD, outline consultation models for use with college faculty and staff and identify avenues for community partnership. Finally, the authors discuss the process of supervision and how one might successfully integrate school psychology graduate students into a support program for students with autism at the college level.

Keywords Autism · ASD · Asperger's · Autistic · College Autism program · University ASD services

Considerations for School Psychology University Faculty: Developing and Implementing Services for Students with ASD

The number of college/university programs for students with autism spectrum disorder (ASD) is rapidly springing up all over the United States as universities attempt to keep up with the growing number of students on the spectrum attending college. It is estimated that approximately 433,00 college students with ASD are expected to

---

J. Cleveland (✉)
The University of Texas at San Antonio, San Antonio, TX, USA
e-mail: jenc@sunpsychological.com

E. Williams
Darien Public Schools, Special Education and Student Services Department, Darien, CT, USA

© Springer Nature Switzerland AG 2022
K. D. Viezel et al. (eds.), *Postsecondary Transition for College- or Career-Bound Autistic Students*, https://doi.org/10.1007/978-3-030-93947-2_12

be enrolled in college during 2020 (Cox, 2017). Presently, there are 198 school psychology graduate programs approved by the National Association of School Psychologists (NASP) in the United States and approximately 72 additional programs that are not NASP-approved (NASP, n.d.). School psychology (or similarly allied fields, such as school counseling or clinical psychology) faculty members at these universities are in a unique position to a) develop a program for college students with ASD at their university and/or b) provide resources and information to colleagues and staff members on campus who are working with these students. The present chapter will review the development and implementation of college-based services for students with ASD, highlight methods of improving university culture, outline consultation models for use with college faculty and stakeholders, identify avenues for community partnership, and discuss the process of supervising graduate students.

Before specific support services can be reviewed, the strengths and challenges of students with ASD are important to discuss. College students with ASD vary in terms of their need for and use of services at the college level. In our work with individuals enrolled in our ASD support program, we have noted that individuals with ASD who are college-bound seem to fall into three distinct categories. The first category of students represents individuals with ASD who require no official academic accommodations in college, but apply to an ASD support program for help with the general transition process, assistance with executive functioning abilities, as well as help in social and/or daily life skills (Adreon & Durocher, 2007; Van Bergeijk et al., 2008). These students may have accessed special education services at earlier periods in their academic development but feel they have outgrown the need for special education services by the time they apply for college. Colleges and universities are governed by the Americans with Disabilities Act (ADA), which stipulates that individuals cannot be "excluded from participation." However, universities are not mandated to provide specialized instruction, only ensure that students have equal access to education (ADA, 1990).

The second category of college-bound students with ASD consists of students currently receiving Individualized Education Program (IEP) services in high school, such as resource room assistance, accommodations on standardized tests, and related services (e.g., counseling). These students (oftentimes with influence from their parents) choose to apply to an ASD support program for their college experience in an attempt to model a similar type of service delivery that was provided in high school. In addition to the services offered through the ASD support program, these students also typically register with the university disability office to receive academic accommodations in their courses.

The third category of college-bound students with ASD apply to and attend college but do not choose to participate in a specialized ASD support program while in school. This last category of students represents both those who attend college but apply for accommodations through the university's disability office (with ASD as their official disability), and those who have an ASD but choose not to apply for accommodations. A percentage of the students who receive accommodations via the disability office could benefit from the services of a specialized program. Some of the reasons they do not enroll in a specialized ASD support program likely include financial limitations (most specialized ASD programs are expensive, costing an average of over $6000 per academic year based on an informal survey of ASD support programs in the Northeast conducted by Cleveland in 2016). Additional reasons for not enrolling in a specialized program may include lack of knowledge about existing programs, limited or no programs located near hometown residences, or a perceived lack of need for the services.

When developing a new support program for students with ASD, it is important to address the unique needs of these students. Literature supports the fact that college-bound students with ASD struggle with executive functioning skills, social difficulties, and often coexisting mental health issues that negatively impact their ability to be successful in college (Anderson & Butt, 2017). In addition, these same struggles affect their academic functioning (Keen et al., 2016; Kurth & Mastergeorge, 2010). Therefore, a successful college-based ASD support program must provide services that address these four main areas: academic support, executive functioning skills, social skills, and support for coexisting psychiatric issues.

But how does one go about designing a program that successfully addresses all these needs? Program theory modeling uses three components to describe the program: the program activities or inputs, the intended outcomes or outputs, and the mechanisms through which the intended outcomes are achieved (Reynolds, 1998; Rogers, 2000; Sedani & Sechrest, 1999). Applying these principles to a college support program for ASD involves defining the components of the particular program (e.g., which support/therapeutic/academic services will be offered), defining the intended purpose or outcome (e.g., retention rates, GPA's, etc.), and finally designing the frequency and manner in which the services are delivered in order to bring about the desired outcome. The desired outcome in this case is providing enough supports so that an individual with ASD has the same opportunity to be successful in college as an individual without ASD.

Conducting a needs assessment is an important first step in developing and implementing a specialized-support program. One time-efficient solution is to conduct a needs assessment by distributing an online survey via email. Relevant information to consider incorporating into a needs assessment may include: knowledge of/perception of competence in using instructional/behavior management strategies for working with students with ASD, level of support offered by current campus offices (e.g., university disability office) for supporting faculty with students with ASD in their classes, number of instances of staff who sought campus supports for help with a student with ASD in the previous academic year, interest in receiving training for strategies to use when working with students with ASD, and opinions related to whether or not specialized support programs would be helpful. Additionally, it is equally important to consider which personnel from the campus will participate in the survey. Faculty are only a portion of the university community that interact with students with disabilities. Librarians, enrollment services staff, campus safety officers, residence life staff, and tutors are all staff members who have frequent interaction with students. When developing a needs assessment, it may be necessary to create different versions for different members of the campus community. For example, the faculty version may inquire about knowledge of instructional strategies whereas the campus safety officers' version may ask for knowledge of de-escalation strategies.

It is strongly recommended that one designing a new program first investigate all available, preexisting resources at their university (Bennett, 1979). There are many questions to consider during this process: Where will the services be housed? Will the services be an extension to an existing disability office, or will it be part of an existing department on campus, such as education or psychology? Other natural partners include mental health clinics on campus where students are trained. The second issue is to identify available personnel. Utilizing existing staff is often most practical. Support programs such as those for students with ASD are unique opportunities for graduate students to be involved in as providers of various services as well as gaining experience in administrative tasks and responsibilities. If your university does not have sufficient staff, outside staff members should be included in proposed budgets and hired prior to beginning the program. The third issue is that of frequency and type of support services that will be offered. Typically, having at least two times per week of contact with the student is recommended in order to provide services such as individual counseling, group counseling, case management sessions, and/or sessions that focus on executive functioning or adaptive living skills. Increasing your point of contact sessions to three to four times per week is often beneficial to ensure delivery of services, as well as provide consistent monitoring of students' progress so that crises can be averted. In addition to developing a needs assessment and choosing and implementing the first steps for building a program, it is also important to examine the university environment that will support this new program.

Improving University Culture

The success of postsecondary support programs for students with ASD relies, in part, on the feelings of inclusiveness felt by students and their families as well as the degree of comfort experienced by members of the campus community towards the students and the program. Previous research in the area of specialized support programs for students with disabilities has shown that more successful programs occur in institutions where students and educators demonstrate positive attitudes towards individuals with disabilities (Cullen et al., 2010). Inclusive programming has also been shown to foster larger-community acceptance for students with special needs (McDougall et al., 2004). ASD program staff are encouraged to monitor the culture surrounding the integration of students with disabilities at their institution, including ASD. This should include reviewing previously collected data from a needs assessment. If faculty or other campus community members reported themes of concern in a needs survey, it is critical to follow up and address these areas. If a needs assessment was not originally administered at the onset of program development, it may be beneficial to initiate a focus group or institution-wide survey to examine campus culture regarding addressing the needs of students with ASD. It may also be important to collect data over time to determine if program supports are beneficial to the campus community beyond the outcomes of enrolled students. Research conducted in this area reveals that educators' attitudes towards inclusion are amendable over time (Cahill, 2016) and attitudinal change is a multifaceted process relying on several key variables.

Faculty Attitudes Towards Inclusion It is promising to see that research investigating college faculty members' attitudes towards students with disabilities indicates that, in general, faculty report positive attitudes towards the general mission of inclusion (Williams, 2018). However, due to the limited amount of research on faculty members' attitudes towards the specific inclusion of students with ASD, it is important for program staff to keep certain variables in mind when evaluating the culture on their specific campus. For example, past research has demonstrated an important relationship between educators' self-efficacy, attitudes towards inclusion, and successful inclusive programs (Condrey, 2017; Cullen et al., 2010). A link has also been established in the literature between educators' increased knowledge of instructional/classroom management strategies and higher levels of perceived self-efficacy (Condrey, 2017; Wilkerson, 2013).

Identifiable negative attitudes towards inclusion practices have been attributed to anticipated concerns surrounding the education of this population of students (Williams, 2018). When integrating students with ASD in their classrooms, faculty reported expectations of an increased workload and additional stress. Faculty also indicated feeling underprepared to teach this population of students and reported lacking the skills necessary to effectively teach students with ASD. Educators who report feeling underprepared to educate this population of students have also demonstrated low levels of self-efficacy. This lack of confidence in their own abilities to teach students with ASD also results in negative attitudes towards the integration of students with disabilities (Cullen et al., 2010). Addressing concerns about perceived increases in workload, experiences of additional stress, and feelings of unpreparedness to implement instructional and/or classroom management strategies should all be targeted via professional development, training opportunities, and consultation services.

Professional Development Faculty professional development should focus on increased understanding of the core struggles of individuals with ASD as well as successful strategies for addressing difficult behavior (e.g.., providing clear and concrete expectations and feedback). Additionally, professional development should provide an overview of the specific services offered by the support program. This may help faculty members understand the areas being targeted for intervention as well as the specific support services offered to university faculty (i.e., consultation opportunities). Attitudinal change within faculty should begin with improving knowledge about ASD with a goal of targeting perceived self-efficacy. More specifically, 8 h of ASD-specific training was associated with more positive attitudes towards inclusion in one study (Park & Chitiyo, 2011). The purpose of professional development seminars should focus on reviewing the key features of ASD with a specific focus on the manifestation of these symptoms (such as the impact of weaknesses in executive functioning skills and deficits in the social realm) that are specific to a university environment. For example, explaining why a student with ASD may have difficulty when assigned a group project, so that the instructor can plan for and anticipate these challenges. However, it is also critical to highlight the features of ASD that may translate well to academic success, including passion for a particular subject area or attention to detail. Beischer (2012) found that faculty were already aware of the important implications of providing students access to legally mandated accommodations provided through the campus disability office. As a result, this specific area need not be targeted for professional development unless program staff or students notice difficulty in accommodation access at their institution.

Interactions with Individuals with ASD Additional research has shown that having prior interactions with students with ASD was associated with increased attitudes of inclusion (Mahoney, 2008). It is important to note that although exposure to individuals with disabilities may foster more positive attitudes towards inclusion, it does not translate to increased knowledge of ASD. As a result, consultation with faculty and staff (discussed later in this chapter) provides an opportunity to make these interactions meaningful learning experiences. It should be noted, however, that due to privacy laws faculty are usually unaware that a student in their classroom has ASD unless shared by the student or disclosed by program staff with permission from the student.

Student Attitudes Towards Inclusion Faculty are not the only subset of the university contributing to the overall culture of inclusion at a particular institution. Fellow college students are other key players attributing to overall campus culture and general attitudes towards individuals with disabilities. Existing research is mixed, however, regarding the role that knowledge plays in students' overall attitudes towards inclusion (Mahoney, 2008; White et al., 2016). Interpersonal relationships appear to play an especially important role. Although spending more time with an individual with ASD has shown to be important, the quality of the relationship has also been attributed to more positive attitudes towards students with ASD (Mahoney, 2008). In fact, neurotypical students enrolled in classes alongside students with disabilities report having more friends with a disability in comparison to students from institutions that do not prioritize inclusive programming (Bunch, 2004). This is important information for universities to consider as students with ASD are at higher risk for social isolation due to deficits in social communication (Shattuck et al., 2012).

Peer Mentoring In addition to typical classroom and campus interactions, peer mentoring is an additional way for support programs to increase students' exposure to those with ASD as well as foster quality relationships between neurotypical peers and students with ASD. Peer mentoring programs can be tailored in a variety of ways. One method is pairing neurotypical undergraduate students with fellow undergraduate students with ASD. Ideal neurotypical students consist of responsible, motivated individuals (often these students are Psychology majors) and those who are excited to have the mentorship experience be a positive one. Support programs can implement peer mentoring as a standard or optional part of their program. Dyads can meet for social outings for a specific amount of time (e.g., once per week). For example, a student with ASD may be interested in joining a club on campus but may feel uncomfortable about navigating the unexpected social interactions of attending club meetings. A peer mentor can accompany the student to club meetings until they feel comfortable attending independently. The program may also look to sponsor social events for all peer mentors and all program students (e.g., game day, movie night, pizza party).

Program staff should provide training specific to undergraduate student peer mentors, which is separate from faculty professional development. Trainings for peer mentors should include reviewing the core symptomology of ASD as well as strategies for navigating challenging behaviors. Specifically, this should include reviewing the social and communication challenges often experienced by individuals with ASD. Training should also outline scenarios that can be uncomfortable and difficult to manage for students with ASD, including unstructured social settings or crowded and loud environments. Training for undergraduate students should also highlight aspects of the college environment in which students with ASD may thrive (i.e., preference for routines, restricted and passionate interest in a particular area). Undergraduate peer mentors should also be in communication as needed with other program staff in order to help facilitate communication among program staff necessary for mitigating issues that arise.

Peer mentoring benefits both members of the dyad as the peer mentors can highlight leadership abilities and clinical skills on job applications. It is recommended to advertise peer mentor positions to all undergraduate students in order to provide outreach for a broad variety of students. It may be easier to recruit students from rehabilitation or human service majors as these populations of students have shown to exhibit more positive attitudes towards individuals with disabilities. However, in an effort to promote inclusionary practices and increase campus attitudes towards ASD, it would be beneficial to include students from business majors who have previously demonstrated less positive attitudes towards individuals with disabilities (Chan et al., 2002; Schwartz & Armony-Sivan, 2001).

Consulting with Faculty and Staff

One of the most important aspects of creating a comprehensive ASD support program involves educating the campus community about ASD. Providing consultation services to those faculty and staff who have frequent interaction with students with ASD is critical to the success of a support program. Professional development opportunities and consistent contact with key faculty members and administrative staff are both needed to ensure the success of these students. During consultation, it is important to educate and highlight the specific manifestations of

ASD symptomology in the college environment as well as provide strategies for working with this population of students. Benefits of consultation extend beyond student's classroom success and have positive outcomes for university faculty and staff, including equipping faculty with skills to handle similar problems in the future (Erchul & Sheridan, 2014). Consultation services offered by ASD support programs should aid faculty and staff in interacting with students with ASD. This assistance may also be helpful to faculty members when dealing with other students with deficits in similar domains, such as executive functioning, social skills, adaptive skills, and/or problematic classroom behaviors.

Who Should Be Targeted for Consultation? Faculty often have the most contact with students during their college experience and are an obvious population of the campus community to be targeted for consultation. ASD program staff should maintain consistent communication with students' professors, reaching out multiple times throughout the course of each semester. These points of contact should provide an opportunity to request information on students' grades, attendance, class behavior, and completion of assignments. One suggested method for gathering this information is sending a standardized form for each professor to complete and return to the ASD support program staff. If areas of concern are indicated, program staff can follow up with the professor via a phone call for additional information. Program staff should offer education and support during these communications aimed at increasing their knowledge about ASD and/or offering classroom management strategies.

In addition to college faculty, there are other important campus departments with which students have frequent contact, including residence life, the admissions office, the registrar or enrollment services office, and the university's Student Disabilities office. Orientation leaders and dormitory Resident Advisors are often the first point of contact for incoming college students and play a key role in helping undergraduates adjust to university life. It is critical to provide training opportunities and consultation services to these student employees prior to the beginning of the academic year, as well as during the academic year on an as-needed basis. Admissions and/or registrar staff, tutors, health center staff, campus safety officers, counseling center staff, and information technology personnel are additional staff members who have frequent and important interactions with students. These individuals and departments should be targeted for both education regarding ASD symptomatology as well as to provide tips on how to be more effective in addressing the needs of students with ASD on campus.

Knowledge about ASD or other disabilities varies widely among campus staff members in these various offices, yet students with ASD are often in regular contact with these departments throughout their academic career. In order to bridge the communication gap between ASD support programs and other departments on campus, it is recommended that support programs raise awareness on campus about their presence and advertise to all staff that consultation services are available for anyone experiencing difficulty supporting a student with ASD.

Need for Consultation Past research has shown that college faculty members have reported feeling underprepared to educate students with ASD (Beischer, 2012; Williams, 2018). A majority of professors have reported feeling as though they do not have the required knowledge or skills to effectively educate students with ASD and feel as though doing so will increase their workload. They have also expressed specific concerns regarding the integration of this population of students into college classrooms. Despite research demonstrating that the academic achievement of students without disabilities is not impacted by the presence of students with disabilities in their classes (Huber et al., 2001; Rouse & Florian, 2006), faculty have voiced concern over the potential for the grades of other students to suffer upon the inclusion of students with ASD.

The need for consultation services is further highlighted by research showing that prior experience teaching a student with ASD has not been associated with an increase in knowledge of the disorder (Beischer, 2012; Williams, 2018). Therefore, it is important to intervene with faculty quickly and effectively when they have concerns in order to increase the chances that their expanded knowledge base can be generalized to similar students in the future. Consultation models are effective strategies in raising program awareness on campus and for increasing knowledge of ASD while improving competency levels in faculty and staff working with this population of scholars.

Consultation Models Similar to consultation work with elementary, middle, and high school educators, consultation can be used as a method of service delivery at the postsecondary level. Behavioral consultation and mental health consultation are two main models of consultation service provision to employ when working with university faculty and staff. The following includes a description of how each model is employed and a case example comparing and contrasting the utility of using behavioral consultation and mental health consultation with faculty.

Systems-Level Consultation Creating and initiating a newly developed support program requires a substantial amount of systems-level change. This requires that program representatives use systems-level consultation to educate university stakeholders about the utility of specialized support programs for students with ASD in order to address the achievement gap in graduation rates as well as support faculty in educating this growing population of college students with unique needs. Systems-level consultation involves knowledge of the hierarchical and organization structure of an organization (Erchul et al., 2001). In higher education, this may vary from one university to the next, but likely involves consulting with the college dean, provost, disability services coordinator, financial directors, and the campus president.

In order to elicit buy-in and resources from stakeholders, it is important to incorporate the previously discussed needs assessment in order to highlight university needs as well as develop a plan for addressing the reported concerns. This systems-level consultation is a required first step in order to gain institutional support for the development and growth of a program, including any monetary or personnel resources required to run the program. Ongoing systems-level consultation may be required to maintain the university's support as the program evolves and necessary changes/additions are made. After such systems-level goals are achieved, consultation can shift to working with campus faculty and staff to support their interactions with enrolled students in the classroom and beyond.

Behavioral Consultation One of the most commonly used consultation models targets students' problematic behavior through behavioral consultation (BC). Consultees (faculty members/staff) are responsible for implementing the specific recommended strategies to modify students' behavior instead of the consultants (program staff) intervening to manage the students' behavior in the classroom. The BC model involves identifying and objectively defining the problem, planning and implementing a strategy to address that problem, and evaluating the outcome (Dougherty, 2014). Consultees may report many different behaviors as problematic, but it is important to prioritize and address one behavior at a time. In BC consultation, a problematic behavior is often defined as a discrepancy between a student's current level of functioning and expected behaviors. It is important to explicitly discuss the expectations (whether they are behavioral or academic in nature) and how those expectations were communicated to students. Faculty may then require education on ways in which a students' ASD symptoms may be serving as a barrier to successfully meeting this goal. Classroom management techniques and/or instructional strategies may need to be given to the faculty member to better support students with a particular deficit.

When transitioning from high school to college, students experience a shift in expectations for appropriate classroom behavior. Expected classroom etiquette also varies depending on the professor and the particular class. For example, in K through 12 schooling, students are typically expected to raise their hand as a signal that they have a question or comment and wait to be called on before speaking. In college, this expectation is more fluid, as it is often acceptable to participate in group discussions without raising hands. Shifts such as this one are not explicitly stated, yet professors often expect that students follow these unwritten classroom "social rules," which are often difficult for students with ASD to accurately interpret and follow. One possible solution to this problem is for the faculty member to speak to the entire class in order to set guidelines around acceptable behavior for participation.

The behavioral consultation approach is beneficial if there is evidence that a student's behavior is becoming disruptive in class. The instructor may reveal this via a phone call to a staff member of the ASD support program or via feedback on a progress monitoring form. The consultant should discuss the behavior with the consultee to identify and define what "disruptive behavior" includes (i.e., speaking without raising their hand or waiting to be called on and/or dominating group discussions without allowing time for other students to speak) as well as identify the expected behavior for the classroom (i.e., raising hand to speak and/or limiting oneself to five questions or comments per class session). A consultant working from a BC model may recommend that the faculty member explicitly review the aforementioned expected behavior with the student and provide strategies for using concrete, directive feedback in the class when the student does not follow the expected behavior. It is often recommended that professors schedule a meeting (outside of class) with the student to address specific behavior concerns and to review classroom expectations. This allows the professor to more subtly provide directive feedback in the classroom setting, such as using a secret signal or simply saying the student's name to cue expected behaviors.

Mental Health Consultation Some consultation cases may require consultants to target consultees' attitudes towards a student rather than targeting a change in student's behavior. In mental health consultation (MHC), the focus of consultation sessions is the consultee's mindset around the students presenting problems. In order words, the "problem" may lie in the consultee's perception of a student's behavior and perceived rationales for a student's behavior, rather than the actual inappropriate behavior. MHC is used instead of BC when a consultee's perception of the student is distorted. The goal of MHC is to shift elements of a consultee's distorted thinking, which can be achieved through targeted questioning about the faculty's experience with a specific student.

The same classroom behavior described in the behavioral consultation example may be approached using an MHC approach instead of a BC model. In discussing the situation with the faculty member, it may become clear that the student's behavior during a group discussion, for example, is actually consistent with expectations for all students. In this case, a consultant may challenge the consultee's thinking and ask, "How many other students call out during class?" or "How was this expectation relayed to the students?" In this instance, the goal of consultation is to shift the consultee's perception of the concern to a more objective view of the presenting problem. Once a more objective view is established and discussed, the consultee may begin to feel more positively towards the student of concern, negating the need for intervention.

Confidentiality When consulting with faculty and staff, it is important to remember that unless specific release of information and/or consent forms have been signed by students, personal/clinical information cannot be disclosed, including the confirmation of an ASD diagnosis. Consent forms for release of information with campus faculty, staff, or outside providers can be signed by students at the time of admission, along with other programmatic documentation. However, the success of a consultative relationship is not contingent on the disclosure of a student's diagnosis. Although the method of disability status identification may vary from one university to the next, some students with disabilities send letters from the campus disability office to faculty members for accommodations and these forms typically do not disclose a student's diagnosis. In lieu of disclosing a specific diagnosis with faculty and staff, consultation providers can instead discuss students' potential weaknesses in executive functioning abilities, communication practices, or social skills, and then provide suggestions on how an instructor can more effectively accomplish their teaching goals.

Progress Monitoring Progress monitoring is a necessary component of consultation in order to ensure that the provision of consultation services is effective.

Feedback forms eliciting students' classroom performance in the areas of attendance, completion of assignments, and classroom behavior should continue to be utilized to examine the students' broad performance in the class. Consultants working from both BC and MHC approaches can examine differences between pre- and post-consultation to monitor change.

Community Partnerships

In implementing a new ASD support at an existing university, it is important to identify key partners in the community and begin to develop those relationships. Valuable community agencies to include in your list are the following: your state's vocational rehabilitation agency, national and local autism agencies, local high schools whose students may want to attend college at your institution, nearby community colleges who may have students wishing to transfer to a four-year university, and local companies/agencies that might serve as appropriate places for students to work or intern. Establishing connections with these local schools and organizations can spread program awareness and provide avenues for student recruitment. Importantly, students and families may learn that college-based support programs for students with ASD may provide a viable option for allowing a student with ASD to attend a four-year college (even if the student does not attend the specific program being advertised).

Every state has a vocational rehabilitation agency that is funded through the United States Department of Labor. These agencies are set up to assist individuals with disabilities in joining the workforce. The Workforce Recruitment Program (WRP) is a specialized program that has been in existence since 1995. The program recruits and refers college students and recent graduates to federal and private sector employers nationwide. WRP helps with both summer internships and permanent jobs (Employer Assistance and Resource Network on Disability Inclusion, 2018). It is also recommended that program administrative staff locate the name of their state's vocational rehabilitation agency and locate the chapter/regional office nearest your university in order to a) become educated about the services these agencies can offer to the students in your program and b) develop a positive working relationship.

Autism agencies that support both research efforts and services are also important resources. At the national level, Autism Speaks, National Autism Center, and Autism NOW are a few of the key agencies that sponsor events, provide resources, and can potentially connect your institution to students and vice versa. Statewide autism agencies will also be helpful in promoting your program as well as providing resources for your staff in the form of conferences, workshops, and community visibility. State and local autism agencies are also important resources for marketing your new program. Agencies such as Autism New Jersey, New York Families for Autistic Children, The Autism Program of Illinois, the Autism Society of Texas, and the Autism Society of California can serve as avenues for connection to local families who have adolescents with ASD.

Additionally, high schools are important organizations to establish a relationship. Schools that are geographically close in proximity (within 2 h) of your university make excellent natural partners. Public high schools and private special education high schools are especially good partners in attaining applicants to your program who are appropriately college-bound. The most appropriate contact at public high schools is usually the school psychologist, due to their role as case manager for most students receiving special education services. The designated 504 coordinator at each public high school is also an excellent resource and contact.

Once your program has its first cohort enrolled, it will be important to reach out to potential places for internship and job placement for students. We would recommend partnering with your university's career services department, as well as various academic departments that have their own contacts for internships for students in their respective majors.

Teaching and Mentoring Graduate Students

Graduate students can play important roles in assisting ASD programs at the college level. In return, the autism support program can provide invaluable experience to graduate students in school psychology at the programmatic level and at the clinical (service provider) level. School psychology graduate students make particularly good mentees for ASD support programs for several reasons. First, under the supervision of licensed faculty, school psychology graduate students can serve on the frontline of consultative service provision for college faculty and staff. One of the NASP requirements for the accreditation of school psychology graduate programs is a course on consultation (NASP, 2010). After the successful completion of a consultation course, graduate students should possess the knowledge and skills necessary to lead a consultative relationship (under supervision). This model of service delivery provides faculty and staff with meaningful support while also serving as a training experience for graduate students.

Second, graduate students in school psychology can gain important programmatic experience by assisting in the administrative aspects of the program including organizing interview days, facilitating communication among service providers for students in the program, leading weekly meetings regarding programmatic and clinical issues for the program, and assisting in community outreach activities. ASD support programs can provide a unique learning experience for those graduate students interested in administrative and programmatic education. Third, by their involvement in a college support program for individuals with ASD, graduate students are immersing themselves in the world of autism and becoming experts in that particular neurodevelopmental disorder. As the rates for autism have recently increased to 1 in 59 (Baio et al., 2018), Autism is becoming a growing and important population to gain experience and can serve graduate students well as they apply for internships and jobs.

Final Thoughts

School psychology faculty are a population of the university community that possess a unique set of skills that translate well into service provision for college students with ASD and provide an opportunity to enter into a nontraditional role. Not only do school psychologists understand the diagnosis and evaluation of ASD, they are also in a position to understand the inner workings of a university environment as well as the benefits and shortcomings of disability law at the postsecondary level. In particular, this population of faculty have knowledge of the differences between educational law in K-12 schooling (IDEA) and college (ADA). School psychologists are often ideal candidates to implement systems-level change, which is imperative when creating ASD support programs aimed at closing the achievement gap in graduation rates between neurotypical college students and those with ASD by designing services to support students' areas of weakness. These programs can utilize school psychology faculty's knowledge of the strengths and challenges of students with ASD to target specific areas of intervention in college. This includes an understanding and appreciation of the manifestation of ASD symptomology in higher education. School psychology faculty also serve as mentors to graduate students, who can provide additional outlets for research and service delivery. Under supervision, faculty can extend their resources by utilizing graduate students as providers in ASD support programs, thereby increasing the number of program staff and providing meaningful experiences and clinical supervision of graduate students, whether that be supervision of counseling sessions, consultation of university faculty, or communication with parents. As the need for new support programs for students with ASD increases, faculty in School Psychology programs are in an optimal position to successfully initiate and develop these important support programs.

References

Adreon, D., & Durocher, J. S. (2007). Evaluating the college transition needs of individuals with high-functioning autism spectrum disorders. *Intervention in School and Clinic, 42*(5), 271–279.

Americans with Disabilities Act of 1990, 42 U.S.C. § 12101 *et seq.* (1990).

Anderson, C., & Butt, C. (2017). Young adults on the autism spectrum at college: Successes and stumbling blocks. *Journal of Autism and Developmental Disorders, 47*(10), 3029–3039.

Baio, J., Wiggins, L., Christensen, D. L., et al. (2018). Prevalence of autism spectrum disorder among children aged 8 years — Autism and developmental disabilities monitoring network, 11 sites, United States, 2014. *MMWR Surveillance Summaries, 67*(6), 1–23.

Beischer, C. G. (2012). Postsecondary faculty knowledge of Asperger's syndrome and disability law. *Dissertation Abstracts International, 72*, 6375.

Bennett, C. F. (1979). *Analyzing impacts of extension programs.* United States Department of Agriculture.

Bunch, V. A. (2004). Student attitudes toward peers with disabilities in inclusive and special education schools. *Disability and Society, 19*(1), 61–76.

Cahill, J. L. (2016). General education teachers' knowledge, training, and perspectives of children with autism Spectrum disorders and evidence-based interventions: An exploratory study. *Dissertation Abstracts International Section A, 76.*

Chan, C. C. H., Lee, M. C., Yuen, H. K., & Chan, F. (2002). Attitudes toward people with disabilities between Chinese rehabilitation and business students: An implication for practice. *Rehabilitation Psychology, 47*(3), 324–338.

Condrey, J. H. (2017). General education teacher perceptions of self-efficacy regarding teaching students with Autism in inclusion settings. *Dissertation Abstracts International Section A, 77.*

Cox, B. E. (2017). *Autism coming to college (Issue brief).* Center for Postsecondary Success.

Cullen, J. P., Gregory, J. L., & Noto, L. A. (2010). The teacher attitudes toward inclusion scale (TATIS) technical report. Online submission, paper presented at the annual meeting of the eastern educational research association (Feb. 11, 2010). Retrieved August 2, 2014 from http://eric.ed.gov/?id=ED509930

Dougherty, A. M. (2014). *Psychological consultation and collaboration in school and community settings* (6th ed.). Brooks/Cole, Cengage Learning.

Employer Assistance and Resource Network on Disability Inclusion [EARN]. (2018). State Vocational Rehabilitation Agencies. Retrieved from: http://www.askearn.org/state-vocational-rehabilitation-agencies/

Erchul, W. P., & Sheridan, S. M. (2014). *Handbook of research in school consultation, Second edition.* Taylor and Francis.

Erchul, W. P., Martens, B. K., & Brian, K. (2001). The school as a setting for consultation. In *School consultation: Conceptual and empirical bases of practice* (2nd ed.). Kluwer Academic Publishers.

Huber, K. D., Rosenfeld, J. G., & Fiorello, C. A. (2001). The differential impact of inclusion and inclusive practices on high, average, and low achieving general education students. *Psychology in the Schools, 38*(6), 497–504.

Keen, D., Webster, A., & Ridley, G. (2016). How well are children with autism spectrum disorder doing academically at school? An overview of the literature. *Autism, 20*(3), 276–294.

Kurth, J. A., & Mastergeorge, A. M. (2010). Academic and cognitive profiles of students with autism: Implications for classroom practice and placement. *International Journal of Special Education, 25*(2), 8–14.

Mahoney, D. (2008). *College students' attitudes toward individuals with autism.* Dissertation abstracts international: Section B: The sciences and engineering. ProQuest Information & Learning.

McDougall, J., DeWitt, D. J., King, G., Miller, L. T., & Killip, S. (2004). High school-aged youths' attitudes toward their peers with disabilities: The role of school and student interpersonal factors. *International Journal of Disability, Development and Education, 51,* 287–313.

National Association of School Psychologists. (2010). *Standards for credentialing of school psychologists.* Retrieved from: https://www.nasponline.org/standards-and-certification/nasp-standards-revision

National Association of School Psychologists. (n.d.). *School psychology program information.* Retrieved from: https://apps.nasponline.org/standards-and-certification/graduate-education/index.aspx

Park, M., & Chitiyo, M. (2011). An examination of teacher attitudes towards children with autism. *Journal of Research in Special Educational Needs, 11,* 70–78.

Reynolds, A. J. (1998). Confirmatory program evaluation: A method for strengthening causal inference. *American Journal of Evaluation, 19*(2), 203–221.

Rogers, P. J. (2000). Program theory: Not whether programs work but how they work. In D. L. Stufflebeam, G. F. Madaus, & T. Kellaghan (Eds.), *Evaluation models viewpoints on educations and human services evaluation* (2nd ed., pp. 209–233). Kluwer Academic Publishers.

Rouse, M., & Florian, L. (2006). Inclusion and achievement: Student achievement in secondary schools with higher and lower proportions of pupils designated as having special educational needs. *International Journal of Inclusive Education, 10*(6), 481–493.

Schwartz, C., & Armony-Sivan, R. (2001). Students' attitudes to the inclusion of people with disabilities in the community. *Disability and Society, 16*(3), 403–413.

Sedani, S., & Sechrest, L. (1999). Putting program theory into operation. *American Journal of Evaluation, 20*(2), 227–238.

Shattuck, P. T., Narendorf, S. C., Cooper, B., Sterzing, P. R., Wagner, M., & Taylor, J. L. (2012). Postsecondary education and employment among youth with an autism spectrum disorder. *Pediatrics, 129*(6), 1042–1049.

Van Bergeijk, E., Klin, A., & Volkmar, F. (2008). Supporting more able students on the autism spectrum: College and beyond. *Journal of Autism and Developmental Disorders, 38*(7), 1359–1370.

White, D., Hillier, A., Frye, A., & Makrez, E. (2016). College students' knowledge and attitudes towards students on the autism spectrum. *Journal of Autism and Developmental Disorders*, 1–7.

Wilkerson, S. E. (2013). Assessing teacher attitude toward the inclusion of students with autism. *Dissertation Abstracts International Section A, 74*.

Williams, E. (2018). *University Faculty's pedagogical knowledge of autism and attitudes towards the academic integration of college students with autism Spectrum disorder* (Unpublished doctoral dissertation). Fairleigh Dickinson University, Teaneck.

The Need for Relationship and Sexuality Education for Transition-Aged Autistic Youth

Susan Wilczynski, Shawnna Sundberg, Brandon Miller, and Sam Johnson

Abstract Despite the fact that most Autistics are interested in having intimate and sexual relationships, they typically receive little or no sexuality education. Given the importance of sexuality education in reducing risk for abuse and improving quality of life, school professionals who wish to support postsecondary transitions for Autistic youth need to be informed about and support the provision of sexuality education for their Autistic students. We review the concept of sex positivity and its unique importance in creating a supportive climate for Autistic students. We also address the scant research on sexuality education for Autistic people as well as focused interventions addressing sexuality-related issues that have been empirically examined with Autistic people. We conclude by providing recommendations and resources that we generated based on the limited literature available paired with clinical expertise to support school psychologists and other school professionals so they can begin expanding their scope of competence in this critical but often overlooked topic.

Keywords sexuality education · sex positivity · LGBTQ+ · abuse

The Need for Relationship and Sexuality Education and Transition-Aged Autistic Youth

We use identity-first language throughout this chapter because Autistics with sufficient communication skills prefer identity-first language over people-first language (Kenny et al., 2015). We respect that practitioners have used "people-first" language in recent decades and may feel uncomfortable with this shift (Dunn & Andrews, 2015). However, it seems ableist (i.e., discrimination or prejudice against people

---

S. Wilczynski (✉) · S. Sundberg
Department of Special Education, Ball State University, Muncie, IN, USA
e-mail: smwilczynski@bsu.edu

B. Miller
Department of Counseling Psychology, Ball State University, Muncie, IN, USA

S. Johnson
Department of Educational Studies, Ball State University, Muncie, IN, USA

© Springer Nature Switzerland AG 2022
K. D. Viezel et al. (eds.), *Postsecondary Transition for College- or Career-Bound Autistic Students*, https://doi.org/10.1007/978-3-030-93947-2_13

with disabilities) to use terms that maximize our level of comfort while denying Autistics their preference for identity-first language. This same ableist culture has often denied Autistics' self-agency over their intimate or sexual relationships (e.g., failing to provide private time to adult Autistics, failing to educate Autistics about sexuality, etc.; Fish, 2017) and has resulted in a lower quality of life (Branco et al., 2019). We hope this chapter reduces your risk of these well-intentioned but ultimately painful pitfalls.

The literature concerning sexuality education among special education students and the self-report of Autistic adults (Mehzabin & Stokes, 2011) suggests sexuality education is not sufficiently provided to Autistic students. Although the scope and sequence may differ, the overwhelming majority (96% females and 97% of males) of public school students receive sexuality education (Martinez et al., 2010). Unfortunately, students receiving special education services are far less likely to receive sexuality education (43%). Perhaps even more concerning, although nearly half (47.5%) of special education students without intellectual disabilities (ID) receive sexuality education, only 44% of students with mild ID and only 16% of students with moderate to profound ID receive sexuality education (Barnard-Brak et al., 2014).

Autistics and neurotypicals (i.e., people without neurological disorders) develop at the same rate physically and sexually; yet the sexual interests and needs of Autistics are often ignored by families and cultures that infantilize them (Moreno et al., 2017). Perhaps that partially explains why Autistics are less frequently provided sexuality education than their neurotypical counterparts (Mehzabin & Stokes, 2011). However, people on the spectrum consistently report that they are interested in sexual and intimate relationships (Gilmour et al., 2012). In fact, in a survey of 229 Autistic adults, only 7% reported no interest in being in an intimate relationship (Strunz et al., 2017). Even among asexual (i.e., little or no sexual attraction) Autistics, requests for sexual interaction are likely to occur in the context of some of their relationships, so comprehensive sexuality education is needed. Given intimate relationships are generally borne from effective social communication and Autistics receive less sexuality education than neurotypical students, the postsecondary transition can be dangerous, daunting, and depressing.

This chapter begins with an analysis of why sexuality education is essential for Autistics and why it may need to be altered to ensure some Autistics fully benefit from the instruction. Although this is a small but emerging area of study, we identify topics that should be addressed in comprehensive sexuality education of Autistics and more common focused interventions on the topic of sexuality. We include a review of sex positivity and its unique importance in creating a supportive climate for Autistic students who seek intimate or sexual relationships. Finally, we identify issues of sexuality that have been insufficiently explored with the ASD population but that school psychologists, parents, and community professionals may need to address for the well-being of Autistic students. We conclude with recommendations and resources school psychologists can use to expand their scope of competence so they can lead or collaborate with sexuality educators to address sexuality education for Autistics.

Why Sexuality Education Is Essential for Autistics

Sexual Activity

Autistics are likely to enter intimate and sexual relationships even if they have not received formal sexuality education. A survey of 50 Autistic adolescent males (ages 15–18) revealed that 82% had been in love, 90% had experienced an orgasm. More than half (52%) of those surveyed had engaged in "heavy petting" (with clothes on), nearly a quarter (24%) had experienced vaginal intercourse, and more than one-fifth (22%) had engaged in oral sex (Dewinter et al., 2015). Given the emotional and physical risks associated with sexual relationships, the lack of sexuality education provided leaves young Autistics vulnerable. In contrast, Autistic females are less likely to report interest in sexual activity than Autistic males; however, they are more likely to have sexual experience than Autistic males. Unfortunately, the best available evidence suggests that Autistic females are more likely to have experienced negative sexual experience (e.g., unwanted, regretted, etc.) and have been victimized by others (Pecora et al., 2019).

Abuse and Predators

The absence of sexuality education may contribute to the prevalence of abuse among Autistics. Approximately 56% of Autistic adults report experiencing sexual abuse during their lifetimes (Weiss & Fardella, 2018). In the general population, numerous risk factors are associated with child sexual abuse (CSA) and a number of these risk factors may be more common among the ASD population. For example, parent perpetration of CSA is more likely to occur when social isolation and other family problems are present (Assink et al., 2019). Like parents of children with other disabilities and medical disorders (Faw & Leustek, 2015), parents of Autistics often experience isolation from others in their communities. Because parents of Autistic students are more likely to have a history of substance use (Wade et al., 2014) and mental health issues (Cohrs & Leslie, 2017), their risk for committing abuse against their child is even higher. Once another form of abuse (e.g., physical abuse) has occurred, the risk for sexual abuse increases (Assink et al., 2019; Wade et al., 2014). Beyond parents, peers (Kildahl et al., 2019) and other adult authority figures are also potential abusers.

Characteristics of ASD may place Autistics at greater risk for sexual abuse. For example, Autistics may be less able to discern whether a person or environment is "safe" or "unsafe" (Edelson, 2010). Further, because compliance is often expected during their interactions with adults, Autistics may not understand their rights (Wilczynski et al., 2015). When educators regularly use physical prompting as means of teaching Autistic students (Cengher et al., 2016), it conveys the message that authorities have control over your body (as opposed to having self-agency).

Schools typically expect students to comply with classroom and school rules. Autistics receiving medical services from physicians, behavior analysts, and other allied health professionals are often taught explicitly to comply with adult commands. Despite the fact that compliance (i.e., following a direction that is delivered by an authority) among neurotypicals historically lies between 60–80% (Forehand, 1977), Autistics are often expected to comply with adult-delivered instructions at a higher rate. The compliance expectation is, in part, data-driven (i.e., mastery criteria of 90% produces greater maintenance of new skills (Fuller, & Fienup, 2018)). However, the consistently high expectation that Autistics comply with adult-delivered instructions place them at greater risk for abuse. In addition, the weak adaptive skill repertoire (e.g., toileting, bathing) some Autistics have developed paired with the consistent expectation of compliance with adult-delivered instruction means these Autistics will be in close physical contact with adult authorities while in a nude or semi-nude state. Some of these adult professionals will be sexual predators (Sevlever et al., 2013; Wilczynski et al., 2015).

Sex Positivity, Sexual Minorities, and Quality of Life

In contrast to sex negativity (i.e., a perspective regarding sexual expression as inherently dirty, deviant, or risky), sex positivity acknowledges the benefit that sexual satisfaction, pleasure, and self-efficacy can have on a person's well-being (Ivanski & Kohut, 2017; Prause & Williams, 2020). It is associated with acceptance of any sexual expression that is consensual and nonexploitative. Sex positivity maintains that sexual expression can fill an important role in people's lives and, thus, it implicitly pushes back against the historical denial and dismissal of Autistic sexuality prevalent in much of the earlier ASD literature (Kellaher, 2015).

Both sexual activity and degree of sexual pleasure are positively related to quality of life (Kashdan et al., 2018; Rothblum et al., 2020; Stephenson & Meston, 2015). The vast majority of Autistics also seek these experiences (Gilmour et al., 2012). According to the World Health Organization (WHO), quality of life is centered at the intersection of psychological and physical health and safety, social relationships, and personal beliefs, including personal perceptions of one's culture and expectations for oneself. In fact, frustration, sadness, and/or confusion are common among Autistic adolescents and young adults who are interested but unsuccessful in achieving a sexual or intimate relationship. Autistic adults report a need for our culture to acknowledge and respect their sexuality across the life span (Edelson et al., 2020).

Shame persisting around many forms of sexual expression in the broader culture (Mercer, 2018) can challenge the formation of sexual and intimate relationships, which further diminishes quality of life. Although studies with clear and current definitions of gender identity and nonconformity are rare, ASD appears to occur more frequently among gender diverse individuals (i.e., those self-identifying as transgender or nonbinary, not identifying solely as male or female) than in the general population (Stagg & Vincent, 2019; Dewinter et al., 2017), with one study suggesting up to a sevenfold increase in gender variance among Autistics (Strang et al., 2014). Autistics also report a higher rate of nonheterosexual identities (i.e., homosexuality, bisexuality, and asexuality; George & Stokes, 2018). Given the sexual and gender diversity within the autism community, its members are more likely to experience unwanted social contingencies in the schools (e.g., gender-based harassment; Peter et al., 2016) and/or experience shame as cultural restrictions on sexual expression conflict with their sexual and gender identities.

Compared to cisgender and heterosexual individuals, people who identify as a sexual or gender minority experience greater risk of psychological distress, suicide, depression, and anxiety as well as lower quality of life. There are compounding risks for social isolation among LGBTQ+ Autistics due to the potential for sexual identity-based discrimination and social deficits of ASD. LGBTQ+ individuals tend to develop resilience to discrimination and social fallout via social adaptation that can include leaving oppressive relationships and environments, developing new and supportive relationships, and developing connections to an LGBTQ+ community and identity (Asakura, 2017; Higgins et al., 2016;). However, building and effectively utilizing these social networks is likely to be more challenging for Autistics.

Social-Communication Impairments

Social competency is the ability to use social-communication skills (e.g., eye contact, tone and volume of conversation, and understanding facial expressions; Chester et al., 2019) to successfully engage and interact with others (Usher et al., 2015). Most Autistics want intimate relationships; however, difficulties in social-communication skills make developing the relationships challenging (Corona et al., 2016). The social-communication skills needed to successfully navigate relationships as they proceed from the "simple attraction" of early pubescence to sexual and intimate interaction become exponentially more complex. Correctly reading the social-communicative actions of others may lead to misunderstanding social signals about relationship interest (e.g., friendship versus sexual/intimate relationship; Parchomiuk, 2019).

Consent Social-communication differences (e.g., overly literal interpretation of what others say) can be particularly challenging for the process of consent. Consent to engage in sexual activities is a daunting topic for the general population (Kolod, 2018), but social-communication limitations may place Autistics at greater risk for engaging in or experiencing a coercive or assaultive relationship. Consider the ubiquity of the phrase: "When a woman says no, she means yes." A Google search for this phrase conducted in May of 2020 yielded 530,000,000 results; the phrase appears in televisions shows, movies, music, literature, and social media, and its widespread use makes it unlikely that a young Autistic male will avoid hearing it. Given that Autistic people are more likely to interpret what they read or hear literally

(Mitchell et al., 1997), the implications for young Autistic men who hear such a phrase repeatedly are severe. As they request sexual interactions with a woman, they may assume she does not really mean no if she refuses. Confusion or misinterpretation might also arise if a woman says "yes" initially to sexual activity and then "no" as the interaction continues. Similarly, an Autistic female being told "she is asking for it by the way she dresses," may believe her offender and comply with a "request" even if she does not want to engage in a sexual interaction. Communication problems surrounding consent are not limited to heterosexual interactions, but the messages sent about women and sexuality are unique, and this communication problem is most likely to lead to assault and incarceration (or other consequences) for Autistic male and female sexual interactions.

STI and Unwanted Pregnancy Prevention Autistics may have difficulty negotiating the use of contraceptives or prophylactics with partners who are resistant to using them. Resistance to condom use is especially widespread and may manifest in a number of ways, including but not limited to attempts to convince a partner that one is STI-free, one has a latex allergy, sensation is dulled, condoms are not necessary between individuals who trust each other, or by actually sabotaging the condom or physically arousing a partner to the point that they agree to forego condom use (see Davis et al., 2014 for a review). Self-advocacy skills around the use of contraceptives and prophylactics are necessary so Autistics understand it is reasonable to decide prophylactic use is nonnegotiable. Autistics may also need extra education about how to access and to use contraceptives and prophylactics (Brown-Lavoie et al., 2014).

Sexting Between 11–28% of adolescents have engaged in sexting (i.e., sending sexually explicit materials, often photographs via cell phones) despite having an awareness of its risks (Ouytsel et al., 2017). Sexting is more common among sexual minorities than heterosexual students during the adolescent years (Ouytsel et al., 2019). The higher rate of nonheterosexuality among Autistics, the social pressure to send sexts, and the tendency for adolescents to acquiesce to requests for sexts due to fears of losing relationships, individuals with ASD may be at particularly high risk for victimization via sexting (Ouytsel et al., 2017; Ouytsel et al., 2019). In addition to the obvious risks of sexting (e.g., blackmail or distribution for the purpose of revenge or boasting), adolescents who engage in sexting are more likely to be cyberbullied a year or two later (Ouytsel et al., 2018). Sexual education should address sexting and how to respond to requests for sexually explicit messages. In addition, sexual education should include how to manage the consequences if a decision to participate in sexting occurs. This need is perhaps even greater for Autistics due to both the direct and indirect (e.g., cyberbullying) effects of sexting.

Hookup Culture Transition-aged Autistics may be entering into a "hookup" culture whether they enter a college setting or the general community (Garcia et al., 2012; Olmstead et al., 2019) and irrespective of their gender identity or sexual orientation (Lamont et al., 2018). Hooking up might be a behavior but it occurs within the context of a culture that often endorses sexual encounters without commitment. There are a general set of beliefs associated with hookup culture (e.g., sex is fun, hookups give me control over my own sexuality); however not everyone agrees with all of these beliefs which can create problems for Autistics and neurotypical students alike. In addition, sexual decision-making in hookup culture is often associated with who can increase a person's status. Finally, not everyone on college campuses or in the community endorses hookup culture (Aubrey & Smith, 2013). Assessing whether or not a prospective partner intends to share a one-time only sexual encounter, repeated commitment-free sexual encounters, or an intimate/romantic relationship can be challenging for any young person. The social-communication difficulties Autistics experience make this assessment more challenging. In addition, a sexual partner may not communicate their intentions and the mismatch can result in emotional or psychological discomfort or pain for either party. Further compounding these challenges is the fact that hookups often occur in "drunk world" (i.e., a setting in which excessive substance use occurs; Garcia et al., 2012). Substance use can impair the ability to accurately read or deliver social cues about the nature of the emerging encounter/relationship. A failure to provide sexuality education to Autistics that includes a discussion of these complex variables (i.e., hookup culture and drunk world) places them at risk for emotional disappointments or worse, potential accusations of sexual assault when they assume there is no harm in their sexual engagement (e.g., a partner agrees to kissing but then passes out).

Stalking Stalking consists of three main elements: (1) harassment involving repetitive, bothersome, and distressing behavior directed towards an individual that has no reason other than to cause harm to the person; (2) a threat toward a person that causes that person to become fearful for their safety or that causes emotional distress; and (3) conduct that involves a series of acts over time towards a person that causes emotional distress or concern for safety (Proctor, 2003). Although stalking is illegal in the United States (Post et al., 2014), school psychologists must be aware of local definitions, as they vary by state (Snow, 1998). This variability suggests ambiguity about what is and is not acceptable behavior in the general community (i.e., actions may be interpreted differently in different settings but also by different people; Post et al., 2014). Autistics may have greater difficulty differentiating respectful from problematic behavior. Ironically, efforts to improve social skills can unintentionally result in stalking behaviors (e.g., increased and repeated initiations) leaving Autistics confused by how others interpret their actions (Post et al., 2014). The desire to have sexual and intimate relationships among Autistics paired with the denied opportunity for sexuality education can result in romantic overtures that meet the state laws for stalking (Mullen et al., 2000).

ASD traits of excessive preoccupation with specific topics or interests or ritualistic behaviors may also increase risk for engaging in stalking behaviors. For example, if an Autistic person ritually walks in an area often frequented by the person who is the object of their fascination, this may easily appear to be stalking. Similarly, coincidental contact could be interpreted as a "relationship" that includes repeated actions that appear obsessive (e.g., following the person across multiple locations) or threatening (e.g., sexting, discussing topics considered taboo, masturbating in front of the person, etc.) by an uninterested recipient of these actions (Parchomiuk, 2019). Specific instruction on how to differentiate between wishful thinking and reciprocated interest in a sexual or intimate relationship, privacy rules (i.e., masturbating and what would be considered a private place), and social rules would aid in building relationships (Post et al., 2014) and prevent stalking behavior.

Sexuality Education Research and ASD

This section includes a review of the literature on both comprehensive programs and focused interventions involving sexual education for Autistics. Comprehensive sexual education for Autistics is important to ensure their safety, the safety of others, and to enhance their quality of life. Although there are limited studies on sexuality education, the increased efforts to establish an evidence base is promising. A review of the literature shows that the most common articles on Autistics' sexual behaviors have focused on inappropriate behavior that could result in problems for both persons engaging in these behaviors and the community (Beddows & Brooks, 2016). The most common inappropriate behaviors included: hypermasturbation, public masturbation, inappropriate romantic gestures, inappropriate arousal, and exhibitionism. Interviews with caretakers of young Autistics also show substantial interest in hygiene and personal space (Ballan, 2011; Holmes & Himle, 2014). Many of these topics are addressed in the comprehensive sexuality education research. Where evidence specific to Autistics is available, we provide brief review of focused interventions on sexual behavior.

Comprehensive Sexuality Education

Little research on comprehensive sexuality education programs for Autistics have been published. Tackling Teenage Training Program is an 18-session sexuality education program that addresses themes such as puberty, basic biology, sexual orientation, sexual intercourse, dating, and the safe use of the Internet for Autistics with IQs above 75. Research on the Tackling Teenage Training Program was conducted in the Netherlands and has been delivered individually to Autistic participants ranging in ages from 11–19 (Sala et al., 2019). Outcomes included improved knowledge acquisition on sexuality topics (Dekker et al., 2015) and personal boundaries. These improvements were maintained at a 6 month follow-up (Visser et al., 2017).

Like many commercially available programs, we cannot rule out the possibility that sex negativity, heteronormativity, and cis-normativity could have influenced program development. For example, the theme on sexual orientation is entitled, "Doubts and confusion during puberty," suggesting that sexual orientation is a result of confusion rather than biology. Similarly, the theme on abusive relationships addresses abusive boyfriends and targets girls, ignoring the potential for abuse within nonheterosexual and nonbinary relationships. Further, a concern about individually delivered sexuality education is the possibility of sexual abuse from educator. Although there is absolutely no evidence that abuse occurred within the context of this study, literature on sexual abuse suggests isolation with a predator dramatically increases the risk for abuse (Assink et al., 2019). Ideally, sexuality education programs are delivered predominantly in a group format but individualize on as needed to reduce this risk.

Healthy Relationships and Autism is a sexuality education program that has been delivered in a small group format (six White Autistic males between 15–17 years of age) in the United States. It covers a broad array of topics across three modules. Module 1 includes six sessions on basic biological sex education. Module 2 also includes six sessions that address factual information about anatomy and other biological processes but includes common slang that is likely to be used in everyday conversations on the topic. Finally, module 3 includes 11 sessions focusing on developing relationships. The materials must be mastered in earlier modules before students move on to later modules. This format increases the likelihood that foundational knowledge taught earlier in the sequences will support more complex learning of later topics. Knowledge about sexuality topics was acquired and maintained at a one-month follow-up. However, these results have yet to be assessed on a larger group, and it is unknown if knowledge is maintained for more extended periods of time (Pask et al., 2016).

One sexuality education study for Autistics has been conducted on "Ready for Love: Relationship Enhancement[R]," which was originally developed for people with personality disorders, schizophrenia, and intellectual disabilities. The program was delivered in the United States to 38 (30 male; 8 female) 18–50+ year old Autistics, with the majority falling between 18–29 years and having "some college." Ready for Love focuses on dating skills and sexuality within the context of relationships and half of participants also received additional sessions on relationship initiations; effectiveness of the intervention was based on self-report. Autistic participants reported improvements in social awareness, social communication, social motivation, restricted interests and repetitive behaviors, dating, and empathy. The data are based on a larger group, which is encouraging (Cunningham et al., 2016). However, this is only one study and self-reported change does not necessarily translate to observable change in behavior. In addition, although all Autistics should be taught about ongoing sexual and intimate relationships, a more sex-positive program on sexuality education would include sexual activities outside the context of traditional relationships (e.g., hookups) as these are more common in some settings (e.g., among college students).

This section only reviews recent research on sexuality education programs for Autistics. Parent-mediated sexuality education is another promising area for comprehensive sexuality education, given the critical role parents play throughout their children's lives. Although not universal, many parents of Autistics want to play an active role in their education. As noted previously, parents can be taught sexuality education in tandem with their children (Corona et al., 2016) or can be taught to address sexuality education with their children (Pugliese et al., 2020).

Focused Interventions on Sexual Behavior

Three methods of intervention have generally been recommended as focused sexuality interventions. Applied behavior analysis (ABA) is a field of human study that relies on behavioral principles to identify and alter environmental conditions and motivating situations (i.e., motivating operations) to produce skills gains and reduce problem behaviors. Social Stories™ are also recommended by Ballan and Freyer (2017) for addressing sexuality needs of Autistic students. However, given the literature demonstrating Social Stories™ tends not to be effective when used in isolation (Leaf et al., 2019), school psychologists relying on Social Stories™ should plan to adopt behavior analytic interventions in tandem with these narratives. Cognitive behavior therapies (CBT) have been recommended for addressing sexual offending; however, one study using CBT included a small number of participants who had ASD co-occurring with intellectual disabilities. Seventy-five percent of participants with ASD re-offended within six months of completing therapy (Sex Offender Treatment Services Collaborative – Intellectual Disabilities, 2010). For this reason, we are not further reviewing CBT but encourage school psychologists to conduct occasional literature reviews to determine if additional data are available for reducing sexual offending.

Use of Feminine Products

Although there is a lack of research regarding Autistics' knowledge of reproductive organs and hygiene, they can require additional assistance to maintain proper reproductive hygiene (Klett & Turan, 2011). This specific need has received very little attention in the literature and more research is recommended. ABA interventions for teaching menstrual care to Autistic women have been used in isolation (e.g., chaining; Veazey et al., 2016) or in tandem with Social Stories™ (i.e., visual task analysis embedded in narrative; Klett & Turan, 2011).

Masturbation and Public Sexual Intimacy

Inappropriate masturbation is one of the most frequent problematic sexual behaviors among Autistics (Dewinter et al., 2015; Byers et al., 2013). Although masturbation is a natural part of sexual development, Autistics are at risk for unhealthy or inappropriate patterns such as excessive masturbation, masturbation that is vigorous to the point of self-injury, and public masturbation (Ballan & Freyer, 2017; Cicero, 2019). Sexual education should teach Autistics social awareness to avoid engaging in public masturbation. In the absence of a comprehensive sexuality education program, however, reactive interventions may be necessary to avoid self-harm or a criminal record.

Excessive masturbation can result from an ineffective technique that does not lead to an orgasm, resulting in masturbation occurring at inappropriate times, injury to the genitals, an inability to benefit from other activities (e.g., social interactions, academic engagement), and distress due to sexual frustration (Hinsburger, 1994). Historically, interventions for both public and excessive masturbation have involved punishment (Cicero, 2019). Medications like mirtazapine (Coskun et al., 2009) have successfully reduced excessive masturbation but have involved small sample sizes. The side effects of antidepressants like mirtazapine (e.g., decreased libido, delayed orgasm, and increased sexual dysfunction) should be considered prior to its use (Lahon et al., 2011). More positive nonmedical interventions like masturbation training (i.e., completing a series of exercises that reduce orgasm dysfunction) have been suggested but have not been subject to research in Autistic adolescents or young adults. If masturbation training is an intervention being considered for excessive masturbation, school psychologists should avoid modeling successful masturbation techniques, providing video models, or using behavioral techniques like shaping (Kaeser, 1996) themselves. A common clinical recommendation is for parents to purchase videos like "Hand Made Love" from Diverse City Press (see Table 1).

When school psychologists receive referrals for public masturbation, ABA techniques like response interruption (with or without redirection) may be both effective and highly feasible. Response interruption may be preferable when possible because it requires fewer resources (Cividini-Motta et al., 2020) and is likely socially valid given that it mirrors the typical response of neurotypical parents when their children touch their genitalia in public. In addition, school psychologists and families may work together to teach Autistic clients about public versus private behavior. It is best to teach Autistics that private places are secluded settings within one's own residence where others cannot observe the sexual activity (e.g., with the curtains drawn). When faced with students who excessively masturbate, some professionals teach students that it is acceptable to masturbate in a closed stall within a public bathroom in the school because it is relatively private compared to a classroom. However, this incurs risk, as masturbating in other public bathrooms (e.g., at a mall, at a public park, etc.) could lead to criminal charges.

We have primarily discussed public masturbation that is automatically reinforced (e.g., it occurs because it feels good) and not being under stimulus control (i.e., not knowing when/where masturbation could acceptably occur). However, some Autistics masturbate in public to gain attention (Hinsburger, 1994). When public masturbation occurs, at least in part, to obtain the attention of others, alternative behaviors should be identified and reinforced with attention that has the same magnitude (i.e., amount of attention) and frequency of attention as received through public masturbation. As noted previously, comprehensive sexuality education paired

Table 1 Sexuality education and related resources

Resource name	Description	Website
School climate survey	School experiences of LGBTQ+	https://www.glsen.org/research/2017-national-school-climate-survey-0
Association of University Centers on disabilities	Dismantling ableism	https://www.aucd.org/template/news.cfm?news_id=13757&id=17
Center for Disease Control	Sexually transmitted infections	https://www.cdc.gov/std/default.htm
Diversity City press	Educational resources for people with disabilities	https://diverse-city.com/
Excuses for sexual harassment	Self-advocacy for victimization	https://www.vogue.com/article/the-worst-excuses-for-sexual-harassment-and-assault
Gay straight Alliance	School-based alliance for LGBTQ+	https://gsanetwork.org/
Green Mountain self-advocates	Sexuality education resources for disabilities	http://www.gmsavt.org/sexuality/
National Adult Protective Services Assn	Adult protective services resource	https://www.napsa-now.org/get-help/how-aps-helps/
Organization for Autism Research	Sexuality self-advocacy guide	https://researchautism.org/sex-ed-guide/
Safe schools	Sexual harassment prevention in schools	https://www.safeschools.com/blog/sexual-harassment-prevention-in-schools/
SAFE (stop abuse for everyone)	Sexuality resources for educators	https://www.safeaustin.org/our-services/prevention-and-education/expect-respect/resources-for-educators/
Scarleteen	Sexuality resources for teens	https://www.scarleteen.com/
Sexuality information and education Council of the United States	Inclusive sexuality education	https://siecus.org/
Sexuality resource Center for Parents	Sexual development	http://www.srcp.org/for_all_parents/development.html
Sex smart films	Video resources for sexuality education	http://www.sexsmartfilms.com/
Youth power	Nonconsensual sex	https://www.youthpower.org/youthpower-issues/topics/non-consensual-sex
Books (B), podcasts (P), and videos (V)		
S.E.X. (B)	Sexuality guide for teens and twenties	Heather Corinna
Behavioral observations: Episode 60 (P)	Sex education for people with disabilities	Matt Cicero with Sorah stein as guest
Sexology (P)	Experts in sexuality and intimacy	Dr. Nazanin Moali

(continued)

Table 1 (continued)

Resource name	Description	Website
Autism and sexuality (V)	Conversation (two Autistic women)	https://www.youtube.com/watch?v=25sUhR-oA0g
Effectively addressing sexual ableism (V)	Delivered by an adult with cerebral palsy	https://www.youtube.com/watch?v=lLNMLsJhxWo

with affording Autistics the dignity of engaging in intimate and sexual relationships in the same way as neurotypicals experience is most likely to address public masturbation for the purpose of partnered sexual activity.

Masturbation is not the only public display that can create problems for Autistics. Limits on public expressions of sexuality are defined both by laws and social norms. Norms governing public expressions of sexuality pose a unique issue for Autistics by complicating the process of discriminating between settings and appropriate behaviors. For example, some behaviors that would be acceptable in a nightclub (e.g., grinding) would not be acceptable in a place of worship or a workplace. Public expression of sexuality or intimacy may need to be considered through the lens of heterosexual or white privilege in some locations (Steinbugler, 2005). Same-sex and interracial couples have reported experiences of verbal or physical harassment after having engaged in an "appropriate" public expression of their sexuality. Given the greater rate of nonheterosexuality among Autistics, focused sexuality education may require discussion of these risks. However, school psychologists and other professionals providing this instruction should ensure they retain a sex-positive attitude while providing these warnings. For example, school professionals should not shame students' sexual identity; shaming can be associated with higher risk of victimization and suicidal actions (Mereish et al., 2018). Lower rates of victimization in schools has been evidenced when professionals access resources (e.g., The Gay Straight Alliance) and improve the social climate for LGBTQ+ students (Marx & Kettery, 2016).

Recommendations

Collaboration and Scope of Competence

Most school psychologists have not been trained as sexuality educators, making sexuality education outside their scope of competence. School psychologists should collaborate with certified sexuality educators already employed in their schools, while recognizing that sexuality educators do not typically have expertise in the accommodations Autistic students may need to benefit from sexuality education. In addition, special educators and school psychologists may need to develop follow-up learning activities and monitor knowledge acquisition.

School psychologists require continuing education and should consider training in sexuality education or related areas. In addition, they should self-evaluate their own views about sexual behavior to address potential biases. Many cultures send sex-negative messages with great frequency (Prause & Williams, 2020). Given that digitally mediated sexual experiences (Dewinter et al., 2015) and fetishes (Fernandes et al., 2016) are more commonly observed among Autistics, a sex-positive perspective may help providers distinguish between forms of sexual expression that are unhealthy and those that are simply nonnormative. The advantage of exploring one's own sex-positive/sex-negative views is that it is a nonpublic way to approach the topic of sexuality. Although no scale has been empirically developed to date, themes relevant to sex positivity that can be explored include factors such as one's personal belief (e.g., whether or not you see sex as good), your views around sexuality education, the extent to which you value health and safety, the extent to which you respect other people's control over their choices (e.g., abstinence through empowerment), and an evaluation of the positive nature of your own relationships, with an emphasize on factors like acceptance and inclusivity (Ivanski & Kohut, 2017). Given many people are uncomfortable discussing the topic of sexuality, this might be a way to ease into your views on sex positivity and sexuality education.

School psychologists may also expand their scope of competence to include issues unique to the LGBTQ+ community. For example, individuals who identify as LGBTQ+ must balance the need to embrace their sexual and/or gender identity with considerations of when, where, and how to come out as an LGBTQ+ person. Myriad social factors influence how prudent it might be to come out at a given time or place. Autistics may be less adept at recognizing those factors and safely navigating the conflict between those factors and their own need for authentic self-expression. School psychologists may need to help LGBTQ+ Autistics find outside qualified providers that can help educate clients about these decisions or assist their Autistic students in identifying universities that have strong supports for their LGBTQ+ college students. This may be particularly necessary given some school leaders actively resist staff obtaining expertise about the needs of their LGBTQ+ students (Payne & Smith, 2017).

School psychologists should be aware of the especially high risk for becoming a victim of bullying when Autistics are also sexual or gender minorities (Forrest et al., 2020; Ashburner et al., 2019). When other students merely perceive Autistic classmates to be sexual or gender minorities, the risk for bullying from neurotypicals and heterosexual, gender-conforming peers is great (Marshall & Allison, 2019). School psychologists involved in bullying prevention programs should ensure that educators are well-informed about this additional risk factor so that bullying prevention does not focus exclusively on the symptoms of ASD.

Abuse

Given the risk of abuse can be increased from the overapplication of physical prompting when teaching, school psychologists can train teachers and paraprofessionals to minimize their use of physical prompting whenever feasible and beginning as early as possible. Physical prompts could be avoided for some students by creating an environment in which they are motivating to make an attempt at an answer. For example, an individualized token economy could be used to increase an Autistic third grader's academic engagement by using the student's special interest in rocks (i.e., in lieu of stickers or tokens, small rocks could be used as tokens). When asked to select the correct picture from an array of pictures (e.g., "Show me the picture of the one people drive," with a car, a plane, and a helicopter as options), the correct answer could initially be presented closer to the student. A physical prompt is not necessary when the student is offered small rocks for correct responding and the correct answer is easiest to find. The position prompt could gradually be faded. Without incorporating special interests into the token economy, motivation might be lacking and a physical prompt is more likely to be used to get the student to attempt the activity. Even when a physical prompt may be necessary, school psychologists can help create an educational environment in which consent for touching the child is commonplace.

Professionals working with Autistics should receive trauma sensitivity training to minimize their failure to detect sexual abuse. Practitioners may not actively consider abuse as a possible explanation for distress and diagnostic overshadowing (i.e., attribution of symptoms to the diagnosis of ASD instead of considering alternative explanations) can result in a failure to detect sexual abuse (Kildahl et al., 2019). School psychologists must seek additional training regarding abuse given the number of Autistic students who may be experiencing abuse or have a trauma history that influences their actions in school. School psychologists will also want to encourage students to seek appropriate resources not only in their current state, but in states where Autistics may travel to seek postsecondary education. Just as school psychologists will benefit from partnering with sexuality educators in the schools, they will benefit from collaborating with and learning from professionals with expertise in domestic violence. These professionals are more likely to detect not only symptoms but risk factors for abuse (Hickson et al., 2013).

Parents

Professionals are often well-served by letting parents tell us where some of our greatest concerns should lie. One of the greatest concerns identified by parents of Autistic preteens and young adolescents is that their children will be viewed as engaging in sexually problematic behaviors when the behaviors are actually a result of their traits of ASD (Ballan, 2011). For example, an Autistic child might have been taught to demonstrate affection by hugging others. Overgeneralizing this behavior to their teachers may be perceived as endearing in early elementary school but may be viewed as sexually inappropriate as the child ages. Similarly, an Autistic adolescent girl might be fascinated by paisley and, while riding the bus, rub her hand on the paisley patterned skirt of another girl on the bus; the other children on the bus call them both lesbians and the parents of the other girl want to file assault charges. We see these are not unrealistic concerns and sexuality education can effectively teach about personal space.

Some parents are concerned that their Autistic children are unable to understand sexuality education or, like many people in the larger community, they wonder if it is really needed. Paradoxically, parents worry about their child's risk for becoming victims of sexual abuse. As children reach an age when sexuality becomes a prominent concern, parents often recognize the risk associated with teaching their children to comply with adult commands (Ballan, 2011).

Early research in which parents are taught about sexuality education alongside their Autistic children (Corona et al., 2016) or trained to provide sexuality education to their children are encouraging both in terms of increased knowledge acquisition for parents and their Autistic children and improved parental efficacy in addressing sexual health issues (Pugliese et al., 2020). School psychologists can encourage parents to seek both types of training. Some sexuality education for parents is easily available through web-based training (e.g., Elevatus), although such trainings may currently lack empirical support. Finally, although sexuality education is extremely important and parents should play a role in this process, it is important to understand that socio-cultural norms may influence the adoption of sexuality education strategies even among professionals (Hanass-Hancock et al., 2018). School psychologists should assume that parents may select to adapt sexuality education based on their own religious or cultural values or norms. However, the implications of adaptations should be presented (e.g., parents who elect not to teach about contraception because they believe in "abstinence only" programs should know the risk for an unwanted pregnancy).

Vocational Training

Many students receive vocational training in schools, which often includes development of work and social skills needed to secure competitive employment. Sexual harassment in the workplace is not consistently included in vocational training programs. Given the exceedingly low rate of competitive employment for Autistic adolescents and adults, it is reasonable that work and social skill acquisition is the primary focus. However, school psychologists should work with vocational rehabilitation specialist to ensure Autistic students know how to identify sexual harassment. In addition, Autistic adolescents and young adults must be taught how to respond to sexual harassment when it occurs and understand that they have recourse after the event.

Sexual Entertainment and Social Media

Autistics, like all people in modern culture, may acquire knowledge of various sexual practices, possibly including information about public expressions of sexuality, through numerous informal channels such as via electronic media or peers (Gougeon, 2009). This information may be inaccurate, incomplete, or easily misinterpreted by Autistics. School psychologists wishing to address a smooth transition to vocational or postsecondary settings will need to be creative in considering issues connected to sexual entertainment and social media because no focused interventions have been published, to date. A survey of 15–18 year old Autistic boys reveals that a large percentage have already accessed a pornographic magazine (36%), video clips with nudity (70%), sexual movies on TV (22%) or DVD (8%), and the Internet (76%). More concerning is the percentage that have shared sexual activity in some form via the Internet. Although a small percentage had sent naked pictures of themselves (6%) or others (8%), shown their genitals (8%), or engaged in cybersex (12%; Dewinter et al., 2015), these behaviors can meet the criterion for child pornography if the participants are young and can place the Autistic male at risk for exploitation even if they are above legal age. On the other hand, the flirting (38%) or even talking about sex on the Internet may be safer as long as partners are not victimizing nor being victimized by Autistics (Dewinter et al., 2015).

Social media abounds with inaccurate information, and it has been used to actively recruit disenfranchised young people. Risk factors for extremism may include a need to belong, a sense of having been humiliated, and having a world view that is rigid (Borum, 2014). Given the high interest in sexual and intimate relationships Autistics report (Gilmour et al., 2012) paired with frustration or sadness when these relationships do not emerge (Edelson et al., 2020), and the likelihood that multiple risk factors for extremism are present for a subset of the population, Autistics may be particularly at risk of being recruited by incels (i.e., involuntarily celibate). The term 'incel' originated from a nonviolent group who connected via the Internet out of a shared desire to find intimate and sexual relationships but being unsuccessful in this endeavor. The term has morphed over time and now represents an organized group who advocate male supremacy and is associated with violence against women (Veer, 2020). Autistic males may find a sense of belonging in the group that they have not found elsewhere and may be unable to successfully evaluate the dangers of associating with what is often considered a terrorist group.

Conclusions and Resources

We hope it is clear that avoiding the issue of sexuality and sexual education is risky in numerous ways (Gougeon, 2009). Sexual knowledge may mediate Autistics' risk for victimization (Brown-Lavoie et al., 2014), providing a compelling argument for comprehensive sexuality education. Research on every sexuality and ASD intervention addressed in this chapter is in its infancy, but research in the area is on a clear upward trajectory. School psychologists using an evidence-based practice decision-making model will need to select the optimal intervention for each student they serve by evaluating the best available evidence along with client and contextual variables (Wilczynski, 2017). Psychologists working in the schools should utilize single-subject research design whenever possible so they can contribute practice-based research to the autism intervention literature. In this way, the most commonly occurring school-based problems as well as practical and effective solutions involving sexuality education for Autistic students could lead to a burgeoning and useful literature base.

School psychologists may be ideally situated to implement popular interventions for problematic sexual behavior that have not yet been empirically examined. For example, Social Behavior Mapping (Winner et al., 2007), a cognitive behavior therapy, has been suggested as a means of addressing public masturbation by asking Autistics to consider whether behaviors are expected or unexpected, thus requiring individuals to consider social norms and the perception of peers (Ballan & Freyer, 2017). In addition to teaching Autistics to evaluate behaviors with an "appropriate" versus "inappropriate" binary, Social Behavior Mapping acknowledges that expected behavior may vary by context, so social behavior mapping could help Autistics consider the invisible social rules of a given social setting (Ballan & Freyer, 2017). As promising as this approach seems, it remains an empirical question if it is effective for addressing public masturbation. If it should be demonstrated to effectively reduce public masturbation, providers will still need to know whether there are parameters of effectiveness (e.g., it may be ineffective with Autistics who have a comorbid severe intellectual disability). School psychologists may identify Autistic students who they believe could benefit from Social Behavior Mapping and use single-subject research design to answer these questions.

Until a wealth of research is available, school psychologists may need to consider purchasing resources that have not yet been submitted to empirical investigation or relying on free websites that share information that is relevant but not autism-specific. Table 1 includes a number of commercially or freely available products (e.g., websites, podcasts, books, videos) that can be mined for possible supports for transition-aged Autistic students. This table does not include an exhaustive list but it can be a helpful starting point.

References

Asakura, K. (2017). Paving pathways through the pain: A grounded theory of resilience among lesbian, gay, bisexual, trans, and queer youth. *Journal of Research on Adolescence, 27*(3), 521–536.

Ashburner, J., Saggers, B., Campbell, M. A., Dillon-Wallace, J. A., Hwang, Y. S., Carrington, S., & Bobir, N. (2019). How are students on the autism spectrum affected by bullying? Perspectives of students and parents. *Journal of Research in Special Educational Needs, 19*(1), 27–44.

Assink, M., van der Put, C. E., Meeuwsen, M. W. C. M., de Jong, N. M., Oort, F. J., Stams, G. J. J. M., & Hoeve, M. (2019). Risk factors for child sexual abuse victimization: A meta-analytic review. *Psychological Bulletin, 145*(5), 459–489.

Aubrey, J. S., & Smith, S. (2013). Development and validation of the endorsement of the hookup culture index. *The Journal of Sex Research, 50*(5), 435–448.

Ballan, M. S. (2011). Parental perspectives of communication about sexuality in families of children with autism spectrum disorder. *Journal of Autism and Developmental Disorders, 42*, 676–684.

Ballan, M. S., & Freyer, M. B. (2017). Autism spectrum disorder, adolescence, and sexuality education: Suggested interventions for mental health professionals. *Sexuality and Disability, 35*(2), 261–273.

Barnard-Brak, L., Schmidt, M., Chesnut, S., Wei, T., & Richman, D. (2014). Predictors of access to sex education for children with intellectual disabilities in public schools. *Mental Retardation, 52*(2), 85–97.

Beddows, N., & Brooks, R. (2016). Inappropriate sexual behaviour in adolescents with autism spectrum disorder: What education is recommended and why. *Early Intervention in Psychiatry, 10*(4), 282–289.

Borum, R. (2014). Psychological vulnerabilities and propensities for involvement in violent extremism. *Behavioral Sciences and Law, 32*, 286–305.

Branco, C., Ramos, M. R., & Hewstone, M. (2019). The association of group-based discrimination with health and well-being: A comparison of ableism with other 'isms'. *Journal of Social Issues, 75*(3), 814–846.

Brown-Lavoie, S. M., Viecili, M. A., & Weiss, J. A. (2014). Sexual knowledge and victimization in adults with autism spectrum disorders. *Journal of Autism and Developmental Disorders, 44*(9), 2185–2196.

Byers, E. S., Nichols, S., & Voyer, S. D. (2013). Challenging stereotypes: Sexual functioning of single adults with high functioning autism spectrum disorder. *Journal of Autism and Developmental Disorders, 43*(11), 2617–2627.

Cengher, M., Shamoun, K., Moss, P., Roll, D., Feliciano, G., & Fienup, D. M. (2016). A comparison of the effects of two prompt-fading strategies on skill acquisition in children with autism spectrum disorders. *Behavior Analysis in Practice, 9*, 115–125.

Chester, M., Richdale, A., & McGillivray, J. (2019). Group-based social skills training with play for children on the autism spectrum. *Journal of Autism and Developmental Disorders, 49*, 2231–2242.

Cicero, F. R. (2019). Shaping effective masturbation in persons with developmental disabilities: A review of the literature. *Sexuality and Disability, 37*, 91–108.

Cividini-Motta, C., Moore, K., Fish, L. M., Priehs, J. C., & Ahearn, W. H. (2020). Reducing public masturbation in individuals with ASD: An assessment of response interruption procedures. *Behavior Modification, 44*(3), 429–448.

Cohrs, A. C., & Leslie, D. L. (2017). Depression in parents of children diagnosed with autism spectrum disorder: A claims-based analysis. *Journal of Autism and Developmental Disorders, 47*, 1416–1422.

Corona, L. L., Fox, S. A., Christodulu, K. V., & Worlock, J. A. (2016). Providing education on sexuality and relationships to adolescents with autism spectrum disorder and their parents. *Sexuality and Disability, 34*(2), 199–214.

Cunningham, A., Sperry, L., Brady, M. P., Peluso, P. R., & Pauletti, R. E. (2016). The effects of a romantic relationship treatment option for adults with autism spectrum disorder. *Counseling Outcome Research and Evaluation, 7*(2), 99–110.

Davis, K. C., Stappenbeck, C. A., Norris, J., George, W. H., Jacques-Tiura, A. J., Schraufnagel, T. J., & Kajumulo, K. F. (2014). Young men's condom use resistance tactics: A latent profile analysis. *The Journal of Sex Research, 51*(4), 454–465.

Dekker, L. P., van der Vegt, E. J. M., Visser, K., Tick, N., Boudesteijn, F., Verhulst, F. C., Maras, A., & Greaves-Lord, K. (2015). Improving psychosexual knowledge in adolescents with autism spectrum disorder: Pilot of the tackling teenage training program. *Journal of Autism and Developmental Disorders, 45*, 1532–1540.

Dewinter, J., Vermeiren, R., Vanwesenbeeck, I., Lobbestael, J., & Van Nieuwenhuizen, C. (2015). Sexuality in adolescent boys with autism spectrum disorder: Self-reported behaviours and attitudes. *Journal of Autism and Developmental Disorders, 45*(3), 731–741.

Dewinter, J., De Graaf, H., & Begeer, S. (2017). Sexual orientation, gender identity, and romantic relationships in adolescents and adults with autism spectrum disorder. *Journal of Autism and Developmental Disorders, 47*(9), 2927–2934.

Edelson, G. (2010). Sexual abuse of children with autism: Factors that increase risk and interfere with recognition of abuse. *Disabilities Studies Quarterly, 30*(1), 189–200.

Edelson, S. M., Nicholas, D. B., Stoddart, K. P., Bauman, M. B., Mawlam, L., Lawson, W. B., Jose, C., Morris, R., & Wright, S. D. (2020). Strategies for research, practice, and policy for autism in later life: A report from a think tank on again and autism. *Journal of Autism and Developmental Disorders*, 382–390.

Faw, M. H., & Leustek, J. (2015). Sharing the load: An exploratory analysis of the challenges experienced by parent caregivers of children with disabilities. *Southern Communication Journal, 80*(5), 404–415.

Fernandes, L. C., Gillberg, C. I., Cederlund, M., Hagberg, B., Gillberg, C., & Billstedt, E. (2016). Aspects of sexuality in adolescents and adults diagnosed with autism spectrum disorders in childhood. *Journal of Autism and Developmental Disorders, 46*(9), 3155–3165.

Fish, R. (2017). Already doing it: Intellectual disability and sexual agency. *Disability & Society, 32*(3), 430–432.

Forehand, R. L. (1977). Child compliance to parental requests: Behavioral analysis and treatment. In M. Hersen, R. M. Eisler, & P. M. Miller (Eds.), *Progress in behavior modification* (Vol. 5, pp. 111–147). Academic Press.

Forrest, D. L., Kroeger, R. A., & Stroope, S. (2020). Autism spectrum disorder symptoms and bullying victimization among children with autism in the United States. *Journal of Autism and Developmental Disorders, 50*(2), 560–571.

Garcia, J. R., Reiber, C., Masseey, S. G., & Merriwether, A. M. (2012). Sexual hookup culture: A review. *Review of General Psychology, 16*(2), 161–176.

George, R., & Stokes, M. A. (2018). A quantitative analysis of mental health among sexual and gender minority groups in ASD. *Journal of Autism and Developmental Disorders, 48*(6), 2052–2063.

Gilmour, L., Schaloman, P. M., & Smith, V. (2012). Sexuality in a community based sample of adults with autism spectrum disorder. *Research in Autism Spectrum Disorders, 6*, 313–318.

Gougeon, N. A. (2009). Sexuality education for students with intellectual disabilities, a critical pedagogical approach: Outing the ignored curriculum. *Sex Education, 9*(3), 277–291.

Hanass-Hancock, J., Nene, S., Johns, R., & Chappell, P. (2018). The impact of contextual factors on comprehensive sexuality education for learners with intellectual disabilities in South Africa. *Sexual Disabilities, 36*, 123–140.

Hickson, L., Khemka, I., Golden, H., & Chatzistyli, A. (2013). Views and values of professionals. *Journal of Policy and Practice in Intellectual Disabilities, 10*, 207–214.

Higgins, A., Sharek, D., & Glacken, M. (2016). Building resilience in the face of adversity: Navigation processes used by older lesbian, gay, bisexual and transgender adults living in Ireland. *Journal of Clinical Nursing, 25*(23–24), 3652–3664.

Hinsburger, D. (1994). Masturbation: A consultation for those who support individuals with developmental disabilities. *Canadian Journal of Human Sexuality, 3*, 278–282.

Holmes, L. G., & Himle, M. B. (2014). Brief report: Parent-child sexuality communication and autism spectrum disorders. *Journal of Autism and Developmental Disorders, 44*, 2964–2970.

Ivanski, C., & Kohut, T. (2017). Exploring definitions of sex positivity through thematic analysis. *The Canadian Journal of Human Sexuality, 26*(3), 216–225.

Kaeser, F. (1996). Developing a philosophy of masturbation training for persons with severe or profound mental retardation. *Sexuality and Disabilities, 14*, 295–308.

Kashdan, T. B., Goodman, F. R., Stiksma, M., Milius, C. R., & McKnight, P. E. (2018). Sexuality leads to boosts in mood and meaning in life with no evidence for the reverse direction: A daily diary investigation. *Emotion, 18*(4), 563–576.

Kenny, L., Hattersley, C., Molins, B., Buckley, C., Povey, C., & Pellicano, E. (2015). Which terms should be used to describe autism? Perspectives from the UK autism community. *Autism, 20,* 442–462.

Kildahl, A. N., Helverschou, S. B., & Oddli, H. W. (2019). Clinicians' retrospective perceptions of failure to detect sexual abuse in a young man with autism and mild intellectual disability. *Journal of Intellectual & Developmental Disabilities, 45*(2), 194–202.

Kolod, S. (2018). You say seduction and I say coercion: The gray areas of consent. *Contemporary Psychoanalysis, 54,* 651–664.

Lahon, K., Shetty, H. M., Paramel, A., & Sharma, G. (2011). Sexual dysfunction with the use of antidepressants in a tertiary care mental health setting-a retrospective case series. *Journal of Pharmacology & Pharmacotherapeutics, 2*(2), 128–131.

Lamont, E., Roach, T., & Kahn, S. (2018). Navigating campus hookup culture: LGBTQ students and college hookups. *Sociological Forum, 33*(4), 1000–1022.

Leaf, J. B., Ferguson, J., Cihon, J. H., Milne, C. M., Leaf, R., & McEachin, J. (2019). A critical review of social narratives. *Journal of Developmental and Physical Disabilities, 32,* 241–256.

Marshall, S. A., & Allison, M. K. (2019). Midwestern misfits: Bullying experienced by perceived sexual and gender minority youth in the Midwestern United States. *Youth & Society, 51*(3), 318–338.

Martinez, G., Abma, J., & Copen, C. (2010). *Educating teenagers about sex in the United States* (NCHS data brief 44). National Center for Health Statistics.

Marx, R. A., & Kettery, H. H. (2016). Gay-straight alliances are associated with lower levels of school-based victimization of LGBTQ+ youth: A systematic review and meta-analysis. *Journal of Youth and Adolescence, 45,* 1269–1282.

Mehzabin, P., & Stokes, M. A. (2011). Self-assessed sexuality in young adults with high functioning autism. *Research in Autism Spectrum Disorders, 5,* 614–621.

Mercer, J. (2018). Sex positivity and the persistence of shame. *Sexualities, 21*(8), 1304–1307.

Mereish, E. H., Peters, J. R., & Yen, S. (2018). Minority stress and relational mechanisms of suicide among sexual minorities: Subgroup differences in the associations between heterosexist victimization, shame, rejection, sensitivity, and suicide risk. *Suicide and Life-threatening Behavior, 49*(2), 547–560.

Mitchell, P., Saltmarsch, R., & Russell, H. (1997). Overly literal interpretations of speech in autism: Understanding that messages arise from minds. *Journal of Child Psychology and Psychiatry, 38*(6), 685–691.

Moreno, A., Laoch, A., & Zasler, N. D. (2017). Changing the culture of neurodisability through language and sensitivity of providers: Creating a safe place for LGBTQIA+. *NeuroRehabilitation, 41,* 375–393.

Mullen, P. E., Pathe, M., & Purcell, R. (2000). *Stalkers and their victims.* Cambridge University Press.

Olmstead, S. B., Noronoa, J. C., & Anders, K. M. (2019). How do college experience and gender differentiate the enactment of hookup scripts among emerging adults? *Archives of Sexual Behavior, 48,* 1769–1783.

Ouytsel, J. V., Gool, E. V., Walrave, M., Ponnett, K., & Peeters, E. (2017). Sexting: Adolescents' perceptions of the applications used for, motivates for, and consequences of sexting. *Journal of Youth Studies, 20*(4), 446–470.

Ouytsel, J. V., Walrave, M., Ponnet, K., & Temple, J. R. (2018). Sexting. In R. Hobbs & P. Mihailidis (Eds.), *The international encyclopedia of media literacy.* Wiley.

Ouytsel, J. V., Walrave, M., & Ponnet, K. (2019). An exploratory study of sexting behaviors among heterosexual and sexual minority early adolescents. *Journal of Adolescent Health, 65,* 621–626.

Parchomiuk, M. (2019). Sexuality of persons with Autistic spectrum disorders (ASD). *Sexuality and Disability, 37*(2), 259–274.

Pask, L., Hughes, T. L., & Sutton, L. R. (2016). Sexual knowledge acquisition and retention for individuals with autism. *International Journal of School and Educational Psychology, 4*(2), 86–94.

Payne, E. C., & Smith, M. J. (2017). Refusing relevance: School administrator resistance to offering professional development addressing LGBTQ issues in schools. *University Council for Educational Administration, 54*(2), 183–215.

Pecora, L. A., Hancock, G. I., Mesibov, G. B., & Stokes, M. A. (2019). Characterizing the sexuality and sexual experiences of autistic females. *Journal of Autism and Developmental Disorders, 49*, 4824–4846.

Peter, C. R., Tasker, T. B., & Horn, S. S. (2016). Adolescents' beliefs about harm, wrongness, and school policies as predictors of sexual and gender-based harassment. *Psychology of Sexual Orientation and Gender Diversity, 3*(4), 426–431.

Post, M., Haymes, L., Storey, K., Loughrey, T., & Campbell, C. (2014). Understanding stalking behaviors by individuals with autism spectrum disorders and recommended prevention strategies for school settings. *Journal of Autism and Developmental Disorders, 44*(11), 2698–2706.

Prause, N., & Williams, D. J. (2020). Groupthink in sex and pornography "addiction": Sex-negativity, theoretical impotence, and political manipulation. In *Groupthink in science* (pp. 185–200). Springer.

Proctor, M. (2003). *How to stop a stalker*. Prometheus Books.

Pugliese, C. E., Ratto, A. B., Granader, Y., Dudley, K. M., Bowen, A., Baker, C., & Anthony, L. G. (2020). Feasibility and preliminary efficacy of a parent-mediated sexual education curriculum for youth with autism spectrum disorders. *Autism, 24*(1), 64–79.

Rothblum, E. D., Krueger, E. A., Kittle, K. R., & Meyer, I. H. (2020). Asexual and non-asexual respondents from a US population-based study of sexual minorities. *Archives of Sexual Behavior, 49*(2), 757–767.

Sala, G., Hooley, M., Attwood, T., Mesibov, G. B., & Stokes, M. A. (2019). Autism and intellectual disability: A systematic review of sexuality and relationship education. *Sexuality and Disability, 37*, 353–382.

Sevlever, M., Roth, M. E., & Gillis, J. M. (2013). Sexual abuse and offending in autism spectrum Disorders. *Sexual Disabilities, 31*(2), 198–200.

Sex Offender Treatment Services Collaborative - Intellectual Disabilities (SOTSEC-ID). (2010). Effectiveness of group cognitive-behavioural treatment for men with intellectual disabilities at risk of sexual offending. *Journal of Applied Research in Intellectual Disabilities, 23*(6), 537–551.

Snow, R. L. (1998). *Stopping stalking: A cop's guide to making the system work for you*. Plenum.

Stagg, S. D., & Vincent, J. (2019). Autistic traits in individuals self-defining as transgender or nonbinary. *European Psychiatry, 61*, 17–22.

Steinbugler, A. C. (2005). Visibility as privilege and danger: Heterosexual and same-sex interracial intimacy in the 21st century. *Sexualities, 8*(4), 425–443.

Stephenson, K. R., & Meston, C. M. (2015). Why is impaired sexual function distressing to women? The primacy of pleasure in female sexual dysfunction. *The Journal of Sexual Medicine, 12*(3), 728–737.

Strang, J. F., Kenworthy, L., Dominska, A., Sokoloff, J., Kenealy, L. E., Berl, M., Walsh, K., Menvielle, E., Slesaransky-Poe, G., Kim, K., Luong-Tran, C., Meagher, H., & Wallace, G. (2014). Increased gender variance in autism spectrum disorders and attention deficit hyperactivity disorder. *Archives of Sexual Behavior, 43*(8), 1525–1533.

Strunz, S., Schermuck, C., Ballerstein, S., Ahlers, C. J., Dziobek, I., & Roepke, S. (2017). Romantic relationships and relationship satisfaction among adults with Asperger syndrome and high-functioning autism. *Journal of Clinical Psychology, 73*(1), 113–125.

Usher, L. A., Burrows, C. A., Schwartz, C. A., & Henderson, H. A. (2015). Social competence with an unfamiliar peer in children and adolescents with high-functioning autism: Measurement and individual differences. *Research in Autism Spectrum Disorders, 17*, 25–39.

Veazey, S. E., Valentino, A. L., Low, A. I., McElroy, A. R., & LeBlanc, L. A. (2016). Teaching feminine hygiene skills to young females with autism spectrum disorder and intellectual disability. *Behavior Analysis in Practice, 9*(2), 184–189.

Veer, R. (2020). *Analysing personal accounts of perpetrators of incel violence: What do they want and who do they target?* International Centre for Counter-Terrorism-The Hague.

Visser, K., Greaves-Lord, K., Tick, N. T., Verhulst, F. C., Maras, A., & van der Vegt, E. J. M. (2017). A randomized controlled trial to examine the effects of the tackling teenage psychosexual training program for adolescents with autism spectrum disorder. *Journal of Child Psychology and Psychiatry, 58*(7), 840–850.

Wade, J. L., Cox, N. B., Reeve, R. E., & Hull, M. (2014). Brief report: Impact of child problem behaviors and parental broad autism phenotype traits on substance use among parents of children with ASD. *Journal of Autism and Developmental Disorders, 44*, 2621–2627.

Weiss, J. A., & Fardella, M. A. (2018). Victimization and perpetration experiences of adults with autism. *Frontiers in Psychiatry, 9*(203), 1–10.

Wilczynski, S. M. (2017). *A practical guide to finding treatments that work for people with autism.* Academic Press.

Wilczynski, S. M., Connolly, S., DuBard, M., Henderson, A., & McIntosh, D. (2015). Assessment, prevention, and intervention for abuse among individuals with disabilities. *Psychology in the Schools, 52*(1), 9–21.

Winner, M. G., Bosmeijer, J., & Horras, J. (2007). Social behavior mapping. .

World Health Organization. (n.d.). WHOQOL: Measuring quality of life. Retrieved May 16, 2020, from https://www.who.int/healthinfo/survey/whoqol-qualityoflife/en/

Index

A
Academic assessment, 46
Academic coaching, 211
Academic majors, 203
Academic needs, 149–151
  classroom demands, 151
  mathematic skills, 151
  peer-reviewed literature, 149
  personal learning styles, 149
  reading comprehension, 150
  writing ability, 150
Academic skills, 14
Acclimation, to workplace, 235
Accommodations, 202, 207
Adaptive Behavior Assessment System –
  Second Edition (ABAS-II), 48
Adaptive Behavior Assessment System
  (ABAS-3), 204
Adaptive behavior measure, 204
Addressing Transition Preparation in Middle
  and High Schools, 8, 9
Alexithymia, 43
Americans with Disabilities Act (ADA), 205,
  233, 244
Anxiety, 19, 201
Application materials, 210
Applied behavior analysis (ABA) therapy, 100
ASD-specific support program, 9
Asperger's disorder, 47, 48, 50
Attention, 14, 50
Attention-deficit hyperactivity disorder
  (ADHD), 42, 201
Attention shifting, 15
Autism and Developmental Disabilities
  Monitoring (ADDM) Network, 138

Autism Brain Imaging Data Exchange
  (ABIDE), 53
Autism Diagnostic Observation Schedule
  (ADOS), 48
Autism New Jersey, 254
Autism Program of Illinois, 254
Autism Society of California, 254
Autism Society of Texas, 254
Autism Speaks®, 25
Autism spectrum disorder (ASD), 2, 3
  barriers to employment, 162, 164–168
  career development, 162
  career inventories, 163
  diagnostic features, 140, 147
  maintaining competitive employment, 166
  supported employment, 165–166
  workforce, 162
Autistic adolescents, 24
Autistic college students
  challenges, 138
  cognitive abilities, 142–144
    academic needs (*see also*
     Academic needs)
    anxiety disorders, 146–147
    behavioral challenges, 147–149
    college community, 152–154
    emotional challenges, 146–147
    executive functions, 143
    intelligence, 142–143
    social challenges, 145–146
    theory of mind, 143–144
    transition plans, 144
  policy and intervention
    implementation, 138
  prevalence and success of, 138–140
  socialization, 141

© Springer Nature Switzerland AG 2022
K. D. Viezel et al. (eds.), *Postsecondary Transition for College- or Career-Bound Autistic Students*, https://doi.org/10.1007/978-3-030-93947-2

Autistic college students *(Cont.)*
strengths of, 140–141
Autistic individuals
academic strengths and weaknesses, 65–67
comorbid specific learning disabilities, 81
computational ability of, 72, 75
general achievement assessments, 80–81
math assessment
math interventions, 74–75
written assessment, 77
written interventions, 77–79
written language, 75–77
mathematical language, 73
normative assessment adaptations, 79
reading, 67–72
assessment, 70
intervention, 70–72
skill development, 68
ToM measures, 69
transition planning, 64–65
verbal comprehension, 68
Autism Work Skills Questionnaire
(AWSQ), 166

B

Barriers to Successful Transition, 6
Behavioral Assessment Scales for Children –
Third Edition (BASC-3), 46
Behavioral consultation (BC), 252, 253
Behavioral rigidity, 20
Behavioral skills training (BST), 167
Boost-A program, 229
Broad autism phenotype (BAP), 145, 146

C

Campus activities, 204
Career One Stop, 230
Centers for Disease Control and Prevention
website, 42
Clinical Evaluation of Language
Fundamentals – Fourth Edition
(CELF-4), 50
College admission, 202
College Autism Network, 208
College-based specialty programs, 202,
208, 209
College community, 152–154
instructors, 154
peers, 152–154
staffs, 154
College funding, 204
College major, 203
College selection
academic majors, 203

academic programs, 203
admission requirements and materials,
209, 210
applying for disability
accommodations, 206
campus activities, 204
change in disability laws entering
college, 205
consultation, 213
cost, 203, 204
disability supports, 205
executive functioning/academic
coaching, 211
factors, 202
location, 204
mental health and social skills support,
211, 212
peer mentoring, 212
program cost, 213
specialty programs, 209
types of college accommodations, 207–209
vocational support, 212
College specialty programs, 209
Commuvnity career services, 233
Community college, 168–171
Community mental health, 233
Community partnerships, 254
Comorbid intellectual disability, 204
Computer-aided diagnosis systems
(CADS), 52
Confidentiality, 253
Conners Continuous Performance Test – Third
Edition (CPT-3), 51
Consultation, 213
Correctional systems, 26
Cost, 203

D

DANN model, 53
Default mode network (DMN), 53
Depression, 19
Diagnostic and Statistical Manual of Mental
Disorders (DSM), 2
Diagnostic and Statistical Manual of Mental
Disorders-5 (DSM-5), 2
Digit symbol, 49
Disability supports, 205
Down syndrome, 201–202

E

Effective transition planning, 225
Employment
acclimation to workplace, 235
appropriate services for workplace, 217

Index   285

benefits, 218, 219
career development, 230, 231
career opportunities selection, 228
collaboration
    cross-agency collaboration to
        employment after school, 231
    processes, 231
community career services, 233
community mental health and other
    providers, 233
high school services and employment
    supports by school staff, 225
hiring process, 234, 235
implications for practice, 237
new tasks and skills, 230
ongoing accommodations, 235, 236
online transition planning, 229
predictor factors for success in
    family factors, 224
    individual factors, 219, 224
    transition services, 224
self-determination, 228
social and independent living skills
    development, 227
transition planning and school
    counseling, 225
vocational rehabilitation, 232, 233
work-based learning experiences, 228
workplace considerations and
    supports, 233
Executive functioning, 51
Executive functioning/academic coaching, 211
Executive functioning coaching, 211
Extracurricular activities, 227

F
Family Education Rights and Privacy Act
    (FERPA), 213
Federal/state vocational rehabilitation
    program, 25
Financial aid, 204
Fragile X Syndrome, 42
Free and appropriate education (FAPE), 203
Free Application for Federal Student Aid
    (FAFSA) form, 204
Freight, 15
Full Scale IQ (FSIQ), 53
Fusiform face area (FFA), 54

H
*Halstead Reitan Neuropsychological
    Battery*, 50
Hands-on training, 172
High-functioning ASD (HFASD), 40–45, 90
    ABA therapy, 100

antecedent interventions, 101
assessment of ASD, 92
    adaptive behavior scales, 94
    behavior rating scales, 95
    diagnostic assessment, 93
    social emotional patterns, 92
    social skills assessment, 96
behavioral presentation, 90
cognitive-behavioral interventions, 102
differential reinforcement, 101
internalizing disorders, 98–99
mood and emotional difficulties, 97–98
peer-mediated instruction and interventions
    (PMII), 102
research-based curricula and
    programs, 103–104
school-based intervention, 99–100
social difficulties, 91
social skills training, 101
video modeling, 101
High-functioning autism (HFA), 160
Hiring process, 234, 235

I
Independent Living Scales (ILS), 45
Individualized education programs
    (IEPs), 5
Individuals with Disabilities Education Act
    (IDEA), 5, 161, 170, 202, 203, 205,
    206, 208, 214
Individuals with Disabilities Education
    Improvement Act of 2004 (IDEA),
    217, 225
Intelligence, 47
iPads, 230
IQ tests, 49

J
Job Accommodation Network, 25
Job shadowing, 230

K
Kaufman Tests of Educational Achievement
    (KTEA-3), 46
Kaufman Test of Educational Achievement
    (KTEA), 80
KeyMath-3 Diagnostic Assessment, 73
K-12 schools, 203, 205, 207, 214

L
Language, 49
LGBTQIA+ spectrum, 10
Location, 204

M

Maintaining competitive employment, 166
Maintaining employment, 162, 164, 166
Memory, 49
Mental health and social skills support, 211
Mental health consultation (MHC), 253
Minnesota Multiphasic Personality Inventory Adolescent (MMPI-A), 46
Minnesota Multiphasic Personality Inventory-3 (MMPI-3), 46
Movement Assessment Battery for Children – Second Edition (MABC-2), 54
Myers-Briggs Type Indicator (MBTI), 163
MyNextMove, 230

N

National Association of School Psychologists (NASP), 5, 237
National Collaborative on Workforce Development for Youth, 25
National Longitudinal Transition Study-2 (NLTS-2), 139, 160, 218
Neuropsychological assessment, HFASD
  academic assessment, 46
  attention, 50
  clinical presentation, 42
  comorbid psychiatric disorders, 43
  executive functioning, 51, 52
  future directions, 52
  gastrointestinal disorders, 44
  incidence and prevalence, 42
  intelligence, 47, 49
  language, 49, 50
  memory, 49
  for school psychologists, 39, 41
  seizure disorders, 44
  social and behavioral functioning, 45
New York Families for Autistic Children, 254

O

Obtaining Appropriate Services in College, 9
Office of Disability Services, 119–122, 129
On-campus housing, 204
Ongoing accommodations, 235, 236
Online transition planning, 229

P

Peer mentoring, 212, 248, 249
Peer mentors and/or job coaches, 168
Perceived burdensomeness, 20
Performance IQ, 53

Perisylvian area, 50
Pervasive developmental disorder not otherwise specified (PDD-NOS), 3, 41
Post-secondary life, 2
Postsecondary transition, 7
Preparation for Successful Employment, 9
Program cost, 213
Problem-solving skills, 15
Progress monitoring, 253
Psychoeducation, 207

Q

Quality of life (QOL), 219

R

Rehabilitation Act of 1973, 205, 225
Resting state fMRI (rs-fMRI), 53
Rett's disorder, 41

S

Scholarship opportunities, 204, 213
School counseling, 225
School psychologists, 5, 39, 41, 42, 44–47, 49–51, 54
School psychologists, 160–173
School psychology university faculty
  community partnerships, 254, 255
  confidentiality, 253
  consultation
    behavioral consultation, 252
    with faculty and staff, 249
    mental health consultation, 253
    models, 251
    need for, 251
    systems-level consultation, 251
    target for, 250
  developing and implementing services for students with ASD, 243, 244, 246
  faculty attitudes towards inclusion, 247
  interactions with individuals with ASD, 248
  peer mentoring, 248, 249
  professional development, 247, 248
  progress monitoring, 253
  student attitudes towards inclusion, 248
  teaching and mentoring graduate students, 255
Securing employment, 165
Seizure disorders, 44
Self-advocacy, 221, 236

Index
287

Self-determination, 228
Self-Determined Career Development Model (SDCDM), 228
Self-Determined Learning Model of Instruction (SDLMI), 228
Self-Directed Search (SDS), 163
Self-management
  antecedent conditions, 115
  attendance policies, 123
  autistic adults monitor, 112
  checklists, 120, 121, 123, 129, 131
  class engagement, 123–124
  external supports, 113, 116, 117
  friendships, 129–130
  IEP meeting, 122
  implementation of, 117, 125
  implementation variants, 117
  independent living skills, 126
  maintenance and generalization, 117
  mental health issues, 126, 127
  nutritional status, 128
  Office of Disability Services, 119–122, 129
  overview, 113–118
  participation in social activities, 131
  physical fitness, 128
  postsecondary education, 119–132
  registering for classes, 123
  reinforcement, 116, 117, 121
  roommate disagreements, 127
  self-advocacy, 113, 122, 130
  self-determination, 112, 113
  sexuality and dating, 130–131
  sleep issues, 128
  social interaction, 129–130
  study habits, 124–125
  target behavior, 114–116
  time management, 112, 125–126
Self-Management for Transition-Aged College-Bound Autistic Students, 7
Self-sufficiency, 20–22
Services in college, 201
Sex education, 10
Sexuality education, 260
  abuse and predators, 261
  cisgender and heterosexual individuals, 263
  collaboration and scope of competence, 271
    abuse, 273
    parents, 273
    school psychologists, 272
    sexual entertainment, 275
    social media, 275
    vocational training, 274

  comprehensive, 266
  focused sexuality interventions, 268
    Feminine Products, 268
    masturbation, 268, 269
  quality of life, 262
  related resources, 270–271
  research and ASD, 266
  sex positivity, 262
  sexual activity, 261
  social-communication
    skills, 263
    consent, 263
    hookup culture, 264
    sexting, 264
    stalking, 265
    STI and Unwanted Pregnancy Prevention, 264
Social and behavioral functioning, 45
Social and independent living skills development, 227
Social communication, 49
Social Communication Questionnaire (SCQ), 54
Social relationships and independence, 17
Special Education programming, 205
Specialty programs, 209
Speech language pathologist (SLP), 80
Suicidal ideation, 19
Supported employment, 165–166
Sylvian fissure, 50
Systems-level consultation, 251, 252

T
Teaching and mentoring graduate students, 255
Theory of mind (ToM), 69, 70, 76, 77
Trade or vocational school, 172
Transition barriers
  academic skills, 14
  anxiety, 19
  attention, 14, 15
  behavioral rigidity, 20
  correctional systems, 26–28, 30
  depression, 19
  mismatch between goals and supports in environment, 22, 23, 25, 26
  organization and planning, 16, 17
  problem-solving skills, 15, 16
  self-sufficiency, 20–22
  social relationships and independence, 17, 18
  suicidal ideation, 19
Transition Goal Generator, 226

Transition planning, 5, 8, 9, 202, 205, 214, 225, 226
Transition planning into young adulthood, 160–162
Transition programs, 179
   academics, 185
   adult agencies, 193
   age-appropriate assessment, 182–183
   career technical educators (CTE), 191
   civic and community groups, 195–196
   core principles, 180
   employers, 194
   employment, 186–187
   families, 196
   general educators, 190
   guidance counselors, 192
   high-quality transition planning, 182
   independent living, 187
   peer relationship, 188
   personnel roles and responsibilities, 189
   postsecondary educational pathways, 195
   recommended transition, 185
   related services, 191
   school administrators, 193
   school psychologists, 189
   schools and communities, 196
   self-determination, 189
   service providers, 193
   social competence, 188
   social skills, 188
   special educators, 190
   strong partnerships, 193
   team-based transition planning, 183–185
   transition specialists, 192
Triangulated Gap Analysis, 226
Tuition costs, 203

U
University location, 204
US Department of Labor's Office of Disability and Employment Policy, 25

V
Valuable community agencies, 254
Verbal IQ, 53
Video modeling, 166, 167, 230
Vineland Adaptive Behavior Scales (Vineland-3), 204
Virtual experiences, 230
Virtual job interviews, 230
Vocational rehabilitation (VR), 160, 161, 232
Vocational support, 212

W
Web coaching, 231
Wechsler Individual Achievement Test (WIAT), 80
Wechsler Individual Achievement Test – Fourth Edition (WIAT-4), 46
Wechsler Intelligence Scales for Children – Fourth Edition (WISC-IV), 48
Wechsler Preschool and Primary Scale of Intelligence – Fourth Edition (WPPSI-IV), 48
Wide Range Achievement Test – Fifth Edition (WRAT-5), 46
Woodcock Johnson Tests of Achievement (WJ ACH), 80
Work-based learning experiences, 228
Workforce Recruitment Program (WRP), 254
Workplace assessments, 166
Workplace training, 166–167

Printed in the United States
by Baker & Taylor Publisher Services